Contemporary Ethics

Contemporary Philosophy

Each volume in this series provides a clear, comprehensive and up-to-date introduction to the main philosophical topics of contemporary debate. Written by leading philosophers, the volumes provide an ideal basis for university students and others who want an engaging and accessible account of the subject. While acting as an introduction, each volume offers and defends a distinct position in its own right.

Published Works

Contemporary Philosophy of Social Science
Brian Fay

Contemporary Philosophy of Mind
Georges Rey

Contemporary Metaphysics
Michael Jubien

Contemporary Philosophy of Religion
Charles Taliaferro

Contemporary Ethics
William H. Shaw

Contemporary Philosophy of Thought
Michael Luntley

Forthcoming

Contemporary Philosophy of Language
Kent Bach

Contemporary Ethics

Taking Account of Utilitarianism

William H. Shaw

Department of Philosophy
San Jose State University

First published 1999

2   4   6   8   10   9   7   5   3   1

Blackwell Publishers Inc.
350 Main Street
Malden, Massachusetts 02148
USA

Blackwell Publishers Ltd
108 Cowley Road
Oxford OX4 1JF
UK

Library of Congress Cataloging-in-Publication Data
Shaw, William H., 1948–
    Contemporary ethics : taking account of utilitarianism / William H. Shaw.
        p.   cm. — (Contemporary philosophy)
    Includes bibliographical references (p.   )
    ISBN 0–631–20293–5 (hb : alk. paper). — ISBN 0–631–20294–3 (pbk. : alk. paper)
    1. Utilitarianism.   I. Title.   II. Series: Contemporary philosophy (Cambridge. Mass.).
    B843.S43   1999
    171'5.—dc21   98–28672
                                                                                   CIP

British Library Cataloguing in Publication Data
A CIP catalogue record for this book is available from the British Library

Typeset in 10 on 12pt Garamond 3
by York House Typographic Ltd, London
Printed in Great Britain by MPG Books, Bodmin, Cornwall

This book is printed on acid-free paper

For Carolyn,
who makes it all worthwhile

Contents

Preface and Acknowledgments

Utilitarianism represents one of the most important and influential currents in ethics and social-political philosophy. Not only is its historical significance undeniable, but today the utilitarian tradition is as alive as ever. In the last two decades, in particular, a number of writers sympathetic to utilitarianism have made innovative and important contributions to the theory and to moral philosophy in general, and these have deepened our understanding of utilitarianism and increased its viability as an ethical theory. As a result, utilitarianism is at the center of a number of contemporary debates in ethics, and discussions of it continue to fill the leading professional journals. Although many philosophers reject utilitarianism, those working in normative ethics, legal theory, or social and political philosophy cannot avoid situating themselves with reference to it.

Intended as a guide to utilitarianism, *Contemporary Ethics* explains the theory sympathetically, elaborates its philosophical implications and practical ramifications, and delves into the problems that it faces. Presupposing little or no familiarity with ethics, the book endeavors to steer the reader through a number of current controversies within and over utilitarianism. In doing so, it reconstructs the theory as plausibly as possible and upholds it against a variety of critics as the most tenable and fruitful orientation open to us in normative ethics and social and political philosophy. As firmly anchored as this book is in the utilitarian tradition, I cannot claim that its ideas are novel or that its arguments have great originality – indeed, much of what I say draws on the insights, not only of contemporary philosophers such as Brandt and Hare, but also of earlier utilitarians such as Mill and Sidgwick. But in clarifying how the theory works, restating the case for it, and answering various objections to it, I hope to show the continuing resilience, vitality, and attractiveness of a utilitarian approach to normative ethics.

ix

Chapter 1 introduces the reader to the theory and to ethics in general. It outlines utilitarianism's principal features and compares the theory to its rivals, in particular, to the ethical systems of Kant and Ross. Focusing on the utilitarian theory of value, Chapter 2 then explicates the different conceptions of well-being that utilitarians have favored. Chapter 3 reviews and reconstructs the arguments for utilitarianism's standard of right and wrong while Chapter 4 presents, and endeavors to answer, the most common objections to this standard. Against this backdrop, Chapter 5 goes on to develop a more subtle conception of utilitarianism, which appreciates the importance of moral rules and which is as concerned with people's motives and characters as it is with the assessment of actions. The final three chapters pursue the implications of this utilitarianism in both the public and private realms. Chapter 6 discusses the utilitarian approach to punishment, explains its view of rights, and – following Mill – argues on utilitarian grounds for a strong commitment to personal liberty. Chapter 7 deals with justice and economic distribution. It contrasts the utilitarian treatment of these issues with that of Nozick and of Rawls and shows the egalitarian implications of a utilitarian approach. Turning from utilitarianism's ramifications for public policy and institutional design, to its implications for personal life, Chapter 8 defends utilitarianism against those philosophers who reject normative theory itself as irrelevant or even harmful to our moral lives. It probes the utilitarian conception of virtue and champions the theory as a plausible and attractive basis around which to organize our moral lives.

Sabbatical leave from San Jose State University made writing this book possible. I am indebted also to the students in my spring 1998 seminar on utilitarianism and to the following friends and colleagues for reading and commenting on the manuscript: John Arthur, Clem Dore, Brad Hooker, Andy Ward, and Joe Waterhouse. Their useful suggestions and helpful criticisms significantly improved the final product, whatever its remaining defects. I also thank Susan Neuhoff for her help in preparing the manuscript and Carolyn Martin Shaw for her generosity, good humor, and wise counsel throughout the project.

William H. Shaw
San Jose

1

Introducing Utilitarianism

The sad but famous case of Karen Ann Quinlan posed a dramatic moral question, one which most people had not previously considered. Is it morally permissible to detach a life support system from a young adult who will (according to a consensus of the medical authorities) never again regain consciousness? Those who favored disconnecting Quinlan, and thus hastening her death, typically argued that doing so would make no difference to her, that it would free her parents and loved ones from an on-going ordeal and allow them to complete the grieving process, and that it would enable the doctors and hospital staff to turn their attention to patients who would benefit more from their efforts.

Those on the other side of the issue, however, were reluctant to dismiss Quinlan's prospects as hopeless. Wasn't a miracle recovery still possible? Further, they worried about the long-run implications of permitting hospitals to terminate the treatment of apparently hopeless patients. Would such a policy lead to giving up on patients who still had a chance? Would patients end up being removed from life support more on the basis of convenience to the family or the hospital than on an objective assessment of their prospects? Might such a policy decrease respect for human life or weaken the commitment of medical professionals to struggle against the odds to keep their patients alive?

As these conflicting perspectives indicate, the Quinlan case raised some challenging issues, and both sides of the debate put forward a number of pertinent points. Later in this chapter we look at Karen Ann Quinlan's eventual fate, but notice that the various considerations I have mentioned, both pro and con, are utilitarian in character. They focus on the results of withdrawing her life support, that is, on its likely consequences – both good and bad, both now and in the long run. Implicitly, the arguments on both sides invite us to weigh and compare the probable positive and

1

negative effects of the alternatives before us on the happiness or well-being of all those who are (or could be) affected by the decision. The consequences of our actions may not be the only thing that concerns people, but the Quinlan controversy illustrates that consequences often appear to be the factor that looms largest and seems the most morally important.

Utilitarianism, Law, and Society

Two fundamental ideas underlie utilitarianism: first, that the results of our actions are the key to their moral evaluation, and second, that one should assess and compare those results in terms of the happiness or unhappiness they cause (or, more broadly, in terms of their impact on people's well-being). Both these ideas have been around for a very long time; one can glimpse hints of them in philosophical and religious writings going back thousands of years. However, as an explicitly and self-consciously formulated ethical theory, utilitarianism is just over two hundred years old. In that time, it has had an enormous influence on moral philosophy, legal and political theory, and social policy. Utilitarian goals have shaped public decision-making in the twentieth century, and the theory has influenced the ethical beliefs of ordinary people. Although, as we shall see, the theory is a controversial one, a number of talented thinkers have upheld it, and they have developed and refined utilitarianism in surprisingly sophisticated and subtle ways. Nevertheless, utilitarianism's guiding impulse is simple and transparent, and many people have found it attractive: human well-being or happiness is what really matters and, accordingly, the promotion of well-being is what morality is, or ought to be, all about.

When we were young, most of us were taught various moral rules, concepts, and ideals. As we have grown older, the precepts and standards that guide our conduct and our thinking about that conduct have been shaped by various influences beyond our early upbringing, including books and movies, the example of those we admire, discussions with friends and family, and our own reflections on our experiences in life. Most of us confidently believe certain things to be morally right and certain things to be morally wrong. Some of these things are general principles or guidelines – for example, that it is wrong to steal, to abuse children, or to discriminate against people on the basis of race. Other moral beliefs of ours concern specific situations – for example, that I ought to keep a promise I made to my sister last November to omit mentioning her husband's illness to our aunt. On reflection, however, we may perhaps be unsure, not whether these things are right or wrong, but why they are. For example, what justifies our conviction that people shouldn't eavesdrop? Why exactly is it wrong for Roberto to interfere with his daughter's career plans? Sometimes, however, we may be unsure whether something is right or wrong in the first place: must I keep my promise to my sister if doing so irritates my spouse? Is it wrong for science teachers to have their students experiment on animals? Is adultery ever morally permissible?

Utilitarianism provides a standard by which we can address these questions, a standard that many thinkers have found deeply compelling.[1] It tells us why actions are right when they are right and why they are wrong when they are wrong. This book explicates the utilitarian theory, defends it against its critics, and attempts to show that it constitutes an attractive and plausible approach to ethics. However, before pursuing the theory further, we need to understand two features of morality, both of which the Quinlan case highlights.

Morality and the Law

The Quinlan controversy was pursued through the courts, and Quinlan's parents eventually won the right to direct the hospital to terminate artificial life support. In the eyes of many observers, the final court decision settled the issue; but law and morality are different things. The question of whether it is morally permissible to do something (for example, withdraw life support from someone in Quinlan's situation) is distinct from the question of whether it is legal or illegal to do so.

On the one hand, an action that is morally right can be illegal. For example, helping a Jewish family to hide from the Nazis was against German law in 1939, but it would have been a morally admirable thing to have done. Of course, the Nazi regime was vicious and evil. By contrast, in a democratic society with a just legal order, the fact that something is illegal provides a moral consideration against doing it. For example, one moral reason for not burning trash in your back yard is that it violates an ordinance that your community has voted in favor of. Some philosophers believe that the illegality of an action sometimes makes it morally wrong, even if the action would otherwise have been morally acceptable. But even

---

[1] In describing his conversion to utilitarianism, the English philosopher Henry Sidgwick (1838–1900) wrote that the theory provided "relief from the apparently external and arbitrary pressure of moral rules which I had been educated to obey, and which presented themselves to me as to some extent doubtful and confused; and sometimes, even when clear, as merely dogmatic, unreasoned, incoherent" (*Methods of Ethics*, xv).

if they are right about this, the fact that something is illegal does not trump all other moral considerations. Nonconformity to law is not always immoral, even in a democratic society. There can be circumstances where, all things considered, violating the law is morally permissible, perhaps even morally required.

On the other hand, an action that is legal can be morally wrong. People sometimes confuse legality with morality, but conformity to law does not guarantee that one's conduct is morally right. It may have been perfectly legal for the chairman of a profitable company to lay off 125 workers and use the money to boost his pay and that of the company's other top managers, as recently happened,[2] but the morality of his doing so is open to debate.

Suppose, to take another example, that you're driving to work one day and see an accident victim sitting on the side of the road, clearly in shock and needing medical assistance. Because you know first aid and are in no great hurry to get to your destination, you could easily stop and assist the person. Legally speaking, though, you are not obligated to stop and render aid. Under common law, the prudent thing would be to drive on, because by stopping you would bind yourself to use reasonable care and thus incur legal liability if you fail to do so and the victim thereby suffers injury. In the U.S., many states have enacted so-called Good Samaritan laws to provide immunity from damages to those rendering aid (except for gross negligence or serious misconduct). But in most states the law does not oblige people to give such aid or even to call an ambulance. Moral theorists would agree, however, that if you sped away without rendering aid or even calling for help, your action might be perfectly legal but would be morally suspect. Regardless of the law, such conduct would almost certainly be wrong.

What, then, may we say of the relationship between law and morality? To a significant extent, law codifies a society's customs, ideals, norms, and moral values. Changes in law tend to reflect changes in what a society takes to be right and wrong, but sometimes changes in the law can alter people's ideas about the rightness or wrongness of conduct (as when the U.S. outlawed racial discrimination by private businesses that serve the public). Utilitarians, in particular, will wish to enact and enforce laws that promote the general good. But even if legislation is sensible and morally sound, it is a mistake to see law as sufficient to establish the moral standards that should guide us. The law cannot cover the wide variety of possible individual and group conduct, and in many situations it is too blunt an

[2] *Newsweek*, May 26, 1997, 54.

4

instrument to provide adequate moral guidance. The law generally prohibits egregious affronts to a society's moral standards and in that sense is the "floor" of moral conduct, but breaches of moral conduct can slip through cracks in that floor.

Ethical Relativism

With the court's permission, Karen Ann Quinlan's parents had her removed from artificial life support. To everyone's surprise, she did not die, but lived for years in a comatose state, sustained only by intravenous feeding. Although the public lost interest in her plight long before she eventually died, her case had a lasting impact. As a result of it, in the United States a popular consensus has evolved that it is morally permissible to withdraw life support in such situations. Likewise, although several decades ago few would have argued that a conscious and rational patient facing a terminal illness has the right to decline medical treatment in order to hasten her inevitable demise, today hardly anyone denies that patients have this right. The law upholds it, and medical practitioners see themselves as morally obliged to accommodate it. On the other hand, moral opinion today is divided over whether a terminal patient has a right to request medical personnel to terminate her life directly or to assist her to commit suicide.

I have just described what I take to be the moral views of most Americans regarding certain life and death choices. Whether my description is accurate is a factual question, one that could be settled by sociologists, anthropologists, or surveyors of public opinion. However, to describe what most people think about right and wrong is not to affirm that their views are sound or that they can withstand critical scrutiny. Agreement in ethical matters does not, just by itself, vindicate the moral beliefs in question.

Some people disagree with this last statement. When they think about right and wrong, they despair of finding any universally valid principles and conclude, as a result, that morality is simply a function of what a particular society happens to believe. This view is called *ethical relativism*. It is the theory that what is right is determined by what one's culture or society says is right. What is right in one place may be wrong in another, because the only criterion for distinguishing right from wrong – and so the only ethical standard for judging an action – is the moral system of the society in which the action occurs.

Abortion, for example, is condemned as immoral in Catholic Ireland but is practiced as a morally neutral form of birth control in Japan. According to the ethical relativist, then, abortion is morally wrong in Ireland but morally permissible in Japan. The relativist is not saying merely that the Irish believe abortion is abominable and the Japanese do not; that is acknowledged by everyone. Rather, the ethical relativist contends that abortion is immoral in Ireland because the Irish believe it to be immoral and morally permissible in Japan because the Japanese believe it to be so. Thus, for the ethical relativist there is no absolute ethical standard independent of cultural context, no criterion of right and wrong by which to judge other than that of particular societies. In short, what morality requires is relative to society.

Those who endorse ethical relativism point to the apparent diverseness of human values and the multiformity of moral codes to support their case. From our own cultural perspective, some seemingly immoral "moralities" have been adopted: polygamy, pedophilia, stealing, slavery, infanticide, and cannibalism have all been tolerated or even encouraged by the moral system of one society or another. In light of this fact, the ethical relativist believes that there can be no non-ethnocentric standard by which to judge actions.

Contrary to the relativist, some people believe that the moral differences between societies are smaller and less significant than they appear. They contend that variations in moral standards reflect differing factual beliefs and diverging circumstances rather than fundamental differences in values. But suppose the relativist is right about this matter. His conclusion still does not follow. The fact that different societies have or have had different views about right and wrong fails to establish that none is true or superior to the others. Disagreement in ethical matters does not imply that all opinions are equally correct. Moreover, ethical relativism has some unsatisfactory implications.

First, it undermines any moral criticism of the practices of other societies as long as their actions conform to their own standards. We cannot say that slavery in a slave society like that of the American South a hundred and fifty years ago was immoral and unjust if that society held it to be morally permissible. Second, and closely related, is the fact that for the relativist there is no such thing as ethical progress. Although moralities may change, they cannot get better or worse. Thus, we cannot say that our moral standards today are any more enlightened than they were in the Middle Ages. Third, it makes no sense from the relativist's point of view for people to criticize principles or practices accepted by their own society. People can be censured for failing to live up to their society's moral code, but that is all. The moral code itself cannot be criticized because whatever a society takes to be right really is right for it. Reformers who identify injustices in

6

their society and campaign against them are only encouraging people to be immoral – that is, to depart from the moral standards of their society – unless or until the majority of the society agrees with the reformers. The minority can never be right in moral matters; to be right it must become the majority.

The ethical relativist is correct to emphasize that in viewing other cultures we should keep an open mind and not dismiss alien social practices simply on the basis of our own cultural prejudices. But the relativist's theory of morality doesn't hold up. The more carefully we examine it, the less plausible it becomes. There is no good reason for saying that the majority view on moral issues is automatically right, and the belief that it is automatically right has unacceptable consequences.

But if society isn't the final arbiter of right and wrong, what is? Utilitarianism provides a possible answer. By making happiness the moral standard, it provides an objective, non-relative guide to right and wrong, one that is independent of the particular moral code taught by the society in which we live. Because the importance of happiness is hard to deny, utilitarianism supplies a basis for morality that seems truly universal. We can use that standard to critically assess the moral practices of other societies as well as the moral code taught by our own society. At the same time, utilitarianism acknowledges that the sources of human happiness are complex and that they vary between cultures and over time as well as between different human beings. Because of this, the actions that promote happiness in a particular society or in a particular cultural or historical context may differ from the actions that promote happiness in another society or in another context. In this way, utilitarianism permits right and wrong to vary from society to society while still upholding a non-relative moral standard.

Understanding Utilitarianism

The ethical views of a number of early philosophers contain elements of utilitarianism, and by the eighteenth century Francis Hutcheson, Claude-Adrien Helvétius, and William Paley were promulgating an essentially utilitarian approach to ethics. However, the English philosopher Jeremy Bentham (1748–1832), who coined the term *utilitarian*, is generally considered to be the founder or at least the first systematic expounder of utilitarianism. In politics and ethics Bentham and his followers saw themselves as fighting on behalf of reason against dogmatism, blind adherence to tradition, and conservative social and economic interests.

They were social reformers who used the utilitarian standard as the basis for assessing and criticizing the social, political, and legal institutions of their day. They rejected many of those institutions (such as the penal code, the reform of which was of particular interest to Bentham) as backward or even harmful, and they dismissed much of the accepted morality of their day as unenlightened, prejudiced, and repressive.

Among Bentham's backers were his friends James Mill and Mill's son John Stuart Mill (1806–1873), who went on to become the most important English philosopher of the nineteenth century. Ardently interested in economics and public affairs, John Stuart Mill was an able defender of utilitarianism, and used the doctrine to champion individual liberty and to urge the emancipation of women. Mill, in turn, was followed by Henry Sidgwick, the last of the great nineteenth-century utilitarians. Unlike Bentham and Mill, Sidgwick was a university professor with a strong academic interest in the history of ethics. His writings developed and refined utilitarianism as a moral philosophy, bringing it to full intellectual maturity.

Let's examine how these three important utilitarians stated their theory, beginning with Bentham. On the first page of his earliest work, Bentham wrote that "it is the greatest happiness of the greatest number that is the measure of right and wrong."[3] Later, in his important work *The Principles of Morals and Legislation*, he stated the utilitarian ethical doctrine this way:

> By the principle of utility is meant that principle which approves or disapproves of every action whatsoever, according to the tendency which it appears to have to augment or diminish the happiness of the party whose interest is in question. (2)

Although the phrase "the party whose interest is in question" is rather open-ended, Bentham was not advocating an egoistic ethical theory. A passage on the following page clarifies this: "An action then may be said to be conformable to the principle of utility . . . when the tendency it has to augment the happiness of the community is greater than any it has to diminish it." According to Bentham, in determining whether a course of conduct is right or wrong, one must take into account the happiness or unhappiness of everyone affected by the action.

Although nowadays the concept of utility has a technical meaning for economists, most people find the word vague and uninformative, and the

[3] "Fragment on government," 227 (emphasis omitted). The phrase "the greatest happiness of the greatest number" is not original to Bentham. See Hutcheson, *Our Ideas of Beauty and Virtue*, 177.

definition of "utilitarian" that most dictionaries give is misleading and not what Bentham and subsequent philosophers mean by it. Indeed, Bentham himself came to prefer "the greatest happiness principle" to the "principle of utility" because

> the word *utility* does not so clearly point to the ideas of *pleasure* and *pain* as the words *happiness* and *felicity* do: nor does it lead us to the consideration of the *number*, of the interests affected ... which contributes, in the largest proportion, to the formation of the standard here in question; the *standard of right and wrong*, by which alone the propriety of human conduct, in every situation, can with propriety be tried. (1)

Like Bentham, John Stuart Mill associated happiness with pleasure and unhappiness with pain although, as we shall see in Chapter 2, his thinking about pleasure and pain differed significantly from that of Bentham. Although Mill, too, acknowledged the misleading connotations of the word "utility," he considered it too late to abandon the name "utilitarianism." In his famous work *Utilitarianism*, Mill expounded its defining principle as follows:

> The creed which accepts as the foundation of morals "utility" or the "greatest happiness principle" holds that actions are right in proportion as they tend to promote happiness; wrong as they tend to produce the reverse of happiness. (7)

Unfortunately, a couple of vague phrases mar this statement of the theory. The phrase "right in proportion" suggests that there can be degrees of rightness, implying that acts A and B could both be right and yet A be "righter" than B. It also implies that if A promotes happiness for some and unhappiness for others, then it is both right to a certain extent and wrong to a certain extent. Although not incoherent, these ideas are somewhat obscure. It is also unclear how the phrase "tend to promote" applies to an individual action. For example, although as a general matter telling lies tends to promote unhappiness, it would seem that a particular falsehood doesn't "tend" to do anything; it either does or does not produce happiness.

By contrast, the definition that Sidgwick gives in *The Methods of Ethics* is more precise:

> By Utilitarianism is here meant the ethical theory, that the conduct which, under any given circumstances, is objectively right, is that which will

produce the greatest amount of happiness on the whole; that is, taking into account all whose happiness in affected by the conduct. (411)

Despite its awkward syntax, this statement makes it clear that utilitarianism instructs us to act so as to bring about as much happiness as we can.

The Basic Utilitarian Standard

Because it is the most recognizable and influential form of utilitarianism, we might call the theory Sidgwick states the standard or basic version of utilitarianism. It is what philosophers, economists, and political theorists usually have in mind when they speak of utilitarianism. Some philosophers call this theory *act utilitarianism*, but this label is a little misleading because the utilitarian standard can be used to assess, not only actions, but also rules, laws, policies, and institutions as well as people's motivations and character traits. In later chapters, our understanding of utilitarianism and of how to apply it in practice will grow more sophisticated, but in the meantime we shall focus on the basic utilitarian standard. According to this,

> an action is right if and only if it brings about at least as much net happiness as any other action the agent could have performed; otherwise it is wrong.

A few points of interpretation are in order. First, in line with what I just said, for "action" we should understand "action or other object of appraisal." Second, the phrase "at least as much" allows for the possibility that two actions might produce equal amounts of happiness. In that case, either action would be right. Putting aside the possibility of ties, the utilitarian principle instructs us to perform the act that brings about the greatest net happiness. Third, the "net" happiness of an action is the happiness it produces minus any unhappiness it causes. We are interested not just in the positive results of actions but in their overall outcome. Finally, the theory states that if an action is not right, then it is wrong. This tallies with the way most people use the words "right" and "wrong."

Utilitarianism is a simple, bold, and direct ethical theory. It takes happiness as its standard and uses it to assess the morality of the actions we perform. We act rightly only when we bring about as much happiness as it is possible for us to bring about. When we are deciding how to act in a given situation, utilitarianism instructs us to assess the consequences of each of the various actions we could perform (including doing nothing at all). In addition to their immediate results, we must consider any long-term consequences and any indirect repercussions that these alternative

10

actions may have. For example, lying might seem a good way out of a tough predicament, but if the people you deceive find out, not only will they be unhappy, but your reputation and your relationships with them will be damaged.

In assessing actions, we must take into account not only their consequences for us, but also their consequences for other people. The utilitarian standard is not egoistic but universalistic because we are to consider the happiness or unhappiness of everyone affected by our actions, with no one person's happiness given more value than another's. We are to count the consequences to ourselves, whether good or bad, as having the same weight as the consequences to others. We are not to ignore our own happiness, but neither are we to treat it as more important than the happiness of anyone else. "Each to count as one, and no one as more than one" was Bentham's motto.

Utilitarianism tells us to sum up the various good, bad, or indifferent consequences for everybody of each possible action we could perform and then to choose the action that brings about the greatest net happiness. This is the action that is morally right and, hence, required of us. As mentioned, if several, mutually exclusive actions have equally good outcomes (and nothing we could do would have better results), then although there is no single right action, we act rightly as long as we choose one of them. Thus, utilitarianism states that we should always act so as to maximize happiness. It holds, in other words, that in whatever situation we find ourselves, the morally right course of conduct is that course of conduct, whatever it is, that brings about the greatest amount of happiness (or, to be more precise, that brings about at least as much net happiness as would have been brought about by any other course of conduct open to us).

Welfarism and Consequentialism

As contemporary moral theorists see it, utilitarianism has two distinct philosophical components. The first of these is *welfarism*. This is the value thesis that welfare or well-being is all that ultimately matters; it is the sole good, the only thing that is intrinsically valuable. Welfarism entails that nothing is good unless it is good for individual people. Accordingly, utilitarianism assesses actions based on whether they benefit or harm people, that is, based on their impact on people's well-being. It seeks to promote what is good for people, and the supreme utilitarian goal is that people's lives go as well as possible.

Bentham, Mill, and Sidgwick focused on happiness, which they equated with pleasure and the absence of pain. Because of this, their utilitarianism is sometimes called hedonistic. But these three writers were concerned with happiness only because they identified it with well-being, that is, with what is good for people. In their view, our lives go well, we have well-being, just to the extent that our lives are pleasurable or happy. Implicitly, then, welfarism is prior to, and underlies, their commitment to happiness. As we shall see in Chapter 2, however, happiness is not the only way to spell out the idea of well-being, and not all contemporary utilitarians understand welfare as happiness (and still fewer equate either concept with pleasure). Although for convenience I shall go on using "happiness" interchangeably with "well-being" (or "welfare"), what matters for utilitarianism is well-being, whether or not one understands it in terms of happiness.

The second philosophical component of utilitarianism is its consequentialist or teleological (goal-oriented) approach to right and wrong. *Consequentialism* is the thesis that the rightness or wrongness of an action is a function of its results or outcome. It is not an action's intrinsic nature or whether it is an instance of a certain permitted or forbidden type of act (for example, the keeping of a promise or the telling of a lie) that determines its rightness or wrongness, but rather its specific consequences in a particular situation. Utilitarianism is not only consequentialist; it is also universalistic, aggregative, and maximizing. It is universalistic because it takes into account everyone's interests equally, and it is aggregative because it combines the happiness or unhappiness of each person affected by an action to determine its overall value. Finally, utilitarianism is a maximizing doctrine because it states that the right action is that which produces the greatest amount of happiness the agent can produce.

Four Points about Utilitarianism

To avoid possible misinterpretation, four points should be clarified or elaborated:

1   Actions can have both good and bad results. As mentioned, the "greatest happiness principle" does not tell us to choose the action that has as part of its outcome the single effect with more happiness than any other effect we might have produced. Rather, it tells us to choose that action whose net outcome, taking into account all of its effects, is the happiest (or the least unhappy). It's probably impossible to measure happiness and unhappiness with mathematical precision, but to illustrate the above point let's pretend that we can. Imagine, then, that a particular action would produce eight units of happiness and four units of unhappiness. Its net

worth would thus be four units of happiness. An opposed action, let us imagine, would create ten units of happiness and seven units of unhappiness. The net worth of this action would be only three units of unhappiness. In this case utilitarianism implies that we should choose the first action over the second. In the event that both lead not to happiness, but to unhappiness, and there is no third option, we should choose the action that brings about the fewest units of unhappiness.

2   Actions affect people to different degrees. Your playing the stereo loudly might bring slight pleasure to three of your neighbors, cause significant discomfort to two others who do not share your taste in music or are trying to concentrate on something else, and leave a sixth person indifferent. The utilitarian theory is not that each individual votes on the basis of his or her happiness or unhappiness with the majority ruling, but that we add up the various pleasures or pains, however large or small, and go with the action that results in the greatest net amount of happiness. Because any action will affect some people more strongly than others, utilitarianism is not the same as majority rule. For example, in the United States today it would probably increase overall happiness to permit homosexuals to marry, even though the thought of their doing so makes many heterosexuals slightly uncomfortable. This is because such a policy would affect the happiness or unhappiness of the majority only slightly, if at all, while it would profoundly enhance the lives of a small percentage of people. Even if banning homosexual marriages makes most people happy, it doesn't bring about the most happiness.

As quoted earlier, Bentham famously said that the utilitarian standard is "the greatest happiness of the greatest number." Although often repeated, this formulation is misleading. The problem is that it erroneously implies that we should maximize two different things: the amount of happiness produced and the number of people made happy.[4] Correctly understood, utilitarianism tells us to do only one thing, maximize happiness. Doing what makes the most people happy usually produces the most happiness, but it may not – as the example of homosexual marriages illustrates. For utilitarianism, it is the total amount of happiness, not the number of people whose happiness is increased, that matters.

3   When utilitarians talk about the results or consequences of one's actions, they stretch the word "result" beyond its usual meaning of something that (i) comes after an act and (ii) is caused by it.[5] On the one

---

[4] In an unpublished essay in 1829, Bentham acknowledged this problem with his formulation. See Parekh, "Bentham's justification of the principle of utility," 98–9.
[5] Kagan, *Normative Ethics*, 27.

hand, utilitarians don't limit results to causal effects in a narrow sense because they are interested in the consequences, not just of one's acting in various positive ways, but also of one's refraining from acting. For example, it would seem odd to say that, by ignoring a panhandler's request for rent money, I "caused" his family to sleep outside tonight. Still, this may be one result of my not stopping to help him; if so, then utilitarians will take it into account in assessing my conduct.

On the other hand, in evaluating an action, utilitarians do not assume that there must be a firm line between it and the effects that flow from it, and they do not tell us to concern ourselves only with the latter. Rather, it is the overall outcome of each alternative action that we are to assess and compare, and this includes the positive or negative value, if any, of the action viewed by itself as well as the positive or negative value of its subsequent effects. Utilitarians have two reasons for focusing on an action's outcome in a broad sense rather than on its subsequent effects in a narrow sense.

First, happiness and unhappiness sometimes accompany, rather than follow, an action. For example, most of the pleasure Sally gets from stretching her arms after being hunched over her desk for an hour is contemporaneous with the stretching rather than a subsequent result of it. If so, then action A might produce more happiness than action B even though A's subsequent effects are no better than B's.

Second, the line between what you do and what results from what you do is a function of some chosen description of the situation. One and the same action can be described in various ways – for example, as "extending your arms," "pushing on a plank of wood," "opening the gate," "hurrying home," or "being rude to one's companion." "Pushing on a plank of wood" is a subsequent effect of my action when that action is described as "extending my arms," but not when it is described as "opening the gate." Because of this, it would be arbitrary and pointless to insist that in concerning itself with the consequences of our actions utilitarianism must focus only on their subsequent effects, rather than their overall outcomes.

4 Our actions can also affect the welfare of non-human animals. Although the implicit focus of the discussion so far has been on human beings, many species of animals feel pleasure and pain, and some animals can plausibly be said to experience happiness and unhappiness. For this reason, utilitarianism takes into account, not just human welfare, but also animal welfare or, more generally, the welfare of all sentient creatures. As we shall see when we return to this issue in Chapter 2, Bentham was one of the first philosophers to give direct moral weight to the suffering of

animals. For ease of exposition, however, this book discusses utilitarianism in terms of the welfare or happiness of human beings, but most of what it says can be extended or modified without distortion to take into account the happiness or unhappiness of other sentient creatures.

One Common Criticism of Utilitarianism

Critics of utilitarianism frequently point out that we can never know for certain all the consequences of the things we do. Still less can we know all the future results of every possible action that we might perform at any given point. A Boy Scout who stops to assist a blind man across the street appears to be doing a good thing. But if as a result of the Scout's intervention the man gets to his destination thirty seconds earlier than he otherwise would have, only to have a flower pot fall on his head from a balcony, then the Scout's deed definitely did not maximize happiness. The fact that the causal ramifications of our actions carry indefinitely into the future compounds the problem, seeming to thwart any claim to know what course of conduct is best. Furthermore, comparing one person's happiness or unhappiness with another's is tricky and imprecise at best, and when many people are involved, the matter may seem hopelessly complex. Finally, even if we had all the relevant information and could perform the necessary calculations, there would rarely be time to do so before we had to act.

Utilitarians have several pertinent rejoinders to this line of criticism. First, they can agree that we never know all the results of our actions and can only roughly estimate the value or disvalue of their consequences, and yet argue that this fact does not impugn the utilitarian goal of maximizing happiness. The correctness of that goal is not undermined by shortfalls in our knowledge of how best to attain it. Happiness is still what we should aim at, however difficult it may be to see the best way to bring it about.

Is this to concede that utilitarianism is unworkable in practice, even if it is right in theory? No, answer the utilitarians, because almost every ethical theory puts some moral weight on the results of our actions and will therefore be hampered in practice by the fact that we never have exact and certain knowledge of future events. Moreover, non-utilitarian systems of ethics face their own distinctive uncertainties. Interpreting and applying their principles can be problematic, and sometimes they give rise to conflicting obligations.

The second response that utilitarians can make is that human beings are already well acquainted with happiness and unhappiness, their nature and typical causes. Based on thousands of years of collective experience, we understand many of the sources of suffering and satisfaction, and we know various things that conduce to people's lives going well and various things that do not. In line with this point, Mill's *Utilitarianism* ridicules people who

> talk ... as if, at the moment when some man feels tempted to meddle with the property or life of another, he had to begin considering for the first time whether murder and theft are injurious to human happiness .... It is truly a whimsical supposition that, if mankind were agreed in considering utility to be the test of morality, they would remain without any agreement as to what *is* useful .... There is no difficulty in proving any ethical standard whatever to work ill if we suppose universal idiocy to be conjoined with it. (23)

Our knowledge of the future is far from certain, and we can, it seems, measure and compare people's happiness only coarsely. However, we are not altogether in the dark about which kinds of action promote well-being and which kinds do not, and the knowledge that we do have will frequently suffice to justify our acting one way rather than another. Even when we do not know, say, the very best way to handle a disruptive colleague, we can be confident that it does not involve burning down his house.

Mill's point also answers the criticism that "there is not time, previous to action, for calculating and weighing the effects of any line of conduct on the general happiness" (23). In ordinary circumstances we can and should follow certain well-established rules or guidelines that can generally be relied upon to produce the best results. We can, for example, make it a practice to tell the truth and keep our promises, rather than try to calculate possible pleasures and pains in every routine case, because we know that in general telling the truth and keeping promises result in more happiness than lying and breaking promises. In this vein, Mill emphasized the necessity of "intermediate generalizations" or "corollaries from the principle of utility":

> To inform a traveler respecting the place of his ultimate destination is not to forbid the use of landmarks and direction-posts on the way. The proposition that happiness is the end and aim of morality does not mean that no road ought to be laid down to that goal .... Whatever we adopt as the fundamental principle of morality, we require subordinate principles to apply it by. (24)

For practical purposes, relying on subordinate principles mitigates the no-time-to-calculate problem. It also alleviates another problem. Conscientious agents can make mistakes in their calculations, and bias can infect the reasoning of even a sincere utilitarian, especially when his or her personal interests are at stake. In normal circumstances, however, one is less likely to err and more likely to promote happiness by sticking to certain settled guidelines or tried and true rules of thumb than by trying to calculate from scratch the consequences of various courses of action.

Two Rival Nonconsequentialist Theories

Normative theories of ethics propose some principle or set of principles for distinguishing right actions from wrong actions. We have seen that utilitarianism is a consequentialist theory because it links the rightness of actions to their outcomes. Different consequentialist theories are possible depending on the good that is to be promoted and on the way that the theory ties rightness and wrongness to results. Egoism, for example, is a consequentialist theory with a structure similar to that of utilitarianism except for one important thing: it takes as its guiding principle the individual's self-interest, not the good of all. As an ethical theory egoism holds that an action is right if and only if it best promotes the agent's own happiness or well-being, whereas utilitarianism requires us to take the interests of all into account.

Although people are sometimes selfish, and self-interest motivates many of us much of the time, egoism is an implausible theory of right and wrong. By reducing everything to individual self-interest, egoism permits any action whatsoever – theft, extortion, arson, or murder – as long as it advances the interests of the agent. Yet a moral principle that permits (or, indeed, requires) us to kill a business competitor or to swindle elderly people out of their life savings if (1) doing so advances our interests and (2) we can get away with it, offends almost everyone's understanding of what is right and what is wrong. In fact, some philosophers believe that egoism is not, properly speaking, an ethical theory at all. They contend that egoism misunderstands the nature and point of morality, which is to restrain our purely self-interested desires so we can all live together. If our interests never came into conflict – that is, if it were never advantageous for one person to deceive or cheat another – then we would have no need of morality. The moral standards of a society provide the basic guidelines for cooperative social existence and for the rational resolution of conflicts by appeal to shared principles. It is hard to see how egoism could perform this function.

By contrast with consequentialist theories like egoism or utilitarianism,

17

nonconsequentialist or deontological (duty-based) theories contend that factors besides an action's consequences affect whether it is right or wrong. Nonconsequentialists need not deny that consequences are morally significant, but they believe that other considerations are also relevant to the moral assessment of an action. For example, a typical nonconsequentialist would hold that for Tom to break his promise to Fred is wrong not because (or not just because) its outcome is likely to be bad (Fred's hurt feelings, Tom's damaged reputation, and so on) but because of the inherent character of the act. Even if more good than bad came from Tom's breaking the promise, the nonconsequentialist might still view it as wrong. What matters is the nature of the act in question, not just its results.

To understand nonconsequentialism (and thus, by contrast, to appreciate better what is distinctive about utilitarianism), it will help to look at two influential nonconsequentialist ethical approaches, both of which are important rivals to utilitarianism: Kant's moral theory and Ross's commonsense pluralism. Although there are various different deontological ethical theories, these two important theories illustrate well the character of nonconsequentialist ethical thinking.

Kant's Ethics

Although the preeminent German philosopher Immanuel Kant (1724–1804) provides an excellent example of a thoroughly nonconsequentialist approach to ethics, he is a notoriously difficult thinker to interpret. Kant's writings have generated an enormous secondary literature in several languages, and one could easily devote a whole book to trying to explain and assess his moral philosophy. For our purposes, however, a brief introductory exposition will have to suffice.

Kant sought moral principles that do not rest on contingencies and that define actions as inherently right or wrong apart from any particular circumstances. He believed that reason alone can uncover the correct rules of morality, without appeal to observation, past experience, or factual data. In contrast to utilitarianism, which he harshly repudiated, Kant contended that we do not have to know anything about the likely results of, say, my lying to a colleague in order to know that it is immoral. "The ground of obligation here," Kant wrote, "must not be sought in the nature of the human being or in the circumstances of the world."[6] Rather it is *a priori*, by which he meant that moral reasoning is not based on factual knowledge and

---

[6] Kant, *Practical Philosophy*, 45.

that reason by itself can disclose the basic principles of morality. For Kant, the motivation to follow the principles that reason reveals is at the heart of morality.

Good will. Earlier I mentioned Good Samaritan laws, which shield from lawsuits those rendering emergency aid. Such laws, in effect, give legal protection to the humanitarian impulse behind emergency interventions. They formally recognize that the interventionist's heart was in the right place, that the person's intention was irreproachable. Because the person acted with good intentions, he or she should not be held culpable for making an innocent mistake. This is in line with Kant, who held that nothing is good in itself except a good will. This belief does not entail that intelligence, courage, self-control, health, happiness, and other things are not good or desirable. However, their goodness, Kant believed, depends on the will that makes use of them. Intelligence, for instance, is not good when used by an evil person.

By "will" Kant meant the uniquely human capacity to act from principle. Contained in the notion of good will is the concept of duty. Only when we act from duty, Kant thought, does our action have moral worth. When we act only out of feeling, inclination, or self-interest, our action – although it may otherwise be identical with one that springs from a sense of duty – has no true moral worth. For example, suppose that you are a clerk in a convenience store. Late one night a customer pays for his five-dollar purchase with a twenty-dollar bill, which you mistake for a ten. It's only after the customer leaves that you realize that you shortchanged him. You race out the front door and find him lingering by a vending machine. You give him the ten dollars with your apologies, which he accepts with thanks. Can we say with certainty that you acted from a good will? Not necessarily. You may have acted from a desire to promote business, or you may have acted out of sympathy for the customer. If so, you would have acted in accordance with, but not from, duty. Your apparently virtuous gesture just happened to coincide with duty, but it was not motivated by a sense of duty and therefore lacked moral worth.

According to Kant, then, actions have true moral worth only when they spring from a recognition of duty and a choice to discharge it. But what determines our duty? How do we know what morality requires of us? To answer these questions, Kant formulated his famous "categorical imperative."

The categorical imperative. In contrast with utilitarianism, which allows factual circumstances to determine what is right or wrong, Kant believed that reason alone revealed a basic and absolute moral imperative. This imperative is categorical, meaning that it is necessarily binding on all rational agents, regardless of any other considerations. From this one categorical imperative, this one universal principle, we can derive all the specific requirements of duty, requirements that are absolute and admit of no exceptions. Kant states his *categorical imperative* in several different ways. The following formulation of it is perhaps the clearest and easiest to understand: "I ought never to act except in such a way that I could also will that my maxim should become a universal law" (57).

By "maxim," Kant meant the subjective principle of an action, the principle (or rule) that implicitly or explicitly guides a person's conduct whenever he or she acts. Suppose Cassandra promises the college dean that she and her colleagues will only offer courses for which there is high student demand, but intends to break that promise if it suits her purposes. Her maxim can be expressed this way: "I'll make promises that I'll break whenever keeping them no longer suits my purpose." This is the subjective principle or maxim that guides her action. Kant insisted that the morality of any action depended on whether we could logically will its maxim to become a universal law. Can Cassandra will that her maxim be universally acted on? The answer is no. The maxim "I'll make promises that I'll break whenever keeping them no longer suits my purpose" cannot be universally acted on – it cannot be a universal law – because it involves a contradiction. On the one hand, Cassandra is willing that it be possible to make promises and have them honored. On the other, if everyone intended to break promises whenever they so desired, then people would not believe or accept promises in the first place. A moral law that allowed promise-breaking would contradict the very nature of a promise.

Similarly, a moral law that allowed lying would contradict the very nature of serious communication, for the activity of serious communication (as opposed to joking) requires that participants intend to speak the truth. I cannot, without contradiction, will both serious conversation and lying. In contrast, there is no problem, Kant thinks, in willing promise-keeping or truth-telling to be universal laws. Kant also used suicide as an example. Consider someone who is in despair after suffering a series of major setbacks that have destroyed her health, cost her the love of her family, and undermined her prospects for future happiness. Would it be contrary to duty for this person to take her own life? Kant interprets the maxim in question to be: "From self-love, I make it my principle to shorten my life when its longer duration threatens more troubles than it promises agreeableness" (74). Can this maxim be willed a universal law of nature? Kant thinks not. He argues that the purpose of self-love is to further life and that to take one's life on the basis of self-love contradicts this. Therefore, the maxim in question cannot exist as a universal law of nature.

When Kant insists that a moral rule be consistently universalizable, he is affirming that moral rules prescribe categorically, not hypothetically. A hypothetical prescription tells us what to do if we desire a particular outcome. Thus, "if you want to get on with people, you should try to take an interest in the things they like" and "if you want to go to medical school, you must take biology" are hypothetical imperatives. They tell us what we must do on the assumption that we have some particular goal. If that is what you want, then this is what you must do. On the other hand, if you don't want to go to medical school, then the command to take biology does not apply to you. In contrast, Kant's categorical imperative commands unconditionally. It is binding on everyone, regardless of his or her specific goals or desires and regardless of consequences.

Kant explicitly offered another, memorable way of formulating the core idea of his categorical imperative. According to this formulation, we should always treat others as ends in themselves and never only as means to our ends. This proposition underscores Kant's belief that every human being has intrinsic worth and a basic dignity because human beings are rational agents. As rational agents, things have value for us in relation to our desires, interests, and projects. We are not objects or things to be used or manipulated for the purposes of others. Accordingly, we must always act in a way that respects people's humanity – in a way that treats both others and ourselves as ends and not means. When you lie to people or make promises to them that you know you will not keep, you are manipulating them. Instead of respecting others, you are using them as means to your own goals. Similarly, Kant thought that you must also treat yourself as an end. We fail to do this, for example, if we prostitute ourselves or commit suicide, Kant argued.

Ross's Commonsense Pluralism

For Kant, the categorical imperative provides the basic test of right and wrong, but nonconsequentialists are not necessarily Kantians. The nonconsequentialist moral philosopher W. D. Ross (1877–1971), for instance, firmly rejects utilitarianism, yet advances a theory that differs significantly from Kant's. Ross's normative theory is important because it is closely related to the commonsense morality of ordinary people and because something like his theory is the implicit ethical approach of many critics of utilitarianism.

Ross rejected utilitarianism as too simple and as untrue to the way we ordinarily think about morality and about our moral obligations. We see ourselves, Ross and like-minded thinkers contend, as being under various moral duties that cannot be reduced to the single obligation to maximize happiness. Often these obligations grow out of special relationships into which we enter or out of determinate roles that we undertake. Our lives are intertwined with other people's in particular ways, and we have, as a result, certain specific moral obligations.

For example, as a professor, Garcia is obligated to assist her students in the learning process and to evaluate their work in a fair and educationally productive way — obligations to the specific people in her classroom that she does not have to other people. As a spouse, Garcia must maintain a certain emotional and sexual fidelity to her partner. As a parent, she must provide for the particular, individual human beings who are her children. As a friend to Smith, she may have a moral responsibility to help him out in a time of crisis. Having borrowed money from Tsing, Garcia is morally obligated to pay it back. Thus, different relationships and different circumstances generate a variety of specific moral obligations. In addition, we have moral duties that do not arise from our unique interactions and relationships with other people. For example, we ought to treat all people fairly, do what we can to remedy injustices, and make an effort to promote human welfare generally. The latter obligation is important, but for the nonconsequentialist it is only one among various obligations that people have.

At any give time, we are likely to be under more than one obligation, and sometimes these obligations can conflict. That is, we may have an obligation to do A and an obligation to do B, where it is not possible for us to do both A and B. For example, I promise to meet a friend on an urgent matter and now, as I am hurrying there, I pass an injured person who is obviously in need of assistance. Stopping to aid the person will make it impossible for me to fulfill my promise. What should I do? For moral philosophers like Ross, there is no single answer for all cases. What I ought to do will depend on the circumstances and relative importance of the conflicting obligations. I have an obligation to keep my promise, and I have an obligation to assist people in distress. What I must decide is which of these obligations is, in the given circumstance, the more important. I must weigh the moral significance of the promise against the comparative moral urgency of assisting the injured person.

Ross and many contemporary philosophers believe that all (or at least most) of our moral obligations are prima facie ones. A *prima facie obligation* is an obligation that can be overridden by a more important obligation. For instance, we take the keeping of promises seriously, but almost everyone would agree that in some circumstances – for example, when a life is at stake – it would be not only morally permissible, but morally required, to break a promise. Our obligation to keep a promise is a real one, and if there is no conflicting obligation, then we must keep the promise. But that obligation is not absolute or categorical; it could in principle be outweighed by a more stringent moral obligation. The idea that our obligations are prima facie is foreign to Kant's way of looking at things.

Consider an example that Kant himself discussed.[7] Imagine that a murderer comes to your door, wanting to know where your friend is so that he can kill her. Your friend is in fact hiding in your bedroom closet. Most people would probably agree that your obligation to your friend overrides your general obligation to tell the truth and that the right thing to do would be to lie to the murderer to throw him off your friend's trail. Although you have a genuine obligation to tell the truth, it is a prima facie obligation, one that other moral considerations can outweigh. Kant disagreed. He maintained that you must always tell the truth – that is, in all circumstances and without exception. For him, telling the truth is an absolute or categorical obligation, not a prima facie one.

Ross thought that our various prima facie obligations could be divided into seven basic types: duties of fidelity (that is, to respect explicit and implicit promises), duties of reparation (for previous wrongful acts), duties of gratitude, duties of justice, duties of beneficence (that is, to make the condition of others better), duties of self-improvement, and duties not to injure others.[8] Unlike utilitarianism, Ross's ethical perspective is pluralistic in recognizing a variety of genuine obligations. But contrary to Kant, these obligations are not seen as absolute and exceptionless. On both points, Ross contended that his view of morality more closely fits with our actual moral experience and the way we view our moral obligations.

Ross also saw himself as siding with commonsense morality in maintaining that our prima facie obligations are obvious. He believed that the basic principles of duty are as self-evident as the simplest rules of arithmetic and that any person who has reached the age of reason can discern that it is wrong to lie, to break promises, and to injure people needlessly. However, what we should do, all things considered, when two or more prima facie obligations conflict is often difficult to judge. In deciding what to do in any concrete situation, Ross thought, we are always "taking a moral risk" (30). Even after the fullest reflection, judgments about which of these self-evident rules should govern our conduct in a particular situation remain

[7] Kant, *Practical Philosophy*, 611–15.
[8] Ross, *The Right and the Good*, 21.

"highly fallible" (42). They are only "more or less probable opinions which are not logically justified conclusions from the general principles that are recognised as self-evident" (31).

A good way to bring into focus the differences between utilitarianism and nonconsequentialist ethical theories like Ross's or Kant's is to contrast their way of looking at a specific case. One frequently discussed case is the deathbed promise.

The Deathbed Promise

Tokens of the same act-type can produce different results in different circumstances. Because of this and because utilitarianism evaluates actions only according to their consequences, it follows that if the situation is unusual enough, an action that would normally be considered reprehensible might be the morally right thing to do. For example, although taking people's property without their permission generally produces unhappiness, circumstances can occur in which stealing something would, on balance, produce the best results. If so, utilitarianism would require us to steal.

Utilitarians take this as a strength of their theory: it's realistic, flexible, and empirically based. Right and wrong, they contend, should be a function of the way the world really is, of what will or will not produce good results in any given situation. If doing something that usually causes unhappiness would in fact produce happiness in the present circumstances, then that is what one should do. To act otherwise, to choose to bring about less happiness when one could have brought about more, is wrong. It is simply benighted, utilitarians urge, to close one's eyes to the way things actually are and follow customary moral rules without regard to the actual effects of our actions. Critics of utilitarianism, however, believe this flexibility licenses immoral conduct. Sometimes, they contend, the means are not justified by the ends they are intended to promote.

Consider the frequently discussed deathbed promise case. The case is imaginary, a kind of thought experiment, but it illustrates well some important features of utilitarianism. An elderly woman living alone in poor circumstances with few friends or relatives is dying, and you are at her bedside. She draws your attention to a small case under her bed, which contains some mementos along with the money she has managed to save over the years, despite her apparent poverty. She asks you to take the case and to promise to deliver its contents, after she dies, to her nephew living in another state. Moved by her plight and by your affection for her, you

24

promise to do as she bids. After a tearful good-bye, you take the case and leave. A few weeks later the old woman dies, and when you open her case you discover that it contains $50,000. No one else knows about the money or the promise that you made.

This is an improbable situation, to be sure, but not incomprehensible or totally unbelievable. Now suppose further that the nephew is a compulsive gambler and heavy drinker and that you know that, if you were to give him the $50,000 as promised, he would rapidly squander the money. How can you confidently know this? Perhaps, someone might suggest, the money would enable him to sober up and turn his life around. Perhaps so – after all, one can make up stories however one likes. But the way the deathbed promise story goes, the nephew really would waste the money, and you know it. Suppose also that, instead of giving the money to the nephew, you could anonymously donate it to a local orphanage, enabling it to build a swimming pool and clubhouse that would bring a lot of happiness to many children for years to come. (Or, if you wish, imagine some other use for the money that would bring even more happiness: for example, donating it to an organization that looks after babies who are born addicted to crack cocaine.)

Now what is the morally right thing to do with the money? Should you give it to the nephew or to the orphanage? Assuming that the facts are as we have imagined, for a utilitarian the answer is simple: give the money to the orphanage. For several utilitarian reasons, it is normally wrong to break a promise. The promisee will be disappointed; he or she will be less ready to count on you in the future, and the incident may damage your future relationship with the person. Further, when other people learn what you did, your reputation may suffer, and your action may even erode somewhat the larger social practice of making and trusting promises. However, these sound utilitarian reasons for keeping promises do not apply in this case because the promisee is dead and no one else knows about the promise. To keep your promise and give the money to the nephew, or to hang on to the money yourself, would be wrong because it brings about less happiness than you could have brought about by donating it to the orphanage.

We know, of course, what Kant would say about this. The maxim permitting you to break your promise cannot be universalized; hence, it would be immoral of you to give the money to the orphanage, despite the happiness that doing so would bring. Ross, too, would almost certainly tell us to keep our promise, and his position seems to tally with commonsense morality. For one thing, promise-breaking is usually considered wrong even if it goes undetected, and we do not generally see people as free to break a promise whenever they think they can accomplish more good by breaking it than by keeping it. Furthermore, in our society deathbed promises are a particularly serious type of promise, a kind of promise that many people treat as almost sacred. Moreover, it was the old woman's money to do with as she wished, to bequeath to whomever she chose. And once the money has been bequeathed, however informally, the nephew could be said to have a right to it. Thus, everyday morality provides some strong considerations against giving the money to the orphanage. These considerations do not presuppose that promise-breaking can never be morally justified, but they do imply that in the imagined circumstances breaking your promise would be wrong.

Utilitarians might be tempted to deny that their position collides with commonsense morality, contending that everyday morality cares about promoting happiness as well as keeping promises and that if ordinary people were presented with this situation and thought it through, then they would agree that the money should go to the orphanage. This contention is a factual one. Although it might turn out to be true, this seems unlikely given common attitudes toward promises and deathbed bequests. Probably the most that utilitarians can plausibly claim is that ordinary people may be conflicted about the case and that commonsense morality does not yield an unequivocal verdict about what to do with the money.

Utilitarians are wiser to concede that their theory can sometimes run afoul of commonsense morality and to urge, instead, that our unreflective everyday ideas about right and wrong are not the final word on morality. To stick to everyday moral principles in cases like the deathbed promise is to choose to bring about a world that is less good than the world we could have brought about. It is to sacrifice happiness out of a kind of rule worship. Despite the value that commonsense morality rightly puts on keeping promises and respecting people's right to bequeath their money as they please, utilitarians can argue that if we think about these issues in an objective and dispassionate way, then we will see that we should not let the rules that normally work to boost long-run happiness stand in the way of maximizing happiness in a special case like this. In this way, utilitarians exhort us not to confuse ordinary moral guidelines like "keep your promises" with the real goal of moral conduct.

In addressing the apparent gap between their theory and everyday morality, utilitarians can emphasize three further points. First, utilitarians can contend that, in general, a theory is not rebutted by showing that it conflicts with people's ordinary moral ideas. In particular, once we have been persuaded that an ethical theory is correct, then judgments based on that theory should take priority over the non-theoretical moral sentiments and guidelines of everyday life. The point of an ethical theory, after all, is to illuminate the basic structure of right and wrong and perhaps to amend and improve our ordinary moral practices. We should not assume that the theory's teachings will coincide fully with our everyday moral sentiments, especially when it comes to difficult or unusual cases. Just as commonsense notions about prudent economic conduct sometimes differ from the theoretically informed ideas of economists, so our everyday, unsystematic ideas about morality will sometimes differ from the ideas entailed by the most plausible ethical theory.

Second, utilitarians can acknowledge, even stress, that it is useful for people to have the strong feelings that they do about the importance of keeping promises and respecting the property of others (including those who are recently deceased). Because these feelings and the moral guidelines and practices to which they correspond tend, in general, to produce happiness, it is good that people have them and are thus at least somewhat resistant to doing the utilitarian thing in the deathbed promise case.

Third, utilitarians can emphasize the related point that the deathbed promise case is unusual, even a bit of a gimmick, because one is asked to imagine, unrealistically, that the factors that normally make promise-breaking wrong do not apply. Naturally, our usual ideas about what leads to happiness and what does not, based as they are on what happens in normal circumstances, are going to break down in abnormal cases. While maintaining that, if the facts are as stated, then one should give the money to the orphanage, utilitarians can also underscore not only how improbable this case really is, but also how unlikely it is that, if one were in that situation, one would confidently know that one was. In other words, not only must it be the case, but one must know it to be the case, that no one else was aware of the money or the promise, that the nephew really would waste the money, that the orphanage would put it to better use, and so on. In the real world, these epistemic uncertainties may make keeping the deathbed promise the morally safest thing for a utilitarian to do.

Consequences, Actual and Probable

According to utilitarianism, to determine whether a given action is right or wrong we must compare its results with those of the alternatives open to the agent. The right action is the one that produces the best outcome, that is, the most happiness. In trying to produce the best outcome, however, an agent can sometimes be unlucky. Suppose a conscientious utilitarian carefully chooses the course of action that she judges to be happiness maximizing, but – alas – things go awry, and the outcome is terrible. Suppose further that the course she elected was what any reasonable utilitarian in her situation, knowing what she knew or even all that she could have known, would have chosen. This utilitarian acted intelligently, but the results were bad, significantly worse than if she had done something else instead. Utilitarianism implies that she did the wrong thing. Now compare the unlucky utilitarian's malicious cousin. He spitefully tries to harm his neighbor, but his action backfires and ends up having very good results for his intended victim. In fact, it maximizes happiness all around. Utilitarianism implies that the cousin acted rightly.

The judgment that the unlucky utilitarian acted wrongly and her malicious cousin did the right thing strikes many people as incorrect. Nevertheless, some utilitarians stand by this judgment and insist that it is an action's actual results that determine right and wrong.[9] They believe that it would be paradoxical to say that the unlucky utilitarian acted rightly when her action had bad results and there was an alternative course of conduct open to her that would have produced a better outcome. However, they also argue that we do not and should not blame someone for acting as a reasonable and well-informed utilitarian would have acted under the circumstances. In their view, although we cannot say that the unlucky utilitarian acted rightly, we can say that she is not to blame and acknowledge that she is a good person. On the other hand, we do and should blame the malicious cousin for acting as he did, even though his deed ended up having good results.

Other utilitarians believe that the utilitarian standard should not be the actual consequences of our actions, but rather their expected or foreseeable

---

[9] One has to compare the actual results of the action we perform with what the actual results of any alternative would have been, had we performed it instead. This raises a difficulty. If determinism is false, then the notion of "what the actual results of an alternative action would have been" becomes indeterminate. This is not an indeterminacy in what we can know, but in the way things are: there is no absolute fact of the matter as to what would have happened had we done something other than what we did. However, although quantum mechanics teaches that the world is indeterminate, it also tells us that objective probabilities govern subatomic behavior. If so, then actual-outcome utilitarians might view the outcome of an action as a probability distribution assigning objective likelihoods to each possibly resulting state of affairs. Comparing the outcomes of actions would thus be a matter of comparing their objective probability matrixes. (One should not confuse the notion of objective probabilities with that of expected utility, as explained in the text below.) See Prior, "Consequences of actions," 51–3; Regan, *Utilitarianism and Co-operation*, 12–13; Vallentyne, "Outcomes of actions," 58–62; and Bennett, *The Act Itself*, 52–4.

results at the time we act. They believe that the unlucky utilitarian acted rightly and the malicious cousin acted wrongly. As they see it, the unlucky utilitarian cannot have acted wrongly in choosing an action that she had every reason to think would be for the best. Suppose the odds against the action's having the outcome it did were so slim that anyone in her situation would have done as she did. If the unlucky utilitarian faced the same choice again (and the probabilities haven't changed), then it would be reasonable and right for her to make the same decision again despite the fact that it had an unfortunate result the first time around. To say only that the unlucky utilitarian should not be blamed for making this choice fails to do justice to her situation. To be wrong, an action must be one that a well-enough informed observer could have advised against, and agents who have acted wrongly should have at least a theoretical chance of learning how they could have done better.[10]

As these utilitarians see it, what matters is not the actual outcome of an action, but its probable, foreseeable, or expected outcome. They interpret the utilitarian standard to hold that the right action is not the action that results (or would result) in the most happiness, but the action whose outcome has, on the available evidence, the greatest expected happiness (or greatest expected utility). An action's expected happiness is calculated by multiplying the positive or negative value of each of its possible outcomes or effects by the likelihood of each of those outcomes or effects happening and then summing those values. Imagine, for example, that the agent is deliberating whether to do action A, and that A has three possible outcomes:

outcome 1 (0.7 probability): 3 units of happiness
outcome 2 (0.2 probability): −1 unit of happiness
outcome 3 (0.1 probability): 2 units of happiness

To determine the expected happiness of action A, one multiplies the happiness of each of its possible outcomes by its probability and then adds these values together. Thus, A's expected happiness is 2.1, which equals $(3 \times 0.7) + (-1 \times 0.2) + (2 \times 0.1)$. In deciding what to do, then, the agent must compare the expected happiness of A to the expected happiness of the other actions that he or she could perform.

Suppose that the only alternative to action A is action B, which has an expected value of 1. Action A is clearly what the agent should do because

---

[10] Bennett, *The Act Itself*, 50–1; see also, Howard-Snyder, "Objective consequentialism."

its expected happiness is greater. Imagine, though, that when the agent does A, the result is outcome 2 (that is, −1 unit of happiness). This result is unfortunate, but it doesn't imply that one should have done B instead. Assuming the imagined probabilities are accurate, action A is still the utilitarian thing to do. Because action A's expected value is higher than B's, if one had to choose again between them, one should still choose A.

In calculating expected happiness, whose estimates of happiness and probability do we use? Some expected-outcome utilitarians believe that, in determining right and wrong, it is the agent's own assignment of values and probabilities that counts.[11] This position faces the problem that the agent might be misinformed or negligent or otherwise fail to examine the situation or estimate outcomes as carefully as he or she should. Even if sincere, one's belief that an action maximizes expected utility may be erroneous and unreasonable. As a result, most expected-outcome utilitarians believe that the utilitarian standard is expected happiness as calculated by a reasonable and well-informed agent based on the available evidence. The phrases "reasonable and well-informed" and "available evidence" can be unpacked in different ways, but for our purposes the differences are not so significant. The important point is that the course of action that one judges best can differ from the course of action one should have judged best, given the available information, and it is this latter standard that seems to be the relevant and morally appropriate one for assessing people's actions.

This book favors the expected-outcome interpretation of the utilitarian standard, and henceforth whenever I describe an action as maximizing happiness or producing the best outcome, I shall have in mind its maximizing expected happiness or producing the best expected outcome. In practice, however, there is little difference between actual-outcome utilitarianism and expected-outcome utilitarianism. Because we are not omniscient and never know for certain the exact outcomes of the various actions we could perform, actual-outcome utilitarians will say that the reasonable way for us to proceed is by trying to maximize probable or expected happiness. Doing this may result in our doing the wrong thing, but it is safe to assume that if our actions maximize expected utility, then we will succeed in producing the most happiness over the long run. Expected-outcome utilitarians, on the other hand, say that maximizing expected utility is not only the reasonable way to proceed; it is also the standard of right and wrong.

Thus, whether one is an actual-outcome utilitarian or an expected-

[11] Jackson, "Decision-theoretic consequentialism," 463–5.

30

outcome utilitarian, in practice one must try to act so as to produce the greatest expected happiness. Of course, we can rarely, if ever, assign specific values and precise probabilities to an action's possible outcomes. Nevertheless, the general idea is important. A moral agent must take into account not just the possible good and bad effects of his or her actions, but also their likelihood. If I take my friend's money, unbeknownst to him, and buy lottery tickets with it, there is a chance that we will end up millionaires and that my action will have maximized happiness all around. But the odds are definitely against it, and the most likely result is loss of money (and probably of a friendship). Therefore, no utilitarian could justify my gambling with purloined funds on the grounds that it might maximize happiness.

Average versus Total Happiness

The utilitarian standard requires us to act so as to maximize total (expected) happiness. One possible way to increase total happiness is to increase the number of people in the world. In the eighteenth century, the proto-utilitarian philosopher William Paley noted this fact and argued that the prime political goal of any country should be to expand its population.[12] The contemporary utilitarian writer J. J. C. Smart agrees with Paley that utilitarians should favor a larger population over a smaller population:

> Would you be quite indifferent between (a) a universe containing only one million happy sentient beings, all equally happy, and (b) a universe containing two million happy beings, each neither more nor less happy than any in the first universe? Or would you, as a humane and sympathetic person, give a preference to the second universe. I myself cannot help feeling a preference for the second universe.[13]

Smart quickly adds, however, that he disapproves of an explosive increase in the world's population because "a typical member of an over-populated planet is *not* equally happy with a typical member of a moderately populated planet."

This last point is probably true, but Smart overlooks the fact that a large population of only moderately happy people might spell more total

---

[12] Paley, *Principles of Moral and Political Philosophy*, 588–9.
[13] Smart, "A system of utilitarian ethics," 27–8.

31

happiness than a small population of happier people. If doubling the world's population would decrease average or per capita happiness by less than half, then utilitarianism seems to imply that we should encourage its doubling. Furthermore, if doubling the world's population again would cut the new average by less than half, then we should double it again – and again and again. Utilitarians, it seems, should favor increasing the world's population until the world hosts a truly enormous number of people with a very, very low per capita level of happiness. Derek Parfit has called this "the repugnant conclusion."[14]

Most people agree with Parfit's sentiment. To avoid the repugnant conclusion as well as the related implication that we have a duty to have as many happy children as we can, some utilitarians have modified their theory. As they re-interpret it, the utilitarian goal is not to maximize total happiness (which is the sum we get by adding up each person's happiness), but rather to maximize average happiness or happiness per capita. This revision saves utilitarianism from the repugnant conclusion because it entails that a small population of happy people is better than a much larger population of less happy people. In addition, the average-happiness view implies that we have a duty to bring children into the world only if their level of happiness will be above average, and people are unlikely to know whether their prospective offspring will be happier than average.

Unfortunately, average-happiness utilitarianism implies, implausibly, that in a world of very happy people, it would be wrong to bring into existence a moderately happy person because doing so would lower average happiness. Average-happiness utilitarianism also implies that it would be good if people whose happiness is below average were eliminated. Suppose an enormous tidal wave completely obliterated a coastal country whose inhabitants' level of happiness was below par. By wiping out this group of people, the tidal wave would increase average world happiness. Average-happiness utilitarians would therefore have to applaud this disaster. Most people find this conclusion unacceptable.

As a general matter, it's difficult to believe that adding or subtracting people from an existing group matters morally only insofar as it affects an arithmetical figure, namely, the mean level of happiness. Because of this and because the average-happiness view has disturbing implications, it's worth taking a second look at the total-happiness view. Is it possible to escape the inference from it to the repugnant conclusion? Two lines of argument suggest themselves. The first assumes that procreative freedom and family planning are important to individual autonomy and well-being.

[14] Parfit, *Reasons and Persons*, 388.

If so, then a moral requirement obliging people to produce as many children as possible would significantly diminish people's happiness – too much, one might argue, for such a requirement to be defended on utilitarian grounds. The second argument is that if total happiness is our goal, then in terms of population policy our concern is properly with the whole future course of humanity, which may yet run for millions and millions of generations. We have no reason at all to assume that the best strategy for maximizing human happiness in the truly long run is for human beings living today to increase their population as much as they can. This would be reckless, given that even short-term population policy is fraught with empirical uncertainties and can have profound and unpredictable social and economic consequences.

These two arguments might be challenged. But even if the total-happiness view does not commit us to relentlessly maximizing population growth, it does seem to imply (1) that we have some positive obligation to have children (even if other considerations can override this), (2) that, other things being equal, the more people on earth, the better, and (3) that in principle increasing the number of people can offset a decrease in people's happiness. For these reasons I think that utilitarians should avoid the total-happiness view. This is not because they should instead concern themselves with average happiness, but because they should seek to promote the happiness only of actually existing people. Utilitarianism's real and proper concern is with how well people's lives go, and it makes no sense to say that bringing a child into existence makes his life go better than it did before. Because of this, the theory should be interpreted as striving to make people happy rather than to make happy people. It is not happiness as a disembodied entity – whether total or average – that utilitarians care about; it's people. Too many utilitarians have been led by abstract talk about maximizing happiness to implicitly reify the notion of happiness, forgetting that their morality is really about human beings and their lives, not about happiness as some sort of thing like soybeans, the production of which we are continually striving to boost.

Utilitarianism seeks to increase as much as possible the collective good. That good is a function of the well-being of actually existing people and does not include the possible happiness or unhappiness of merely potential people. To say that it is the happiness of actually existing people that matters is not to ignore future generations. There will almost certainly be actually existing people on earth two hundred years from now, and not only will their happiness matter then, but also some of the things we do now (for example, how we dispose of our toxic wastes) have moral significance just because they will affect those future people for better or worse. Other things being equal, utilitarians want future people to be as happy as possible. But this fact does not imply that utilitarians should try to increase the quantity of future world happiness by multiplying the number of human beings.

Some writers aver that potential people should count, believing that there is no morally relevant difference between them and actual people.[15] But this position seems mistaken. Talk of potential people encompasses more than fertilized eggs on their way to birth; it includes all those human beings it would be biologically possible for existing people to create if they chose to do so. In other words, Tony and Dawn's potential children are not just the embryo Dawn is now carrying and the two other kids they are planning on having and for whom they are buying a house with four bedrooms. Rather, their potential offspring include all those children they could beget if they devoted themselves solely to procreation. Now, we can perfectly reasonably care about the welfare of the people who will end up inhabiting the earth two hundred years from now, and utilitarian morality requires us to take some steps to safeguard and enhance their welfare. But it makes no more sense to care about the well-being of possible but non-existent people than it does to mourn the absence of the siblings you might have had, had your parents decided to have ten children, rather than the five they did have. People who exist or will exist matter; merely potential people don't.

If, as I argue, the goal of their theory is to maximize the happiness of people who exist (both those who exist now and those who will happen to exist in the future), then utilitarians have no reason to choose a policy that increases overall happiness while decreasing the happiness of the average future person; indeed they have reason to disfavor such a policy. And contrary to what Smart says, they should be indifferent between a world of one million happy sentient beings and a world of two million equally happy sentient beings.[16] Again, the reason is that utilitarianism values the happiness of people, not the production of units of happiness. Accordingly, one has no positive obligation to have children. However, if you have decided to have a child, then you have an obligation to give birth to the happiest child you can. It would be wrong for you to have a child now while

---

[15] Haslett, "On life, death, and abortion," 161.

[16] Should they be indifferent between it and a world of 100 (or 12 or 3) sentient beings? The smaller the number gets, the more plausible it is to challenge the assumption that people living in such a world, which would inevitably be socially, culturally, and economically impoverished, would be as happy as those living in a world of one million people.

you are addicted to crack (or are taking a medication like thalidomide that causes birth defects), when by deferring pregnancy you could later have a healthy baby.

2

Welfare, Happiness, and the Good

Utilitarianism makes right and wrong a function of the consequences of our actions, and as its name implies, the theory assesses and compares those consequences in terms of their utility – that is, their usefulness or benefit. But usefulness for what, benefit to whom? The utilitarian's answer is that it is the interests of human beings (or, more generally, sentient creatures) that are at issue, so that by the utility of actions we are to understand their impact on the welfare or well-being of people. Utilitarianism instructs us to promote the good, but by "the good" it means what is good for people. At the end of the day, all that really matters morally is that people's lives go as well as possible. Utilitarianism is thus committed to *welfarism*, to the view that individual welfare or well-being is the only thing that is to be valued for its own sake. It is, ultimately, the only thing with which morality should concern itself. Anything else that we think of as good for people – friendship, say, or individual freedom – is good only because, and to the extent that, it contributes to their well-being.

This last point is worth expanding on. There are many things that we judge good for people, and numerous objects, activities, or experiences that people need, want, or care about. Many of these things pretty clearly have only instrumental value and are good or valuable only because they are means to other things or to other ends that people have and that we deem good. Money, for example, is of purely instrumental value. It is good, not in itself, but only because it facilitates our doing or having other things that we value. A new transmission is good because my car runs better and more dependably with it, which is good because it facilitates my getting to work, which is good because keeping a job makes it possible for me to do a number of things I wouldn't otherwise be able to do – including purchasing a new transmission. Of course, as Aristotle pointed out a long time ago, life would seem fruitless if everything that is good were good

36

only because it was a means to something else.[1] The chain, it seems, must stop somewhere – there must be some thing or things that are good, not instrumentally, but in themselves.

For utilitarians, the chain of instrumental goods stops with welfare or well-being. It is the one thing that is good for people, not as a means, but intrinsically, that is, in itself or for its own sake. To borrow another argument from Aristotle, we value a variety of different things as means to well-being – for example, health or material prosperity. However, we never value happiness or well-being as a means to something else.[2] It is good for its own sake. From the utilitarian perspective, everything that is good for people is good only because directly or indirectly it enhances individual well-being. To be sure, there are things we judge good for people that do not seem to be merely instrumental goods and yet may seem distinct from well-being – for example, deep emotional attachments to others, a sense of achievement, experiencing a beautiful sunset, or getting an education. Still, about these things we can ask, why are they valuable? What makes them good for us? The utilitarian's welfarist answer is that, when we think carefully about these things, we will see that they are valuable because, and only because, they enhance human well-being.

This answer may strike one as unsatisfactory because the concept of well-being seems vague and open ended. What precisely does it mean? What exactly are we to understand by individual welfare? If utilitarianism instructs us to promote what is good for people – or, in other words, to try to make their lives go as well as possible – what specifically is it asking us to do? This chapter addresses these questions, but unfortunately utilitarians disagree about the answers.

We begin with Bentham and Mill. Like other early utilitarians, they equated happiness with pleasure and unhappiness with pain, and they interpreted welfare or well-being as happiness – hence, as we have seen, the principle of utility is also called the "greatest happiness principle." This classical utilitarian position has long had its critics. After examining objections to identifying well-being with pleasurable consciousness or a happy mental state, this chapter probes two alternative conceptions of welfare that many utilitarians have favored – the desire-satisfaction theory and the objective-list theory – and considers the possibility of a consequentialist ethical theory that abandons utilitarianism's commitment to welfarism. The chapter concludes by affirming the viability of utilitarian-

---

[1] *Nicomachean Ethics*, 1094a18–22.
[2] *Nicomachean Ethics*, 1097a35-b6.

37

ism despite the on-going debate over the nature of well-being and the shortcomings in our understanding of what is good for people.

Bentham's Hedonism

Bentham implicitly identified well-being with happiness and explicitly took happiness to be enjoyment of pleasure and security from pain. He affirmed the hedonistic doctrine that pleasure is the only thing that is good in and of itself and pain the only thing that is bad in and of itself and concluded that one state of affairs is intrinsically better than another if and only if it contains a greater balance of pleasure over pain. Bentham catalogued different pleasures and pains, and described their various sources and the factors that influence our experience of them. He saw the value of any given pleasure or pain as a function of its intensity, duration, certainty or uncertainty, and its "propinquity" or remoteness. In addition, when assessing, not the value of a pleasure or pain by itself, but the action that produces it, we must consider the likelihood that the pleasure (or pain) will be followed by other pleasures (or pains) of the same kind (Bentham calls this its "fecundity") and not followed by sensations of the opposite kind (he calls this its "purity"). Further, we must also take into account the number of people affected. In this way, Bentham thought, we can estimate, first, the goodness or badness of an action for any given individual and then, by taking into account all the individuals affected by the action, the overall goodness or badness of the action.

Critics of Bentham have long characterized his theory as crude, and they lampoon the whole idea of a hedonic calculus by means of which the pleasures and pains of individuals are to be weighed and summed. Although his theory probably does overreach itself, Bentham doesn't deserve all the abuse he has received. For one thing, he was not only concerned with sensory or bodily pleasures and pains, but also examines various other forms of gratification, satisfaction, enjoyment, and fulfillment. For example, he discusses the pleasures of memory and of religion and the pain of a bad reputation and of knowing that another is suffering. And although few, if any, subsequent utilitarians have thought that we can weigh and compare pleasures and pains, happiness and unhappiness, with anything like the precision that Bentham hoped for, central to the utilitarian tradition is the idea that the good is aggregative – that is, that we can derive an overall welfare assessment of a given state of affairs based on the welfare or happiness or utility of each individual person. That notion, along with the universalist thesis, also urged by Bentham, that the

38

happiness of each person counts as much as the happiness of any other, gives utilitarianism much of its distinctive character.

All Pleasures Are Equal

Bentham held that all pleasures are equal, famously remarking that "Prejudice apart, the game of push-pin is of equal value with the arts and sciences of music and poetry. If the game of push-pin furnish more pleasure, it is more valuable than either."[3] In saying this, he meant to insist that no pleasure is intrinsically better than any other pleasure. Bentham himself was a refined and educated man, who certainly thought that pleasures involving the intellect, the imagination, and deep human emotions are, as a rule, superior to simple sensory pleasures. But this is because they are generally more pleasurable. Even if playing chess is a less intense pleasure than taking heroin, it is safer, less costly, more permanent, less productive of future pain, and thus for these and related reasons more satisfying in the long run. For a person who can play all three games reasonably well, tick-tack-toe is likely to be a less satisfying pastime than checkers, and checkers a less satisfying pastime than chess. The pleasures of using our higher human faculties are not intrinsically better than simpler pleasures or bodily enjoyments. It's just that complex activities that engage our minds and require us to exercise our talents tend to bring us more pleasure, especially in the long term.

Still, the fact that a pleasure is simple or crude is not, in itself, a strike against it because what matters for Bentham is the amount of pleasure, as assessed by the various factors previously mentioned. The same is true of evil, malicious, or sadistic pleasures. Non-hedonists typically view evil pleasures as having little, no, or even negative value. By contrast, Bentham staunchly states that he is willing to include in the utilitarian calculus "the most abominable pleasure which the vilest of malefactors ever reaped from his crime."[4] Bentham reminds us that, in fact, such pleasure is always vastly outweighed by – "is as nothing to" – the pain (or chance of pain) that the crime causes. But viewed by itself, pleasure is pleasure whatever its nature or source.

Some philosophers have rebelled against this doctrine. For example, G. E. Moore held that it is intrinsically bad to enjoy something that is evil or

[3] Bentham, "Rationale of reward," 253; see also Paley, *Principles of Moral and Political Philosophy*, 18–19.
[4] Bentham, *Principles of Morals and Legislation*, 9.

ugly.[5] A universe that consisted only of such enjoyments would be worse than no universe at all. This was one of his reasons for rejecting Bentham's hedonism. In opposition to this, the utilitarian J. J. C. Smart has written:

> Imagine a universe consisting of one sentient being only, who falsely believes that there are other sentient beings and that they are undergoing exquisite torment. So far from being distressed by the thought, he takes a great delight in these imagined sufferings. Is this better or worse than a universe containing no sentient being at all? Is it worse, again, than a universe containing only one sentient being with the same beliefs as before but who sorrows at the imagined tortures of his fellow creatures? I suggest, as against Moore, that the universe containing the deluded sadist is the preferable one.[6]

Moore and Smart have conflicting sentiments, but the issue is difficult to adjudicate at the intuitive level because pleasures that an opponent of hedonism repudiates as vile, evil, or sadistic are usually associated with vile, evil, or sadistic conduct. In the real world, there are good reasons to discourage or even suppress certain sorts of pleasure, and it is natural that we should find not only cruel or wicked actions repugnant but also the pleasures associated with such conduct.

Some utilitarians differ from Smart in believing that their theory should put no positive weight at all on sadistic or evil pleasures. Whereas for Bentham any pleasure that a demented psychopath would get from torturing an innocent person is outweighed by the pain that the victim would suffer (as well as by the insecurity everyone would feel if such viciousness were permitted), for these writers the psychopath's potential pleasure is not even to be considered. The reason for this is that the utilitarian doctrine itself instructs us to promote happiness. Because the torturer's pleasures are anti-utilitarian in the sense that they rest on the unhappiness of others, utilitarians should not count them at all. This line of argument is problematic, however. No doubt, it would have good results if utilitarians refuse, as a matter of policy, ever to indulge people's sadistic instincts or viciously anti-social inclinations. It is not clear, however, that utilitarians can, consistent with a theory like Bentham's, decline in principle to recognize certain sources of gratification, however much they may attempt to discourage them in practice.

[5] Moore, *Principia Ethica*, 208–9.
[6] Smart, "A system of utilitarian ethics," 25.

Animals

Not only did Bentham treat all human pleasures as of equa[l]
of their source, but he also believed that we should take
pleasures and pains of animals. For this reason, he can be
of the animal rights movement. In a stirring passage in *The Principles of
Morals and Legislation*, Bentham notes the wrongness of human slavery and
goes on to write:

> The day *may* come, when the rest of the animal creation may acquire those
> rights which never could have been withholden from them but by the hand
> of tyranny. The French have already discovered that the blackness of the skin
> is no reason why a human being should be abandoned without redress to the
> caprice of a tormentor. It may come one day to be recognized, that the
> number of legs, the villosity of the skin, or the termination of the *os sacrum*,
> are reasons equally insufficient for abandoning a sensitive being to the same
> fate. (311n)

Bentham denies that animals' inability to speak or their lack of reason
permits us to ignore their interests, arguing that

> a full-grown horse or dog is beyond comparison a more rational, as well as a
> more conversable animal, than an infant of a day, or a week, or even a month,
> old. But suppose the case were otherwise, what would it avail? the question
> is not, Can they *reason*? nor, Can they *talk*? but, Can they *suffer*? (311n)

Bentham's position contrasts sharply with the view of most earlier and
many subsequent philosophers that human beings are not bound to
consider the interests of animals, who are (it is thought) essentially means
or objects that human beings are free to use as they wish for their own
purposes. Although many moralists have opposed cruelty to animals, they
tend, like Kant, to oppose it because such cruelty represents a coarsening of
our humanity, not because it ignores the interests of animals and causes
them pain.

Bentham's stance does not imply that the pleasures and pains of animals
are the same as ours or that their lives are of equal value to those of human
beings. Although some higher mammals probably enjoy rudimentary self-
awareness, their lives lack the complexity and psychological richness of
ours. They have neither the plans and projects that ordinary human beings
do, nor an awareness of how death may thwart the realization of those goals
and hopes. Nevertheless, animals can experience discomfort, pain, and
suffering. For Bentham and subsequent utilitarians that is the key point. If
a creature is sentient, then its well-being is something that can be affected,

for better or worse, by our conduct, and we must, therefore, take its pain or pleasure, happiness or unhappiness, into account along with that of human beings.

The precise implications of utilitarianism for our treatment of animals are open to debate. For his part, Bentham believed that although tormenting animals is wrong, we may nevertheless kill them for food:

> We are the better for it, and they are never the worse. They have none of those long-protracted anticipations of future misery which we have. The death they suffer in our hands commonly is, and always may be, a speedier, and by that means a less painful one, than that which would await them in the inevitable course of nature. (311n)

Some contemporary utilitarians would dissent from this conclusion. Even if utilitarianism justifies hunting animals or raising them for food when they are humanely treated and have a pleasant existence, animals such as chickens, pigs, and veal calves who pass their lives in tiny pens in modern factory farms fall outside this category. Because today most of the meat we eat comes from factory farms, where animals are unable to move freely or exercise their most basic instincts, there is a strong utilitarian case against the eating of meat.[7]

Putting this issue and related controversies aside, the point to remember is that contemporary utilitarians follow Bentham in extending the notion of individual welfare to non-human animals insofar as they are sentient or able to feel pleasure and pain. Of course, the interests of animals differ from the interests of human beings, and their sources of well-being are not the same as ours. Nevertheless, the interests of animals matter, and utilitarianism insists that they be taken into account. As it explores the ins and outs of utilitarianism, however, this book will, for ease of exposition, simplify the discussion by focusing on human well-being, ignoring the fact that utilitarianism concerns itself with the welfare of all sentient creatures, human and non-human. This narrowing of focus should affect nothing of philosophical substance.

Mill's View of Pleasure and Happiness

Like Bentham, John Stuart Mill advocated a broadly hedonistic account of well-being, writing in *Utilitarianism* that "the ultimate end" of human life

---

[7] See Singer, *Animal Liberation*. For a utilitarian perspective on animals opposed to Singer's, consult Frey, *Rights, Killing, and Suffering*.

and action is happiness, which he understood to be "an existence exempt as far as possible from pain, and as rich as possible in enjoyments, both in point of quantity and quality" (11). However, as the last phrase intimates, Mill's account of pleasure differed from Bentham's in an important respect. As we have seen, Bentham maintained that all pleasures are of equal worth if they are equivalent in terms of intensity, duration, and so on. By contrast, Mill thought that one could compare and rank pleasures, not just quantitatively, but also qualitatively. In other words, some kinds of pleasure are better than others, not because they are more pleasurable, but because they are pleasures of a higher or more valuable kind. From Mill's perspective, two activities could involve equal amounts of pleasure as measured by Bentham, yet one of the pleasures be qualitatively superior to the other.

Quantity and Quality

Unfortunately, Mill never works out the implications of his position in detail, and several generations of readers have puzzled over how one is to assess and measure quality and how it is to be compared with and balanced against quantity. Mill did hold, though, that there is a simple test for determining when one pleasure was qualitatively superior to another. This is by appealing to the experience of those who have tried both, especially those with well-developed "habits of self-consciousness and self-observation" (12). We already use something like this test to compare quantities of pleasure. How do we know that having a cold soft drink after playing vigorously in the hot sun is more pleasurable, as a general rule, than drinking a glass of warm water? The answer is simply that people who are familiar with both options (which is almost everybody) prefer one to the other. Similarly, Mill reasons that if those who are equally acquainted with and equally capable of appreciating two pleasures prefer one to the other even though they contain the same amount of pleasure, then the one pleasure is qualitatively superior to the other.

This suggests the idea that one might multiply the Benthamite value of a pleasure by a quality weighting in order to derive its true Mill-adjusted value. Pleasures could then be compared in terms of their Mill-adjusted values. Unfortunately for his readers, Mill provides no specific examples, and when he discusses the quality/quantity comparison, he imagines situations in which people would not forgo a qualitatively higher pleasure for any amount of a qualitatively lower pleasure. Thus, if pleasures of kind A are qualitatively superior to kind B, then the least pleasurable instance of A is better than the most pleasurable instance of B. Do any pleasures pass this demanding test? Mill thinks so. "Few human creatures," he argues,

43

would consent to be changed into any of the lower animals for a promise of the fullest allowance of a beast's pleasures; no intelligent human being would consent to be a fool, no instructed person would be an ignoramus . . . even though they should be persuaded that the fool [or] the dunce . . . is better satisfied with his lot than they are with theirs. (9)

Mill continues:

It is better to be a human being dissatisfied than a pig satisfied; better to be Socrates dissatisfied than a fool satisfied. And if the fool, or the pig, are of a different opinion, it is because they only know their own side of the question. The other party to the comparison knows both sides. (10)

Virtually everyone would agree with the rousing sentiment expressed in these passages, but one can debate their philosophical implications. For instance, a follower of Bentham could try to square his position with what Mill says by arguing that Mill's examples do not require the hedonist to draw qualitative distinctions among pleasures. First, the Benthamite might reject the hypothesis that the pig, fool, or ignoramus has a quantitatively more pleasurable existence than a normal human being does. When we say that we prefer our life to theirs, it is really because we cannot put aside the belief that our life is more pleasurable in Bentham's terms. In other words, we know their pleasures would bore us, and we do not really believe that the fool would become less happy if he were instructed or that we would be more happy if we were stupid. Second, Benthamites can argue that when people say they agree with Mill that the life of the pig, fool, or ignoramus is inferior, they may implicitly be taking broader utilitarian considerations into account. For instance, even if an instructed, but dissatisfied person lives a life that is less pleasant than that of a satisfied ignoramus, his or her life might be better on the whole because it benefits others more. The historical Socrates was a cheery person, but even if he had been unhappy or dissatisfied, his life would still have been better than the fool's, in an important way, because of the positive effect it has had on the world.

Some philosophers criticize Mill from the opposite perspective. Whereas Bentham might have argued that his theory can accommodate Mill's examples, these writers contend that, contrary to his expressed intention, Mill's talk of higher and lower pleasures implicitly repudiates hedonism. They argue that what his attempt to rank pleasures qualitatively really shows is that we care about things other than pleasure. If we prefer a dissatisfied human existence to the life of a satisfied pig, the reason is not that we believe that the former is more pleasurable once quality is taken into account. Rather, it is because we value things other than pleasure. The ambiguities in Mill's discussion make him vulnerable to this line of criticism. Nevertheless, Mill always equated happiness with "pleasure and the absence of pain" and insisted that they "are the only things desirable as ends" (7).

An Expanded Conception of Happiness

As Mill sees it, a happy life is "not a life of rapture, but moments of such, in an existence made up of few and transitory pains, many and various pleasures, with a decided predominance of the active over the passive" (13). In *Utilitarianism*, he addresses the fact that people seem to desire things other than happiness and pleasure. For instance, they sometimes appear to crave power, money, fame, or even virtue, not as means to happiness, but for their own sakes. Strictly speaking, the classical utilitarian thesis that happiness is the only thing that is (intrinsically) good for us does not entail that people never desire anything other than happiness for its own sake. People might, after all, simply fail to grasp what is really important in life and pursue as ends things that are not intrinsically worthwhile. In some cases, at least, this contention seems plausible. Zealots who sacrifice their own happiness or peace of mind for fame or power probably strike us as misguided, perhaps even irrational. From the point of view of their own well-being, their values are askew. However, this line of argument is unlikely to persuade the moralist that there is something defective about one's desiring virtue for its own sake and pursuing it as one's end.

In any case, Mill himself is debarred from taking the position that happiness is the sole good regardless of what people think. This is because *Utilitarianism* defends the thesis that happiness is the only thing that is good in itself on the grounds, first, that everyone desires happiness for himself and thus values it as a good and, second, that people never desire anything else. Because of this, Mill is forced to address the fact that people do seem to desire other things. Subsequent philosophers have lambasted Mill's argument, but hardly anyone would deny the conclusion of the first part of it, namely, that happiness is a good, even if not the only one.[8] Is happiness the only intrinsic good? Mill's argument does not conclusively demonstrate that it is, even if we grant the premise that people never desire

---

[8] Mill's critics contend that his argument for this conclusion commits at least two fallacies. First, they charge that Mill's use of the word "desirable" equivocates between "people do, can, or are apt to desire X" and "X is worthy of being desired." Therefore, the fact that people desire happiness does not prove that happiness is good. Mill, however, does not claim to be offering a rigorous proof, and his larger point seems

anything other than happiness. However, Mill thought that all claims about ultimate ends are, in a strict sense, beyond proof even though one can offer rational considerations in their favor.

What is important here is Mill's response to the "palpable" fact that people "do desire things which, in common language, are decidedly distinguished from happiness" (35), and what this response reveals about his understanding of happiness. Mill first observes that happiness is not something above and beyond the pleasures that make it up:

> The ingredients of happiness are very various, and each of them is desirable in itself, and not merely when considered as swelling an aggregate. The principle of utility does not mean that any given pleasure, as music, for instance, or any given exemption from pain, as for example health, is to be looked upon as means to a collective something termed happiness. They are desired and desirable in and for themselves. (35)

One does not enjoy music or good health only as a means to happiness, in Mill's view. Rather, these things are part of happiness; one's happiness consists of them.

Mill then goes on to remind us that people can come to desire something for its own sake that they originally desired only as a means to something else. For instance, a miser comes to covet money, not as a way of acquiring other goods, but for its own sake, and a person who originally sought power or fame as a way of securing other things may come to treasure it for its own sake. When this happens, what was formerly a means not only becomes an

persuasive, namely, the fact that people desire their own happiness and judge it to be a good provides compelling evidence for believing that happiness is indeed a good.

Mill's critics also lambast his moving from the proposition "that each person's happiness is a good to that person" to the conclusion that "the general happiness . . . [is] a good to the aggregate of all persons." However, Mill did not mean that every human being's happiness is a good to every other human being. As he explained to a correspondent, he "merely meant in this particular sentence to argue that since A's happiness is a good, B's is a good, C's is a good, &c., the sum of all these goods must be a good" (Later Letters, 1414).

For Mill, as for Bentham, the good is additive. The general happiness is just the sum of each individual's happiness, and the more happiness the better. One might conceivably challenge this proposition, however, by arguing that a situation in which happiness is equally distributed might be better than a situation with a greater amount of less equitably distributed happiness. But this challenge is better interpreted as an objection, not to the value thesis that good or happiness is additive, but rather to the normative thesis that it is always right to maximize happiness. We take up this latter objection in Chapter 4.

end, it becomes, Mill writes, "a principal ingredient of the individual's conception of happiness."

> In being desired for its own sake it is ... desired as *part* of happiness. The person is made, or thinks he would be made, happy by its mere possession; and is made unhappy by failure to obtain it. The desire is not a different thing from the desire of happiness any more than the love of music or the desire of health. They are included in happiness. They are some of the elements of which the desire of happiness is made up. Happiness is not an abstract idea but a concrete whole; and these are some of its parts. (36–7)

Thus, in Mill's view, at the end of the day nothing is desired except happiness. Whatever is desired is desired either as a means to something else and, ultimately, to happiness, or it is desired as a part of one's happiness. We may desire fame for its own sake and not under the description happiness, but in so desiring we make it part of our happiness.

As mentioned, Mill advances this argument in order to uphold the contention that happiness is the sole good because it is the only thing that people desire. But this contention is problematic. If happiness is whatever you desire for its own sake, then it seems empty to assert that the value of happiness is shown by the fact that people desire only it. Mill's argument looks like a merely verbal maneuver, and his critics have charged that he has drained the concept of happiness of any content. If happiness subsumes anything that one desires for its own sake, then happiness no longer names some distinctive end.

This is an important criticism, but there are at least two possible responses to it. First, taking a page from Sidgwick's *Methods of Ethics*, one might contend that there is no other way to frame a coherent account of human good, one capable of encompassing the full range of human endeavor and ambition (406). Only an expanded conception of happiness like Mill's permits us to offer a systematic, unifying account of well-being. Second, one can argue, as Mill himself did, that because happiness is intimately linked to pleasure, his expanded conception of it is not empty. Mill contends that introspection and observation show that:

> Desiring a thing and finding it pleasant, aversion to it and thinking of it as painful, are phenomena entirely inseparable or, rather ... two different modes of naming the same psychological fact; that to think of an object as desirable (unless for the sake of its consequences) and to think of it as pleasant are one and the same thing; and that to desire anything except in proportion as the idea of it is pleasant is a physical and metaphysical impossibility. (38)

It follows from this that when we desire something for its own sake, it is both part of our happiness and something we find pleasant. Mill grants that we can will from habit something we no longer desire, but this fact, he thinks, is compatible with "the doctrine that nothing is a good to human beings but in so far as it is either itself pleasurable or a means of attaining pleasure or averting pain" (40).

A critic will point out that Mill does not establish that our goal or motive is always pleasure, but this is not Mill's intention. When he writes that "all desirable things ... are desirable either for pleasure inherent in themselves or as a means to the promotion of pleasure" (7), he does not mean that all desirable things are *desired* by us only for their pleasure. The things we value are not necessarily sought for the pleasure to be had from them. Mill believes that the prospect of pleasure is at least part of the cause of any desire, and that we are made happy by obtaining the thing we desire, but this does not entail that all desire is desire for pleasure. Suppose Mr. Celebrity desires fame for its own sake. The idea of fame is pleasurable to him, and it may be, as Mill suggests, that the association of fame with pleasure explains why Mr. Celebrity originally began to chase after it. Nevertheless, the object of his desire is fame. His motive for passing up a weekend of sensual delight and instead enduring inconvenience and discomfort in order to be able to appear on the *Tonight Show* is fame, not pleasure. But fame brings him pleasure, and he cannot be happy without it.

A Problem for Mental-State Accounts of Well-Being

In their different ways, Bentham and Mill identify well-being or what is good for a person with happiness and, in turn, happiness with pleasure and the absence of pain. They would agree that happiness is, as one utilitarian has recently argued, "being in a state of consciousness whose overall quality is pleasurable."[9] What does this mean? Bentham evidently thought that pleasure is some kind of agreeable, internally identifiable sensation and that all pleasures are homogeneous. By contrast, other hedonistic utilitarians have interpreted pleasure as an experience (or an aspect of an experience) that one likes or that one wishes to continue on its own account. Pain is an experience that one dislikes and wishes to cease. In this view, the pleasure of drinking a cold beer may have no phenomenological tone or experiential quality in common with the pleasure of watching your daughter learning

[9] Sprigge, "The greatest happiness principle," 40–1.

48

to walk; they are pleasures because they are experiences that one wishes (other things being equal) to prolong.

Contemporary philosophers refer to classical utilitarianism as offering a *mental-state* account of well-being because, however we interpret pleasure, a person's welfare or good consists solely in the person's having certain experiences or being in certain mental states. When Mill wrote that a worthwhile life is "an existence made up of few and transitory pains, many and various pleasures," along with some moments of "rapture," he was endorsing a mental-state account of well-being, according to which a person's well-being is a function of the character or quality of the person's conscious experiences.

Classical utilitarianism is committed to the hedonistic thesis that well-being consists entirely in pleasurable consciousness, but other mental-state theories are possible, theories that identify well-being with experiences or states of consciousness other than pleasure or in addition to pleasure. However, regardless of the specific mental state or states that are deemed intrinsically good for a person, there is something attractive about the idea that one's well-being is entirely a function of the quality of one's mental life. After all, without consciousness life would have no value. Mental life, not mere biological existence, is what counts, and most of us believe that a person is no better off being permanently unconscious than she is being dead. In light of this, one can go on to argue that our possessions, activities, and relationships do not matter in themselves; what matters about them is only how they impinge upon our feelings and consciousness, how they are experienced or lived by us. The more we reflect on things, the reasoning goes, the more certain we shall become that nothing has value except in relation to consciousness and that people's good consists solely in the quality of their subjective experiences. Of course, people's experiences of the same or similar situations can differ. Tariq loves speaking before large audiences, but Rebecca hates it. A mental-state account captures the subjective or personal character of well-being, which in turn reflects the important fact that well-being is a matter of how an individual's life is going for her.

From the perspective of a mental-state account, however, there is no difference in value between (1) your enjoying the affection of a spouse who loves you and (2) your enjoying the apparent affection of a spouse whom you falsely believe to love you but who is only acting a part. Without a difference in your conscious experience, there can be no value difference between (1) and (2). Yet, everyone would prefer being in situation (1) to being in (2), and we would feel sorry for our colleague Maria if we learned she was in situation (2) when we had thought she was in (1). We would believe her to be less well-off than we had previously thought. This example draws attention to the fact that people care about things other than the character of their conscious experiences, and it argues that something can affect a person's well-being without affecting her mental state. There is more to our good, the example suggests, than how our lives feel from the inside. If so, then any mental-state account of well-being must prove unsatisfactory.

In a famous thought experiment, Robert Nozick has developed this line of argument in a dramatic form. "Suppose," he writes,

> there were an experience machine that would give you any experience you desired. Superduper neuropsychologists could stimulate your brain so that you would feel you were writing a great novel, or making a friend, or reading an interesting book. All the time you would be floating in a tank, with electrodes attached to your brain. Should you plug into this machine for life, preprogramming your life's experiences? . . . Would you plug in?[10]

Nozick's answer to both questions is no. We want, and rightly so, he argues, to do things and be a certain sort of person, not just have the experience of doing them or of being the kind of person that does them. We desire to remain in touch with reality and are repelled by the idea of living an artificial life in a world created by a machine. We do not want merely to have a succession of experiences or mental states, however valuable or satisfying they are, but to live our own lives and to do so in contact with the real world.

Nozick's thought-provoking example has persuaded many people that it can make a difference to the intrinsic value of an experience whether it is based on reality or not. If one agrees with Nozick that the life of a person hooked up to the experience machine is missing something of intrinsic importance, even though the person is not missing out on any valuable feelings or consciousness, then one must reject a mental-state view of well-being. However, the fact that most people are strongly disinclined to plug into the machine may not conclusively refute a mental-state approach to well-being. Because Nozick's thought experiment "draws upon intuitions about what we want for its own sake which were developed in settings where the drastic split the machine effects between experience and reality does not typically exist," those intuitions may be untrustworthy.[11]

Moreover, two natural and very strong reasons people have for refusing

[10] Nozick, *Anarchy, State, and Utopia*, 42–3.
[11] Railton, "Naturalism and prescriptivity," 170; cf. Haslett, *Capitalism with Morality*, 40.

to plug into the machine are compatible with a mental-state account of well-being.[12] First, we fear doing so because it would make us totally vulnerable. By plugging into the machine, we would be surrendering both our bodies and our minds to whoever operates it. That is a frightening prospect. Second, we may have concerns for other things besides our own well-being. We may, for instance, want to help our children grow up, see our students make it to graduation, or continue campaigning for increased assistance to the homeless. Even if it would be better for me personally if I were on the experience machine, I may quite understandably desire not to desert my family or abandon my real-world projects.

If the machine proved safe, people might be willing to give it a short try and, if they liked it, to plug in for occasional intervals thereafter. Would they be worse off for having tried it once or for using it occasionally? It seems not. Just as it might be good for someone to have immersed himself totally in the imaginative world that Dickens creates in *David Copperfield*, so it might enhance a person's well-being to have experienced that world on Nozick's machine. Likewise, a person might be better off, his or her life might be said to have gone better, for having lived an abridged version of some great human lives of the past — to have experienced their joys and agonies, their hard work, their defeats, their victories.

The experience machine is supposed to be able to create any experience so that it is indistinguishable from the real thing. One wonders whether this is an intelligible supposition. Consider the experience of working hard, persevering through difficult times, and suffering discouraging defeats before achieving eventual success. Or consider the experience of gradually developing intimate relations with and deep emotional attachments to other people, or the experience of becoming better informed, wiser, and more judicious in one's conduct. Can one coherently be imagined to have experiences like these without doing anything? To see the incoherence of supposing that machine experiences are indistinguishable from reality, imagine that what you took to be your whole life until now had been a machine-generated fantasy. You learn this when a technician trips over something, disconnecting you from the machine. The situation is explained to you. Would you repudiate (what you took to be) your life until now as "unreal" or would you beg to be plugged back into the machine, thus returning to "reality" after some kind of bizarre nightmare?

Let us put these experience-machine fantasies aside and return to the more manageable example of Maria, whose happy existence rests on the false belief that her spouse loves and adores her. According to mental-state

---

[12] Goldsworthy, "Well-being and value," 18.

accounts, if her conscious experiences are the same, then Maria is equally well off whether her happiness is based on false beliefs or on true beliefs. But this is a big *if*. In most circumstances in life, a lot can turn on whether our beliefs are true or false. Because we cannot easily put aside this background knowledge, it is difficult for us to imagine that Maria's life really is the same whether her belief in her spouse is true or false. We cannot help thinking that she will discover the truth, and with dire results, or that somehow her experiences will be different with a spouse who is playing a part than with a spouse who genuinely loves her. The risk of discovery and the overwhelming likelihood that one's experiences would, in fact, differ in the two cases are extrinsic considerations, but they may prejudice our answer to the question whether the deceived state is intrinsically worse than the undeceived state.

A final point. We want our experiences to be veridical, and we don't want others to deceive us. We want to be loved by our spouse, not just believe that we are loved. But these facts do not prove that we are better off undeceived or that what is good for us is a function of something besides subjective experience, something besides how our life feels to us from the inside. Regardless of what we want or think we want, a benevolent observer might reasonably believe that we are better off having a certain mental state than we would be knowing the truth. In line with this, most people would think it cruel to tell the truth to a happily deceived person on her deathbed. In this case, the usual practical advantages of true beliefs over false do not muddy the water (for instance, the likelihood that the deceived person will eventually discover the truth and the fact that people generally do better, at least in the long run, the fewer illusions they suffer from). If we put aside the real but extrinsic advantages of knowledge, then it may not be so evident that a person is intrinsically better off undeceived.

Well-Being as the Satisfaction of Desire

Bentham believed not only that pleasure is the sole intrinsic good but also that, as a matter of psychological fact, people tend to seek what brings them the most pleasure or happiness. This second proposition makes a debatable, empirical claim. As Mill points out, people desire a variety of things, and even if getting the things they desire does frequently (or even always) bring them pleasure or happiness, pleasure needn't be their reason for pursuing those things. In fact, one might more plausibly claim that people's well-being or happiness consists in their getting what they want than that all they want is pleasure or happiness. Indeed, Mill's conviction that everything people desire, they desire either as a means to happiness or as part of their happiness, suggests the idea that what ultimately matters is not that people get happiness (which now seems a relatively formal notion), but that they get the things they desire.

Many contemporary utilitarians have endorsed this sort of account of well-being. In their view, something benefits a person, promotes her well-being, or enhances her welfare if and only if it satisfies her desires (or, as economists say, her "preferences"). In other words, what is good for a person is not a certain sort of mental state or experience such as enjoyment or pleasure, but rather her getting what she wants, whatever it is. People may want enjoyment or pleasure, but they want other things as well – for instance, to visit Barcelona, climb Mt. Kilimanjaro, understand calculus, learn French, reconcile with an estranged cousin, or finish writing a poem. Instead of trying to organize these disparate goals under the heading of happiness or pleasure, the desire-satisfaction view of welfare holds that people's well-being consists in their desires being satisfied. Satisfaction here has nothing to do with one's feeling satisfied; it means only that the desired state of affairs has obtained. According to this way of thinking, what matters, and what utilitarianism rightly seeks to promote, is people getting as much as possible of whatever it is they want.

Today the desire-satisfaction theory is probably the dominant view of welfare among economists, social scientists, and philosophers, both utilitarian and non-utilitarian. One reason for this is the prestige of modern economic theory, which defines utility maximization as one's doing what one most prefers and explains market behavior in terms of people's rational pursuit of their ends. If one accepts the standard idealizations of positive economics and the economists' view of rationality, then it follows that what one prefers is what is good for one.[13] But there are at least two other reasons for the popularity of the desire-satisfaction theory.

First, the theory is attractive because it doesn't tell people what specific things are good for them or what they should want. It respects people's desires, taking their wants as they are, without making value judgments about the content of those desires. The idea that what is good for people is their getting what they want, whatever it is, and the related proposition that what should enter into the moral calculus is not what other people think is good for us, but what we want or believe good for us, accord well with the ethos of a liberal and democratic society.

Second, many people gravitate toward the desire-satisfaction theory because it appears to make the notion of welfare less obscure and less

---

[13] Hausman and McPherson, *Economic Analysis*, 73; cf. Broome, "Utility," 3–5.

psychological than a mental-state theory does. This is because people's wants seem easier to identify and compare than do their mental states or pleasures and pains. Proponents of the theory believe that we can more readily determine whether a person's desire has been satisfied – for instance, Frank's desire to see Graceland – than what his mental state is. Moreover, there are behavioral indices of the intensity of people's desires, wants, and preferences, and decision theorists have taught us how to rank the strength of people's desires in terms of the choices and trade-offs they are willing to make. People sometimes say that you can't compare apples and oranges, but if, when given a choice between an orange or a 50 percent chance of winning an apple, Alice values the outcomes equally (or, as economists say, is "indifferent" between them), then we can rank fairly precisely the relative strength of her respective desires for oranges and apples.

Nevertheless, the desire-satisfaction theory of welfare faces serious difficulties.

One problem, or set of problems, arises from the fact that people's desires can and do change. As a boy, Wayne desires to own a cow when he grows up, but as an adult he no longer has this desire. Giving the adult Wayne a cow will not enhance his welfare, but it is not clear that the desire-satisfaction theory can ignore his earlier desire simply because it is past. One cannot say that past desires don't count because fulfilling them brings no satisfaction without moving back toward a mental-state theory. Indeed, sometimes we may believe it worthwhile to fulfill a person's past desire. We might, for example, judge it good that the strong desire Heather once had to see her poetry published is satisfied, even though that desire expired when repeated failure caused her literary ambitions to wither. Moreover, if we are permitted to dismiss a desire because it is past, can we ignore a person's present desire if we truly believe that it will eventually fade away? These puzzles for the desire-satisfaction theory are made worse by the fact that people's current desires sometimes conflict among themselves. If happiness is not our guide, how are we to decide which desire to satisfy?

A second problem is that a person's desires may be based on false beliefs as when Fred desires to build up his muscles or move to a new apartment because he incorrectly thinks that Donna will love him if he does. Or a person's desires may result from coercion or manipulation or be based on some problematic psychological mechanism such as cognitive dissonance, wishful thinking, or not wanting something because you don't think you can have it (sour grapes). There seems to be little or no value in satisfying desires based on erroneous beliefs, and it is doubtful that gratifying desires that are irrational or the product of manipulation enhances people's welfare or makes them better off.

A third difficulty with the desire-satisfaction theory is that a person's desires can be satisfied without his or her realizing it. When Angela visits a small village in Africa and is moved by its poverty, she may strongly desire that someday it prosper. Later, after Angela has returned home and resumed her normal life, the village's economic fortunes improve markedly, and her desire is realized. Yet word of the village's success never reaches her. In such a case, it seems odd to say that satisfying Angela's desire has enhanced her welfare.

A fourth problem is that there is no guarantee that, when my desire is satisfied, I will like it or enjoy it. Indeed, satisfying my desire may cause me unhappiness. Attracted by its sophistication and glamour, I want to spend a year in Manhattan. My desire is realized, but I find the city noisy, dirty, dangerous, and unfriendly, and I hate the experience. Here again one's welfare seems divorced from the satisfaction of one's desires.

Finally, the desire-satisfaction theory implies that it would enhance a person's well-being for her to cultivate desires that are easy to satisfy, thus boosting her overall level of desire satisfaction. Some ancient and modern moralists advise us to moderate our wants and cease to worry about or avidly pursue material goods. They do so because they believe that if we give up these wants, then our lives will be more tranquil and satisfying – in short, that we will be happier. Far less plausible is the proposition that we should have easily satisfied wants (and as many of them as possible) in order to maximize the only thing that is intrinsically good for us, namely, the satisfaction of our desires.

Many proponents of the desire-satisfaction view of welfare attempt to dodge these objections by modifying their theory in various ways. Frequently, they stipulate that the desires must be those I would have only if I were properly informed, reflective, and rational, or they require that my desires not result from conditioning or from some undesirable psychological mechanism. Some theorists also recommend excluding malicious or malevolent desires. One might go further and bar desires for states of affairs – for example, the prosperity of the African village – the realization of which does not enter into my experience or even presuppose my existence. But it is hard to know on what grounds the desire-satisfaction theorist can exclude certain desires in principle, and to require that a satisfied desire affect one's experiences starts the theorist down the road to a happiness or mental-state theory.

Weeding out desires that are irrational, malformed, or based on false beliefs does, to be sure, make the desire-satisfaction theory a more plausible account of one's good, but it also costs the theory some of its original appeal. This is because my welfare no longer involves the satisfaction of the

55

desires that I actually have, but rather the desires I would have if rational, properly informed, and so on. What matters now is not getting what one wants, but getting what one should want. Furthermore, even a revised desire theory cannot eliminate all possible gaps between desire satisfaction and (what we normally take to be) well-being. To be sure, one's welfare is greatly affected by whether one's wants and desires are satisfied, and no one can be truly happy or well-off whose most important desires in life are thwarted. But satisfying people's desires does not automatically make them better off, as the desire-satisfaction theory requires. Even if my desire is informed and rational, satisfying it may not bring me satisfaction or enhance my welfare. There is more to well-being, it seems, than having your dreams come true.

Objective Theories of Well-Being

The revised desire-satisfaction theory focuses on what a person would want under idealized conditions, that is, if he or she were rational, fully informed, and so on. From here it is a short step to asking what people should want or what it is good for them to have regardless of what they actually do want or think they want. In this way, the revised desire-satisfaction theory slides towards an objective theory of well-being. Sometimes called the *objective-list* approach,[14] this is the view that human well-being is a matter of one's life comprising certain objectively valuable things – for example, friendship, rational activity, a sense of achievement, or an appreciation of true beauty.[15] Just as these things are good for people, so are certain things bad – for example, ignorance, being deprived of dignity, being coerced, manipulated, or deceived, or having the development of one's natural talents thwarted. According to the objective-list approach, these things are good (or bad) for a person regardless of whether the person desires them or enjoys them. One is better off with a life that contains more of these desirable things or contains a better, more balanced mix of them.

Some philosophers happily affirm that certain things benefit a person or that the person must have them for her life to go well regardless of what she herself happens to think. After all, common sense accepts the idea that people do not always know what is best for themselves. Their desires may

[14] Parfit, *Reasons and Persons*, 499; Scanlon, "Value, desire, and quality of life," 188–9.
[15] For some sample lists, see Brink, *Moral Realism*, 231–5; Finnis, *Natural Law*, 85–90; Griffin, *Value Judgement*, 29–30; and Crisp, *Mill on Utilitarianism*, 62.

be twisted; their goals foolish; their sources of satisfaction self-destructive. Because of their upbringing or restricted circumstances, people may find gratification in base activities or disdain cultivated pleasures in favor of vulgar ones. Because of this, we are reluctant to chain the concept of human good to the way people happen to be, rather than to the way they should be. Although the notion of well-being must to some extent connect with the way a person actually is, few would deny that sometimes people would be better off if their desires or sources of gratification were other than they are or if they were to engage in different activities or develop other aspects of themselves.

A mental-state theorist and a desire-satisfaction theorist can readily grant that the items on the objective list are sources of welfare. Things like friendship, accomplishment, and knowledge typically make people happy and are generally desired by them. However, objective-list theorists are not merely inventorying the things that can affect well-being or that typically make people better off. Rather, they are trying to reveal the nature of well-being and explain what it means for a person to flourish. For objective-list theorists, well-being consists in having the recommended goods.

How is one to identify the things that are good and bad for people? How is one to specify the objective constituents of human well-being? Objective-list theorists cannot avoid value judgments because empirical claims about what people desire or enjoy do not settle what is good for them. Instead, these theorists rely on their intuitions about what is good for people, about what makes our lives valuable ones for us. In defending judgments about well-being, objective-list theorists may appeal to what rational, ideally informed people would want or enjoy, but one should not be misled by this. The claim is that rational, ideally informed people will desire the things on the objective list because they realize that those things are good for them. It is not their being desired, even by rationally and ideally informed people, that makes them good.

Let's consider an example. John Finnis has argued that knowledge is intrinsically good for us. It enhances our well-being regardless of whether we like it, value it, or desire it. He writes:

> It is obvious that a man who is well-informed, etc., simply *is* better off (other things being equal) than a man who is muddled, deluded, and ignorant, that the state of the one is better than the state of the other, not just in this particular case or that, but in all cases, as such, universally, and *whether I like it or not*. Knowledge is better than ignorance.[16]

[16] Finnis, *Natural Law*, 72.

Probably everyone will agree that, generally speaking, knowledge is better than ignorance and that a well-informed person is better off than an ignorant person. But these generalizations do not establish that in itself knowledge is always and necessarily good for us. Some knowledge seems utterly worthless, and some knowledge may even be harmful. Counting the bricks on my office wall does not make me better off, and learning what my neighbors say about me to their friends would hurt.

Putting aside trivial or painful knowledge, one might argue, more modestly, that some knowledge is, in itself, good for us to have. For example, one might contend that scientific or theoretical knowledge is valuable even when it has no practical use. However, the value we place on such knowledge can be accounted for in various ways, without supposing that it is, in itself, necessarily good for us. Besides helping us in subtle or unexpected ways in the future, such knowledge may improve our intellectual abilities, enhance our self-confidence, gratify our curiosity, or give us a sense of satisfaction.[17] If so, then it becomes plausible to assert that such knowledge is good for us, not in itself, but only because, and to the extent that, it tends to make us happy or satisfy our desires.

These comments on the value of knowledge may rebut Finnis, but they do not sink the whole objective-list approach to well-being. Perhaps future philosophical dialogue will establish the thesis that there are some goods, the possession of which, in itself, necessarily makes one's life better. Right now, though, there are no decisive arguments for that thesis, and the attempts of various philosophers to identify the goods that constitute well-being have only produced conflicting lists – lists that seem to reflect only the tastes of their different authors.

Perfectionism

One historically influential objective account of well-being is *perfectionism*. Descended from Aristotle, this is the view that we are to assess the goodness of an individual's life by standards derived from the species or other natural kind to which the individual belongs. These standards determine what is an ideal or excellent life for a being of that kind. The life of an individual is good to the degree that it approximates that ideal. For an Aristotelian, human beings have certain natural and distinctive capacities, and it is the full development of these capacities that constitutes an excellent human life – the life that it is appropriate, fitting, and good for a human being to lead.

---

[17] Goldsworthy, "Well-being and value," 12–13.

Human well-being consists in living such a life. Perfectionism, however, faces at least two difficulties.

The first is to identify and defend certain reasonably specific traits or capacities as ideal. Aristotle thought that a good human life is one in which a person exercises the distinctively human side of his soul – that is, his rationality – in accordance with virtue or excellence. Aristotle's writings are rich and suggestive, but this thought is an elusive one, and commentators disagree about how best to spell out his understanding of human excellence. Moreover, most modern thinkers have difficulty accepting Aristotle's belief that human beings have an essential function (namely, the exercise of their reason) and that like acorns, caterpillars, and other living things their development has a natural and proper course. Not sharing Aristotle's teleological worldview, we find dubious the idea that any one mode of human functioning can be seen as essential either to an individual person or to the whole species.

Like Aristotle, Nietzsche can be interpreted as advocating a kind of perfectionism. Nietzsche is a challenging and provocative writer, and many have found inspiring his vision of the *übermensch*, the yet-to-be realized ideal existence toward which the most talented members of our species are implicitly striving. Yet Nietzsche's perfectionist ideal is nebulous and seems to express only his own predilections, a fact that can be obscured by his dramatic rhetoric. To say the least, his value judgments are contestable. "Life itself," he writes, "is *essentially* appropriation, injury, overpowering of what is alien and weaker." Moreover, he is prepared to subordinate everything to help bring about a superior form of human existence. "Society must *not* exist for society's sake," he proclaims, "but only as the foundation and scaffolding on which a choice type of being is able to raise itself to its higher task and to a higher state of *being*."[18] Elsewhere he asks, "how can your life, the individual life, receive the highest value, the deepest significance? How can it be least squandered?" His answer is disturbing, and not just to utilitarians: "Certainly only by your living for the good of the rarest and most valuable exemplars, and not for the good of the majority."[19]

The second problem with perfectionism is that, in specifying what constitutes a good or excellent human existence, it loses contact with a crucial aspect of the notion of welfare or well-being – namely, that

---

[18] Nietzsche, *Basic Writings*, 392, 393. Cf. *Untimely Meditations*, 161: "Mankind must work continually at the production of individual great men – that and nothing else is its task."

[19] Nietzsche, *Untimely Meditations*, 162.

something enhances a person's welfare if and only if it is good for the person. In other words, for something to promote a person's well-being, it must make her life go better for her. As L. W. Sumner writes:

> Welfare assessments concern what we may call the prudential value of a life, namely how well it is going *for the individual whose life it is*. This . . . is one of the deepest features of the language of welfare: however valuable something may be in itself, it can promote someone's well-being only if it is also good or beneficial *for her*.[20]

Sumner goes on to argue that perfection diverges from welfare because there is no guarantee that the better human specimens will have lives that are better than other people's.

He develops this point with an example. You stumble into philosophy as an undergraduate and begin taking it seriously because you are good at it and find the exercise of your intellectual abilities satisfying. You progress rapidly, making important contributions to the field and going on to be a professor at a prestigious university. As time passes, however, dissatisfaction haunts you. Although you continue to flourish professionally, you come to doubt that this is how you wish to spend your life. The prospect of building yourself a cabin and pursuing organic farming tempts you. You persist in your career, but become irritable and depressed, feeling trapped and driven by your own talents. Eventually, you leave the university and take up farming and cabin building. You do not feel as challenged as you did before, but you are relaxed and at peace with yourself. You are now doing less to develop your capacities, but your life is more satisfying and fulfilling to you.[21]

A perfectionist might challenge this particular example based on his or her particular theory of the ideal existence. But the larger point still holds. Because perfectionism derives its standards from our capacities and nature, and not from our choices and satisfactions, it risks imposing on people a life-design that they do not themselves ratify. Developing your distinctively human capacities or becoming a close approximation of the human ideal may or may not be good for you; it may or may not make your life go better for you. Because of this, perfectionism founders as an account of well-being.[22]

---

[20] Sumner, "Two theories of the good," 4.

[21] Sumner, "Two theories of the good," 4–5.

[22] Although perfectionists typically resist or overlook this point, Thomas Hurka explicitly concedes it. See Hurka, *Perfectionism*, 17, but cf. Sher, *Beyond Neutrality*, 234.

Beyond Welfare?

Perfectionism implicitly breaks (or is close to breaking) with utilitarianism's commitment to welfarism, to the proposition that individual welfare or well-being is the only thing that is to be valued for its own sake. However, welfarism is not beyond question, and some philosophers balk at it. Philosophers who reject welfarism rarely deny that welfare is good but, rather, assert that some things or states of affairs other than well-being are also intrinsically good. Moreover, although they abandon welfarism, many of these philosophers cling to the consequentialist component of utilitarianism so that right and wrong are still, in their view, determined by the outcomes of our actions, by the goodness or badness of their consequences. Although we are to act so as to bring about as much good as possible, well-being is not the only thing we are to promote; it is not the only thing that is good in itself.

Some of the things or states of affairs that such non-utilitarian consequentialists identify as intrinsically good involve people – for example, distributive equality, fairness, reward in accord with merit, retribution for wrongdoing, or the mutual acknowledgment and reciprocation of affectionate feelings. However, the goodness of these states of affairs is not a function of individual well-being. Rather, these things are valuable regardless of whether they enhance any individual's welfare or make anyone's life go better. A non-utilitarian consequentialist might also identify, as intrinsically good, things or states of affairs that do not affect or involve human beings at all. For example, one might urge that biodiversity is good for its own sake or that beauty is intrinsically valuable even if no one is conscious of it.[23]

G. E. Moore used the method of isolation to identify the things that possess intrinsic value and the degree to which they possess it.[24] The method simply consists in asking what value we should attach to a thing if it existed all by itself, stripped of the things that usually accompany it. Something is intrinsically good if and only if its existence by itself would be good, and one compares the relative value of different things by comparing the value that attaches to each in isolation. Alternatively, one can imagine a universe that has x and compare it with a universe that lacks x but is identical in every other respect. Is the universe with x better? In these ways, one tries to focus one's intuitive judgments of value. Following

---

[23] This second view once tempted G. E. Moore; see his *Principia Ethica*, 83–4 and 189.

[24] Moore, *Principia Ethica*, 187.

this method, Moore rejected hedonism and urged, instead, that there are an immense variety of intrinsically good and bad things, that these things need share no characteristics in common, and that their positive or negative value does not rest on the value of their constituent parts in any simple or straightforward way.

Contemporary philosophers who, like Moore, endorse consequentialism but not welfarism favor the same method to support their non-welfarist judgments of intrinsic value.[25] In response, utilitarians contend that the goods identified by the non-welfarist are intrinsically valuable only insofar as they promote human well-being. Things like mutual affection, aesthetic appreciation, equality of opportunity, or the punishing of misconduct are valuable only if, directly or indirectly, they benefit people, if they improve our lives for us. If we think carefully about these things, utilitarians argue, we shall see that they have no value beyond their impact on human well-being. Furthermore, from the utilitarian perspective the function of morality is, ultimately, to make our lives go better. Even if, ex hypothesi, there were intrinsic values other than welfare, they would not matter in a moral sense. Neither individually nor collectively would we have reason to promote those supposed values.

The issue is difficult to resolve, and there are no knock-down arguments for or against welfarism. Take biodiversity as an example. Many environmentalists value biodiversity, but is it good for its own sake or only because of its impact on sentient creatures, including human beings? Compare for example a world with 350,000 different species of beetles with an otherwise identical world with 400,000 species of beetles.[26] Assume that the number of individual beetles is the same in both worlds, that the difference in the number of beetle species affects the well-being of no living thing, and that nobody in either world has a clue how many species of beetles there are. Is the more beetle-diverse world a better, more valuable world?

It is difficult to believe that it is, but suppose nevertheless that someone affirms the superiority of the beetle-diverse world. There is still the question whether the putative value of biodiversity has normative repercussions. In particular, would it give one a reason to strive to increase beetle diversity for its own sake? Does it give one moral grounds for imposing some cost on himself or any other sentient creature in order to promote beetle diversity? These questions are abstract and perplexing, but I, for one,

---

[25] See Railton, "The demands of morality," 149n.
[26] Scientists have now described 350,000 different species of beetles, but the number may ultimately reach into the millions (*National Geographic*, March 1998, 101).

find it implausible to affirm that species diversity is valuable for its own sake.

Where This Lack of Consensus Leaves Utilitarianism

Utilitarians can judge a person's life to be morally good even when its overall level of welfare is not particularly high. Although the person's life could have gone better for her, she may have made the world a better place by enhancing the well-being of others. Imagine someone who dedicates her life to aiding poor migrant laborers and succeeds over the years in significantly improving their lot. Presumably, she finds pleasure in her work, and her life brings her satisfaction. Yet, we may also imagine that her overall level of well-being is lower than that of some of her less socially engaged acquaintances. Perhaps she suffers from health problems, has experienced personal tragedy, or is estranged from her adult children. Perhaps she would have experienced even more satisfaction in her life had she pursued a more conventional, less altruistic career. In any case, although she is an admirable person, and utilitarians will hold her up as an exemplar, her life is not as high in personal well-being as it might have been and as many other, less praiseworthy lives are.

Utilitarians, however, are not interested in moral goodness for its own sake, any more than they want, as the perfectionist does, to create ideal or admirable human specimens. Rather, utilitarians aim to increase the well-being of people in general, to enhance as much as possible the goodness of their lives for them. As we have seen, though, there is no consensus among utilitarians or other philosophers about how best to understand the concept of well-being. All the theories we have surveyed face difficulties. On the other hand, they all offer some important insights.

Even if there is, as Nozick's experience machine suggests, more to our lives going well than how they feel to us, happiness or mental-state theories rightly emphasize the role of experience in well-being. In particular, enjoyment, satisfaction, and pleasure are, at the very least, important components of well-being, and no one denies that pain, suffering, and unhappiness tend to undermine welfare and destroy our well-being. Desire-satisfaction theories wrongly cut this link to experience. After all, the reason we care about fulfilling people's desires is that we believe that it will bring them satisfaction. We buy our children the presents they want, throw our friend the party he desires, and vacation where our spouse wishes because we believe that doing so will make them happy.

On the other hand, desire-satisfaction theories highlight the pertinent fact that a person's good or welfare is intimately connected to the realization of her desires, especially her central and most important desires. Nobody's life can go well if her enduring goals remain unrealized or her most basic wants thwarted. Furthermore, what people want is generally a reliable guide to what will please them or make them happy, and even when it isn't (or we can't be sure that it is), it may be best on various other grounds to provide them with what they want, rather than what we think will be good for them.

Objective theories of well-being rightly point out that certain goods are reliable sources of well-being, even if such accounts err in supposing that possession of those goods constitutes what we mean by well-being. Such theories draw attention to the fact that we can often make reasonably objective judgments about the types of things that enhance welfare. A person's life cannot go well – it will be a poor life for that person – if it lacks such basic human goods as proper nourishment, physical health, self-respect, liberty, meaningful work, a sense of achievement, leisure or play, and feelings of love and affection for others, especially when those feelings are reciprocated. We can judge that something is good for people even if particular individuals do not desire the thing or find little satisfaction in it. But the link to what people want or to what they find gratifying cannot be fully severed without sliding toward perfectionism and away from welfarism. One requirement might be that the items on the objective list be ones that would be endorsed by those whose lives contained them, at least when they took a reflective and long-term view of their lives.

New Directions

If philosophers are to develop a satisfactory theory of well-being, they will probably have to incorporate elements from more than one of the approaches we have discussed. One possibility is to blend together elements of a mental-state and an informed desire-satisfaction account of well-being. D. W. Haslett, for instance, links welfare to the experiences that one would prefer to have if fully informed.[27] In a related vein, Richard Brandt has recently suggested "that what is intrinsically better for a person is a total segment of one's life marked by enjoyments *and/or* by satisfaction of desires, which one would *prefer*, from the long-range point of view, given full relevant information." He calls this an *informed-gratification theory* of well-being.[28]

[27] Haslett, "What is utility?" and *Capitalism with Morality*, 24–41.
[28] Brandt, *Facts, Values, and Morality*, 48.

64

Haslett's and Brandt's approaches place value on the satisfaction of people's informed desires, but they retain the link with experience, which seems essential to a satisfactory account of well-being. At the same time, they circumvent the experience-machine problem. This is because well-being is a function of the experiences one would desire to have if fully informed, and being fully informed about an experience would certainly include knowing that a machine was producing it. In addition, by explicitly restricting his account to desires that are for particular experiences, Haslett's conception of well-being eliminates the problem posed for standard desire-satisfaction theories by desires for states of affairs, the realization of which seems intuitively to have no impact at all on one's own well-being.

A different approach is to take a second look at the concept of happiness, which looms so large in the utilitarian tradition. At the end of the last section, I suggested that an objective theory of well-being might rely on the notion of one's affirming the goodness of the major constituents of one's life. A number of thinkers believe something like this is central to the concept of happiness. In their view, one is living happily only if one realizes that one is attaining the important things one values (or is coming close to this standard).[29] Happiness is the condition of being satisfied or fulfilled by the circumstances of one's life, and my life is a happy one only when I can endorse or affirm it in terms of my own priorities.[30]

When we talk about an evaluative dimension to happiness, we obviously do not have in mind happiness in the sense of one's feeling happy (being in a cheery mood) or one's being a happy person (having a sunny disposition). Rather, we mean being happy in the long-term sense of one's living happily or having a happy life. In order to be happy in this sense,

> it is necessary that one like ... those parts of one's total life pattern and circumstances that one thinks are important. To say that one likes them is in part to say that one is "satisfied" with them – that one does not wish them to be substantially different, and that they measure up, at least roughly, to the life ideal one had hoped to attain.[31]

As L. W. Sumner explains, happiness in this sense is really a matter of life satisfaction. As such, it involves both an affective and a cognitive component. The former consists in what we usually call a sense of well-being; that

---

[29] Kraut, "Two conceptions of happiness," 228; Taylor, *Principles of Ethics*, 138–41; Keyes, *The Examined Life*, 161–4.
[30] Sumner, "Welfare, happiness, and pleasure," 220; cf. Barrow, *Utilitarianism*, 76.
[31] Brandt, "Happiness," 413.

is, experiencing your life as fulfilling or enriching. On the other hand, the cognitive component consists

> in a positive evaluation of the conditions of one's life, a judgment that, at least on balance, it is measuring up favorably against one's standards or expectations for it. . . . It represents an affirmation or endorsement of (some or all of) the conditions or circumstances of one's life, a judgment that, on balance and taking everything into account, one's life is going well for one.[32]

If something like this captures the concept of happiness, is happiness identical with well-being? Sumner has argued that it is only if the person's self-evaluation is genuine or authentic, that is, if it accurately reflects the person's own point of view. This requires that the self-assessment be informed and autonomous. If one is deceived or deluded about one's circumstances, then one is not endorsing the conditions of one's life as they really are. On the other hand, the values, standards, and expectations that underlie a positive evaluation of one's life must not be a function of external manipulation through conditioning, indoctrination, or brainwashing. As Sumner sees it, then, welfare consists in authentic happiness.

Open-Ended Utilitarianism

Haslett's hybrid theory, Brandt's informed-gratification account, and Sumner's concept of authentic happiness all represent new and promising lines of philosophical research. It's clear, though, that more work is needed to clarify and refine the notion of well-being and to enhance our understanding of the factors that contribute to it. In addition to conceptual analysis and substantive theorizing, philosophers will need to draw on the insights of psychology and the other human sciences. Philosophers sometimes overlook this. However, as Russell Hardin writes, "value theory is constantly subject to revision and improvement as social scientific understandings of psychology and social interactions advance. . . . Any notion of human welfare, for example, depends on objective understandings of the nature of humans and their pleasures and pains."[33]

In reflecting on these matters, one must bear in mind that the shortcomings and inadequacies in our understanding of what is good for human beings also constitute a problem for non-utilitarian ethical theories, for other normative domains like law and economics, and for human self-

[32] Sumner, "Is virtue its own reward?" 28; *Welfare, Happiness, and Ethics*, 172.
[33] Hardin, *Morality within the Limits of Reason*, 168–9.

comprehension generally. Because of this, deficiencies in our grasp of the nature and sources of well-being do not, by themselves, vitiate a utilitarian approach to ethics. Utilitarians seek to promote human well-being, however it is best understood, and they do not have to pretend to have the final word on how best to understand it. They can leave room for further empirical research and philosophical assessment and debate.

Individual well-being has yet to be adequately conceptualized, and we do not understand perfectly the factors that enhance or diminish it. This fact leaves utilitarianism rather open ended. Yet, as a practical matter, its predicament is not dire because we still have a fair amount of knowledge about human well-being. In particular, there is reasonably widespread agreement about the things that are good for people and a consensus that certain other things – like pain – damage their interests and make their lives go less well. Because of this, disputes over the precise nature and meaning of well-being are not fatal to utilitarianism. In practice, as Mill remarks, "utility, or happiness, [is] much too complex and indefinite an end to be sought except through the medium of various secondary ends, concerning which there may be, and often is, agreement among persons who differ in their ultimate standard."[34] Whatever specific account of well-being one endorses, there will be little or no doubt about some of the steps that we can take to prevent suffering and reduce misery. Despite theoretical uncertainties and an imperfect understanding of human beings, then, agreement about Mill's "secondary ends" – about the factors that typically affect people's well-being for better or worse – provides utilitarianism with more than enough content for it to have reasonably specific implications for conduct.

---

[34] Mill, "Bentham," 110.

3

Arguing for Utilitarianism

Utilitarianism assesses and ranks the goodness of outcomes in terms of their utility or benefit. Because it understands utility to mean well-being, utilitarianism's account of the good is *welfarist*. It is also *aggregative* and *universalistic* because the theory holds that the goodness of outcomes is a direct, additive function of the welfare of all the individuals affected or potentially affected by our actions. Each person counts as one, and the general good is simply the sum of individual welfare.

As we saw in the previous chapter, there are competing ways of spelling out the notion of well-being. For ease of exposition, and in line with classical utilitarianism, I will continue to use "happiness," "welfare," and "well-being" interchangeably, but this is not intended to foreclose the substantive debate among utilitarians over the nature of well-being. All sides to that debate would agree that more work is necessary to improve our conception of welfare and our grasp of the things that make people's lives go better or worse. However, as previously argued, neither a lack of consensus about the meaning of well-being nor the deficiencies in our understanding of the factors that affect it defeat a utilitarian approach to ethics.

Turning, then, from utilitarianism's value theory to its normative account of right and wrong, the theory is, as we saw in Chapter 1, *consequentialist* in its general ethical orientation because it links the right-ness of actions to the goodness of their outcome. In particular, it holds that morality is ultimately or fundamentally about the promotion of well-being. Moreover, utilitarianism is not only a consequentialist, but also a maximizing doctrine because it states that the right action is the one with the best possible expected outcome. As standardly interpreted, utilitarianism requires us always to act so as to maximize well-being.

This chapter is concerned with the normative structure of utilitarianism

– that is, with its consequentialist and maximizing approach to right and wrong rather than with its welfarist theory of value. After assessing Jeremy Bentham's and John Stuart Mill's arguments for utilitarianism, the chapter examines efforts to ground the theory on self-evident axioms or base it on certain linguistic principles. It then goes on to investigate utilitarianism's complex relationship with ordinary, everyday morality. After examining utilitarians' critique of appeals to commonsense moral intuition and their criticisms of deontological theories of ethics, the chapter concludes by reviewing the values and ethical ideas that favor a utilitarian account of ethics.

Bentham and the Principle of Utility

Bentham writes that according to the principle of utility "human suffering and enjoyment – pain and pleasure" are "the only sources and tests of right and wrong."[1] This ethical standard accords with experience because, or so Bentham believes, pleasure and pain motivate human conduct. The famous opening passage of his *Principles of Morals and Legislation* states his view clearly:

> Nature has placed mankind under the governance of two sovereign masters, *pain* and *pleasure*. It is for them alone to point out what we ought to do, as well as to determine what we shall do . . . . They govern us in all we do, in all we say, in all we think . . . . *The principle of utility* recognises this subjection, and assumes it for the foundation of that system.

In light of this declaration, Bentham has been frequently but erroneously accused of arguing to his utilitarian conclusion from the premise that individuals are naturally motivated only to pursue pleasure and avoid pain. This would, indeed, be an invalid argument. One cannot use the supposed fact that people are hedonistic egoists to prove the utilitarian theory of right and wrong because how people tend to behave doesn't settle the question how they ought to behave. In fact, Bentham did not believe that one could logically derive utilitarianism from a description of human motivation. He did think, though, that his ethical theory accorded with the known facts about human conduct:

> It is by experience, and by that alone, that the tendency of human conduct, in all its modifications, to give birth to pain and pleasure, is brought to view: it is by reference to experience, and to that standard alone, that the tendency

[1] Bentham, "Rationale of judicial evidence," 238.

69

of any such modifications to produce more pleasure than pain, and consequently to be *right* – or more pain than pleasure, and consequently to be *wrong* – is made known and demonstrated.[2]

By itself, this passage does not advance very far the case for a utilitarian account of right and wrong, but it does reflect the naturalistic orientation to ethics that is characteristic of utilitarianism and surely one of its attractive features. From Bentham on, utilitarians have sought to anchor our understanding of good and bad, and thus right and wrong, in facts about human nature and in an empirically grounded understanding of the mainsprings of human well-being. Bentham believed that on most occasions, whether they are aware of it or not, people assess their own actions and the actions of others in terms of the happiness they produce. This natural human concern with happiness and unhappiness, he thought, enhances the plausibility of the utilitarian principle. Bentham was right about this, but he also believed, much more debatably, that this concern for happiness ruled out any rival, non-utilitarian ethical system.

Despite using the word "demonstrated" in the last passage quoted, Bentham held that it was both unnecessary and impossible to prove the greatest happiness principle. "That which is used to prove every thing else, cannot itself be proved," he states in *Principles*; "a chain of proofs must have their commencement somewhere" (4). Bentham probably took the principle of utility to be self-evident,[3] and he maintained that those who try to argue against the principle inevitably tangle themselves in inconsistencies by drawing on considerations and arguments that are implicitly utilitarian. In effect, they end up arguing only that the principle has been misapplied. Bentham's position reflects his belief that human beings generally guide themselves by the utilitarian principle in practice, even if they quarrel with it in theory.

Bentham held that no plausible principle could be opposed to the utilitarian principle and that opposition to it was inevitably based on subjective sentiment, muddled thinking, or sinister interest. This was rather dogmatic on his part because he identified and explicitly discussed only two rival ethical principles: the principle of asceticism and the principle of sympathy and antipathy. The first principle approves of actions insofar as they tend to diminish happiness, whereas the second principle approves or disapproves of certain actions "merely because a man finds himself disposed to approve or disapprove of them" (16).

[2] Bentham, "Rationale of judicial evidence," 238.
[3] Mill, "Bentham," 111.

Bentham's emotionally charged rejection of the principle of asceticism takes for granted what the ascetic denies, namely, that pain and misery are bad. He is right, of course, that the principle that one should act so as to diminish happiness is repellant. However, this principle is so preposterous, and its supposed proponents are so vaguely described, that it is hard to believe that he is not attacking a straw man.[4] Bentham asserts that a person "who reprobates any the least particle of pleasure, as such, from whatever source derived, is *pro tanto* a partizan of the principle of asceticism" (9). But this is tendentious. One can deny the intrinsic value of certain pleasures and even the intrinsic value of pleasure itself without believing that morality requires the pursuit of pain. Of course, whenever one acts contrary to the principle of utility, one fails to bring about as much pleasure or happiness as one could have. But it is unfair to infer, as Bentham does, that one is therefore advocating asceticism or approving of actions because they tend to diminish happiness.

In Bentham's eyes, the second non-utilitarian principle, that of sympathy and antipathy, is not really a principle at all, except in name. This is because "a principle is something that points out some external consideration, as a means of warranting and guiding the internal sentiments of approbation and disapprobation" (16), and the principle of sympathy and antipathy does nothing of the kind. According to this principle, to determine what is right and wrong, one need merely consult one's feelings or opinions, and that "whatever you find in yourself a propensity to condemn, is wrong for that very reason."

Bentham maintains that all the various non-utilitarian normative systems reduce to the principle of sympathy and antipathy. Systems that appeal, for example, to a moral sense, the law of nature, natural justice, the fitness of things, right reason, common sense, or naturalness and unnaturalness are really only covert appeals to one's own sentiments and prejudices, which are simply taken for granted and not argued for. For example:

> One man says, he has a thing made on purpose to tell him what is right and what is wrong; and that it is called a *moral sense*: and then he goes to work at his ease, and says, such a thing is right, and such a thing is wrong – why? "because my moral sense tells me it is." (17n)

In this vein, Bentham ridicules all these supposed systems of ethics as merely using "the author's sentiment or opinion as a reason for itself." Bentham also dismisses talk of natural rights as empty rhetoric, as

[4] Mill, however, defended Bentham on this point ("Whewell on moral philosophy," 176).

71

"nonsense on stilts," because instead of justifying moral claims it only dresses up one's unreflective sentiments in verbal finery.[5] Likewise, appeals to the will of God simply assume that something is God's will because it conforms to some ethical principle the person already accepts. We may be sure, Bentham writes, that whatever is right conforms to God's will, but that still leaves the task of determining the standard of right and wrong.

Bentham does not claim that our moral sentiments reflect or correspond to an action's utility or disutility, nor does he assert that we derive our everyday notions of right and wrong from an assessment of outcomes. "I do not know: I do not care," he writes (19n). Bentham is a moral reformer. It is not his project to explicate, still less to defend, ordinary moral ideas. What matters is only whether our notions of right and wrong, our sentiments of approbation and disapprobation, can be justified. As we have seen, Bentham can see no standard for assessing them other than the utilitarian one. Non-utilitarian ethical systems are either hostile to human pleasure or serve to cloak prejudice and unsubstantiated ethical opinions.

Mill: Proof and Sentiment

Like Bentham, John Stuart Mill was sharply critical of those who appeal to a supposed moral faculty capable of supplying them with general ethical principles, the truth of which is a priori and self-evident. In his view, either such moralists simply take for granted the validity of the commonsense precepts of everyday morality, or else they propose some more general foundation for them that is less authoritative and less generally accepted than the precepts themselves. Moreover, whether they realize it or not, the principle of utility plays an important role in their theorizing. This is because people's moral sentiments are greatly influenced by what they believe to be the effects of things on their happiness.

Mill believed that Kant's ethical philosophy illustrates these points. As explained in Chapter 1, Kant's categorical imperative states that one should always act so that the maxim governing one's conduct could be adopted as a moral law by all rational agents. Mill contends in *Utilitarianism*, however, that the categorical imperative fails "almost grotesquely" to expose as contradictory even the most outrageous conduct. It is neither logically nor physically impossible for rational beings to adopt totally

[5] Bentham had other arguments against natural rights, which he considered both "absurd in logic" and "pernicious in morals." See Sumner, "Rights denaturalized," 27–9, 33–6.

immoral rules of conduct (4). The most that Kant succeeds in showing is that people would not choose to incur the consequences of adopting such rules. The only sensible way to construe Kant's principle, Mill concludes, is to interpret it in a quasi-utilitarian fashion as saying that we ought to shape our conduct by a rule that all rational beings might adopt "with benefit to their collective interest."[6]

Besides being quick to repudiate appeals to moral intuition and impressed by the implicitly utilitarian strains running through most ethical theories, Mill also agreed with Bentham that the utilitarian theory cannot be proved – at least not in a strict sense of proof. Again, this is because one is dealing with first principles. "To be incapable of proof by reasoning is common to all first principles," Mill writes, "to the first premises of knowledge, as well as to those of our conduct" (34). However, Mill believes that one can still rationally discuss first principles and, further, that considerations "capable of determining the intellect" can be advanced in favor of utilitarianism. This is what Mill does in Chapter IV of *Utilitarianism*, "Of What Sort of Proof the Principle of Utility Is Susceptible."

This famous "proof" divides into two parts. First, Mill argues from the fact that people desire happiness to the conclusion that happiness is a good and, thus, one of the criteria of morality. In the second part, he argues that everything people desire they desire either as a means to happiness or as part of their happiness and that therefore happiness is the only thing that is good for its own sake. From this it follows that the promotion of happiness is "the [sole] criterion of morality." In discussing happiness, the previous chapter has already touched on several aspects of Mill's proof. What interests us now is the case Mill makes for the consequentialist and maximizing aspects of utilitarianism, rather than his understanding of the nature of happiness or his argument that it is the only intrinsically valuable end.

Let us assume, then, that happiness is the one thing that is good in and of itself or, as Mill puts it, that happiness is "the sole end of human action" (38), "the ultimate end, with reference to and for the sake of which all other things are desirable" (11). It is the step from this value premise to a consequentialist approach to morality that now concerns us. In *Utilitarianism* Mill explicitly makes this move twice, but each time he does so quickly and with precious little argument. The first time is in Chapter II. Having affirmed that happiness is the ultimate end, he immediately writes that it is "necessarily also the standard of morality, which may accordingly be

[6] Mill, *Utilitarianism*, 51. Cf. Hare, "Could Kant have been a utilitarian?" 2.

defined as 'the rules and precepts for human conduct'" that will secure the happiest existence for all (12).

In Chapter IV Mill expands slightly on this. At the end of his argument that happiness is the only thing that is desirable for its own sake (because everything we value, we value either as part of happiness or as a means to happiness), he states:

> If so, happiness is the sole end of human action, and the promotion of it the test by which to judge of all human conduct; from whence it necessarily follows that it must be the criterion of morality, since a part is included in the whole. (38)

Mill's argument here seems to be that the utilitarian standard is the proper one for any assessment of human conduct and that therefore it is the proper basis of specifically moral assessment. But this broad assertion is problematic for it is debatable whether all assessments of human conduct turn on happiness. For instance, it seems doubtful that aesthetic appraisals do. Prudential assessments probably do turn on happiness, but they concern the happiness of the individual agent, not general happiness.

In a passage at the beginning of *Utilitarianism*, Mill writes that "All action is for the sake of some end, and rules of action, it seems natural to suppose, must take their whole character and color from the end to which they are subservient" (2). And in his *Logic*, Mill states that we need a general principle for the practice of life and that if it is well chosen, it will "serve quite as well for the ultimate principle of Morality, as for that of Prudence, Policy, or Taste."[7] However, at best these remarks illuminate, rather than vindicate, Mill's guiding teleological assumption that moral and other rules must derive from the ultimate end of all human endeavor.

What we find, then, is that in his famous "proof" Mill simply takes for granted the validity of a consequentialist approach to right and wrong and assumes that any plausible ethical theory must make right and wrong serve the promotion of some good. Implicitly, the only controversial or difficult ethical question for Mill is the nature of the good to be pursued. Mill made this clear in another essay:

> Whether happiness be or be not the end to which morality should be referred
> – that it be referred to an *end* of some sort, and not left in the dominion of

---

[7] Mill, *Logic*, 951. Mill goes on to reaffirm his conviction "that the general principle to which all rules of practice ought to conform, and the test by which they should be tried, is that of conduciveness to the happiness of mankind, or rather, of all sentient beings."

vague feeling or inexplicable internal conviction, that it be made a matter of reason and calculation, and not merely of sentiment, is essential to the very idea of moral philosophy; is, in fact, what renders argument or discussion on moral questions possible. That the morality of actions depends on the consequences which they tend to produce, is the doctrine of rational persons of all schools; that the good or evil of those consequences is measured solely by pleasure or pain, is all of the doctrine of the school of utility, which is peculiar to it.[8]

Mill's position is, I think, an attractive one. Certainly, the belief that moral assessment turns on consequences and, in particular, that the promotion of what ultimately matters ought to be the guiding principle of ethics lies at the heart of utilitarianism. But simply to state this belief is not to refute a nonconsequentialist approach to ethics. Indeed, the defining characteristic of nonconsequentialism is that right and wrong are not a function of some antecedently identified good like happiness. Such theories insist that there is more to duty, more to right conduct, than acting to promote the good. Like Bentham before him, Mill firmly rejects nonconsequentialism, but he has not disproved it.

The Social Feelings of Mankind

In Chapter III of *Utilitarianism* Mill discusses what motive there would be to obey the principle of utility or what sanctions would support it, were we to adopt it as our ethical standard. He argues that what ultimately underwrites any moral standard are "the conscientious feelings of mankind" (28) and that these feelings can sustain a utilitarian ethic just as well as they can any rival moral system. Moreover, one of utilitarianism's strengths is that it is firmly grounded in "the social feelings of mankind – the desire to be in unity with our fellow creatures" (30–1).

Mill believes this desire is already an important aspect of human nature. "The deeply rooted conception," he writes, "which every individual even now has of himself as a social being tends to make him feel it one of his natural wants that there should be harmony between his feelings and aims and those of his fellow creatures" (33). True, in most of us this desire to be in unity with our fellows is weaker than our selfish instincts, and Mill concedes that some people may lack it altogether. However, the trend of social evolution is to strengthen people's social feelings and sympathetic regard for others, a development which education and other social institutions can enhance. As civilization progresses, it becomes less and less

[8] Mill, "Bentham," 111. Cf. *Logic*, 951.

possible to organize society on any other basis than one that takes the interests of all into account. Thus, the development of society and the closer ties among people not only "give to each individual a stronger personal interest in practically consulting the welfare of others," they also lead "him to identify his *feelings* more and more with their good" (31).

Through external sanctions and early training, it is possible, Mill believes, to inculcate in people almost any moral principles, even quite absurd and socially counterproductive ones. But social progress fosters analysis and reflection, and these inevitably tend to undermine the emotional force of moral principles and convictions that "are wholly of artificial creation" or lack "foundation in human nature." By contrast, utilitarianism rests on a "powerful natural sentiment," which analysis does not weaken (30). In other words, the social sentiments and feelings of solidarity with others that undergird a commitment to utilitarianism are not only a normal and integral part of our nature, but they can withstand rational scrutiny – in part, because the moral principle they favor is a reasonable one.

Although Mill does not present these considerations as an argument for utilitarianism, they do have some suasive force. To be sure, if one believes that the basic principles of morality reflect certain objective facts that are built into the universe and exist independently of human society, only waiting to be discovered by rational beings, then one may view the psychological considerations Mill mentions as irrelevant. However, if one views morality as essentially a human creation, or at least as having a social function to perform, then it is a point in favor of a recommended moral system that it is socially and psychologically stable – that is, that it connects with and is reinforced by deep and enduring aspects of the human personality.

Stability and Rational Choice

In his impressive and influential work *A Theory of Justice*, John Rawls addresses the issues Mill raises, but argues that his own principles of justice provide a more stable basis for organizing society than does the utilitarian principle (496–504). Chapter 7 discusses Rawls's theory in some detail, but notice that his stability argument presupposes that the case he presents for his principles of justice is an intellectually convincing one. Principles that lack a compelling rationale will, in his view, be unable to furnish a psychologically stable foundation for society.

A Theory of Justice engages the reader in a thought experiment, asking one to imagine rational, self-interested people meeting to choose the principles that are to govern their society and doing so without knowing anything about their particular interests or abilities or about the positions they will ultimately occupy in that society. Under this veil of ignorance, Rawls argues, people will choose two non-utilitarian principles. However, this conclusion has been challenged by some utilitarians. For example, John Harsanyi examines rational choice under conditions similar to those that Rawls imagines. Like Rawls, Harsanyi supposes that the choosers do not know in advance what their social positions will turn out to be. He also stipulates that each person can reasonably assume that he has an equal chance of ending up in any given social position. (By contrast, Rawls supposes that the choosers can make no probability estimates at all and that they are extremely risk averse.) Under these conditions, Harsanyi argues, a rational self-interested individual would want society to be governed by whatever principle resulted in the highest average utility. That principle is, of course, the utilitarian principle.[9]

Eschewing Rawls's whole hypothetical construction, some utilitarians argue more directly that it is rational for people who are fully informed (and not behind a veil of ignorance) to support a welfare-maximizing moral code.[10] Others argue for utilitarianism on the grounds that any normative principle must claim the assent of all rational beings, and the only principle that can do this is the utilitarian principle because it alone takes the interests of all as equally worth satisfying.[11] We cannot pursue these arguments about rational choice here. The relevant point is simply that if it is rational (at least under certain conditions) to choose the utilitarian principle to govern one's society, then this fact will buttress the social feelings and desire for unity with others that, at least in Mill's eyes, give the utilitarian principle its motive force. Rationality and benevolence will thus push in the same direction, with both our heads and our hearts favoring the principle of utility.

Self-Evidence and the Language of Morality

Like Bentham and Mill before him, Henry Sidgwick held that it is impossible to prove any first principle because such a proof would pre-

---

[9] Assuming, that is, either that population is constant or that average happiness, not total happiness, is the goal of utilitarianism. See Harsanyi, "Theory of rational behaviour," 44–8.

[10] Brandt, *Morality, Utilitarianism, and Rights*, 141; *Theory of the Good and the Right*, Chs. 10–15.

[11] Narveson, *Morality and Utility*, 292.

suppose premises that would be more fundamental than the initial "first" principle. Critical of Mill's argument for utilitarianism, Sidgwick maintained instead that the greatest happiness principle "must rest on a fundamental moral intuition" (xix). In his book *The Methods of Ethics*, he identifies as self-evident several distinct axioms that, taken together, underwrite the case for utilitarianism.[12]

The first of these ethical axioms reflects Kant's influence on Sidgwick. It is that whatever an individual judges to be right for himself, he implicitly judges to be right for all persons in similar circumstances. More specifically, "it cannot be right for A to treat B in a manner in which it would be wrong for B to treat A, merely on the ground that they are two different individuals" without there being some relevant difference in their natures or circumstances (380). This principle and the related requirement that similar cases should be treated similarly dictate impartiality and consistency in applying or following any general moral rule. They do not, however, specify what rule or rules we should follow. In other words, Sidgwick's first axiom is compatible with, but does not entail, utilitarianism. For that, other axioms are required.

Sidgwick approaches these additional axioms through a discussion of prudence. Rational self-interest, he argues, dictates that one should have equal concern for all the temporal parts of one's conscious life. A self-interested person may rationally discount future happiness or unhappiness to the extent that it is less certain, but not merely because it lies in the future. Temporal order is not, in itself, a reasonable basis for a person to regard any one moment of life as more important than another. My feelings a year hence should be just as important to me as my feelings five minutes from now, assuming I can make an equally sure forecast of them (124n, 381). Allowing for differences in certainty, a truly prudent person will not prefer a smaller present good to a greater future good.

Now, Sidgwick argues, just as we can form a conception of what is "good on the whole" for ourselves based on the different parts or moments of our lifetime, so we can form the notion of "universal good" by comparing and integrating the goods enjoyed by different individuals. Reflection on this – on the relations among parts and between them and the whole they compose – leads Sidgwick to affirm as self-evident two further axioms. The first is that "the good of any one individual is of no more importance, from the point of view (if I may say so) of the Universe, than the good of any other." A page later Sidgwick puts this important point in a different way

---

[12] In *Sidgwick's Ethics* (290–7), Schneewind identifies several variants of the axioms discussed below.

when he states that the proposition that "I ought not to prefer my own lesser good to the greater good of another" is just as self-evident as "I ought not to prefer a present lesser good to a future greater good." The second axiom is "that as a rational being I am bound to aim at good generally, – so far as it is attainable by my efforts, – not merely at a particular part of it" (382).

From these two fundamental principles – that I ought to promote what is good generally and that my own good is neither more nor less important than the good of others – Sidgwick deduces what he calls "the maxim of Benevolence." According to it, "each one is morally bound to regard the good of any other individual as much as his own." In this way Sidgwick claims to have arrived at "the fundamental principle of Utilitarianism" (387). However, the transition from Sidgwick's two principles to the utilitarian account of right and wrong falls short.

Further argument is needed, first, to justify moving from his two self-evident principles to the consequentialist conclusion that morality is entirely a matter of promoting the good and, then, to justify moving from that conclusion to the further conclusion that one should always act so as to bring about as much good as possible. The problem is that Sidgwick has not eliminated the possibility that rival moral considerations might thwart both of these moves. Even if his axioms are genuinely self-evident, other ethical principles might be equally self-evident but nonconsequentialist in character. If there are such principles, then the obligation to promote the good of all impartially would be, at best, just one duty among others.

To be fair to Sidgwick, however, he does not aver that his axioms deductively establish the principle of utility. Although they support and reinforce it, they do not logically entail the principle, which ultimately remains an ethical intuition. Thus, in the concluding section of *The Method of Ethics*, Sidgwick writes, "I find that I undoubtedly seem to perceive, as clearly and certainly as I see any axiom in Arithmetic or Geometry, that it is 'right' and 'reasonable' for me . . . to do what I believe to be ultimately conducive to universal Good or Happiness" (507).

Moore on Self-Evidence

Following Sidgwick, G. E. Moore and a number of early twentieth-century moral theorists held it to be self-evident that the morally right action is the one with the best overall outcome. In his book *Ethics*, Moore asserts that something is intrinsically good if and only if it ought to be preferred to nothing at all, and one thing is intrinsically better than another if and only if the first thing ought to be preferred to the second (28). "It would always be wrong," he continues, "to prefer a *worse* set of total consequences to a *better*" (68). Accordingly, "it must always be the duty of any being who had to choose between two actions, one of which he *knew* would have *better* total effects than the other, to choose the former" (71). Thus, it is "quite self-evident that it must always be our duty to do what will produce the best effects *upon the whole*" (100).

More recent writers in the utilitarian tradition have endorsed the first part of Moore's reasoning. For instance, Shelly Kagan writes, "To say that from the moral standpoint one outcome is objectively better than another, is to say that *everyone* has a reason to choose the better outcome."[13] Some non-utilitarian writers agree with this, at least in part. They concede that insofar as we are dealing with objective goods, we have an impersonal, agent-neutral reason to promote them. Thus, for example, Thomas Nagel holds that pain is something that is objectively bad, not simply bad relative to a particular individual's perspective. Pain is something, toward which the objective response is simply "*This experience* ought not to go on, *whoever* is having it." Accordingly, Nagel believes that everyone has a reason to act so as to mitigate pain, wherever it occurs.[14]

However, unlike a utilitarian, Nagel denies that all values are objective. As Kagan explains:

> On one level, to say that there is a pro tanto reason to promote the good is actually to make a trivial claim. Everyone has a standing reason to promote the objectively best outcome, because the existence of such a reason is in part just what it *is* for something to have objective value . . . . The substantive question is only whether there is anything that *has* objective value. (61)

Thus, even if a non-utilitarian agrees that objective values are to be promoted, he will deny, whereas a utilitarian will affirm, that all value is objective value (or, alternatively, that the only values that matter morally are objective values). Suppose, for example, that Kofi desires to master the piano or to climb to the top of a treacherous mountain. For the utilitarian, although these activities do not have objective value per se, the satisfaction or well-being that stems from Kofi's pursuing his projects does. Well-being is an objective good, which everyone has some reason to promote. By contrast, non-utilitarians like Nagel hold that the furthering of a person's projects is an agent-relative good, not an objective, agent-neutral value. Kofi has a reason to further his own projects, which other people lack.

[13] Kagan, *The Limits of Morality*, 61.
[14] Nagel, *The View from Nowhere*, 161.

Kagan's comment brings out two gaps in Moore's reasoning. The first is that, like Sidgwick, he assumes that the good is an objective, agent-neutral value, that states of affairs can therefore be assessed as better or worse, and thus that everyone has a reason to prefer a world with more good to a world with less. For utilitarians, this assumption comes easily. They readily affirm that welfare is an objective good. In their eyes, Nagel and other non-utilitarian philosophers get hung up on the simple fact that other people cannot promote Kofi's happiness or well-being by climbing the mountain or practicing the piano for him (167–8). However, as discussed in Chapter 2, the fact that people have different desires and pursue different projects is perfectly compatible with the utilitarian claim that the pursuit of our individual desires and projects is a major source of human well-being, which is an objective good.

The second gap in Moore's position is more problematic. It involves the step from his claim that one ought to prefer the better state of affairs to the worse state of affairs, to the proposition that one should always act so as to maximize good. From the fact that one state of affairs is better than another it follows, for Moore, not only that we ought to prefer the former state of affairs but also, much more controversially, that we ought always to strive to bring about as much good as possible. To put the point in different terminology, Moore moves from saying that everyone has a reason to pursue the greatest good to saying that everyone has a conclusive and overriding reason to do so. This step is hardly self-evident. Indeed, many non-utilitarians affirm that one has a duty to promote the good but, in contrast to utilitarianism, explicitly hold that this is only one among other, equally fundamental duties.

In ethics, assertions of self-evidence are tricky, and few of them are beyond challenge. For his part, Moore continued throughout his career to affirm as logically equivalent the proposition that I ought to do X and the proposition that X will make the world better than anything else I could do. Although their meanings are distinct, the two propositions are necessarily and reciprocally connected.[15] By contrast, Moore's contemporary W. D. Ross explicitly denied that these propositions are co-extensive. The assertion that they are, he argued, is not self-evident, nor can it be proved either deductively or inductively.[16]

Many people find the principle that the morally right action is the action that best promotes the good at least initially plausible. Yet reflection on examples like the deathbed promise case of Chapter 1 leads most people to

[15] Moore, "Reply to my critics," 562–3.
[16] Ross, *The Right and the Good*, 36.

doubt that this principle is self-evidently true or even to doubt that it is true at all. As we shall see in the next chapter, the critics of utilitarianism vigorously oppose the theory on various grounds and challenge it with a vivid array of putative counterexamples. Utilitarianism's defenders can, I shall argue, rebut many of these criticisms and disarm many of the supposed counterexamples. However, at this stage of the debate, it will not do for utilitarians simply to declare that a consequentialist and maximizing approach to ethics is self-evidently correct.

A Linguistic Argument

We have seen that Moore thought it self-evident that one should always act so as to maximize the good. In his early and most famous work *Principia Ethica*, he went further than this, contending that "morally right" simply means "maximizes the good." "The assertion 'I am morally bound to perform this action' is," he wrote, "identical with the assertion 'This action will produce the greatest amount of good in the Universe' " (147). Were this contention correct, then (assuming that welfare is the sole good) utilitarianism would be true by definition. But Moore's contention is false, as Bertrand Russell and others were quick to argue,[17] and Moore, to his credit, soon abandoned it.

Although Moore's position in *Principia Ethica* is untenable, the contemporary moral theorist R. M. Hare has advanced a more powerful and more influential linguistic argument for utilitarianism, one that has been refined over several decades and developed in countless publications. Put concisely, Hare argues that moral judgments are universal prescriptions and that, because of this, moral language itself entails a utilitarian approach to ethics.

Moral judgments are prescriptive, Hare thinks, because they are evaluative and action guiding. They express our preferences about the way things should be. Whether spoken aloud or to oneself, moral judgments are a kind of command that one should act in a certain way. Applied to ourselves, the prescriptivity of moral judgments entails that we are being insincere if we agree that we ought to act in a certain way and then do not try to do so. Hare also maintains, just as Sidgwick and Kant did, that moral judgments must be universalizable. This means that any given moral judgment implicitly applies to all precisely similar situations and that we contradict ourselves if we make different moral judgments about situations that we

---

[17] See Russell, "The meaning of good," 330, and Ross, *The Right and the Good*, 8–9, and *Foundations of Ethics*, 42.

admit to be identical. For example, one cannot with logical consistency say that it would be right for Sonny, but wrong for Cher, to act a certain way in the same exact situation.

Because moral judgments are both prescriptive and universalizable, as moral agents we can make moral judgments only when we are prepared to prescribe for all like situations. From this it follows that to make a universal prescription, we must identify an action that will be acceptable to us after we have put ourselves in the shoes of each person affected by the action. Hare writes: "It is in the endeavour to find lines of conduct that we can prescribe universally in a given situation that we find ourselves bound to give equal weight to the desires of all parties . . . and this, in turn, leads to such views as that we should seek to maximize satisfactions."[18] In imagining myself successively in the position of each affected person, I identify with the preferences of each. I prefer, in turn, what each of them would prefer. In representing their preferences to myself in this way, I now have preferences regarding what should happen to me, were I in each person's position with his or her preferences. I can then compare the strengths of their preferences by comparing the strengths of my own corresponding preferences. To arrive at a moral judgment in a given situation, then, I must coordinate these different preferences into a total preference which is impartial among them.

In this way, then, the requirement, inherent in our moral language, that we universalize our prescriptions leads us, Hare believes, to utilitarianism (couched in terms of preference satisfaction rather than happiness). Together, universalizability and prescriptivity entail that I treat the preferences of each person as of equal weight with my own and that I form a total preference that accommodates these individual preferences. In prescribing the act that impartially maximizes the satisfaction of these preferences, I am doing what utilitarianism recommends. Hare sums up his thinking this way:

> The thesis of universalizability requires that if we make any moral judgement about [a] situation, we must be prepared to make it about any of the other precisely similar situations . . . . What critical thinking has to do is find a moral judgement which the thinker is prepared to make about this conflict-situation and is also prepared to make about all the other similar situations. Since these will include situations in which he occupies, respectively, the positions of all the other parties in the actual situation, no judgement will be acceptable to him which does not do the best, all in all, for all the parties. Thus the logical apparatus of universal prescriptivism . . .

[18] Hare, *Freedom and Reason*, 123.

will lead us ... to make judgements which are the same as a careful act-utilitarian would make.[19]

Hare's arguments are controversial, and the debate over his ideas is lively.[20] Some philosophers challenge his meta-ethical analysis of moral language, others his derivation of utilitarianism from the implicit logic of moral discourse. Whatever the final verdict on Hare's argument, however, no one denies that moral judgments must be universalizable, and his notion that morality requires one to be impartial and to take into account the interests of all strikes many people as clearly correct. If Hare's linguistic argument fails (and no similar argument can be made to work), then an allegiance to impartiality and to the idea that morality requires you to put yourself in the shoes of others is a substantive value commitment rather than a logically inescapable entailment of moral language itself. But this is a conclusion that many utilitarians would be willing to live with.

Some contemporary utilitarians influenced by Hare (and indirectly by Sidgwick and Mill) make the simple but powerful point that if I take my own interests or welfare as mattering, then I must grant that everyone else's interests matter too. I cannot reasonably claim that my interests count but the interests of others don't, or that my interests count more than theirs, simply because they are mine. Because my interests are neither more nor less important than the interests of others, objectivity requires me to take the interests of all into account, and simple rationality requires me to weigh, balance, and maximize them as best I can. This line of thinking, although it may not conclusively establish the utilitarian principle, does provide at least a presumptive case for it, and it is arguable that the onus is on those who would reject utilitarianism in favor of some kind of non-consequentialism.[21]

Utilitarianism and Commonsense Morality

As we have seen, Bentham and Mill vehemently criticized non-utilitarian moralists for relying on intuition instead of argument and for asserting as self-evidently correct ethical propositions that only reflect received moral opinion and customary practice. Although Sidgwick based his utilitarianism on a fundamental moral intuition, he conscientiously sought to make

[19] Hare, *Moral Thinking*, 42–3.
[20] See Seanor and Fotion, *Hare and Critics*.
[21] See Singer, *Practical Ethics*, 12, and Narveson, *Morality and Utility*, 275.

his appeal to self-evidence as rational and objective as possible. In particular, he identified three conditions that must be met for a proposition to be considered self-evident (338–42). First, its terms must be clear and precise. Second, careful reflection must eliminate subjective sentiments and feelings, the support of authority and tradition, and adherence to the customs and laws of society as possible bases for judging the proposition to be self-evident. Third, propositions accepted as self-evident must be mutually consistent. In addition, one's claim that a proposition is self-evident is weakened if it conflicts with the judgments of others. Sidgwick contends that the principle of utility and the other supporting axioms he identifies satisfy these criteria.

In *The Methods of Ethics* Sidgwick puts these criteria to another use. Guided by them, he critically examines the various maxims of commonsense morality, carefully sifting the principles that seem to underlie our everyday thinking about justice as well as a variety of ordinary moral precepts like "I ought to speak the truth" and "I ought to keep my promises." In his assessment, the precepts and principles of commonsense morality fail as fundamental ethical axioms. Their air of self-evidence is illusory. Typically, they are too general and too vague to be genuinely self-evident, and attempts to make them more definite either miscarry or lead to clearly unacceptable results. Sidgwick concludes his discussion this way:

> We have examined the moral notions that present themselves with a *prima facie* claim to furnish independent and self-evident rules of morality: and we have in each case found that from such regulation of conduct as the Common Sense of mankind really supports, no proposition can be elicited which, when fairly contemplated, even appears to have the characteristic of a scientific axiom. (360)

Sidgwick's critique of commonsense morality is hardly surprising. Although utilitarians may judge certain teachings of ordinary morality to be useful and worthy of support, its rules do not represent basic moral truths or self-standing ethical norms.

In contrast, many non-utilitarian moralists and certainly many ordinary people take commonsense morality to be obviously correct and treat its precepts as reflecting elemental ethical principles that need no independent justification. That people view ordinary morality this way is far from astonishing because, as Mill writes in *Utilitarianism*, "customary morality, that which education and opinion have consecrated . . . presents itself to the mind with the feeling of being *in itself* obligatory." Indeed, Mill continues, "when a person is asked to believe that this morality *derives* its obligation from some general principle round which custom has not thrown the same halo, the assertion is to him a paradox" (26). Because it offers a general principle by which to assess ordinary morality, utilitarianism is reformist, and its supporters approach everyday morality with a skeptical eye.

As we shall see in the next chapter, philosophers who reject utilitarianism because of its consequentialist, maximizing approach to morality typically do so because its injunctions clash with those of everyday, commonsense morality. In dismissing utilitarianism, they typically appeal to "intuition," by which they mean the sincere moral beliefs or "considered moral judgments" of people like themselves. For example, some critics attack utilitarianism for allegedly giving the wrong answer in the deathbed promise case. Because it tells us to confer the money on the orphanage, the critics argue that utilitarianism ignores or places insufficient moral weight on the keeping of promises – as judged by how we ordinarily think about these things. It must therefore be rejected as a satisfactory normative theory.

In response, utilitarians frequently play down the differences between utilitarianism and ordinary morality and attempt to show that in practice their theory, when carefully and intelligently applied, constitutes no serious affront to commonsense moral thinking. In addition, utilitarians argue that ordinary morality is far from sacrosanct. Because people's upbringing, social environment, and cultural tradition strongly influence their beliefs about right and wrong, appeals to ethical intuition will all too often simply reflect the values, norms, and customary moral practices that individuals have uncritically absorbed from those around them. For this reason, Bentham harshly attacked utilitarianism's critics for what he called "ipsidixism" – that is, for contending that something is right (or wrong) solely on the basis that that is how things appear to them. One cannot settle a moral issue by simply appealing to one's own moral convictions, no matter how firmly felt they may be, or so utilitarians argue.

Reflective Equilibrium

With some justification Bentham and other early utilitarians saw their critics as moral conservatives reflexively upholding customary ideas of right and wrong, for which no cogent arguments could be mustered. By contrast, contemporary critics of utilitarianism are reflective and insightful thinkers who challenge the moral status quo as often as utilitarians do. They do not appeal directly and uncritically to conventional morality. Rather, most non-utilitarian thinkers implicitly follow an ethical methodology that

86

involves carefully sifting and balancing intuitive ethical judgments about specific cases (it would be wrong to lie to Thelma to assist Fred out of a jam) and higher-level normative beliefs (racial discrimination is wrong) in an effort to identify a consistent system of principles that weaves our particular ethical judgments and our general normative beliefs into as coherent and attractive a package as possible. This methodology permits us to adjust, revise, or ignore some of our initial intuitions in order to forge, in Rawls's famous phrase, a "reflective equilibrium" which preserves as many of our most important beliefs as possible. This is a coherentist approach to ethical justification, which sees it as "a matter of the mutual support of many considerations, of everything fitting together into one coherent view."[22]

Nevertheless, it remains an open question why a normative principle or theory like utilitarianism should be tested against our considered beliefs, or why an intuitive ethical belief must be compatible with our other normative intuitions if it is to be acceptable. Utilitarians are skeptical of the notion, implicit in the reflective equilibrium methodology, that our firmly believing a proposition provides a justification for it, even if that justification is only presumptive and the proposition can be abandoned, if necessary, to achieve overall coherence. As Hare explains:

> The appeal to moral intuitions will never do as a basis for a moral system. It is certainly possible, as some thinkers even of our times have done, to collect all the moral opinions of which they and their contemporaries feel most sure, find some relatively simple method or apparatus which can be represented, with a bit of give and take ... as generating all these opinions; and then pronounce that that is the moral system which, having reflected, we must acknowledge to be the correct one. But they have absolutely no authority for this claim beyond the original convictions, for which no ground or argument was given. The "equilibrium" they have reached is one between forces which might have been generated by prejudice, and no amount of reflection can make that a solid basis for morality. It would be possible for two mutually inconsistent systems to be defended in this way; all that this would show is that their advocates had grown up in different moral environments.[23]

Hare and other utilitarians argue that the reflective equilibrium method can never generate results that are more secure than the intuitions with which it begins. Many non-utilitarian moral philosophers maintain, to the contrary, that, by refining and perhaps revising our ordinary moral judg-

---

[22] Rawls, *Theory of Justice*, 21.
[23] Hare, *Moral Thinking*, 12.

ments in order to weave them into a coherent and systematic package, the reflective equilibrium approach rightly increases one's confidence in the ethical beliefs that make up that equilibrium. They also believe that there is simply no alternative to starting with our settled moral convictions and working from there. Whether they are correct about this or whether utilitarians are right to eschew reliance on our considered moral beliefs is an issue that runs through this book. It is also one of the most disputed points of contemporary ethics.

Sidgwick's Argument from Commonsense Morality

Sidgwick intends his critical examination of commonsense morality to eliminate its rules and precepts as rivals to the utilitarian principle. Most utilitarians adopt a largely defensive posture toward commonsense morality, endeavoring to show that any discrepancies between it and utilitarianism are not fatal to their theory. Sidgwick himself, however, goes on to contend that utilitarianism, and only utilitarianism, is capable of explaining and systematizing (within broad contours) commonsense morality. This fact, he believes, provides an independent argument for utilitarianism. Instead of posing a challenge to utilitarianism, commonsense morality strengthens the case for it.

Sidgwick perceives utilitarianism and ordinary morality as overlapping or coinciding in their content to a significant extent. On the one hand, a utilitarian estimate of consequences broadly supports existing moral rules as well as their generally understood limits and qualifications. On the other hand, when disputes arise over the precise scope and meaning of the ordinary moral rules or when those rules come into conflict, commonsense morality typically turns to utility to settle the issue.

It is possible, of course, that an alternative normative approach – for instance, the reflective equilibrium method – might provide as coherent a basis around which to unify, synthesize, and reconstruct ordinary morality as utilitarianism does. However, Sidgwick maintains not only that utilitarianism and ordinary morality roughly coincide, but also that everyday morality is unconsciously utilitarian (453). Although commonsense morality is not expressly utilitarian, and ordinary people do not view its rules as binding because they perceive them to promote happiness, nevertheless over the long run society tends to abandon rules that do not (or no longer) promote happiness. Moreover, the differences between the ethical codes of different countries or historical periods correspond, to a great extent, to differences in the results, or the perceived results, that apparently similar actions have in different social contexts (454). Sidgwick believes, further, that utilitarianism is the morality toward which human ethical development has always been tending (456–7).

If ordinary morality is unconsciously utilitarian in these ways and if there is a significant overlap between the practical content of the two, then Sidgwick's claim that utilitarianism, and only utilitarianism, can explain and unify the tenets of commonsense morality would be very compelling. In turn, utilitarianism's ability to synthesize ordinary morality would enhance its plausibility as a normative theory and justify using it as the basis for reforming and improving everyday morality. However, because Sidgwick's thesis involves a bundle of bold philosophical, sociological, and historical claims, establishing it would be difficult, and it is fair to say that on this point Sidgwick has failed to win many converts. Although contemporary utilitarians hold that their theory should be used to reform and revise conventional morality, they shy away from contending that their theory is justified because it already captures the gist of that morality.

From a utilitarian perspective, Sidgwick is absolutely correct to emphasize both the limits to the rules and principles of commonsense morality and the need, if those rules and principles are to be retained, to situate them within a secure philosophical framework. Although, as I have said, contemporary utilitarians do not assert that commonsense morality is implicitly utilitarian, like Sidgwick they are far from rejecting it as a working guide for everyday conduct. For one thing, most people operate on commonsense moral principles rather than the principle of utility, and utilitarians must coordinate their actions with these non-utilitarians by following certain generally accepted rules. Moreover, ordinary morality does contain significant utilitarian elements, and many of its familiar rules and precepts can be defended as tending to promote total welfare. Even when commonsense morality appears to diverge from utilitarianism, there may be utilitarian grounds for supporting ordinary morality. For example, from a utilitarian perspective, it will certainly have better results to teach children that they should always tell the truth and to instill in them a commitment to veracity in all circumstances rather than to instruct them that they should tell the truth only if they believe that doing so will maximize total welfare.

The Challenge of Egoism

As we have seen, Sidgwick argues for utilitarianism on two independent grounds. First, "such abstract moral principles as we can admit to be self-evident are not only not incompatible with a Utilitarian system, but ... furnish a rational basis for such a system" (496). Second, "careful and systematic reflection on ... Common Sense, as expressed in the habitual moral judgments of ordinary men, results in exhibiting the real subordination of these rules" to the utilitarian principle (497). However persuasive one finds Sidgwick's reasoning, he himself was troubled by his inability to undermine egoism as a rational alternative to utilitarianism.

The egoist takes his own happiness as his only end and the measure of his conduct. In response, Sidgwick argued convincingly that if the egoist affirms that his happiness is not merely good for him but objectively good – a component of the general good – then the egoist is inexorably led to utilitarianism. For the egoist cannot claim that, from a universal perspective, his happiness is more important than the happiness of any other individual. However, Sidgwick recognized that an egoist could avoid this dialectical trap by declining to affirm that his good is part of the general good.[24] Instead, the egoist affirms only that he ought to take his own happiness as his ultimate guide.

Many moralists have argued that enlightened self-interest directs people to cooperate with others, to be trustworthy and fair, and to follow established moral rules. Honesty, they tell us, pays. This is true, no doubt, but only as a generalization. It remains the case that what utilitarianism or any normative theory other than egoism requires of one can at least sometimes diverge from what would best promote one's own interests. In particular, utilitarianism affirms, and egoism denies, that it is "right for me to sacrifice my happiness for the good of the whole of which I am a part."[25] In cases of genuine conflict between self-interest and duty, Sidgwick thought, practical reason is divided against itself.

This conclusion troubled Sidgwick, who wrestled with it for years, having hoped to eliminate all rational alternatives to utilitarianism. However, no rival ethical system can refute egoism, either. Any non-egoistic ethic will sometimes clash with self-interest, for instance, by forbidding crimes that would benefit the perpetrator but go undetected. This truth is a commonplace, but Sidgwick seems to have overlooked it. Moreover, his ambition was probably misguided to begin with. One vindicates a moral system by showing that it provides the most plausible or best justified account of right and wrong. One needn't demonstrate that there can be no divergence between duty, as the theory understands it, and rational self-interest. Indeed, demonstrating this is not only unnecessary, but probably impossible. Self-interest and morality are simply different things. To aspire

---

[24] G. E. Moore thought that Sidgwick conceded too much to the egoist. For more on this issue, see Shaw, *Moore on Right and Wrong*, 79–80; Narveson, *Morality and Utility*, 268–71; and Mackie, "Sidgwick's pessimism."
[25] Sidgwick, *Methods of Ethics*, xvi.

to eliminate any potential gap between them reveals a failure to grasp their essential natures. So, however troubling it was to Sidgwick, his inability to prove egoism irrational does not weaken his case for utilitarianism.

The Case against Deontology

Critics of utilitarianism's consequentialist and maximizing orientation to ethics believe that at least some moral rules or principles are valid, independently of the goodness or badness of their results. In particular, they believe that sometimes it is wrong to act in the way that would maximize good (*deontological restraints*) or that sometimes it is permissible to act in a way that does not maximize the good (*deontological permissions*), or both. Contrary to what Sidgwick suggests, commonsense morality seems to contain significant nonconsequentialist or deontological elements. Utilitarians, therefore, attempt to buttress their theory not only by challenging the authority of commonsense morality and of people's "considered moral judgments," but also by directly attacking nonconsequentialism and debunking the belief that there are moral rules, requirements, or principles that can be justified without reference to utility.

Nonconsequentialist systems of ethics come in various shapes and colors, but utilitarians challenge all of them along certain general lines, two of which are particularly important. First, they argue that deontologists, when pressed to defend their restrictions and permissions, typically fall back on two ethical distinctions that cannot withstand critical scrutiny. Second, they contend that deontological restrictions on conduct are paradoxical and that this fact points to an irrationality at the nucleus of all deontological systems.

Doing versus Allowing, Intending versus Foreseeing

Utilitarians believe that if the outcome is the same and if all other things are equal, then it is morally irrelevant whether the outcome results from my acting or from my not acting. That is, they believe that the difference between my doing something or making it happen and my allowing or letting it happen is not, by itself, morally significant. For example, if their motives are the same, then there is no morally relevant difference between Smith's drowning his young nephew in the bath and Jones's refusing to rescue his nephew from the bath after he has accidentally bumped his head and slipped under the water.[26] In contrast, almost all nonconsequentialists

---

[26] See Rachels, "Active and passive euthanasia."

believe that there can sometimes be a significant, possibly weighty, moral difference between making something happen and allowing it to happen – between acting and refraining from acting – even when the outcome is the same and all other factors are equal.

Utilitarians also believe that if the outcome is identical, and all other things are the same, then there is no morally significant difference between an outcome that I intentionally bring about and an outcome that I merely foresee will result from what I do. In other words, my acting in a way intended to produce a particular result (either as a goal or as a means to something else) is, considered in itself, neither better nor worse than my acting in a way that I foresee will have that same result as a likely or inevitable side effect but which I do not seek to bring about. Many deontologists believe, to the contrary, that sometimes there is a morally significant difference between intending and foreseeing. The thesis that there is a difference is called the *doctrine of double effect*. It states that it is sometimes permissible to bring about as the merely foreseen consequence of one's action a harm that it would not be permissible to bring about intentionally, either as one's goal or a means to one's goal.

The doctrine of double effect implies that the following situations are different in a morally important way. In the first, a pilot bombs an enemy railroad station in order to kill the civilian passengers inside (perhaps in an effort to dampen enemy morale). In the second, a pilot bombs the same station in order to disrupt enemy transportation. Although he foresees that the civilians will die, this is not his goal; it is only a side effect of his conduct. Many deontologists believe, as Kant does, that to kill an innocent person is categorically forbidden; it is something we must absolutely never do, under any circumstances. If so, then by intentionally blowing up the innocent civilians, the first pilot acts immorally even if he fights in a just war. However, because the second pilot did not intend to kill anyone, the doctrine of double effect views his conduct in a different moral light. Assuming he is performing a militarily useful maneuver in a just war, then the pilot may have done nothing wrong. By contrast, utilitarians believe that whether a person intends or merely foresees that his action will have a certain result is immaterial to the assessment of the action itself (although it may be relevant to the assessment of his character). In determining whether an action is right or wrong, all that matters is its expected outcome (as compared to the expected outcomes of the alternative actions open to the agent).

Utilitarians believe that, in defending deontological restraints and deontological permissions, non-utilitarian moralists inevitably rely on the proposition that there is (sometimes) a morally weighty distinction between doing x and letting x happen or that there is (sometimes) an important moral difference between intending x and foreseeing that x will happen. Utilitarians maintain that neither proposition can withstand critical scrutiny and that deontologists fail to explain exactly when and why these distinctions should matter morally. In and of themselves, utilitarians argue, these distinctions are morally neutral: if all other pertinent moral factors are the same, then neither distinction makes any moral difference. If I must choose between option A and option B, then what matters is the difference between the expected outcome of A and the expected outcome of B, not whether one of the options involves doing rather than letting, or intending rather than foreseeing.

These are philosophically contested matters, and the debate over them involves intricate metaphysical issues. However, two important writers sympathetic to utilitarianism have recently argued at length and with great subtlety that all efforts to breathe life into these deontological distinctions fail.[27] If sound, their arguments definitely strengthen the case for a utilitarian ethic.

The Paradox of Deontological Restrictions

Utilitarians stress that whenever a rival moral theory leads one to perform an action that runs counter to utilitarianism, then one is bringing about less welfare or happiness than one could have brought about. In other words, if one does the non-utilitarian thing, then there is less good in the world than there could have been. The proposition that it can be right, intentionally and knowingly, to act in a way that brings about less, rather than more, well-being strikes utilitarians as deeply implausible. If ethics is about anything, they think, it has to be about doing good.

Deontologists, however, readily affirm that the right can diverge from the good. The consequences of our actions may be relevant to their assessment, but the good, they believe, does not fully determine the right. It follows from this that morality can require an agent to perform a suboptimal action, that is, an action the expected outcome of which is less good than that of some other action open to the agent. To be sure, if a deontologist believes, say, that the deathbed promise ought to be kept, then he or she believes that, morally speaking, this is the best thing to do. But, in this view, the morally best action is not necessarily the action that produces the most good, where good is identified independently of right

[27] Kagan, *The Limits of Morality*, and Bennett, *The Act Itself*.

and wrong (as it is by utilitarians, who define it as well-being or happiness).

The deontologist sees it as an important fact about our moral lives that an action can sometimes be wrong even though its outcome would be superior to that of alternative actions. Now suppose that somehow your violating a certain deontological restriction (call it R) would result in there being fewer violations of R overall. According to the deontologist, it would still be wrong for you to violate R. This is puzzling, even paradoxical, and it is natural to ask, as Robert Nozick has: "If nonviolation of R is so important, shouldn't that be the goal? How can a concern for the nonviolation of R lead to the refusal to violate R even when this would prevent more extensive violations of R?"[28]

Admittedly, this is an abstract question, but one can imagine circumstances in which only by telling a lie (breaking a promise, killing an innocent person) can one prevent several other people from telling lies (breaking promises, killing innocent people). Faced with such situations, deontological theories will, at least sometimes, forbid an action of a certain type even when performing it would result in fewer actions of the forbidden type. This point does not presuppose that the deontologist is an absolutist. Even a very moderate deontologist endorses restrictions that it would be wrong for me to violate, at least in some circumstances, even though my doing so would minimize violations of the very same restriction. This seemingly paradoxical feature of deontological restrictions suggests to some moral philosophers that an irrationality lurks at the heart of nonconsequentialism. For how can a normative theory plausibly say that it is wrong to act so as to decrease immoral conduct (that is, conduct that the theory itself identifies as immoral)? To these philosophers it seems illogical for a theory to forbid the performance of a morally objectionable action when doing so would reduce the total number of such actions and would have no other relevant consequences.[29]

Deontologists lack an answer to this challenge, or at least an answer that satisfies their critics.[30] They tend either to ignore the issue or to address it only by restating their initial position in different words. Yet, if this is so, then this paradoxical, possibly irrational, feature of deontological restrictions significantly weakens, perhaps even obviates, many standard challenges to utilitarianism, challenges that presuppose the soundness and rationality of such restrictions.

---

[28] Nozick, *Anarchy, State, and Utopia*, 30.
[29] Scheffler, "Agent-centred restrictions," 409.
[30] Shaw, "Paradox of deontology," 102–5.

The Appeal of Utilitarianism

Although they offer considerations in favor of utilitarianism that many have found compelling, none of the utilitarian moral theorists canvassed in this chapter can be said to have conclusively established the utilitarian principle. Indeed, only Hare even claims to be able to prove the theory in any strict sense. Likewise, the criticisms utilitarians make of commonsense morality and deontological ethics, although important, are insufficient to demonstrate beyond any doubt the superiority of the utilitarian approach. In this respect, however, utilitarianism is in no worse shape than its rivals. Serious objections have crippled all attempts heretofore to rigorously establish some non-utilitarian normative system, and there is little reason to anticipate that such efforts will be successful in the future. Mill was probably right, therefore, to insist that first principles cannot themselves be proved because argument must stop somewhere. If so, then it seems plausible to say that any normative theory is "necessarily grounded in intuitions of truth or value that cannot be objectively demonstrated or disproved."[31]

If this is correct, then utilitarianism as a normative ethic ultimately stands or falls based on whether one finds its core ethical ideas or values intuitively compelling. The first of these ideas is that morality is ultimately or fundamentally about the promotion of well-being. This is the specifically utilitarian version of the more general consequentialist contention that the morality of our actions is in some way or other a function of the goodness of their outcomes. The second core idea builds on the first, asserting further that we should act so as to bring about as much well-being as possible. This is the specifically utilitarian version of the general maximizing principle that an action is right if and only if it brings about the best outcome the agent could have brought about. Neither self-evident nor beyond rational criticism, these two theses are the foundation of utilitarianism. They represent the fundamental convictions or intuitions upon which the theory rests.

Utilitarianism's rivals also, of course, rely on unproved moral assumptions or else appeal to our considered moral judgments. And we have seen that utilitarians are extremely critical of them for this, castigating theorists who invoke intuition to support their normative theories, moral principles, or other ethical claims. But can utilitarians consistently criticize non-utilitarian theorists for relying on intuition if their own theory ultimately

[31] Hardin, *Morality within the Limits of Reason*, 179.

rests on certain moral convictions or assumptions that are themselves beyond proof? Are utilitarians guilty of the same sin of which they accuse others? Defenders of utilitarianism argue that their reliance on intuition is less objectionable than that of their opponents.

First, utilitarianism requires a very small number of ethical assumptions, and these yield a powerful but structurally simple normative theory, capable of unifying our understanding of a diverse range of ethical phenomena. By contrast, most nonconsequentialist approaches to ethics (such as the popular reflective equilibrium method or Ross's commonsense pluralism) have recourse to intuition at an array of different points. In practice, the result can be a hodgepodge of rules, principles, and injunctions of varying degrees of generality. Second, the ethical assumptions on which utilitarians rely are not only few in number, but also very general in character, whereas non-utilitarian theorists utilize various more specific, lower-level intuitions, concerning the legitimacy of particular rules or the moral necessity of particular deontological permissions and restraints. Intuitions about the rightness or wrongness of specific types of conduct seem more likely to be distorted by the authority of cultural tradition and the influence of customary practice than are the more abstract, high-level intuitions upon which utilitarianism relies. Thus, what draws the fire of utilitarians is the comparatively specific, promiscuous, and unsystematic character of their opponents' appeals to intuition. By contrast, the values or ethical ideas that underlie utilitarianism are general and architectonic.

Finally, the ethical assumptions that utilitarians make tally with the postulates that guide us in other areas of life. In particular, their goal-oriented, maximizing approach to ethics coheres with what we implicitly believe to be rational conduct in other contexts, in particular, when it comes to assessing prudential behavior. As one recent writer explains,

> whereas the consequentialist [or utilitarian] line on how values justify choices is continuous with the standard line on rationality in the pursuit of personal goods, the non-consequentialist [or deontological] line is not. The nonconsequentialist . . . position . . . is without analogue in the non-moral area of practical rationality.[32]

In other words, when seeking to advance our personal interests, we take for granted that practical rationality requires us to weigh, balance, and make trade-offs among the things we seek in order to maximize the net amount of good that we achieve. Only a utilitarian or consequentialist approach to ethics fits with that.

[32] Pettit, "Consequentialism," 238.

96

Ultimately, utilitarians believe that the ethical ideas, values, or assumptions that inspire the theory are more attractive and more convincing than those that guide non-utilitarian approaches to ethics, and that their theory in turn provides the most coherent, systematic, and plausible orientation to ethics that one can find. This chapter has uncovered a number of considerations that utilitarians see as strongly supporting their theory, making it the most credible basis around which to orient our moral thinking. A concluding review of these considerations should serve to illuminate what is distinctive to, and attractive about, the utilitarian approach to normative ethics.

The Goal of Morality

Most utilitarians implicitly accept Mill's idea that morality must have an end or goal or point – that there must be some reference point against which our ideas of right and wrong can be measured and assessed. This is an attractive notion, but it is not easy to refute the contrary idea that morality has no external end but is simply a free-standing human activity (perhaps like art or certain areas of mathematics) that people pursue for its own sake. In this view, although there are norms and standards implicit in the moral point of view, there is no overarching goal toward which right and wrong are (at least indirectly) oriented. However, many philosophers, both utilitarian and non-utilitarian, are inclined instead to view morality as a social institution that, like law, performs certain important, indeed necessary, functions in human society. It is not a system of abstract truths that are simply built into the universe, unrelated to the human predicament.

Although admittedly rather vague, this general way of looking at morality is buttressed by our knowledge of moral development in human beings and by sociological and historical study of the moral codes of different societies. From the premise that morality is primarily a social institution, it doesn't follow that morality has only a single end or that there is some simple criterion in terms of which it is to be assessed. But it has seemed plausible to many philosophers that, in the words of C. I. Lewis, "without reference to what is good and what is bad there could be no determination of anything as right or wrong."[33] He elaborates:

> If it were not for the fact that some things gratify and some things grieve,
> nobody would have any concern over what he, or anybody else, should bring
> about. If there were no such fact as good and bad in the experience of life,

[33] Lewis, *Values and Imperatives*, 30–1.

there would also be no such fact as right and wrong in what is done. Nobody would have any reason to care. (25)

Lewis goes on to affirm the thesis (reminiscent of Mill) that it is the consequences of acts that give them their content – if asked what I am doing, the only answer I can make, Lewis says, is in terms of the consequences I expect or am trying to bring about. Together with this thesis, the passage quoted above leads Lewis to conclude that "no judgment of right and wrong can validly be made except by reference to appraisal of predictable consequences of the act in question as good or bad" (30).

Lewis believes that right and wrong must be tied to good and bad and, thus, to the consequences of our actions. From these attractive ideas, it is a small step to the proposition that

there is one ultimate moral aim: that outcomes be as good as possible[34]

and then to the more specific injunction that

so far as morality is concerned, what people ought to do is to minimize evil and maximize good, to try, in other words, to make the world as good a place as possible.[35]

Human Well-Being

Some moral philosophers such as G. E. Moore embrace the above propositions but reject utilitarianism's welfarist account of good. However, for many people it is the fact that utilitarianism equates the good with individual well-being or happiness that makes its consequentialist, maximizing approach to morality so appealing. The idea that human well-being is what ultimately matters, and all that ultimately matters, is so powerful that many people who accept it can see no other remotely plausible basis for morality. As a recent commentator has written:

It seems evident to people that there is such a thing as individuals' being made better or worse off. Such facts have an obvious motivational force . . . . Further, these facts are clearly relevant to morality as we now understand it. Claims about individual well-being are one class of valid starting points for moral argument. But many people find it much harder to see how there could be any other, independent starting points. Substantive moral requirements independent of individual well-being strike people as intuitionist in

[34] Parfit, *Reasons and Persons*, 24.
[35] Scheffler, *Consequentialism and Its Critics*, 1.

an objectionable sense . . . . There is no problem about recognising it as a fact that a certain act is, say, an instance of lying or of promise breaking. And . . . such facts as these often have (derivative) moral significance . . . because of their consequences for individual well-being. The problems, and the charge of "intuitionism," arise when it is claimed that such acts are wrong in a sense that is not reducible to the fact that they decrease individual well-being.[36]

This long passage makes three important points. The first is that a concern for well-being motivates people. Not only do people care about their own welfare and the welfare of those close to them, but also they can easily see and appreciate that other people are quite reasonably concerned about their own welfare and the welfare of those close to them. This connects with the second point: namely, that ordinary morality already makes individual well-being a touchstone. No one doubts that the impact of our conduct on individual well-being is always a morally relevant issue. Moreover, not only is well-being a morally relevant factor, it is so relevant that, and this is the third point, many people find it difficult to imagine how any important moral considerations could fail to be somehow connected to welfare, even if only indirectly.

As we saw earlier, Mill urged that human beings have social feelings and a desire for unity with others and that this concern for the well-being of other people is natural and cannot be subverted by critical analysis. Accordingly, the attachment of human beings to their fellows and our natural desire for solidarity with others make utilitarianism a workable morality in practice – make it a moral system that, because of its commitment to the well-being of everyone, can win people's hearts and retain their allegiance.

Utilitarians have long emphasized benevolence as one of the wellsprings of utilitarianism, but this benevolence is a generalized, long-term regard for the good of all, not simply the immediate sympathy or good will that one human being sometimes feels toward a specific person. As Bentham writes, "the dictates of utility are neither more nor less than the dictates of the most extensive and enlightened (that is *well-advised*) benevolence."[37] In a similar vein, the contemporary utilitarian J. J. C. Smart writes that in setting up their system of normative ethics, utilitarians appeal to the "sentiment . . . [of] generalized benevolence, that is, the disposition to seek happiness, or at any rate, in some sense or other, good consequences, for all mankind, or perhaps for all sentient beings," later suggesting the possibility that "many sympathetic and benevolent people depart from or fail to

---

[36] Scanlon, "Contractualism and utilitarianism," 108.
[37] Bentham, *Principles of Morals and Legislation*, 121.

attain a utilitarian ethical principle only under the stress of tradition, or superstition, or of unsound philosophical reasoning."[38]

Impartiality

Utilitarians have sometimes appealed to the hypothetical notion of an *ideal observer*. The concept can be spelled out in different ways, but the ideal observer is usually imagined to be empathetic and dispassionate, and to enjoy an omniscient and disinterested perspective. Above the fray, so to speak, and with an equal and impartial concern for all, the ideal observer enjoys the big picture. An old and venerable philosophical tradition holds that the notion of an ideal observer captures and elevates to perfection the qualities that are essential to one's taking the moral point of view. Accordingly, in this view, morally right actions are those that would be approved by an ideal observer. What actions are these? Utilitarians claim, and many non-utilitarian philosophers would agree, that the actions an ideal observer would approve are co-extensive with those that a perfectly informed utilitarian would advocate.

The device of the ideal observer highlights the idea, which many moral philosophers embrace, that morality itself implies a commitment to impartiality and hence to the equal consideration of interests. Morality can and often does permit self-interested behavior, but when we speak of people taking the moral point of view, we have in mind their transcending self-interest and personal bias and examining the situation from an objective and impartial perspective. From that perspective it is obvious that no one person's happiness or well-being is of greater or lesser value than another's (except, of course, insofar as the amount of happiness differs). Accordingly, as utilitarians see it, objectivity and impartiality require one to take other people's interests into account and to weigh them equally with one's own. Simple rationality then requires one to compare and balance those interests and to promote as much as possible the well-being of all.

Thus, a cluster of related ideas and values support the utilitarian approach to right and wrong. In particular, a commitment to impartiality, a concern for individual welfare, and a belief that morality must have an end, in light of which we can appraise conduct, underwrite the utilitarian conviction that human well-being is all that ultimately matters morally, as well as the more specific proposition that we ought always to act so as to bring about

---

[38] Smart, "A system of utilitarian ethics," 7, 31.

as much well-being as possible. Despite the undeniable appeal of utilitarianism, many contemporary thinkers charge that grave difficulties plague the theory and that upon extended examination its initial attractiveness dissolves. These critics raise such powerful and damning objections to the theory that utilitarianism cannot possibly win our allegiance unless it can survive this attack and answer its critics. Whether utilitarianism can meet the challenge of its critics is the subject of Chapter 4.

4

Objections to Utilitarianism

Utilitarianism reflects the conviction that because well-being is what ultimately matters, conduct should be assessed solely in terms of its impact on how well people fare. After examining in Chapter 2 utilitarianism's theory of value and considering different ways in which well-being can be understood, we reviewed in Chapter 3 a variety of arguments in favor of the consequentialist orientation to right and wrong that is characteristic of utilitarianism. As we have seen, a cluster of closely connected ideas and values supports the proposition that the right action is that which produces the greatest net good or the most happiness for all. However, even if one finds the considerations that underwrite this normative thesis compelling, the real test is whether, when one examines it closely, utilitarianism provides a lucid and coherent normative system, an account of right and wrong and of how we ought to live that is both intellectually compelling and morally attractive.

Many philosophers today deny that utilitarianism provides such an account. They believe that its view of right and wrong is profoundly flawed and contend that the theory faces crippling objections. This chapter scrutinizes the most significant and frequently voiced objections to utilitarianism. These can be grouped into four categories: (1) that the theory requires immoral conduct, (2) that it cannot do justice to promises and other special obligations, (3) that it is indifferent to the distribution of welfare, and (4) that it requires too much of moral agents. If utilitarianism is to establish itself as a plausible theory, let alone prove itself to be more satisfactory than alternative ethical approaches, then it must rebut these criticisms and overcome the reservations of its critics. In this chapter I address objections to utilitarianism in terms of the basic or standard version of it explicated in Chapter 1, but in the next chapter I will begin elaborating a more sophisticated account of utilitarianism. Only as that account is filled out over the remainder of the book will the issues raised by the critics be entirely laid to rest.

Utilitarianism Condones Immoral Conduct

As the deathbed promise case of Chapter 1 illustrates, utilitarianism seems sometimes to conflict with the injunctions of ordinary, everyday morality. However, Chapter 1 argued that in the deathbed promise case itself this apparent conflict poses no genuine challenge to utilitarianism. For one thing, people's intuitions about the case may be conflicted or uncertain so that the claim that commonsense morality unhesitatingly instructs us to give the money to the nephew rather than the orphanage is open to doubt. Moreover, even if utilitarianism does clash with everyday morality in this case, it is far from obvious that one ought, in these unusual circumstances, to cleave to the quotidian rules and pass the money on to the nephew.

Nevertheless, critics of utilitarianism contend that in an array of situations utilitarianism not only diverges from ordinary morality but also has implications that are ethically repugnant. For example, Richard B. Brandt has written that standard-version utilitarianism

> implies that if you have employed a boy to mow your lawn and he has finished the job and asks for his pay, you should pay him what you promised only if you cannot find a better use for your money . . . . It implies that if your father is ill and has no prospect of good in his life, and maintaining him is a drain on the energy and enjoyments of others, then, if you can end his life without provoking any public scandal or setting a bad example, it is your positive duty to take matters into your own hands and bring his life to a close.[1]

Relying on examples like these, many philosophers argue that utilitarianism must be rejected on moral grounds. For instance, A. C. Ewing contends that "utilitarian principles, logically carried out, would result in far more cheating, lying and unfair action than any good man would tolerate."[2]

Before we consider whether utilitarianism really does have these startling ramifications, we must first examine whether and why it would be a problem for utilitarianism if it did. Utilitarianism provides a normative standard by which we are to assess actions. To denounce utilitarianism on the ground that an action it judges right is in fact immoral presupposes the

[1] Brandt, "Toward a credible form of utilitarianism," 109–10.
[2] Ewing, *Ethics*, 40.

correctness of some non-utilitarian moral theory and thus seems to beg the question against utilitarianism. The critic is implicitly assuming the truth of an alternative theory and, on that basis, claiming to show that utilitarianism is untenable. Logically, such a procedure no more establishes that utilitarianism is incorrect than it proves the correctness of the rival theory the critic is presupposing. The point here is simple. If there are solid grounds for accepting utilitarianism as a general normative theory, then there are grounds for doing what the theory says it is right to do in particular cases even if the theory's instructions seem surprising or appear to differ from common sense.

In response, critics who wield the immoral-conduct argument against utilitarianism typically claim that they are not presupposing the truth of any particular non-utilitarian ethical theory. They assert that it is simply a datum, a given, that refusing to pay the boy for mowing your lawn is wrong. No theory here, they say, just a moral fact, which any normative theory must respect, just as any scientific theory must be true to the observational facts if it is to be taken seriously. However, the philosophy of science teaches us that the relation between theory and observation is no simple matter, and when it comes to ethics, it certainly seems that the judgments people make about the rightness or wrongness of different actions reflect, at least in part, a socially and historically shaped moral sensibility. Because what strikes people as obviously right or obviously wrong has varied tremendously in different times and places, one can reasonably doubt that, in wielding the immoral-conduct argument, the critic is countering utilitarianism with some simple moral fact that is epistemologically prior to any normative theory and against which we can and must test our basic principles and more general moral beliefs.

Nevertheless, many philosophers would bridle at the suggestion that our moral judgments about particular situations have no evidentiary warrant in their own right and rebuff the contention that our moral beliefs are simply a function of values and moral attitudes which we have uncritically absorbed from those around us. Although contemporary philosophers differ in their views on such meta-ethical issues as whether moral statements have truth value or whether there are moral facts, most of them would probably agree that there are some moral judgments about which it would make little or no sense to say that we could be mistaken. We are far more confident, and rightly so, it seems, of the correctness of some of our particular judgments about right and wrong than we could ever be of the soundness of some general moral theory. A man rapes a woman and then blinds her so that she cannot identify him; a sadistic soldier tortures an enemy to death; a boy burns down a randomly chosen home in order to win acceptance into a local gang. These are crimes, the wrongness of which is beyond debate. If something calling itself a moral theory did not condemn these actions, it could not plausibly be said to be a theory of right and wrong at all.

Therefore, even if utilitarians are right, as I believe they are, to insist (1) that if one accepts a general normative theory, then one has grounds for following its directives in particular cases, (2) that the injunctions of ordinary morality have no privileged status just because they are widely accepted, and (3) that, to win acceptance, a moral theory is not required to tally with commonsense moral beliefs, nevertheless it is the case (4) that there are certain ethical judgments with which no moral theory could conflict and still claim our allegiance as a moral theory. Critics of utilitarianism who advance the immoral-conduct argument claim to be able to identify cases where utilitarianism runs afoul of (4). Against this argumentative strategy, utilitarians pursue two lines of defense. First, they argue that in practice their theory does not have the implications for conduct that its critics claim it has; second, they argue that even if their theory does have the implications it is alleged to have, closer inspection shows that this fact does not require us to reject utilitarianism.

Consider the supposition that it would maximize benefit for you not to pay the boy the $10 you owe him for mowing your lawn. Utilitarians will be quick to dispute this possibility. They will urge that there are no realistic circumstances (1) in which you face only a simple choice between paying and refusing to pay and (2) in which the happiness created by doing something else with your money will be sufficient to outweigh the boy's disappointment and resentment, the indignation of his parents, the damage to your reputation, and the certainty that the boy will never work for you again. One is hard pressed to conceive what alternative use of your money would produce enough happiness to counterbalance these deleterious effects. Moreover, we must assume that you could not have envisioned this alternative use before you employed the boy. Having a newly mowed lawn may bring you pleasure, but reneging on the deal has such obvious bad effects that if you had known in advance that there was some other demand on your money, then as a utilitarian you would not have engaged the boy in the first place or would have asked him to accept payment later or to work for free.

Suppose, however, that the critic simply stipulates that an unpredicted emergency occurred between the time when you hired the boy and when payment fell due and that there is now a demand on the money owed to the lad sufficiently important to outweigh the unhappy consequences of not paying him. Perhaps you lost your job and your life savings on the same day and were then robbed, so that you now need what little cash you have on hand to buy food for your children. Yet if we suppose these are the facts, then it is far from obvious that it is wrong of you not to pay the boy. We can imagine a conscientious person explaining the situation to the boy and his parents and promising to find some way to make it up to him in the future. Common moral sense suggests that the boy would be wrong to insist on being paid then and there if it means that your children go hungry.

The Wrongness of Killing

Utilitarians can wield the two above-mentioned lines of defense to good effect against almost all the different versions of the immoral-conduct argument that fill the philosophical literature. Brandt's example of murdering your parent to promote overall happiness is even less plausible than the example of not paying the boy for mowing your lawn. To try to get the example off the ground, the critic has to stipulate an either-or situation, imagine one to have knowledge one is unlikely to have, and make unrealistic assumptions about the emotions and feelings of the people involved. On the other hand, utilitarians may well favor euthanasia in some circumstances – at least if it is assumed that there are medical and legal safeguards sufficient to prevent any abuses. Yet on this point, utilitarianism is probably in step with contemporary non-utilitarian moral thinking.

Critics of utilitarianism sometimes charge, though, that the theory cannot satisfactorily explain what is wrong with killing.[3] Instead of appealing to well-being, they favor notions like the sanctity of life, or they contend that killing is intrinsically wrong because it transgresses the victim's autonomy, violates her right to life, or fails to respect her as a person. Like utilitarians, however, most of these critics do not view killing as categorically wrong, that is, as impermissible always and in every circumstance whatsoever, and they differ among themselves over such controversial issues as war, euthanasia, and capital punishment. Nevertheless, these theorists believe that the normative concepts they favor provide a theoretically more acceptable moral basis for denouncing killing than does utilitarianism. I do not challenge that belief here, but I do reject the suggestion that, when it comes to killing, utilitarianism has implications that most people would find shocking and that therefore the theory must be abandoned.

[3] See Henson, "Utilitarianism and the wrongness of killing."

From a utilitarian perspective, the negative consequences of killing are obvious. In addition to whatever pain the victim suffers, killing the person deprives him of the future well-being he would have had. For this reason it is ordinarily one of the most serious harms that can befall a person. Killing someone also typically brings sorrow and grief to family and friends, and murder can easily spread fear, worry, and insecurity through society. All societies firmly prohibit killing other people, at least under ordinary circumstances, and there is a fully compelling utilitarian case for their doing so. Without such a prohibition, social existence would barely be possible.

However, its critics argue that utilitarianism does not condemn killing as strongly and unequivocally as it should. Imagine, they say, an old tramp who is miserably depressed and unhappy, whose future will be one of continued misery, and who has no family or friends. If it can be done painlessly and without anyone noticing, and assuming that the killer would enjoy doing it or that he or others would benefit from the tramp's death in some other way, then killing the tramp would appear to be justified on utilitarian grounds. Yet surely, the critic argues, killing him would be foul and immoral, and because utilitarianism condones it, one must repudiate utilitarianism as a normative theory.

To this argument utilitarians can respond that the critic's scenario assumes knowledge about the future that one is most unlikely to have. And even if all the supposed empirical contingencies are exactly as the critic stipulates – and that's a big *if* – one is unlikely to know, or have compelling grounds for believing, that killing the tramp would maximize happiness, all things considered and in the long run. Furthermore, permitting people to kill others whenever they are firmly convinced that doing so is for the best would have disastrous social consequences. "If it were thought allowable for any one to put to death at pleasure any human being whom he believes that the world would be well rid of," Mill writes, then "nobody's life would be safe."[4] Finally, a readiness to kill others (especially without their consent) expresses, as a recent writer says, "an attitude of such negativeness to another that it is for the good of us all that we should, so far as possible, never feel it towards our fellows."[5] Because utilitarianism is based on a concern for people's well-being, it seeks to foster attitudes and sentiments that tend to promote welfare. Real utilitarians cannot love and assist others as they should and yet be as ready to kill people as the unhappy tramp case imagines.

---

[4] Mill, "Whewell on moral philosophy," 182.
[5] Sprigge, "Utilitarianism and respect for human life," 19.

Lying

An important and more plausible variant of the immoral-conduct argument focuses on lying, with the critics arguing that utilitarians take truthfulness less seriously than they should. Utilitarians, however, rejoin that there are firm and compelling consequentialist grounds for telling the truth. As moralists of all persuasions have recognized, experience teaches that although lying sometimes appears an attractive short-term expedient, all too frequently it leads to unhappiness in the long run. When people learn that they have been deceived, they are made unhappy, trust among human beings is damaged, and the liar is likely to suffer adverse effects. Further, when mendacity becomes widespread, it has debilitating social effects. As Mill remarks in *Utilitarianism*, lying weakens "the trustworthiness of human assertion, which is . . . the principal support of all present social well-being." A lack of veracity, he continues, "does more than any one thing that can be named to keep back civilisation, virtue, [and] everything on which human happiness on the largest scale depends" (22). Not only does a general social practice of telling the truth promote the interests of all, truthfulness is also sound policy from the point of view of one's own self-interest.

In response, the critics contend that utilitarians oppose lying for the wrong reason. Utilitarians are against lying because of its consequences, not because of its intrinsic wickedness. With his characteristic and instructive forthrightness, Bentham unambiguously endorses the position that utilitarianism's critics repudiate:

> Falsehood, take it by itself, consider it as not being accompanied by any other material circumstances, nor therefore productive of any other material effects, can never, upon the principle of utility, constitute any offence at all. (223)

This statement reflects the utilitarian thesis that no action is right or wrong simply in view of the kind of action it is, apart from its circumstances and effects. Rather, it is the outcome of lying that makes it wrong. As Bentham goes on to say, "there is scarce any sort of pernicious effect which [falsehood] may not be instrumental in producing." By contrast, nonutilitarian writers urge that lying is wrong, and inherently so, not because of its results, but because it is exploitative and violates the respect we owe other rational creatures.[6]

---

[6] Fried, *Right and Wrong*, 67; Donagan, *Theory of Morality*, 89.

Who is right about this? Unfortunately, the contrast is not as sharp as non-utilitarians think it is. After all, utilitarians are also against exploitation, and they too urge us to respect the interests of others. The fact that lying almost always involves taking advantage of others or ignoring their interests can be seen as part of the consequentialist case against it. Presumably, though, the critic wants to insist that any given lie (for example, Jill's complimenting Jack on his new car when Jill actually dislikes its styling) is wrong because exploitative even if its outcome is better than that of any alternative action open to Jill (such as keeping her mouth shut or refraining from commenting directly on the merits of Jack's purchase). Whether utilitarianism would authorize Jill's lie depends on further details about the situation and the ramifications of her saying or avoiding saying different things. In weighing the alternatives, utilitarians will also consider the risk that Jill's conduct will reinforce a character trait that she would be better off without, namely, a ready inclination to fib in awkward circumstances.

Let us assume, though, that from a utilitarian perspective Jill is right to prevaricate. Has she nevertheless exploited Jack or failed to extend him the respect owed a rational creature by complimenting him on his new car? The claim that she has exploited him seems doubtful. On the other hand, if the critic insists that in telling a lie Jill has exploited Jack, it is not obvious that this fact makes the lie wrong, especially if it is, ex hypothesi, the best thing she could have done under the circumstances. In assessing utilitarianism on this point, we must bear in mind that commonsense morality does not view lying as absolutely or categorically wrong. Indeed, apart from Kant, few moral theorists have affirmed that we have an absolute duty to tell the truth and, thus, that it is always and under all circumstances wrong to lie.

A critic might argue that ordinary morality nevertheless differs from utilitarianism because it views lying as prima facie wrong, that is, as something one always has a duty not to do even though more stringent ethical concerns can sometimes outweigh this duty. Utilitarians, however, can agree that there is a general moral presumption against lying. This is because "most lies *do* have negative consequences for liars, dupes, all those affected, and for social trust."[7] The fact that lying usually has bad results is a reason for presuming, until it is demonstrated to the contrary, that any particular lie will fail to maximize happiness in the long term. This presumption is strengthened by the fact that when it is in our interest to lie, bias is likely to warp our assessment of the likely consequences.

However, this utilitarian presumption against lying does not amount to

[7] Bok, *Lying*, 50.

saying that lying is inherently wrong or that falsehood is bad in itself. If, therefore, the statement that lying is prima facie wrong entails, not simply that there is a presumption against it, but rather that there is something intrinsically wrong about any lie (even when it is morally justified all things considered as, for example, when saving a friend necessitates lying to the murderer), then there would be a contrast between utilitarianism and the position being attributed to commonsense morality. But this interpretation of commonsense morality forces it into a prefabricated and possibly distorting theoretical mold. It is far from clear that the everyday moral beliefs of ordinary people distinguish between the Rossian proposition that lying is inherently but not absolutely wrong and the utilitarian proposition that lying is generally wrong, still less that commonsense morality favors the former view over the latter.

Some moralists complain that everyday morality is too permissive about lying. They believe that these days too many people countenance white lies, paternalistic lies, and inflated letters of recommendation, and turn a blind eye to hyperbolic advertisements, to the dissembling of politicians, and to deception by investigators and others claiming to act for the public good. If these moralists are correct, then everyday morality probably permits more lying than it should on utilitarian grounds because these practices have bad long-term effects, which are ignored by those who condone or engage in them. A less mendacious world would be a happier place. The critic of utilitarianism is, therefore, a long way from establishing that utilitarianism permits more lying than ordinary people can stomach or than a person of conscience should abide.

However, the critic might respond that the (supposedly) relaxed attitude of ordinary people toward lying reflects the corrupting impact of utilitarianism on everyday moral attitudes. Having adopted a utilitarian orientation toward truth and falsehood, people are prepared to lie if and when they perceive the consequences to warrant it. But because people are fallible in their moral calculations and tend to rationalize their behavior when their interests are at stake, this utilitarian attitude leads them to tell falsehoods in situations when accurate, long-term utilitarian calculation would not warrant it. Although open to debate, this line of criticism does raise a novel question: could it happen that encouraging people to adopt a utilitarian perspective has results that are less than ideal from the point of view of utilitarianism itself?

We will return to this issue in the next chapter, but it needs stressing here that utilitarianism does not require moral agents to attempt to calculate in every situation whether to lie or tell the truth. Utilitarians know that there are good, tried and true grounds for veracity. Accordingly, they should firmly adhere to a policy of telling the truth unless they have very good reason for believing there is something unusual or exceptional about the circumstances they are in, at which point they may stop to calculate more carefully the best course of conduct overall. To make honesty not just a rule of thumb, but a habit – indeed, a reflex – has good results. Not only does it save time, but the risk that rationalization or an erroneous calculation of outcomes will lead even well-intentioned utilitarians to lie when they should not is greater than the risk that by making it a habit to tell the truth they will fail to lie when they should.

Promises and the Particularity of Obligation

From a utilitarian point of view, breaking a promise is not always wrong. It is wrong only when the results are bad – worse than the results of keeping the promise. Although contingent, the utilitarian case for keeping promises is nevertheless strong. Broken promises generally result in unmet expectations and disappointment – even hurt, anger, and a sense of betrayal. In addition to the good that may come from keeping a particular promise is the good that results from supporting a system or practice in which people make and rely on one another's promises. As a rule, when philosophers discuss promising, they focus on gratuitous promises (such as deathbed promises) where there is no evident benefit to the promisor and ignore promises that facilitate the exchange of goods and services or that coordinate people's actions and facilitate their accomplishing some joint purpose.[8] However, exchange promises and coordination promises are of greater practical importance than gratuitous promises, and their utilitarian rationale is unmistakable. Indeed, the practice of keeping them not only benefits society generally but is also in one's self-interest.

Nevertheless, utilitarianism's critics frequently insist that it fails to treat promises seriously enough. Not only, in their view, does utilitarianism too readily permit promises to be broken but also, because of its consequentialist perspective, the theory misunderstands what promises are and fails to grasp the distinctive character of the obligation they create. The critics further contend that utilitarianism's inadequate treatment of promises is symptomatic of its inability to do justice to the special obligations that give each person's moral duty its specific, individualized character.

The critics, however, have never adequately supported their allegation

---

[8] Hardin, *Morality within the Limits of Reason*, 60.

that utilitarianism is too lax about breaking promises. In particular, they have yet to demonstrate that it requires one to break a promise in circumstances where doing so would be undeniably immoral. The deathbed promise case asks us to imagine that we have knowledge that we are unlikely to have about future utilities, and the supposition that it would promote happiness for you not to pay the boy for mowing my lawn, as you said you would, is inane. Yet even if one grants these factual assumptions for the sake of argument, it is still far from clear that breaking the promise would be so patently immoral that any moral theory that permits or requires it can have no claim on one's allegiance.

The critics of utilitarianism tend to exaggerate the seriousness with which everyday people take promising. No one denies that ordinary morality permits one to break minor promises when one has a sufficiently good reason. From its perspective, we have at most a prima facie, not an absolute, obligation to keep our word. Indeed, ordinary people break promises all the time – not just when the duty to keep their promise is overridden by a more stringent obligation, but also when they find it convenient to break them. They do this without a qualm when the promise is of little importance and when the other person is unlikely to mind ("I'm sure he'll understand").[9] How important it is to keep a promise depends on what sort of expectation it has created, on how much trouble other people have taken in relying on it, and on the extent to which breaking it will inconvenience them. Far from being lax about promising, utilitarianism is at least as stringent about it as everyday moral practice is.

How We Think about Promises

This last point is also germane to the critic's charge that the consequentialist orientation of utilitarians conflicts with the way ordinary people think about promising. As W. D. Ross writes:

> When a plain man fulfils a promise because he thinks he ought to do so, it seems clear that he does so with no thought of its total consequences, still less with any opinion that these are likely to be the best possible . . . . What makes him think it right to act in a certain way is the fact that he has promised to do so – that and, usually, nothing more. That his act will produce the best possible consequences is not his reason for calling it right.[10]

[9] Narveson, *Morality and Utility*, 193.
[10] Ross, *The Right and the Good*, 17.

There are elements of truth in what Ross says, but only elements. When an ordinary person tells the truth, keeps a promise, stops to help a child, or sends a check to a charity, the person may be thinking only that this is the right thing to do. Even if this ordinary person is a utilitarian, he or she may still act from habit or on the basis of simple everyday rules without thinking about total consequences. That I made a promise to Gretchen to meet her for lunch is my reason for dragging myself away from something I would prefer to be doing and hurrying across town to the restaurant we agreed upon. Normally, to explain and justify my conduct it suffices for me to say "because I promised." However, this fact is consistent with there being an underlying utilitarian rationale for what I do, a rationale that, perhaps with some prodding, I both could and would provide: after having intentionally led Gretchen to rely on me, if I stand her up, then I will have wasted her time, inconvenienced her, and perhaps hurt her feelings.

Ross writes as if, when questioned about why he should keep his promise, the "plain man" can only say "because I promised" and nothing more. But he can say a lot more than this. Otherwise we could not explain why ordinary morality sometimes permits us to break our promises. Suppose that Alice, who is Gretchen's close friend and works near the restaurant, has agreed to join us. If Alice is there, as I can safely assume she will be, Gretchen is unlikely to mind my absence at all. So I call the restaurant and leave a message for Gretchen, "Sorry that I can't join you and Alice today, but I can't get away. Let's try another time."

Ross argues his point from yet another angle. Suppose, he writes, that keeping my promise to person A will produce 1000 units of good for him, but that by breaking it I can produce 1001 units of good for person B. Surely a promise cannot be set aside to obtain such a small increase in good (35). Even if we take into account A's disappointment and the collateral damage done to my credibility (and, to a lesser extent, to the whole system of mutual reliance and confidence built around promising), it will still be the case, Ross argues, that if the imagined benefit to B is great enough, then there will be a point at which the good that comes from breaking the promise slightly outweighs the good that comes from keeping it. At this point, utilitarianism requires me to break the promise. Here, concludes Ross, utilitarianism conflicts with the way people ordinarily view promising and the moral obligation it creates (38).

Ross's discussion suffers from false precision, for one can give no meaningful content to the hypothesis that breaking a particular promise would, all things considered, produce one-tenth of a percent more good. Even if one had an account of good that theoretically permitted states of affairs to be ranked as exactly as this, no one could claim to know these rankings with the imagined degree of precision. Nevertheless, suppose that, in the long run and all things considered, slightly more good would come from breaking a promise than keeping it and that one could reasonably be said to know this. Ross's point is that the advantage of breaking the promise over keeping the promise can be very slight, but as long as the advantage exists, utilitarianism requires one to break his promise. As we have seen, Ross believes that this conflicts with our ordinary moral ideas. However, it has been argued above that when one colors in some realistic details, as in the example of meeting Alice and Gretchen for lunch, it is far from evident that it would either be wrong or conflict with our ordinary moral ideas to break a promise to achieve the greater benefit that doing so makes possible.

Some non-utilitarian writers, however, reject this line of argument. For example, John Rawls writes: "What would one say of someone who, when asked why he broke his promise, replied simply that breaking it was best on the whole? Assuming that his reply is sincere ... one would question whether or not he knew what it means to say 'I promise.'"[11] If a child used this excuse, Rawls continues, we would correct his mistaken understanding of what promising means. But Rawls goes too far. The excuse that breaking the promise would be best on the whole is, if well supported, a legitimate one. Indeed, it is not clear what we would make of someone who agreed that it would be best on the whole to break a promise and yet insisted that it ought nevertheless to be kept.[12]

What lies at the bottom of the complaints of writers like Ross and Rawls is this: utilitarianism seems entirely future oriented. It tells me to do what is best, independently of what I have promised. If it would promote the most good to do what I have promised, then that is what I should do; if not, then I should do something else instead. But this makes promising irrelevant, or so the argument goes. However, this line of attack overlooks the fact that the past structures the utilities of the future alternatives open to me. It is precisely because I have promised, that my acting or not acting in a certain way will have the specific consequences it does. Utilitarians can easily grant that what is best for me to do depends on what I have done in the past.

A final argument stemming from Ross is that utilitarianism cannot do justice to ordinary people's sense that, when one justifiably breaks a promise, one still has a lingering obligation to the promisee. Suppose circumstances force you to break a lunch date with me in order to assist the

---

[11] Rawls, "Two concepts of rules," 17.
[12] Narveson, *Morality and Utility*, 188.

victims of an automobile accident. Critics of utilitarianism claim that the theory does not capture the regret we feel about breaking our promise:

> Commonsense morality implies, rightly I think, that you *owe* me an explanation and an expression of regret that you were sidetracked. A utilitarian cannot *simply* express sincere regret here. Once [my] dissatisfaction was outweighed by the prevention of more serious dissatisfaction for the accident victims, there was either nothing to be regretted or at least the expression of regret is viewed as a completely separate act, whose rightness or wrongness is determined exclusively by a separate calculation of its consequences rather than [as] a backward-looking expression of genuinely felt emotion.[13]

The implicit premise here seems to be that if one does what is right, all things considered, then one owes no apologies and need express no regret. But that premise is false. Because it was right to aid the accident victims, you should not regret, nor need you apologize for, acting as you did. Nevertheless, you can rue the disappointment and inconvenience others suffered because an emergency prevented you from keeping your word. By analogy, parents rightly have their children inoculated against various childhood diseases, however much their children may hate shots. Yet the rightness of what the parents do is no barrier to their feeling and expressing genuine regret over the pain inflicted on their children.

Do you *owe* the other person an explanation and an expression of regret when you break a promise that both utilitarians and non-utilitarians agree you should have broken? Whatever meaning one gives to "owe," it is obvious that you should explain, and the sooner the better, because you want to reduce the other person's unhappiness at having been stood up as well as to prevent any ill will toward you. Your expression of regret is in effect a statement that you took the other person's interests into account in deciding how to act. If you miss an appointment in order to aid the victims of an accident, customary practice may require you to say "I'm sorry," but it equally requires the other person to say, upon learning the facts, "Oh, don't give it a second thought." Once one thinks about how people really act and are expected to act in situations like this, it is hard to see anything at all in the charge that utilitarians look at promises in some alien way or fail to take them seriously enough.

[13] Harwood, "Eleven objections to utilitarianism," 147.

Special Claims and Duties

As we have seen, the critics argue that utilitarianism's consequentialist orientation skews its view of promising and that the theory cannot grasp the significance of promises or do justice to the moral burden they create. This contention connects to the more general criticism that utilitarianism is untrue to the way we ordinarily think about morality and about our moral obligations. As Ross argues, ordinary people see themselves as being under various moral obligations that cannot be reduced to the single requirement to maximize overall happiness. Often these obligations grow out of special relationships into which people enter or out of determinate roles that they undertake. Each of our lives is intertwined with the lives of other people in very specific contexts. As a result, one has certain specific moral obligations – to spouse, children, and in-laws, to colleagues, friends, and business associates, to creditors, benefactors, and collaborators, and to one's employer, profession, and country.

Critics like Ross allege that utilitarianism overlooks the pluralistic character of duty, failing to see the distinctive, individual character of our moral lives, shaped as they are by special obligations to particular individuals. Utilitarianism, writes Ross, "seems to simplify unduly our relations to our fellows. It says, in effect, that the only morally significant relation in which my neighbours stand to me is that of being possible beneficiaries by my action." He continues:

> They do stand in this relation to me, and this relation is morally significant. But they may also stand to me in the relation of promisee to promisor, of creditor to debtor, of wife to husband, of child to parent, of friend to friend, of fellow countryman to fellow countryman, and the like; and each of these relations is the foundation of a *prima facie* duty, which is more or less incumbent on me according to the circumstances of the case.[14]

In other words, Ross and other critics charge that, by requiring us to promote impartially the good of all, the utilitarian formula ignores, in the words of Sidgwick, "the special claims and duties belonging to special relations, by which each man is connected with a few out of the whole number of human beings" (432).

This issue will be examined more closely in Chapter 8. In response to Ross, however, utilitarians can follow Sidgwick in arguing that "generally speaking, services should be rendered to the persons commonly recognised

---

[14] Ross, *The Right and the Good*, 19; see also Kymlicka, *Contemporary Political Philosophy*, 23.

as having such claims rather than to other persons" (439). Sidgwick suggests at least three reasons for this. First, people expect that "commonly recognised ties and claims" (433) will be acknowledged and upheld, and disappointing these expectations will be painful. Second, these ordinary ties and claims generally represent the most effective channels for our beneficence. Not only does Jones know in some detail what is good for her students, colleagues, friends, and family, but also she is generally better placed to advance their good than she is the good of strangers. Third, natural affection underlies many of the ties and claims that Ross emphasizes – for example, our obligations to friends, family members, and those who have been kind to us in the past. Encouraging this natural affection in its "normal channels and courses" (439) promotes happiness. This affection is also a source of pleasure in its own right. Moreover, reinforcing people's concern for the well-being of those around them prepares the ground for a more extensive altruism. It is difficult for people to come to care for strangers without having first learned to attend to the needs of family and friends. In this sense, charity can be said to begin at home.

Contrary to what its critics imply, utilitarianism accepts the whole complexity of human social existence and the full richness of our emotional bonds. Although utilitarianism seeks to promote well-being as much as possible, it does not view human beings simply as potential providers or consumers of welfare, stripped of all social context and without relationships, commitments, and emotional attachments to particular people. For instance, nothing obliges utilitarians to pretend that parents can care about other people's children as much as they do their own, whom they have raised and looked after. Nor, for the reasons Sidgwick suggests (and which Chapters 5 and 8 develop further), does the theory imply, as its critics claim it does, that parents really should strive to care no more for their own children than they do for other children.

The Distribution of Welfare

We have reviewed the charge that utilitarianism licenses immoral conduct and examined the contention that it ignores the particularity of our obligations and the special moral ties that bind us to others. These criticisms dovetail with the frequently heard complaint that utilitarianism is indifferent to the distribution of welfare. Because the theory recognizes only one fundamental imperative – namely that welfare be promoted as much as possible – it does not matter, in itself, how that welfare is allocated. As a result, the critics argue, utilitarianism too easily permits one person's happiness to be sacrificed for the benefit of others. It ignores considerations of justice and fairness or, at best, subordinates them entirely to the principle of utility.

But this is a tendentious way of framing the issue. To be sure, utilitarians believe that only the principle of utility has foundational moral status, but as we shall see in later chapters, utilitarians use their theory to identify and defend more specific ethical principles. Because no such principle has independent moral status, claims of justice, fairness, and desert derive ultimately from utilitarian considerations. But the word "ultimately" is important here. To say that a more fundamental principle shapes the content of a secondary principle is not to debunk that subsidiary principle or dismiss as insignificant the factors or considerations that are its proper province. This point should become clearer as the book proceeds, in particular after the next three chapters have discussed the utilitarian view of rules, rights, and justice.

Equality

In the eyes of most philosophers, the concept of equality is closely linked to that of justice, and some critics fault utilitarianism for giving no independent moral weight to equality. Because utilitarians believe that social well-being should be promoted in whatever manner will maximize it overall, it follows that the precise way in which welfare is distributed among individuals – in particular, whether some individuals end up enjoying greater well-being than others – is, in and of itself, unimportant.[15] From a utilitarian perspective, considerations of overall well-being determine "whether and when and in what way and to what extent people ought to be treated equally."[16] At the end of the day, what matters is how well or ill people's lives go, not how they compare to one another.

It is this apparent subordination of equality to welfare that the critics of utilitarianism find objectionable. For example, they invite us to compare two hypothetical societies. Equality reigns in society E, which consists of five peasants each with two units of happiness, whereas happiness is very unequally distributed in society U. It consists of four agricultural laborers each with one unit of happiness working for a fifth person who enjoys seven units of happiness. Because total happiness is greater in society U, the

---

[15] For some wavering by Bentham on this point, see Dinwiddy, *Bentham*, 26–7.
[16] Goldstick, "Distributive justice and utility," 70.

objection goes, a utilitarian would have to favor it over its more egalitarian rival E. But in favoring U over E, the critics continue, utilitarianism goes astray. Because it is a more equal place, society E is morally preferable to society U, and any satisfactory normative theory should acknowledge this fact.

Utilitarianism does indeed recommend that a society adopt whatever system of production and distribution will maximize social welfare in its particular cultural, historical, and economic circumstances. Chapter 7 returns to this topic, but in the meantime utilitarians can rejoin that the contrast between societies E and U lacks any social detail or historical realism. One wonders, for instance, how society U manages to generate so much well-being for that one lucky person. Moreover, the example, as presented, ignores the fact that the distribution of well-being is distinct from the distribution of wealth, income, property, and other means to well-being. Money and possessions may bring happiness, but they are not proxies for it, or even very reliable indicators of it. Distributing them, which is all that society can distribute, is not the same as distributing happiness. If the example is recast accordingly, then the critics who rebuke utilitarianism for being insufficiently committed to economic equality – call them economic egalitarians – are asking us to imagine a situation in which distributing land and wealth equally (society E') results in less total well-being than distributing it unequally (society U'). This is certainly possible, but at the very least one needs some socially and psychologically plausible story of how and why in the imagined circumstances inequality promotes well-being better than equality does.

One possibility is that the unequal society contains some ill or disabled people and that giving them extra resources to meet their special needs enhances net well-being more than a strict division of goods would. Another possibility is that an unequal distribution of economic goods boosts social well-being overall because it gives people an incentive to work and produce that they would otherwise lack. However, if inequality maximizes well-being for one of these reasons, then (depending on how the precise details are filled in) we may not find it morally troubling. Some critics ask us to imagine that certain people get so much more well-being from any given unit of wealth or income that society can only maximize total well-being by giving them a disproportionately larger share of its resources. In other words, because these "utility monsters" derive so much pleasure from money, the rest of us should tighten our belts to see that they get it. By contrast with the case of the ill or handicapped person, it may strike one as unfair to give extra resources to a few utility monsters. In practice, however, there is no problem. Even if there were utility monsters (a doubtful supposition), we could never reliably know who they were. Moreover, if it were public policy to identify and assist utility monsters, everyone would have an incentive to profess to be one and thus to stake a claim to extra social resources.

Many contemporary philosophers are economic egalitarians and favor a radical redistribution of wealth and income. Although egalitarians disagree among themselves about the exact dimension of equality that is of fundamental importance – is it equality of wealth, equality of resources, equality of opportunity, or equality of something else? – they agree that it has an intrinsic moral importance that utilitarianism neglects. It is true, of course, that utilitarians subordinate economic equality to well-being and do not prize it for its own sake. Nevertheless, in the real world eliminating gross economic disparities would almost certainly boost social well-being, and Chapter 7 argues that there is a strong and convincing utilitarian case for a much more equal distribution of economic goods and services. Moreover, in prosecuting utilitarianism for its allegedly deficient commitment to economic equality, the theory's critics cannot plausibly purport to be siding with the moral sentiments of ordinary people, at least in the United States where growing economic inequalities have generated barely a ripple of popular moral protest.[17]

As I have said, talk about distributing well-being or happiness is somewhat misleading because we cannot parcel it out as we can money and other resources. Still, whether we have in mind government policy or the conduct of an individual person, alternative actions can obviously result in individuals enjoying very dissimilar levels of well-being. Further, different courses of action might produce the same overall sum of welfare and yet yield different amounts of happiness to different people. According to the utilitarian standard, if different actions produce the same amount of happiness, and no alternative could produce more, then those actions are equally right. Does this pose a problem?

Sidgwick and some subsequent utilitarians have thought so. They have urged that ties be broken in favor of equality. In other words, when several courses of action have equally optimal results, we should elect the course that distributes welfare the most equally. Sidgwick himself made the point that a tie-breaking principle is important, not because there will often be ties, but because we are often unable to estimate welfare reliably or predict the outcomes of our actions with much accuracy. In other words, we must often choose between different distributions of happiness, where the amount of happiness in question seems, as far as we can discern, equivalent.

---

[17] See Ryan, "Conservatives, nice and nasty," 27.

"In all such cases, therefore, it becomes practically important to ask whether any mode of distributing a given quantum of happiness is better than any other" (416).

Some friends of utilitarianism see a tie-breaking principle of equality as an independent moral principle – second in priority to the principle of utility, to be sure, but having independent warrant. By contrast, Sidgwick sees a commitment to equality as implicit in Bentham's formula, "everybody to count for one, and nobody for more than one." In his view, the utilitarian commitment to the equal consideration of people's interests and to weighing the happiness of each equally would ground both the principle of utility (as discussed in Chapter 3) and the supplementary principle of equality. A third possibility is that one could modify one's utilitarianism by abandoning welfarism and incorporating considerations of equality into one's concept of good, so that the overall goodness of an outcome is not just a function of the well-being it contains but also a function of how that well-being is distributed.

I think, however, that utilitarians are wrong to modify their theory to accommodate the non-utilitarian belief that equality is important in and of itself – that is, that it has intrinsic, inherent, or underived moral value.[18] Utilitarians strive to treat the interests of each impartially, but what matters for them is how people fare, not whether they are treated the same as others along some favored dimension or other.

Although utilitarians may want to follow supplementary decision-making principles in circumstances where utility estimates are likely to be too vague and uncertain to provide much guidance, those principles must be grounded on the promotion of welfare. In other words, the advice to follow a particular rule or decision-making procedure in certain sorts of situations must rest on an argument that following such a procedure best promotes well-being in the long run. Sometimes, what Sidgwick calls "pure equality" may be the appropriate rule to follow, but there is no reason to think that this will be the best way to proceed in all decision contexts. Moreover, because there are different respects in which we can treat people equally or unequally, the idea of "pure equality" is itself vague. By equality, pure or otherwise, Sidgwick has in mind the equal distribution of happiness – as opposed to the equal distribution of income and wealth (417n) – but equality of happiness is unlikely to be a very useful secondary principle because estimating it is no easier that calculating total happiness.

---

[18] I do not mean to imply that all non-utilitarians hold this belief. For one who doesn't, see Frankfurt, "Equality and respect."

The Slavery Argument

The objection that utilitarianism fails to take equality seriously enough is one variant of the more general criticism that the theory is indifferent to the distribution of welfare. Another variant of this criticism is that utilitarianism permits unfair, unjust, or morally repugnant social arrangements if they maximize well-being. Some critics believe that the underlying problem is that utilitarianism ignores the separateness of persons; we examine that contention in the next section. Here we look at the most popular version of the argument that utilitarianism condones unjust or iniquitous distributions of welfare, namely, the argument from slavery.

That argument goes like this. We are to imagine that social and historical circumstances are such that legal slavery would produce more overall welfare than freedom would, perhaps because the enhanced well-being of the owners more than offsets the decreased well-being of the slaves. This situation may not be probable, but it is at least theoretically possible. Now, if slavery did maximize well-being in a certain context, then utilitarianism would condone or even recommend it. But to recommend slavery, urge the critics, would be outrageous. If we are sure of anything, it is that slavery is unjust and immoral. If utilitarianism is ever prepared to countenance it, then something is terribly wrong with the theory.

The slavery argument against utilitarianism can be seen as a variant of the inequality argument based on the contrast between societies E and U. But that argument was too schematic to pack much of a punch, and not everyone is troubled by the possibility that utilitarianism might favor an unequal distribution of welfare or an unequal distribution of resources if this is necessary to produce greater well-being overall. By contrast, slavery is almost universally condemned today as profoundly unjust. This conviction is so firm a part of our modern moral sensibility that any ethical theory that approved slavery would be, it seems, so utterly out of step with our thinking about right and wrong as to deserve immediate rejection. As a result, many people believe the slavery argument conclusively refutes utilitarianism.

R. M. Hare, however, has decisively rebutted the slavery argument.[19] Because of the importance of the argument, Hare's rejoinder is worth rehearsing. Hare begins by elaborating the slavery argument in a way that is intended to make as plausible as possible the critic's supposition that slavery might, in certain circumstances, maximize well-being. He tells the story of two imaginary Caribbean islands, Juba and Camaica, which

---

[19] See Hare, "What is wrong with slavery."

develop different institutions after declaring themselves independent from European rule in the nineteenth century. In Juba, the government retained the institution of slavery, but brought it under state control and reformed it by improving work conditions, prohibiting cruel punishments, and paying wages. The island became prosperous, and its citizen-slaves the envy of impoverished Camaica, where the government had abolished slavery but was unable to stimulate economic development. While slave Juba flourished, free Camaica stagnated. Hare embroiders this scenario in some detail to give the critics what they want: a case where one might reasonably believe that a slave system produces more overall benefit than a system of free labor would. Utilitarians, it seems, would have to oppose the abolition of slavery in Juba, and yet this pro-slavery stance profoundly affronts our sense of justice, or so the critic of utilitarianism contends.

Hare then launches a two-pronged response to the slavery argument. Either the defenders of utilitarianism are permitted to challenge the imagined facts of Juba and Camaica, or they are not. Assume, first, that they are not allowed to contest the example. Utilitarians must then agree that, as the situation is portrayed, abolishing slavery in Juba would be wrong. Liberty usually promotes happiness, but there can be exceptions, and this is one of them. If ordinary people considered the case on its merits and without confusing it with truly detestable forms of slavery, then they would agree.

Hare then argues that utilitarians have, with respect to the first prong of their two-part response, a further, more sophisticated argument open to them. They can acknowledge that many people will reject the proposition that slavery is permissible in Juba. Opposed to slavery on principle, these people are unwilling even to consider the possibility that in an exceptional case it might be better than freedom. However, utilitarians can applaud this categorical opposition to slavery, maintaining that it is a good thing that people have principles that lead them to repudiate slavery across the board. This is because utilitarians are concerned with the rules and principles that it is desirable for people to have and to act on in the real world, not when dealing with fantastic cases. In the real world, slavery is never as benign as we are imagining it to be in Juba; it is always worse than freedom. In the real world, then, it will always be right to oppose slavery. Thus, utilitarians can consistently affirm both that it would be wrong to do away with slavery in Juba and that it is a good thing that people believe that slavery should be abolished everywhere, even in Juba.

Assume now, to take the second prong of the argument, that utilitarianism's defenders are permitted to challenge the facts of the example. They will certainly question many of the imagined details of Juba, wondering, for example, why slavery is so crucial to its prosperity. Why couldn't a system of free labor achieve comparable affluence? And why must one suppose that the government of Camaica has been so incompetent? Furthermore, utilitarians can make the deeper point that human nature is such that people who are enslaved always, or nearly always, find it to be an intolerable condition. Familiarity with the actual history of slavery in different cultures and times shows this. Among other things, even ordinary, otherwise decent human beings exploit those over whom they have absolute power, and while both animals and slaves can be abused, slaves can be terrorized, in a way no animal can be, by the threat of future punishment. Human psychology and social dynamics being what they are, slavery will never in fact be a happiness-maximizing institution.

The fact that slavery might, in some unreal but logically possible world, maximize happiness is an irrelevant basis of critique. To imagine, as the critics do, slavery without its socially and psychologically necessary consequences is idle. Hare writes that "the wrongness of slavery, like the wrongness of anything else, has to be shown in the world as it actually is" (121), and he argues that it is a strength of utilitarianism that it can illuminate so tellingly what is wrong with slavery. We condemn slavery so strongly precisely because of the misery we know it brings to human beings as they actually are. For this reason, Hare believes that utilitarianism accounts for the immorality of slavery in the real world more aptly and effectively than other moral theories. The wrongness of slavery is a firm and reliable principle, but it is grounded on the bedrock principle of utility along with certain basic features of the human condition. By analogy, punching people with your fists is wrong because of the pain and injury it causes. If we were creatures with an elephant-like exterior, then perhaps punching us would not be wrong. But the wrongness of punching, in the world as it really is, is not diminished by the fact that it depends on certain contingent features of human beings.

Separateness of Persons

Hare, I believe, convincingly rebuts the slavery argument, yet many critics of utilitarianism are still troubled by the fact that, in the eyes of utilitarians, no principle of just distribution has independent moral weight. Because utilitarianism concerns itself with issues of distribution only insofar as they affect net well-being, the critics believe that the theory inevitably leads to unfair results. In the past twenty-five years, many philosophers have been persuaded by John Rawls that the root problem is that utilitarianism ignores "the separateness of persons." So widespread is this contention, that it has become a virtual mantra. What does the phrase mean, and does it really identify some irremediable defect of utilitarianism?

As Rawls sees it, utilitarianism illegitimately extends to society as a whole the sort of decision-making procedure that is appropriate only for an individual. In *A Theory of Justice* he writes:

> Just as an individual balances present and future gains against present and future losses, so a society may balance satisfactions and dissatisfactions between different individuals . . . . The principle of choice for an association of men is interpreted as an extension of the principle of choice for one man. Social justice is the principle of rational prudence applied to an aggregative conception of the welfare of the group. (24)

As a normative theory, utilitarianism is simply the natural result of applying to society the principle of choice that governs rational individuals:

> The most natural way, then, of arriving at utilitarianism . . . is to adopt for society as a whole the principle of rational choice for one man . . . . On this conception of society separate individuals are thought of as so many different lines along which rights and duties are to be assigned and scarce means of satisfaction allocated . . . so as to give the greatest fulfillment of wants. The nature of the decision . . . is not, therefore, materially different from that of an entrepreneur deciding how to maximize his profit . . . or that of a consumer deciding how to maximize his satisfaction by the purchase of this or that collection of goods. (26–7)

Rawls concludes that utilitarianism fails to recognize the separateness of persons:

> This view of social co-operation is the consequence of extending to society the principle of choice for one man, and then, to make this extension work, conflating all persons into one through the imaginative acts of the impartial sympathetic spectator. Utilitarianism does not take seriously the distinction between persons. (27)

It is true, of course, that utilitarianism treats each person's happiness or unhappiness equally, aggregates the well-being of different individuals as best it can, and seeks to enlarge overall welfare as much as possible. Indeed, Rawls's remarks tally with the way that Sidgwick and a number of other utilitarians argue for their theory (as we saw in Chapter 3). In their view,

125

just as it is prudent for individuals to make trade-offs, accepting a cost here to reap a benefit there, so as to maximize their overall satisfaction, so it is right to make trade-offs among people in order to maximize net well-being.

The separateness-of-persons argument can be interpreted either as the metaphysical objection that utilitarianism does not adequately recognize that people are distinct individuals or as the moral objection that it does not treat people as individuals, each with a separate life to live.[20] When Rawls mentions the idea of a sympathetic utilitarian spectator viewing the well-being of all in the same way that a rational and prudential person views the stages of his or her own life, this suggests that he has in mind the metaphysical objection that utilitarianism overlooks the boundaries between people, collapsing them into one social organism. In line with this objection, David Gauthier writes that theories like utilitarianism "suppose that mankind is a super-person, whose greatest satisfaction is the objective of moral action."[21] And Thomas Nagel asserts that any such theory "treats the desires, needs, satisfactions, and dissatisfactions of distinct persons as if they were the desires, etc., of a mass person."[22] Alternatively, however, one can see the sympathetic spectator idea merely as a vivid way of capturing the core utilitarian conviction that the good of each person has an equal claim on us. We are not forced to interpret the utilitarian commitment to impartially promoting well-being as based on the premise that people are merely interchangeable components of a larger organism or as derived from a prior belief that society is best seen as an individual entity choosing rationally how best to pursue its interests.

Even if there is a sense in which utilitarians assimilate social choice to individual choice, it doesn't follow that they fail to appreciate the metaphysical distinctness of persons. Whether they do or not depends, in part, on the nature of personal identity and on exactly how metaphysically distinct persons are. In *Reasons and Persons* Derek Parfit has argued with great subtlety that personal identity is only a matter of certain relations of psychological connectedness (such as memory and the persistence of character and motivation) holding between different temporal stages in an individual's life. Because these relations can be stronger or weaker, the connection between an individual at an early point in time and the

---

[20] Brink, *Moral Realism*, 284.
[21] "But this is absurd," Gauthier continues. "Individuals have wants, not mankind; individuals seek satisfaction, not mankind. A person's satisfaction is not part of any greater satisfaction" (*Practical Reasoning*, 126).
[22] Nagel, *The Possibility of Altruism*, 134; also 138.

individual at a later point in time is less firm than we often think, more like the relation between one person and another person. If so, then utilitarianism becomes more plausible. As Parfit writes:

> If we cease to believe that persons are separately existing entities, and come to believe that the unity of a life involves no more than the various relations between the experiences in this life, it becomes more plausible to be more concerned about the quality of experiences, and less concerned about whose experiences they are. This gives support to the Utilitarian View .... Since persons are not separately existing entities, the impersonality of Utilitarianism is less implausible. (346)

Parfit's discussion raises important, difficult, and controversial issues in the philosophy of mind,[23] but at the very least he demonstrates that further argument is needed if the critic is to establish that utilitarianism commits one to a metaphysically deficient view of people.

More often, the separateness-of-persons argument is pursued as the moral objection that utilitarianism permits us to benefit some by inflicting costs on others. Robert Nozick, for one, repudiates utilitarianism for this reason. Each of us sometimes chooses to undergo some present pain or sacrifice for a greater benefit later. "Why not," he asks, "hold that some persons have to bear some costs that benefit other persons more, for the sake of the overall social good?" Nozick's answer is that

> there is no *social entity* with a good that undergoes some sacrifice for its own good. There are only individual people, different individual people, with their own individual lives. Using one of these people for the benefit of others, uses him and benefits the others. Nothing more .... To use a person in this way does not sufficiently respect and take account of the fact that he is a separate person, that his is the only life he has.[24]

However, contrary to what Nozick implies, Bentham and all subsequent utilitarians have rejected the idea of a social entity with a good above and beyond the various goods of individual persons. If utilitarianism appeals to the greater good to justify imposing costs on some individuals, then this greater good is simply the cumulative good of yet more individuals.

Nozick writes as if an individual's interests should never be made to

---

[23] It also raises a problem for the view of Sidgwick and others that it is irrational for one to prefer a lesser present good to a greater future good.
[24] Nozick, *Anarchy, State, and Utopia*, 32–3.

yield to those of others. However, for no normative theory (aside from egoism) does the fact that people are distinct, that they have separate lives to live, imply that they are free to advance their interests without regard to the cost to other people. Sometimes morality obligates us to subordinate our interests to those of others. We do not, however, normally view the fact that we are forbidden to take the possessions of others or are required to play our part in the defense of the community as wrongfully sacrificing our interests. Moreover, most normative theories follow everyday morality in permitting (and sometimes requiring) trade-offs among people. The rich are taxed to assist the poor; a teacher decides to spend more time with students who are struggling with the material even though this means that other students are bored; if we can rescue either a group of three people or a group of thirty, and cannot save both, then we rescue the larger group. But we do not ordinarily see such trade-offs as ignoring the distinctness of persons.

To be at all plausible, the moral version of the separateness-of-persons complaint must be that utilitarianism licenses unfair or immoral trade-offs. Suppose for instance that sacrificing the basic interests of one person somehow saves each of a large number of other people from some small loss, and that these losses, though individually slight, are cumulatively sufficient to justify the cost imposed on the one person. Critics charge that it would be unfair to sacrifice this person for the benefit of others. Would it? Getting a handle on the hypothesized scenario is difficult because it is so vague, but utilitarians can accept the idea that in principle we would be justified in taking an innocent life in order, say, to prevent a sufficiently large number of headaches.[25] However, they will also insist, as they did in the slavery argument, on three further propositions: (1) in practice, that is, in the real world as opposed to some hypothetical world, utilitarianism does not lead to outcomes that violate ordinary non-utilitarian ideas of justice, (2) the fact that utilitarianism can have disturbing and counter-intuitive implications in some artificially constructed world is no cause for alarm, and (3) utilitarianism can explain why injustices such as slavery or inflicting harm on some isolated individual really are wrong. In response, Rawls, Nozick, and other critics would still contend that there is something suspect about utilitarianism's summing and maximizing procedures. However, if (1), (2), and (3) are plausible, then it is hard to see the argumentative force of the charge that utilitarianism "does not take seriously the distinction between persons."

---

[25] For a vigorous defense of the utilitarian position, see Norcross, "Comparing harms."

Is Utilitarianism Too Demanding?

Its advocates see the moral version of the separateness-of-persons argument as underwriting the charge that, in its indifference to distribution, utilitarianism permits injustice, condoning in the name of the general good things (like slavery) that it ought not tolerate. But the argument also connects to the opposite charge that utilitarianism requires too much of us, with its critics now asserting, not that utilitarianism is too lax, but that it is too demanding, to be an acceptable moral theory.

The utilitarian criterion states that an action is right if and only if its expected outcome is at least as good as anything else the agent could have done; otherwise it is wrong. This sets a high standard, and critics of utilitarianism have frequently balked at it. At many points in our day, when we are innocently relaxing, talking with friends, or simply at work doing our job, we could probably be doing something else instead that would bring more happiness into the world. For example, instead of watching television tonight, we could visit a nursing home to chat and play cards with its elderly residents. Instead of going to the beach with friends, we could work with the homeless. Instead of buying a new car, we could make do with our old one and give the rest of the money to a charitable cause. And so on: our lives are rarely so productive of good that it would be impossible for us to do yet more.

In response, utilitarians make three points, which the next chapter discusses in more detail. The first turns on the distinction between right and wrong, on the one hand, and praise and blame, on the other. A person who gives 20 percent of her income to famine relief fails to live up to the utilitarian standard, if the benefit to others from her giving more would outweigh the increased sacrifice on her part. Yet, from a utilitarian perspective, it is hard to see that the person should be criticized for not doing more when most people are doing far less. In these circumstances, reproaching her may yield little or no good and might even do harm. Rather, utilitarians will probably wish to encourage others to do more by praising the agent and holding her up as a model.

The second point is that although utilitarianism makes the promotion of well-being its standard of right and wrong, it does not entail that a desire to increase the general good must be our constant and only motive. In *Utilitarianism* Mill relies on this point to answer those who criticize the theory on the ground that it demands that people continually seek to boost social utility. They urge that "it is exacting too much to require that people shall always act from the inducement of promoting the general interest of society." To this Mill responds that the critics "mistake the very meaning

129

of a standard of morals and confound the rule of action with the motive of it" (17). Utilitarianism wants people to act in ways that promote well-being, but it does not require that general happiness be their only end.

Nevertheless, it would appear that, whatever our motives are, most of us could be doing more to live up to the utilitarian standard than we do now, by assisting needy strangers. However, both Mill and Sidgwick argue – and this is the third point – that on most occasions we do best to attend to the happiness of the people we know (including ourselves). As Sidgwick puts it in *The Methods of Ethics*, "*practically* each man, even with a view to universal Good, ought chiefly to concern himself with promoting the good of a limited number of human beings, and that generally in proportion to the closeness of their connexion with him" (382). Several considerations support Sidgwick's position. The closer we are to people, the better we know their needs and desires and the better situated we are to promote their happiness. (And, of course, we are in a unique and advantageous position to advance our own happiness.) As a result, we can generally increase well-being more effectively by focusing our efforts on the people around us – not just friends and loved ones, but also colleagues, co-workers, and acquaintances. In addition, ties of love and affection link our interests to family and friends, so that promoting their well-being is likely to be less burdensome to us than would making similar sacrifices for strangers; indeed it may augment our own happiness. If it does, then focusing on the good of those who are dear to us may produce more good than would seeking to benefit strangers. In practice, it may also be a more realistic and thus a more effective way for most people to attempt to maximize well-being, given the fact that human altruism is finite.

These are important points, which Chapters 5 and 8 examine further, but they fall short as a response to the objection that utilitarianism is too demanding. The main reason is that the world has changed since the days of Mill and Sidgwick. Rapid worldwide communication and increased international ties enable many of us now to have an impact on the lives of distant strangers, whose circumstances we could not, in previous decades and centuries, have known of, still less affected. For instance, almost all of us in affluent countries could be doing more than we do now to combat famine, hunger, and poverty in underdeveloped nations, if only by giving money to the appropriate charitable organizations.

It is hard to deny, then, that the world being the way it is, almost all of us should, according to the utilitarian standard, be doing substantially more to aid strangers in distress. But where does the obligation to aid others end? Are we to be enslaved to the general good, as utilitarianism's critics claim, working around the clock to promote happiness? Some

130

utilitarians have embraced the implication that morality requires us to do as much as possible – specifically, that it requires us to sacrifice to the point of marginal utility, that is, to the point at which, if we were to do more, we would make ourselves worse off than the people we were trying to aid. However, as the remainder of this book deepens our understanding of utilitarianism, we shall see that in practice the theory's implications are not so drastic.

Suppose, however, that one grants that utilitarianism implies that morality demands much, much more of us than one might have supposed. It does not follow that one must reject utilitarianism. To be sure, many people believe strongly that their obligations to others are circumscribed well short of what (we are assuming) utilitarianism demands. But intuitions about how much money (or time or energy) morality obliges us to give to assist those in serious distress are an unreliable foundation for normative theorizing because those intuitions reflect social expectations and customary practice in a socioeconomic system the legitimacy of which is itself open to assessment. No doubt, the proposition that they are morally obliged to give thousands of their hard-earned dollars every year to famine relief would strike most middle-class Americans as preposterous. Yet it remains a fact that, in the larger scheme of things, such a sacrifice would pale into insignificance when compared to the benefits to those whose lives are imperiled by famine or disease. The point here is that the perceived irksomeness of living up to the demands of a proffered normative theory does not by itself refute the theory.

It is only fair to note, though, that how one looks at this matter will be influenced by one's meta-ethical views, in particular, by whether one thinks of morality as something that is true or false or as something that we choose. A full discussion of this matter is beyond the scope of this book, but compare for example the views of Derek Parfit and Jonathan Bennett, both of whom are sympathetic to a utilitarian-like approach to ethics. Parfit writes:

> [If] a moral theory is something that we *invent* . . . it is plausible to claim an acceptable theory cannot be unrealistically demanding. But, on several other views about the nature of morality, this claim is not plausible. We may *hope* that the best theory is not unrealistically demanding. But, on these views, this can only be a hope. We cannot assume that this must be true.[26]

From a perspective like Parfit's, if utilitarianism is the correct moral theory, and if it places extreme demands on people, then that is simply a fact about

---

[26] Parfit, *Reasons and Persons*, 29.

morality. Whether we like it or not, it happens that the best justified moral theory calls on us to do more than most of us want to, perhaps more than most of us can.

By contrast, Bennett writes:

> To accept a moral principle, in my non-realist view, is not to recognize a truth but rather to take a stand or adopt a policy – to be or become willing to hold oneself to certain standards of behaviour. For me, then, the proposed morality is too demanding (not to be *plausible*, but) to be *acceptable*: I am unwilling to hold myself to such a standard.[27]

Some utilitarians who are non-realists may be able to accept what Bennett cannot; they may be able to embrace the utilitarian standard while acknowledging that they cannot fully live up to it. This does not discredit Bennett. If his non-realist view of morality is right, then he cannot be criticized for refusing to endorse, after full and careful reflection, a normative standard because it is too demanding for him to accept. However, a possibility to be explored in Chapter 8 is that, whatever utilitarianism, considered abstractly, dictates in principle, in practice the theory must temper its demands on people in light of what they are capable of doing. To demand what is beyond most people is not only unrealistic, it may be counterproductive. In any given situation, what utilitarianism specifically requires is a function of the actual circumstances, and among those circumstances will be the facts of human nature, including our limited capacity for altruistic behavior.

---

[27] Bennett, *The Act Itself*, 162.

5

Refining Utilitarianism

The previous chapter surveyed and attempted to answer several standard objections to utilitarianism. Despite their initial plausibility, few of these criticisms withstand sustained examination. Too often, the critics' arguments rest on their own prior (and unargued for) non-utilitarian moral convictions, or their attacks hinge on contrived examples or presuppose completely unrealistic hypothetical scenarios. Moreover, the critics frequently make overly simplistic, sometimes even absurd, assumptions about how utilitarians would or should apply their theory in practice. Utilitarianism is a relatively simple theory to state, but it is far from simple-minded. Chapter 4 endeavored to show this and to establish that utilitarianism is, when intelligently handled, a surprisingly subtle ethical doctrine.

The present chapter develops this thesis further, highlighting the theory's operational complexities and making explicit the normative resources at its command. After discussing the utilitarian approach to praise and blame, the chapter examines the motivations, dispositions, and character traits that it would maximize utility for people to have, contrasting utilitarianism understood as a criterion of right and utilitarianism as a procedure for making moral decisions. Building on this, the chapter then underscores the importance of secondary rules in guiding our actions and probes the different ways that utilitarians have incorporated rules into their theory. In exploring these issues, we shall push beyond the basic version of utilitarianism, which we have had in view so far, toward a less direct but more nuanced normative theory. If this makes utilitarianism a less simple ethical approach, it also makes it more viable in practice and more credible in theory.

Second-Order Moral Judgments

First-order moral judgments concern the rightness or wrongness of conduct: Frank acted rightly in returning the wallet to its owner; Sally would be wrong to break her date with Leslie. Second-order moral judgments concern the appropriateness of praise and blame, of assigning people credit and discredit for their conduct.[1] Second-order judgments ("Sally is to blame for that") presuppose first-order judgments ("That was the wrong thing for her to have done"), but various other considerations can influence them. Whether Frank is to be praised or Sally criticized depends on more than the rightness or wrongness of what they did. For one thing, virtually all ethical theories allow for the possibility of mitigating or exculpatory excuses so that someone may do wrong but not be blameworthy.

Blame, Criticism, Rebuke

At first glance, one might infer that a utilitarian would always criticize people for not guiding themselves by the principle of utility, blaming them whenever they bring about less happiness than they could have – at least if they are of sound mind and acted intentionally. But this is not so. For utilitarians, the wrongness of an action is one issue; whether to blame or criticize the agent for it (and, if so, how severely) is an entirely separate matter. Utilitarians use their normative standard to determine whether it would be right to criticize someone for failing to maximize expected happiness. In particular, they will blame people only when doing so is likely to have good results, and they will let the consequences determine how much censure to measure out.

People find it unpleasant to have their conduct criticized, and this sort of negative reinforcement can trigger or strengthen their feelings of guilt and remorse. Although hurtful, blame, criticism, and rebuke can have good results by encouraging both the agent and other people to do better in the future. On the other hand, neglecting to reproach misconduct increases the likelihood that the agent (or others) will act in the same unsatisfactory way in the future. However, in some circumstances to blame or criticize someone for acting wrongly would be pointless or counterproductive – for example, if the person did so accidentally, was innocently misinformed, or was suffering from extreme emotional distress. In such circumstances, chastising the person for not living up to the utilitarian standard might do more harm than good.

---

[1] Bennett, *The Act Itself*, 46.

This way of looking at moral criticism tallies with common sense. Indeed, utilitarianism can explain and justify most of our everyday refusals to censure people for acting wrongly: for instance, our reluctance to hold toddlers, the mentally deranged, or people under great duress responsible for their misconduct. True, we sometimes speak of someone's *deserving* to be blamed or rebuked, but this way of speaking may not signal a genuinely non-utilitarian attitude. It does so if it expresses a belief that one's moral desert, and it alone, justifies blame and thus that blaming someone can be morally appropriate even if no good comes from it. Utilitarians, of course, resist this notion. Desert is not a foundational moral concern for them. Rather, talk of desert, if it is to be meaningful, must derive from utility. However, in saying that a person deserves to be blamed, the ordinary speaker may mean only that it is right, appropriate, or good to blame the person. This, of course, is perfectly compatible with a utilitarian approach.[2]

Our everyday views about who is to be blamed, and when, and how much are often subtle, but these details can be skipped here because a utilitarian approach seems to be more or less in tune with them. (One reason for saying "more or less" is that people's everyday views may be incomplete and inconsistent.) Suppose, however, that a critic disagrees, arguing that our pre-theoretical intuitions about the assigning of blame do sometimes significantly diverge from a utilitarian approach. Yet, it is difficult to see how one could stick to the intuition that an agent should be blamed for something after one has been convinced that criticism could do no possible good and might even have bad results.[3] Might there, however, be cases in which it would be useful to blame people for actions or omissions for which commonsense morality does not now criticize them? Perhaps. But if doing so would have good results, then we should reassess ordinary practice. For instance, how people spend their money is often

---

[2] For utilitarians, an agent is blameworthy if and only if blaming the agent is likely to have better results than not blaming the agent. Bernard Williams believes that if people understood this, then utilitarian blame would become ineffective ("Critique of utilitarianism," 23). But this conjecture is implausible. Suppose acquaintances warmly upbraid me for having been rude or thoughtless or dishonest. Knowing that they are utilitarians doesn't make it any easier for me to shrug off their reproaches.

[3] Some writers charge that the utilitarian position confuses two distinct things: judging a person blameworthy and communicating that judgment. However, utilitarians can coherently contrast the two. For instance, a utilitarian can consistently believe that someone is blameworthy (in the sense that some sort of criticism or reproof is appropriate on utilitarian grounds) and yet judge that she should not express that blame herself.

considered a private matter so that wealthy people who selfishly give little or nothing to charity are not criticized severely (or even at all). But maybe it would be right to reproach them for not being more generous.

Utilitarians, then, believe that their approach to blame broadly agrees with people's everyday ideas and that if any gaps do exist between the two, then it is people's ordinary beliefs that should be adjusted. For our purposes, though, the point that matters is that when an agent falls short of the utilitarian standard, it remains an open question for utilitarians – and one to be answered using the utilitarian standard itself – whether the agent should be blamed for this. Indeed, on utilitarian grounds, it can be wrong to blame someone for doing wrong even when none of the commonly recognized moral excuses is applicable. Realizing that it may not be right to criticize someone for violating the utilitarian standard is to take the first step toward a more sophisticated form of utilitarianism.

Suppose, for instance, that an agent acted in a beneficial way, but she could have produced even more (expected) good. Should utilitarians criticize her? Depending on the circumstances, the answer may well be no. Suppose that she acted spontaneously but in a way that was unselfish or showed regard for others, or suppose that she could have produced more good only by violating a generally accepted rule ("do not say hurtful things about others"), the following of which usually produces good results. Or imagine that pursuing the second course of action would have required a disregard for self-interest that is more than we normally (or, perhaps, can reasonably) expect from human beings. In these cases, blame would seem to have little or no point. Indeed, if the agent behaved in a way that usually produces good, we may want to encourage others to follow her example (that is, adhere to the same rule or act from the same motive) when they encounter similar situations.

Thus, utilitarians can consistently judge both that an action is wrong and that it would be wrong for one to criticize it. On the other hand, they can also consistently judge both that an action is right and that it would be right to criticize an agent for doing it. This is easiest to see in cases where the agent did the thing with the best expected outcome, but where her acting in this way was only a fluke. If the agent acted recklessly or if she thoughtlessly disregarded the normal rules or the risk she was imposing on others, criticism may be called for. This is because we do not want the agent to act that way in the future, and we want to discourage others from imitating her.

Praise

For reasons it should now be easy to grasp, praising an agent for an action that fails to live up to the utilitarian standard can sometimes be right. Utilitarians applaud instances of act-types that they want to encourage, and they commend motivations, dispositions, and character traits they want to reinforce. For instance, they extol generosity or the disposition to tell the truth because these traits generally lead to actions that have good results. It is possible, of course, that although a particular disposition – for example, a prudent concern for one's physical health – generally leads to actions that are right, the disposition is sufficiently strong and widespread as to need no further reinforcement. Although utilitarians would judge the disposition good, they might not praise it.

From a utilitarian perspective there are some actions that it is right to praise, but the non-performance of which it would be wrong to criticize. In this way, the theory accommodates conduct that people normally regard as saintly, heroic, or supererogatory – conduct that is, so to speak, above and beyond the call of duty.

Imagine, for example, a respected professional who forsakes a lucrative career and an affluent suburban existence to devote her life to working for, and living among, the homeless and dispossessed of the inner city. At some cost to herself, she works tirelessly and effectively over the years, accomplishing a great deal of good. Utilitarians will praise this person, holding her up to others as an exemplar to be admired and imitated. Judging strictly, however, one might say that this fine woman does only what the principle of utility morally requires of her or of anyone – namely, to maximize expected happiness. Still, she is a kind of moral hero, and utilitarians will single her out for acclaim, because she has done far more good and acted with far less regard for her personal interests than the average person does. Expecting most ordinary people to make similar sacrifices and accomplish as much good in their lives would be unrealistic, and criticizing them for their unheroic lives might produce more harm than good. But implicitly encouraging people to do better by holding this excellent woman up as an ideal would be beneficial.

With regard to praise, then, we can see, just as we did with regard to blame, that utilitarians carefully distinguish between first-order moral judgments and second-order moral judgments and that they frequently rely on the differences between them when elaborating the practical implications of their theory and defending it against critics. As J. J. C. Smart writes, "many fallacious 'refutations' of utilitarianism depend for their plausibility" on overlooking the "distinction between the utility of an action and the utility of praise or blame of it."[4] For one thing, this distinction weakens the objection, discussed in the previous chapter, that the utilitarian moral standard demands too much from us. It also blunts the practical force of the criticism that utilitarianism can require us to act in wicked or despicable ways. For, as we shall see below, if it is useful to encourage people habitually to act in certain ways – for example, to keep their word or to refrain from hurting others – it may well be counter-productive to criticize them for not violating those rules in an effort to capture a marginal increase in utility.

Motives, Dispositions, and Traits of Character

Non-utilitarians characteristically urge that the rightness or wrongness of an action does not depend entirely on its outcome. Some people agree with this because they believe that the motive from which an action is done affects whether it is right or wrong. They may believe, for instance, that any action done from a good motive is right. Or they may believe, more plausibly, that a good motive is a necessary rather than a sufficient condition of rightness so that no action can be right unless done from a good motive.

By contrast, utilitarians strive to keep the rightness or wrongness of an action distinct from the goodness or badness of the actor's motives. Thus, a man who saves a child from a burning building acts rightly whatever his motive – whether it be a sense of duty, a humanitarian impulse, hope for a reward, a longing for public acclaim, or a desire to put the child's parents in his debt. For utilitarians, assessments of people's motives and characters are second-order moral judgments. They depend on first-order judgments about the rightness or wrongness of the things the agent is disposed to do because of the motive or character trait in question. But the reverse is not true. First-order moral judgments are entirely independent of assessments of the goodness or badness of the agent's motive or character.

Historically, humankind took a step forward when, in making moral judgments, people began putting weight on motives.[5] We rightly judge someone who does something with bad consequences but from an honorable motive differently from someone who does the same thing from a wicked motive. Yet, for a utilitarian, the assessment of motives does not

---

[4] Smart, "A system of utilitarian ethics," 53.
[5] Moore, *Ethics*, 77

affect whether the action itself was right or wrong. The idea that someone can act wrongly from the best of motives is perfectly intelligible, as is the less familiar idea that an ill-motivated person might act rightly. Good motives do not make right an action that would otherwise be wrong, and bad motives do not make wrong an action that would otherwise be right. This is a simple point, but one that is often overlooked. For example, many critics of the Gulf war repudiated American policy on the ground that, high-flown rhetoric notwithstanding, the Bush administration was really motivated by a concern for oil (or for regional stability, international credibility, or domestic political advantage). But even if the motive for repelling the Iraqis from Kuwait was ignoble or self-serving, it doesn't follow from this that doing so was wrong.

Although an agent's motives are irrelevant to the rightness or wrongness of her conduct, they are pertinent, as we have seen, to whether, and to what degree, the agent deserves praise or blame. For utilitarians the main factor influencing the rightness or appropriateness of blame is whether blaming the agent will do good by deterring her (or others) from doing similar actions in the future. Suppose an agent acted wrongly only from a good motive; that is, she acted on the basis of considerations that utilitarians want people to be swayed by. If so, blaming her will produce little or no good. Thus, there is in general a strong utilitarian case for blaming people less (or not at all) when they do wrong from a good motive.

From a utilitarian point of view, good motives are those that tend to produce right conduct whereas bad motives are those that promote wrong-ful conduct. Utilitarians assess dispositions, behavioral patterns, and character traits in the same instrumental way. They determine which are good, and how good they are, by looking at the actions they lead to. G. E. Moore, however, deviated from this approach in an interesting way even though he had a consequentialist orientation to ethics and agreed that motives are irrelevant to judgments of right and wrong. For Moore believed that certain motives, dispositions, and character traits are intrinsically – not just instrumentally – good or bad and that their presence or absence makes a difference to the overall value of a state of affairs.

In Moore's view, if Geraldo acts from an intrinsically good motive, this fact does not affect the rightness or wrongness of what he does, but the overall state of affairs is better than it would have been had he acted from some other motive. Moore's position is intriguing, but utilitarians will be wary of it. The idea that certain motives are good in and of themselves, and not because of their typical effects, fits ill with most theories of human well-being. Furthermore, Moore's position encounters a problem that throws its consistency into question. If one grants that certain motives have

139

inherent value or disvalue, it is hard to see how one could avoid letting this fact influence the normative assessments of actions, so that the right thing for Geraldo to do is not simply to act in a certain way but to act that way from an intrinsically good motive.[6]

A passage in one of John Stuart Mill's early writings harmonizes with Moore's position. After asserting that all actions presuppose "certain dispositions, and habits of mind and heart," he stated that these dispositions and habits "may be in themselves states of enjoyment or of wretchedness."[7] This remark might be read as suggesting that certain motives or dispositions are direct components of well-being and thus have intrinsic value. Mill did not clarify exactly what he meant, and he seems not to have pursued the idea further.

This passage apart, Mill looked at motive and character in an unquestionably instrumental manner. However, they do, in his view, appertain to the rightness or wrongness of actions in one significant way. This is because a person's actions can affect his or her own character and future motivations. In particular, performing an action tends to "fix and perpetuate the state or character of mind in which itself has originated." Thus, utilitarians need to consider not just the consequences that actions have on the "outward interests of the parties concerned (including the agent himself)" but also their "consequences to the characters of the same persons." "It often happens," Mill wrote, "that an essential part of the morality or immorality of an action or a rule of action consists in its influence upon the agent's own mind," making it either more or less likely that she will act in a certain way in the future. "Many actions, moreover, produce effects upon the character of other persons besides the agent." Although Mill did not believe that an action can be wrong just because it is done from an objectionable motive or disposition, it may be wrong because it reinforces "habits of mind and heart," both in the agent and others that will have negative consequences in the future. Mill criticized Bentham for allegedly overlooking this point and for failing to appreciate that an act "though not in itself necessarily pernicious, may . . . form part of a *character* essentially pernicious, or at least essentially deficient in some quality eminently conducive to the 'greatest happiness.'"[8]

---

[6] Shaw, *Moore on Right and Wrong*, 91–2.
[7] Mill, "Remarks on Bentham's philosophy," 7.
[8] Quotations in this paragraph are from Mill, "Remarks on Bentham's philosophy," 7, 8, and "Sedgwick's discourse," 56.

What Motives and Dispositions Should People Have?

Putting Moore aside, the mainstream utilitarian position is clear. Motives as well as character traits and other dispositions are good if, and to the extent that, they lead to actions that have good results. It might seem that the only motive that utilitarians should value is universal benevolence, but (as mentioned in the previous chapter) utilitarians have long insisted that their theory does not imply that one's only motive must be to maximize happiness in general. Thus, Mill writes in *Utilitarianism* that "it is the business of ethics to tell us what are our duties, or by what test we may know them; but no system of ethics requires that the sole motive of all we do shall be a feeling of duty" (17). Sidgwick echoes this important thought:

> The doctrine that Universal Happiness is the ultimate *standard* must not be understood to imply that Universal Benevolence is the only right or always best *motive* of action. For . . . it is not necessary that the end which gives the criterion of rightness should always be the end at which we consciously aim. (413)

Mill and Sidgwick argue that motives other than pure universal philanthropy are frequently more conducive to general happiness. "If experience shows," Sidgwick continues, "that the general happiness will be more satisfactorily attained if men frequently act from other motives than pure universal philanthropy, it is obvious that these other motives are reasonably to be preferred on Utilitarian principles" (413). The phrase "if experience shows" highlights the fact that this is a contingent, empirical claim, not an a priori ethical axiom. Although such things as a passion for truth or fairness, love for others, or some personal ideal to which one is committed may lead a person to act without regard for general happiness, such motivations can nevertheless be justified from a utilitarian perspective. This is so if, because of these motivations, there is more happiness in the world than there would otherwise have been.

In addition to the pointing out that it will often produce better results to have people motivated by goals other than general happiness, both writers emphasized that in general one does best to focus on the welfare of that limited number of human beings to whom one is closely connected. One reason is that one is rarely in a position to promote happiness on a wide scale. As Mill explains:

> The great majority of good actions are intended not for the benefit of the world, but for that of individuals, of which the good of the world is made up;

141

and the thoughts of the most virtuous man need not on these occasions travel beyond the particular persons concerned . . . . The occasions on which any person (except one in a thousand) has it in his power to [promote happiness] on an extended scale – in other words, to be a public benefactor – are but exceptional; and on these occasions alone is he called on to consider public utility; in every other case, private utility, the interest or happiness of some few persons, is all he has to attend to. (18-19)

In other words, people generally produce more happiness when they are motivated by and focus on the welfare of those relatively few people with whom their lives are intertwined and whose good they can directly affect, rather than on happiness in general.

Three decades before Mill's *Utilitarianism*, the utilitarian philosopher and legal theorist John Austin struck essentially the same note in a lighter key:

Though [the utilitarian] approves of love because it accords with his principle, he is far from maintaining that the general good ought to be the motive of the lover. It was never contended or conceited by a sound, orthodox utilitarian, that the lover should kiss his mistress with an eye to a common weal.[9]

Because the common weal or general good is only the sum of the welfare of various individuals, often the most effective way for an agent to maximize general happiness is by increasing the happiness of the particular individuals around him. Nor should we forget that the agent's own happiness is also part of the general good – indeed, it will usually be the part that he has the greatest power to affect, one way or another. As Mill writes, "the good of all can only be pursued with any success by each person's taking as his particular department the good of the only individual whose requirements he can thoroughly know," namely himself.[10]

Accordingly, kissing his beloved may be the greatest contribution to the happiness of all that the lover can make at that moment. However, if the lover's only desire were for the general good, then he would be less likely to kiss her in the first place, and if he were to kiss her only out of a desire to promote happiness generally, such a kiss would be unlikely to create as much pleasure for either of them, as it would if it were a spontaneous display of emotion. Over the long run, the lover's caring about, and having

---

[9] Austin, *Province of Jurisprudence Determined*, 97.
[10] Mill, *Later Letters*, 762.

an attachment and commitment to, a particular person is the source of much happiness for both of them – happiness that would go unrealized if his only commitment were to the general good or if his only motive were a generalized benevolence for all humankind.

A sophisticated utilitarian understands that people are likely to create more happiness in the world if, in addition to a commitment to the general good, they have other, more particular motivations, commitments, and dispositions. However, this position implies that a person who has a character or motivational structure that utilitarians would applaud will sometimes miss opportunities to maximize happiness.[11] The person is, let us suppose, kind to loved ones, generous with friends, and helpful and supportive to colleagues. Being the kind of person he is, he acts in these characteristic ways without calculating closely (or at all) the consequences of acting as he is inclined to act – for example, volunteering without a moment's thought to aid his daughter with her homework or to work late in the evening helping a friend finish a project. His spontaneous generosity towards those he cares about sometimes prevents him from thinking whether his time or money might be better spent in some other way, as will sometimes be the case.

We can even imagine that on a particular occasion this admirable person realizes that his devotion to his loved ones or his concern for his friends and colleagues is leading him to act in a way that does not maximize happiness. Yet, although he is aware that, in the larger scheme of things, he could probably be doing something better with his time, for example, using his business skills to help Oxfam fight hunger, he continues helping his daughter with her homework (or working late with a colleague) because he is truly devoted to her (or genuinely concerned for the colleague). Although his particular attachments sometimes outweigh his concern for general welfare, he may nevertheless be the kind of person utilitarians would want him to be.

Does the fact that this person acts from motives or as a result of a character that utilitarians would want him to have imply that he is acting rightly in choosing to help his daughter even though (we are supposing) he could do yet more good by using this time to raise money for Oxfam instead? Some writers suggest that this is so. But unless utilitarians modify their theory, they must acknowledge that, in failing to maximize happiness, this fine person acts wrongly.[12] Yet if the person acts from a good character, and especially if he acts from a character that it would be difficult

---

[11] Railton, "The demands of morality," 158.
[12] Johnson, *Moral Legislation*, 94–5.

to improve upon, then utilitarians will find it counterproductive to criticize him. Indeed, they will probably wish to hold him up as an exemplar, for he does more good than most people do.

Criterion of Right versus Decision Procedure

Utilitarianism states that an action is right if and only if it produces at least as much (expected) happiness as anything else the agent could have done in the circumstances; otherwise it is wrong. As we have interpreted the theory heretofore, it instructs us to assess carefully whatever decision situation we are in and then act so as to maximize well-being overall. In other words, we are always to act using the utilitarian standard as our guide. Faced with any decision, we are to examine carefully the various possible outcomes of each of the actions we might perform. Then, weighing the happiness of each possible outcome and taking into account its likelihood, we are to choose that course of action, whatever it is, that maximizes expected happiness. So understood, utilitarianism provides the standard of rightness – the criterion or test for determining whether an action is right or wrong – and says also that this standard is to be the direct basis of moral decision-making.

It is natural to assume that utilitarianism "is meant to give a method of deciding what to do,"[13] and thus that if one adopts the utilitarian standard as one's criterion of right and wrong, then one thereby accepts it as the appropriate basis for making moral decisions, that is, as one's direct and immediate guide to action. However, as Mill, Austin, and Sidgwick argue, things are not so simple.

For one thing, a utilitarian should not try to compute the probabilities of all possible outcomes before each and every action. Even if this were humanly possible, it would be absurd and counterproductive. At least in trivial matters and routine situations, stopping and calculating will generally lead to poor results. One does better to act from habit or do what has proved right in similar situations in the past or what seems intuitively or at a glance to be the best course of conduct. Thus, utilitarianism implies that one should not always reason as a utilitarian or, at least, that one should not always reason in a fully and directly utilitarian way. Indeed, as we have seen, better results may come from people acting in accord with other principles, procedures, or motives than the basic utilitarian one.

This last statement may sound paradoxical, but the utilitarian standard itself determines in what circumstances we should employ that standard as

---

[13] Smart, "A system of utilitarian ethics," 44.

our direct guide to acting.[14] The proper criterion for assessing actions is one matter; in what ways one should deliberate, reason, or otherwise decide what to do (so as to meet that criterion as best one can) is another issue altogether. Utilitarians will naturally want to guide their lives, make decisions, and base their actions on principles, procedures, and motives, the following of which will produce the best results over the long run.[15] These principles, procedures, or motives may or may not involve one's directly applying the utilitarian standard by carefully calculating and comparing the expected outcomes of all possible actions one might perform. Appreciating the difference between accepting the utilitarian standard as the criterion of right and using it as a direct guide to action or as a basis for making decisions takes us another step toward a more sophisticated utilitarianism. It also brings us to the importance of secondary moral rules in pursuing the utilitarian goal.

The Importance of Secondary Rules

As we saw in Chapter 1, John Stuart Mill held that any fundamental principle of morality requires secondary principles for its successful application, and he praised Bentham for being "the first who . . . deduced a set of subordinate generalities from utility alone, and by these consistently tested all particular questions." From a utilitarian perspective, it is not enough simply to state that happiness is the ultimate goal; people need "secondary or middle principles" to steer by.[16] There are at least four reasons for this.

First, secondary rules help resolve the no-time-to-calculate problem. Having been around for a long time, human beings have extensive, collective experience of how various types of actions affect well-being. On this basis certain rules and precepts can be laid down, and people can be "advised to take one direction rather than another."[17] One does not need to calculate afresh, every day and in each situation one faces, whether breaking

---

[14] In *Principles of Morals and Legislation*, Bentham remarks, " 'The principle of utility, (I have heard it said) is a dangerous principle: it is dangerous on certain occasions to consult it.' This is as much as to say, what? that it is not consonant to utility, to consult utility: in short, that it is *not* consulting it, to consult it" (5n).

[15] "If our conduct were truly adjusted to the principle of general utility, our conduct would seldom be determined by an immediate or direct resort to it" (Austin, *Province of Jurisprudence Determined*, 57).

[16] Mill, "Whewell on moral philosophy," 173.

[17] Mill, *Utilitarianism*, 24.

one's word, taking another's property, or punching someone in the nose will tend to cause happiness or unhappiness. We already know these things. Because in most situations we can safely act on well-established precepts, we do not need to stop and do a full utilitarian reckoning before each and every action.

Second, for similar reasons secondary rules help utilitarians to deal with the future-consequences-are-hard-to-foresee problem. Whatever action we choose to perform, it will be impossible to foresee its full and exact causal ramifications. We will almost always be ignorant of some of the immediate and intermediate consequences of the choices we make. Moreover, those choices have causal effects that continue indefinitely into the future and are exceptionally hard to discern because crisscrossed by other events. Given these uncertainties, it is possible that doing something truly dreadful, like running over the pedestrian who calmly walks in front of my car while I am stopped at a red light, might somehow have good results. (Perhaps she will soon die anyway in a yet more terrible way. Perhaps if she lives, she will have evil children who cause the world great harm.) But past human experience teaches that running over the pedestrian is exceedingly unlikely to maximize long-term happiness. This is a precept or "intermediate generalization" on which I can safely rely. I don't need to study the situation further or speculate about remote and unlikely possibilities.

Third, reliance on secondary rules can counteract the fact that even conscientious moral agents can err in estimating the likelihood of a particular result and thus the expected happiness or unhappiness of an action. In particular, when our interests are engaged or when something we care about is at stake, bias can unconsciously skew our deliberations, leading us, say, to overestimate the good to us, and underestimate the harm to others, from telling a lie, ignoring a prior commitment, or declining to help another person. Freeing ourselves from partiality and achieving a truly objective perspective are hard. Even if we are sincerely trying to do the right thing, rationalization and wishful thinking can sometimes distort our judgment. For this reason, a utilitarian is less likely to go wrong and more likely to promote happiness by cleaving to well-established secondary rules.

Finally, when the secondary rules are well known and generally followed, then people know what others are going to do in certain routine or easily recognizable situations, and they can rely on this knowledge. This improves social coordination and makes society more stable and secure. For example, the overall results are better when people can assume that others generally tell the truth and keep their promises. They can reasonably assume this, of course, only if people make it a general practice, and are

146

known to make it a general practice, to tell the truth and keep their promises. However, if it were known to be the case that moral agents told the truth or kept their promises only if they calculated that doing so would, in the circumstances, maximize happiness, then people could not safely assume that on any given occasion others will tell the truth or keep their promises. The less predictable the conduct of others becomes, the harder it is to navigate through life.

An analogy with traffic laws and regulations illuminates these points. Society's goal, let's assume, is that the overall flow of automobile traffic should maximize happiness by getting everyone to his or her destination as safely and promptly as possible. Now imagine a traffic system with just one law or rule: drive your car so as maximize happiness. It's easy to see that such a one-rule traffic system would be far from ideal. We do much better in terms of total human well-being to have a variety of traffic regulations telling us, for example, to drive on the right side of the road, to stop for pedestrians, and to obey traffic signals. Without secondary rules, drivers would be left to do whatever they thought best in any given situation – for instance, whether to slow down, stop, or cruise straight through an intersection – depending on their interpretation of the traffic situation and the probable results of alternative actions. Drivers would often find it difficult to calculate the best thing to do, and their own goals and personality quirks could easily warp their decisions. Moreover, they could never be confident what other drivers would do. We clearly get much better results from a system in which people follow a variety of secondary traffic rules, and can be relied on to do so, than from a system in which people are free to drive in whatever way they think will maximize happiness.

Some philosophers seem to think that if people were smart enough and well informed enough, and if time and effort were no consideration, then secondary rules would be unnecessary: they could just use the utilitarian principle to determine, on each and every occasion, what act would be optimal. But this is a delusion, as Brian Barry explains:

> The optimal course of action for me depends upon what I expect others to do, while the optimal course of action for others depends upon what they expect me to do . . . . Expectations can be coordinated only by a system of rules (such as that enjoining promise-keeping) which are adhered to without regard to consequences. Only within a matrix of stable expectation created in this way does it make sense for people to make judgements about the likely consequences of acting in one way or another.[18]

[18] Barry, *Justice as Impartiality*, 220.

For the reasons we have canvassed, then, people should not try to apply the utilitarian standard directly to every situation they encounter. Utilitarians of all stripes agree about this. They all believe that in pursuit of the utilitarian goal one should, at least sometimes, rely and encourage others to rely on secondary rules, precepts, and guidelines. However, they disagree over the precise status of those rules and precepts, their relation to commonsense morality, and how firmly and under what circumstances one ought to adhere to them.

Secondary Rules as Rules of Thumb

Some utilitarians think of secondary rules merely as rough empirical generalizations, practical guidelines or, as J. J. C. Smart puts it, "rules of thumb." He writes that as utilitarians,

> we may choose to habituate ourselves to behave in accordance with certain rules, such as to keep promises, in the belief that behaving in accordance with these rules is generally optimific, and in the knowledge that we most often just do not have time to work out individual pros and cons . . . . The act-utilitarian will, however, regard these rules as mere rules of thumb, and will use them only as rough guides.[19]

Smart believes that as a practical matter utilitarians are well advised generally to guide themselves by rules of thumb. This is especially true when there is little time to think, when there is time to think but no reason to suppose that fuller utilitarian computation will lead to a different answer, and when the utilitarian suspects that personal bias might distort his or her calculation of consequences. By schooling themselves to adhere to certain useful rules of thumb, utilitarians can save time and mental energy and reduce the possibility of error. Thus, for example, they should habituate themselves routinely to tell the truth and keep promises and to act without hesitation to save people in distress. In this way they will accomplish more good, and do the right thing more often, than if they always stopped and tried to calculate the consequences before acting.

Guiding ourselves by empirically grounded rules of thumb tallies with common sense. We all know that certain kinds of conduct, however enticing they might appear, tend to decrease happiness in the long run. For instance, rude, cruel, dishonest, or deceptive conduct is, other things being equal, less conducive to happiness than behavior that is considerate, kind, honest, and straightforward. Knowledge that an action of a certain type

---

[19] Smart, "A system of utilitarian ethics," 42.

148

typically leads to unhappiness rather than happiness provides the agent with presumptive grounds for not acting that way. In addition to general knowledge, the agent may also know things about himself – for example, that he tends, if not careful, to be curt on the telephone or too generous when grading the work of attractive students – and, as a result of this knowledge, attempt to adopt better habits or follow certain countervailing policies.

Adherence to certain secondary rules of thumb can produce happiness-maximizing results. Summarizing past experience, these rules are entirely pragmatic guidelines. They tell us what conduct has been found (by ourselves and others) to produce good results in the past. In themselves, however, rules of thumb have no normative weight and can and should be put aside whenever one reasonably believes that doing so would have better results. One can make mistakes, of course, for there are no firm rules about when one should make an exception and depart from the usual guidelines. But this possibility is not deeply troubling, a utilitarian like Smart can argue, either in theory or practice. Just as experience suggests the reasonableness of following certain policies, so it can suggest their limits. If we err by deviating from a rule, we can learn from our mistake to be less quick to put the rule aside in the future.

Secondary Rules as Moral Rules

Mill, Sidgwick, and many subsequent utilitarians differ from Smart in their view of secondary rules. They see these rules, not as mere rules of thumb or practical aids to decision making, but as moral rules, and the question that interests them is what moral rules a utilitarian would support or seek to establish for his or her society.

We have seen the reasons why utilitarians need secondary rules, but why should these be moral rules rather than rules of thumb? Why should utilitarians seek to promote any moral rules other than the principle of utility itself? The answer to these questions turns on the way that moral rules differ from rules of thumb. As part of the specific "machinery of rules, habits, and sentiments" that constitutes morality,[20] moral rules or principles have a motivational force that rules of thumb or merely pragmatic guides to conduct lack. Normally, a person feels no compunction about deviating from a rule of thumb, when he judges doing so to be for the best, nor any regret or guilt afterwards. But a person who has internalized a rule

---

[20] Sidgwick, *Methods of Ethics*, 475.

as part of his or her personal moral code does not look at the rule so instrumentally – it is not something that the person can simply pick up or put down as the occasion demands.

When a rule or principle is part of a person's moral code, that person will be strongly motivated toward the conduct required by the rule and against behavior that conflicts with it.[21] The person will tend to feel guilt when his or her own conduct fails to live up to that rule and to disapprove of those who act contrary to the rule. The person will also believe that the conduct in question is important and that his or her attitudes toward it are justified. If a society recognizes and generally observes a moral rule, then something like this set of dispositions in its favor will be widespread. The more strongly and widely embedded the relevant dispositions, the more consistently people will act in the desired ways. Shared moral rules also serve, in a way that rules of thumb cannot, as a basis for punishment and praise, which further reinforce the favored behavior. Further, a general commitment to shared rules, and public knowledge of this, enhances mutual trust and security.[22]

Because people are much more strongly motivated to adhere to moral rules than to rules of thumb, many utilitarians have held that the full benefits of having secondary rules can only be reaped when those rules are treated as moral rules. Having people strongly inclined to act in certain rule-designated ways, to feel guilty about failing to do so, and to use that standard to assess the conduct of others can have enormous social utility. Recognizing that they are human and thus limited in their abilities, even a society of utilitarians would find it advantageous to inculcate in themselves a firm commitment to certain secondary moral rules. This is because it produces good results to have people strongly disposed to act in certain predictable ways, ways that generally (but perhaps not always) maximize happiness. "Any other plan," Mill wrote, "would not only leave everybody uncertain what to expect, but would involve perpetual quarrelling: and hence general rules must be laid down for people's conduct to one another, or in other words, rights and obligations must . . . be recognised."[23] In addition, it is easier to monitor a person's compliance with rules and norms than to determine whether she performed that act, of those open to her, with the greatest expected utility.[24]

---

[21] See Brandt, *Theory of the Good and the Right*, 165–70, and *Facts, Values, and Morality*, 66–8.

[22] Johnson, *Moral Legislation*, 26.

[23] Mill, *Later Letters*, 762.

[24] Barry, *Justice as Impartiality*, 221.

The Rules of Ordinary Morality

Although almost everyone has some utilitarian sentiments, few people in our society look at morality in a fully utilitarian way. Rather, most people accept as at least part of their personal moral code certain non-utilitarian moral injunctions. We have seen that utilitarians emphasize the importance of secondary moral rules, but what stance should they take toward the moral rules that people already embrace? In particular, does commonsense morality supply adequate secondary rules for utilitarians to follow?

Let's begin with Smart's way of looking at these questions. The rules of thumb that he recommends we follow include some of the ordinary rules of everyday non-utilitarian morality. This is because many of these rules – tell the truth, respect the property of others, keep your promises – are reasonably reliable guides to happiness-maximizing behavior, even if ordinary people do not necessarily think about them in this light. In line with this, Mill wrote in *Utilitarianism* that "mankind must by this time have acquired positive beliefs as to the effects of some actions on their happiness; and the beliefs which have thus come down are the rules of morality for the multitude" (23). Similarly, Sidgwick affirmed that "the current morality expresses, partly consciously but to a larger extent unconsciously, the results of human experience as to the effects of actions" (463).

Of course, the customary moral practices and established ethical rules of one's society are likely to fall short of what a utilitarian like Smart would want. His attitude toward the moral code of the society around him will therefore be somewhat detached, critical, and reformist. Even Sidgwick, who stressed the implicitly utilitarian character of much of ordinary morality, was quite clear that it does not express a "*consensus* of competent judges, up to the present time, as to the kind of conduct which is likely to produce the greatest amount of happiness on the whole" (467). Nevertheless, general adherence to at least some of the core rules of ordinary morality is probably the best course for a utilitarian like Smart to follow.

This is for two reasons. First, these rules often do identify, at least in a rough and ready way, conduct that tends to produce happiness. Utilitarians will certainly support the ordinary moral rules to the extent that they channel people's behavior in happiness-maximizing directions. Second, the fact that people accept a certain moral rule, follow it themselves, and expect others to do so increases the utility of one's adhering to the rule. The accepted rules of morality structure the social world and shape people's expectations about the conduct of others. Even if the rules are less than ideal, breaching them disrupts that world, upsetting expectations and

151

causing frustration and unhappiness. It also invites censure and disapprobation, which are negative consequences in themselves. For these reasons,
some positive utility almost always comes from adhering to customary
moral practice and the accepted moral rules.

Yet, even if a utilitarian like Smart makes it a general practice to follow
the ordinary rules of morality, he won't always do so. They are for him, at
most, only useful precepts or convenient rules of thumb. Therefore,
whenever he deems it appropriate, he will take a directly utilitarian
approach and encourage others to do so as well. This task is made somewhat
easier by the fact that the principle of utility is already one of the principles
of ordinary morality and because appeals to utility are already considered
legitimate grounds for settling potential conflicts among the different rules
and precepts of ordinary morality. Although a utilitarian like Smart will
willingly debate moral issues with his neighbors, their rules are not rules he
truly accepts – at least not in the way his non-utilitarian neighbors accept
them.

In this respect, his attitude toward their moral opinions will sometimes
resemble that of an anthropologist living in a strange and exotic society.
Some of the rules that the foreign society follows may seem sensible to her,
and she can see the negative consequences of violating them. She may even
discuss those rules with her hosts. Nevertheless, they are not rules she
accepts for herself but, rather, are part of an alien social reality she is trying
to understand and negotiate. Although she prudently adjusts her conduct
in light of the group's beliefs and practices and although she may even
justify her actions to them by appealing to their own rules, she views those
rules from an external perspective. She does not internalize them; she does
not embrace them as a genuine "basis for claims, demands, admissions,
criticism, or punishment."[25]

Sidgwick's Moral Elitism

Smart's view can be usefully contrasted with that of Sidgwick. Like Mill
before him, Sidgwick recognized the importance of utilitarians not just
heeding certain rules of thumb, but also upholding and following secondary moral rules. Sidgwick approached the rules of ordinary morality with
respect, arguing that a utilitarian "cannot possibly construct a morality *de
novo* either for man as he is . . . or for man as he ought to be and will be"
(473–4). Rather, utilitarians must "start . . . with the existing social order,
and the existing morality as part of that order" and work gradually and

[25] Hart, *Concept of Law*, 88.

incrementally to improve it. This is a sensible message. Sidgwick also made the reasonable but frequently overlooked point that the task for utilitarians is often less one of correcting and improving existing morality than of strengthening and re-enforcing its existing provisions. However, Sidgwick sometimes appears to fall into a kind of worshipful awe toward the established rules of morality, which has strengthened the image of him as a conservative defender of Victorian morality. Thus, he writes that a utilitarian

> will naturally contemplate [established morality] with reverence and wonder, as a marvellous product of nature, the result of long centuries of growth, showing in many parts the same fine adaptation of means to complex exigencies as the most elaborate structures of physical organisms exhibit: he will handle it with respectful delicacy. (475–6)

Sidgwick respected established morality and saw its provisions as providing moral rules that, with few exceptions, utilitarians should support and follow. Even if these rules are less than optimal, by and large they tend to promote happiness, and general conformity to them is extremely beneficial. Sidgwick was ever alert to the dangers of undermining established rules or weakening people's allegiance to them. Nevertheless, he thought that from a utilitarian perspective "a slight admixture of irregularity along with a general observance of received rules" will produce even better results than will universal adherence to them (487). Although deviating from established and generally useful moral rules is risky, utilitarians are sometimes justified in doing so.

Influenced by Kant, Sidgwick held that when a utilitarian does conscientiously violate an established moral rule, he is simply acting on a more complex and delicate rule. This is because if an exception is justified in the present case, then it will be justified in any similar case. When, in order to maximize happiness, a utilitarian makes a justified exception to the simple, generally useful, and socially accepted rule "Never do X," the utilitarian is simply following the more refined rule "Never do X, unless in situation S." Although the utilitarian rightly follows the new rule, it may nevertheless sometimes be better, Sidgwick thought, for him to continue to uphold and teach the simpler rule instead of the revised moral rule. Advocating the revised rule could do more harm than good if it is too subtle or too complicated for people of average intelligence and self-control to follow successfully. Although rare, there will thus be cases when a utilitarian rightly violates an established moral rule, does so on the basis of a superior moral rule, and yet believes that it is the former rule, not the superior rule, that should be generally observed.

In Sidgwick's view, then, there can and sometimes will be different, but fully justified moral codes in the same society. Although the same conduct cannot be both right and wrong in the same circumstance,

> two contradictory opinions as to the rightness of conduct may possibly both be expedient; it may conduce most to the general happiness that A should do a certain act, and at the same time B, C, D should blame it. (491)

Sidgwick pursued this line of thought in a couple of passages that have struck subsequent readers as remarkably elitist:

> Thus, on Utilitarian principles, it may be right to do and privately recommend, under certain circumstances, what it would not be right to advocate openly; it may be right to teach openly to one set of persons what it would be wrong to teach to others; it may be conceivably right to do, if it can be done with comparative secrecy, what it would be wrong to do in the face of the world; and even ... what it would be wrong to recommend by private advice or example. (489)

Although Sidgwick granted that these conclusions seem paradoxical and that common morality repudiates them, he held them to be theoretically sound. There are, however, utilitarian grounds for maintaining the common moral conviction that it cannot be right to do in secret that which it would be wrong to do openly. Thus, Sidgwick continues,

> a Utilitarian may reasonably desire, on Utilitarian principles, that some of his conclusions should be rejected by mankind generally; or even that the vulgar should keep aloof from his system as a whole, in so far as the inevitable indefiniteness and complexity of its calculations render it likely to lead to bad results in their hands. (490)

Those who live in societies that are more democratic, better educated, and less class stratified than was Victorian England will probably find Sidgwick's position elitist and offensive. An air of unreality pervades its abstract logic, which is insensitive to some key aspects of human psychology. Experience suggests that if people publicly champion a moral code that they themselves do not follow, they open the door to rationalization, self-serving exceptions, and other moral abuses. The possibility that utilitarianism requires this is too remote to take seriously. Moreover, as subsequent theorists of various persuasions have emphasized, public moral dialogue – involving the analysis, justification, and refinement of our moral principles – is itself an important good for society. Utilitarians will want, not to try to manipulate that on-going debate, but rather to contribute to it in an open and positive way.

Moore on Accepted Moral Rules

G. E. Moore was less taken with the glories of ordinary morality than Sidgwick, whose student he had been. Although Moore is widely thought to have upheld all of established morality, in fact he argued only that utilitarian analysis could vindicate some of its rules. He identified as crucially important certain core moral rules – for example, those against theft and murder – which are widely, perhaps universally, recognized and which are usually backed up by criminal sanctions. The general observance of these rules would be useful in any society, Moore thought. They are needed to preserve social stability – sometimes, indeed, needed for any sort of civilization at all. Utilitarian analysis can also underwrite some of the other rules of everyday morality although their utility rests on social conditions that do not hold in all societies. In fact, a significant source of their utility follows simply from the fact that people already observe them. Given common practice, following an existing rule may be better than following some other rule or no rule at all (other than the principle of utility).

Moore didn't believe that utilitarian analysis would validate all the rules of conventional morality. For one thing, some of those rules have poor results. In addition, Moore was wary of exhortations to follow various moral rules that society does not in fact generally observe. This is because most of the benefit of following a specific rule (as opposed to simply following the principle of utility) results from the fact that the rule already governs people's behavior and structures their expectations. Moore doubted the utility of adhering to any proffered moral rule not generally complied with. Rather, where there is no rule that is both useful and generally observed, one should, Moore thought, simply act so as to bring about as much goodness as possible. Indeed, many of Moore's readers found his *Principia Ethica* fresh and exciting back in 1903 because they saw it as breaking with established morality by giving so much moral freedom to the individual.

With regard to those moral rules that utilitarian analysis does vindicate, Moore argued – again from a utilitarian perspective – that one should always stick to them. Although he acknowledges in principle that sometimes neglecting an established utility-promoting rule would be for the best, *Principia Ethica* nevertheless maintains that "the individual can . . . be confidently recommended *always* to conform to rules which are both

155

generally useful and generally practised" (164). But how can Moore believe this? "Surely it will be irrational," one is inclined to say, "to obey even the most useful rule if in a particular instance we clearly see that such obedience will not have the best results."[26]

However, for three interconnected reasons Moore doubted that we can ever clearly see that disobedience would be best. First, if it is useful to observe the rule in most cases, then it is probable that breaking it in the present case will have shoddy results. Second, because we can predict only poorly the consequences of our actions, it is doubtful that an individual's judgment that violating a rule will prove beneficial can outweigh the general probability that any action of that kind will prove wrong. Third, such judgments will generally be biased by our own desire for the results in question. "In short, though we may be sure that there are cases where the rule should be broken, we can never know which those cases are, and ought, therefore, never to break it" (162–3).

Moreover, even if we could be sure that the rule should be broken, Moore worried that doing so would create a bad example, encouraging others to violate rules in situations where they shouldn't. What will impress people's imagination, he thought, is not the exceptional circumstances that justify our rule-breaking action but its resemblance to other actions that really are wrong. Even the agent himself, having once condoned or engaged in an action that is generally wrong, will be more likely to do so in cases where it is not warranted.[27]

A lack of examples hampers Moore's discussion, as does his propensity to think of moral rules as simple and categorical. It seems to have escaped him that a moral rule might acknowledge exceptions to itself or permit other, more stringent rules to outweigh it. Still, his line of argument raises some pertinent points that utilitarians must consider when deciding whether to break a generally useful moral rule. He is right to stress that it is far more difficult than textbook examples make it seem to be confident that breaking such a rule really would have superior results in the long run. Moreover, rationalization can certainly affect one's judgment, and it may be that breaking a rule in one case, even if theoretically justified, can make one more ready than one should be to break it in other cases. Nevertheless, Moore's arguments fail to establish his strong conclusion. It is implausible

[26] Foot, "Utilitarianism and the virtues," 198 (emphasis omitted).
[27] John Austin made the same point: "If the act were permitted or tolerated in the rare and anomalous case, the motives to forbear in the others would be weakened or destroyed. In the hurry and tumult of action, it is hard to distinguish justly" (*Province of Jurisprudence Determined*, 44).

to believe that there will never be situations when a utilitarian could reasonably judge that more good will come from breaking a generally useful moral rule than from sticking to it.

Several Things Moore Could Have Said

Although Moore did not mention them, several further considerations bolster the conclusion that utilitarians will not readily license people to override useful, generally observed moral rules. First, authorizing people to neglect such rules reduces the benefit to society of having those rules in the first place. The greater the number of exceptions, the less frequently the rule is being heeded and, thus, the less safely one can rely on others observing it. When we permit or encourage people to neglect established moral rules and act on their own judgments of what it would be best for them to do, those rules become less firm and people's conduct less predictable.[28]

Second, the finite set of tried and true rules, which Moore thinks should always be obeyed, structure existing social practices, fix people's expectations, and coordinate their conduct, thus helping to create a secure and stable framework for the pursuit of happiness. Once one appreciates the benefits of stability and security that respect for rules brings, one will be less tempted to violate them whenever it appears that doing so would achieve more good in the case at hand. Rules that are generally useful and socially observed constitute practices that have beneficial effects above and beyond the cumulative, immediate utility of the individual actions that are in accord with them. Violating these rules, even in a good cause, tends to disrupt the stable social order that those rules foster. For utilitarians these rules are a vehicle for collectively maximizing social utility – in particular, for obtaining the utility that would be lost if each of us acted directly to maximize the good. Accordingly, a utilitarian can rationally permit this collective endeavor to take precedence over her individual efforts to maximize utility. She will follow socially beneficial rules just because she is committed to maximizing happiness and sees the necessity of collective efforts to do so.[29]

A third consideration concerns what is involved in an individual's adhering to a moral rule in the first place. Sometimes Moore rather

---

[28] In "Whewell on moral philosophy," Mill wrote: "If one person may break through the rule on his own judgment, the same liberty cannot be refused to others; and since no one could rely on the rule's being observed, the rule would cease to exist" (182).
[29] Johnson, *Moral Legislation*, e.g., 4, 220.

carelessly describes a moral rule as a generalization stating that a certain type of action has better results than alternative ways of acting.[30] But individuals who have internalized a rule as part of their moral code will not look at that rule so instrumentally. As previously mentioned, when a rule is part of a person's moral code, the person will be motivated to act in accord with the rule and to feel guilty if he or she fails to live up to it. Moral agents who genuinely accept a moral rule are unlikely to break it whenever they believe that doing so will marginally increase overall utility. They may perhaps deviate from the rule in truly exceptional circumstances or when it conflicts with some other internalized rule. But breaking the rule in an effort to procure a relatively modest gain in net utility – indeed, even routinely considering the advantages of breaking the rule – is inconsistent with its being a firm part of one's moral code. Utilitarians will be more concerned about instilling in people a strong disposition to follow certain basic rules (the general utility of which has been established), than they will be desirous of harvesting the extra utility that might hypothetically come from people shrewdly deviating from those rules. Encouraging people to be on the lookout for exceptions to the basic moral rules is incompatible with reinforcing in them a firm commitment to those rules.

A final consideration is that utilitarians will not blame or criticize a person for adhering to a useful, generally observed moral rule in the rare case in which deviating from it would have had better results and the person was in a position to know this. As we have seen, utilitarians draw a sharp distinction between an action's failing to maximize happiness and the appropriateness of blame. Criticizing someone for misapplying a rule or disregarding a generally recognized exception to it makes sense. But it is hard to imagine what benefit could possibly come from criticizing people for following, in the appropriate circumstances, the very moral rules that one is trying hard to inculcate in them. These rules are an important part of the shared public morality of one's society; they constitute the norms against which behavior is normally judged. To uphold these standards yet criticize people for sticking to them would be counterproductive.

The considerations we have been discussing are ones to which contemporary utilitarians are more alert than Moore was. We turn now to two of the most influential of these writers – R. M. Hare and Richard B. Brandt.

---

[30] Moore, *Principia Ethica*, 155, 162.

Two Levels of Moral Thinking

In his important book *Moral Thinking* R. M. Hare distinguishes two levels of moral reasoning – one he calls the intuitive level, the other the critical level. The intuitive level is the level at which most of us think about moral matters most of the time. As a result of our upbringing and moral training, almost all of us have internalized moral principles which are associated with deep feelings and reasonably firm behavioral dispositions. We rely on these relatively simple, specific, and intuitive moral principles to guide us in the routine circumstances we normally encounter. A person will resist acting contrary to his or her intuitive moral principles and tend to feel guilty about violating them.

These principles are prima facie, not absolute, because almost any given intuitive principle can sometimes be overridden by other principles. Thus, I may believe that I should keep my promise to take my young nephew to the children's zoo this afternoon and also that I should assist an old and dear friend from another country who has arrived in town unexpectedly and now needs my help dealing with some problem. Since I cannot both keep my promise and assist my friend, one of my principles must give way. However, even if I believe that I am doing the right thing, say, by breaking my promise, I will still feel some compunction about the prospect of doing so and experience some regret afterwards. This is because keeping promises is not simply a rule of thumb but one of my moral principles. It is part of my character.

Some moral philosophers and most ordinary people do their moral thinking entirely or almost entirely at the intuitive level. They operate on the basis of their intuitive principles, weighing and comparing their instructions as best they can in situations where the principles conflict, and that is the end of the matter. However, it is also possible to reflect on the intuitive principles one has; that is, to step back, as it were, and to critically assess those principles, perhaps refining, revising, or rejecting some of them. This is the level of critical thinking. As a utilitarian, Hare believes that to think at this level is essentially to think, or try to think, as an ideal, superhuman utilitarian would – that is, as a utilitarian who could foresee all the possible consequences of the alternative actions open to him, grasp their exact likelihoods, and weigh and compare the value of their different effects. Perfect in his reasoning ability and calculating power, this "archangel," as Hare calls him, is also perfectly impartial and free of any personal bias.

159

The Relation between the Levels

Hare believes that, strictly speaking, the morally right thing to do is what the archangel would advise doing. However, we are not archangels,[31] and for reasons already discussed we need in practice to rely on intuitive principles: it is "an indispensable help in coping with the world," Hare writes, to encourage "the formation in ourselves of relatively simple reaction-patterns ... which prepare us to meet new contingencies resembling in their important features contingencies in which we have found ourselves in the past." To do otherwise, to confront each situation afresh and try to perform a cost–benefit analysis before acting, would be, Hare says, like driving a car without having ever done it before and "deciding *ab initio* at each moment what to do with the steering wheel, brake and other controls" (36). In addition, by building firmly into our characters certain dispositions and a commitment to certain intuitive principles we reduce the risk of rationalization, wishful thinking, and special pleading that afflicts real human beings trying to apply the utilitarian principle directly to their conduct. It is all too easy, for example, to persuade oneself that telling a lie to get out of a jam would not hurt anyone else, even though, objectively considered, the costs outweigh the gains.

Thus, Hare writes:

> The principles which we have to follow if we are to give ourselves the best chance of acting rightly are not definitive of "the right act"; but if we wish to act rightly we shall do well, all the same, to follow them. (38)

And:

> Our common intuitions are sound ones, if they are, just because they yield acceptable precepts in common cases. For this reason, it is highly desirable that we should all have these intuitions and that our consciences should give us a bad time if we go against them. (49)

Accordingly, utilitarians should seek to inculcate in themselves and to

---

[31] In an early essay, Mill attributes to some human beings certain superior qualities, which bring to mind Hare's archangel. Given their higher natures – vigorous intellect, strong will, and loving hearts – it is better for these people to follow their own judgment rather than any moral principles or maxims. Mill and Mill, *Essays on Sex Equality*, 69.

foster in others that set of intuitive moral principles whose acceptance will, given the realities of human behavior, yield as close an approximation as possible to what the archangel would recommend.

When examining and selecting our intuitive principles, we operate at the critical level. In addition, we must sometimes move to this level to resolve conflicts between those principles. In some cases, to be sure, we can work through a clash of principles (keeping a promise versus helping a friend) at the intuitive level, weighing them as best we can to determine which is the more important. In other cases, however, especially when the stakes are high, we will need to put our intuitive principles aside and repair to the critical level in order to think in a detailed and directly utilitarian way about the dilemma facing us. In such cases and in other unusual circumstances, which our intuitive principles were not meant to accommodate, we try to think through the situation just as the archangel would. Also, when our intuitive principles clash in a serious way, we need to move to the critical level to determine whether they should be qualified or revised in some way to reduce the risk of future conflict.

Hare's two-level model provides a powerful rejoinder to the standard criticism that utilitarianism can sometimes require us to do something despicable — for example, kill an innocent person — in the name of the greater good. As a general matter, Hare thinks such scenarios are only the fancy of anti-utilitarian philosophers. Even if the moral agent were in the imagined situation, he would probably not be warranted in believing himself to be in it — would, in other words, probably lack evidence sufficient to justify doing something (killing an innocent person) that is normally vile and wicked. Furthermore, and this is Hare's more distinctive point, a person who has internalized a moral principle will find it very difficult, perhaps impossible, to deviate from it. Even if he thinks that breaching one of his principles by destroying a guiltless person would be for the best, he may find himself unable to violate his conscience. Moreover, Hare believes that it is good that the person holds this principle as firmly as he does — that it is good, say, that his whole being rebels at the idea of slaying an innocent victim.

Is a Two-Level Perspective Stable?

This is a powerful line of argument, but some of Hare's critics argue that his two-level approach is unstable because "it represents the intuitive responses as deeply entrenched, surrounded by strong moral emotions, sufficiently robust to see the agent through situations in which sophisticated reflection might lead him astray, and so on; and yet at the same time explains those responses as a device to secure utilitarian outcomes."[32] These critics see Hare's model as psychologically unrealistic; people cannot reasonably be expected to look at their intuitive principles in the instrumental way advocated by Hare. They argue, further, that utilitarian reflection on one's intuitive principles will tend to erode or undermine one's commitment to them, thus scuttling Hare's whole approach.

Hare denies this, responding that people can have strong intuitive principles and also think critically about them. Indeed, this sort of reflection is what ethics requires:

> It has always seemed to me that this objection ... will not be sustained by anyone who has experience even of *trying* to live a morally good life. It is perfectly possible at the intuitive level to treat moral duty or virtue as ultimate ... while at the same time to recognize that in order to establish that those traits of character really do constitute virtue, and that those moral principles really are the ones we should observe, requires more thought than the mere intuition that this is so.[33]

Hare's rejoinder seems persuasive, but Bernard Williams has pursued this line of attack further, arguing that the objection to Hare's two-level approach is not merely a psychological one:

> In saying that you "cannot combine" these two things [intuitive and critical thinking], I do not mean that as a matter of psychological fact it is impossibly difficult .... The point is that the thoughts are not stable under reflection: in particular, you cannot think in these [intuitive] terms if at the same time you apply to the process the kind of thorough reflection that this theory itself advocates. That is not a merely psychological claim. It is a philosophical claim, about what is involved in effective and adequate reflection on these particular states of mind.

A couple of pages later, Williams restates his point:

> The difficulty is, in summary, that one could not think at the "intuitive" or everyday level in the way that the theory requires while one was fully conscious of what one was doing: in particular, while one fully understood in terms of the theory itself what one was doing.[34]

---

[32] Williams, "The structure of Hare's theory," 189–90; see also Alexander, "Comment," 824.

[33] Hare, "Could Kant have been a utilitarian?" 10–11.

[34] Williams, "The structure of Hare's theory," 190, 192.

Hare finds Williams's argument baffling,[35] and indeed it is difficult to pinpoint exactly what his objection is.

The criticism seems to be that one cannot look at the world from inside one's intuitive principles and also look at those principles from the outside, from the utilitarian point of view.[36] But merely to remind us that the critical and intuitive perspectives are different is not to establish that there is anything problematic about looking at the moral world in both ways. Many people seem able both to be firmly committed to certain intuitive principles and at the same time to think in a detached way about the content of those principles, as well as their rationale, justification, and limits, slipping back and forth between the two perspectives as circumstances demand. Indeed, the ideal of the examined life which philosophers have long upheld seems to imply the importance, indeed the moral necessity, of being able to step back and critically reflect on one's own values and commitments. What Williams overlooks is that Harean agents believe that they are fully justified in having the principles and moral feelings they do. Neither psychologically nor philosophically, then, is there anything unstable, incoherent, or inauthentic about the two-level model in either theory or practice.

Rule Utilitarianism

Hare's two-level theory appreciates that the general good will not be maximized by people always applying the principle of utility directly to their actions. If they do so, then not only are errors likely, but also their conduct will be less predictable, and society less stable, than if they simply follow certain generally useful rules. For these reasons, it is good that one's reliance on intuitive moral principles limits the occasions on which one has direct recourse to the principle of utility. As we have seen, earlier utilitarians stressed the importance of secondary rules and intermediate principles, but some of them overlooked what it means for an agent to internalize a moral principle. For an agent to act contrary to her sincere moral commitments would be to violate her conscience, which Mill's *Utilitarianism* aptly describes as "a mass of feeling which must be broken through in order to do what violates our standard of right, and which, if we do nevertheless violate that standard, will probably have to be encountered

---

[35] See Hare, "Comments," 289: "I cannot understand why Williams makes such heavy weather . . . of the combination of critical with intuitive thinking."
[36] See Williams, *Ethics and the Limits of Philosophy*, 108.

afterwards in the form of remorse" (28). Hare rightly emphasizes that someone who has internalized a moral principle cannot and will not put it aside lightly. She may deviate from it when it conflicts with other intuitive principles or in truly exceptional circumstances. But the person will not be on the lookout for opportunities to breach her principles, nor will she be willing to violate them in an effort to reap a marginal increase in utility.

Because it advocates firmly entrenching intuitive moral principles, Hare's moral theory resembles a hybrid version of utilitarianism known as *rule utilitarianism*. Rule utilitarianism maintains that the utilitarian standard should not be applied to individual actions, but should instead be used to determine the appropriate moral rules to follow. Those rules, in turn, determine what one ought to do. The guiding thought behind rule utilitarianism is the now familiar one that overall utility will be greater if people follow rules instead of attempting directly to maximize utility through their actions. But rule utilitarians differ from Hare and other writers who recommend that utilitarians pursue the good indirectly because rule utilitarians assert that whether an action is right or wrong is entirely determined by the utility-derived rules, and not by its results.

Although different writers state the theory in slightly different ways, rule utilitarianism is, essentially, the view that an action is morally right if and only if it accords with that set of rules, the general acceptance of which would result in more happiness than any alternative set of rules. (To distinguish it from rule utilitarianism, many philosophers refer to standard utilitarianism as *act utilitarianism*.) For rule utilitarians, first-order moral appraisal thus involves two steps. We assess moral rules in terms of utility, selecting those rules, the acceptance of which would maximize utility; we then judge individual actions in terms of those rules. If an action complies with the rules, it is right, and if it conflicts with them, it is wrong. The rules are not secondary rules but, rather, define what is right and wrong. There is no direct appeal to utility.

The rules in question cannot be too detailed or complex. If the rules were detailed and specific enough to anticipate every possible exception, so that in every situation any action that accorded with the rules would maximize utility, then in practice there would be no difference between the rule-utilitarian approach and using the act-utilitarian standard as one's direct guide to action. For when an act utilitarian approves an individual action because it maximizes happiness in a particular situation S, he could be seen as following the rule "Do an action just like X in circumstances exactly like S." More important, the rules need to be simple enough that people can learn them and guide their conduct by them for otherwise the rules will not maximize happiness. It is also important that the rules be appraised in context and as a set, not one by one. For example, one cannot assess the benefits of a rule assigning adult children responsibility for the care of their elderly parents without knowing what other norms, rules, and institutions provide its backdrop.

As early as 1712, Bishop Berkeley distinguished between act utilitarianism and rule utilitarianism (although he did not use that terminology) and came down strongly in favor of the latter. We should conform our conduct, he wrote, to "certain, universal, determinate rules or moral precepts, which, in their own nature, have a necessary tendency to promote the well-being of the sum of mankind." Although the rules are "framed with respect to the good of mankind ... our practice must be always shaped immediately by the rule."[37] Several utilitarian thinkers in earlier centuries also adopted or came close to adopting such a view. For instance, John Austin urged that "Utility [should] be the test of our conduct, ultimately, but not immediately ... Our rules [should] be fashioned on utility; our conduct, on our rules."[38]

Although some scholars disagree, John Stuart Mill is better interpreted, I believe, as an act utilitarian than as a rule utilitarian. Nevertheless, some of his remarks in the final chapter of *Utilitarianism* have stimulated interest among contemporary philosophers in the rule-utilitarian approach. For example, Mill writes:

> We do not call anything wrong unless we mean to imply that a person ought to be punished in some way or other for doing it – if not by law, by the opinion of his fellow creatures; if not by opinion, by the reproaches of his own conscience. This seems the real turning point of the distinction between morality and simple expediency. (47)

This passage suggests the following line of thought. As utilitarians, we should not judge an action to be morally wrong just because it is inexpedient or fails to maximize happiness. Instead, we should reserve the label *morally wrong* for conduct that is sufficiently damaging to the general good that it would maximize benefit to criticize people for such conduct and for them to feel guilty about it. In other words, we should use the principle of utility to determine the standards on the basis of which guilt feelings, criticism, and perhaps other sanctions would be appropriate. To criticize people or have them feel guilty every time they fail to do as much good as they might have done is unlikely to maximize happiness. Rather, it better promotes long-term happiness to have people firmly committed to

[37] Berkeley, "Passive obedience," 22, 34.
[38] Austin, *Province of Jurisprudence Determined*, 49.

following certain moral rules and to use these more specific rules as the basis for assessing their own conduct and that of others.

Brandt and the Ideal Moral Code

Richard B. Brandt, the leading contemporary exponent of rule utilitarianism, expounds a theory like that adumbrated by Mill in the passage above. According to Brandt, the rule utilitarian asks what moral code or set of moral rules a particular society should adopt to maximize happiness. In other words, the rule utilitarian seeks to determine the moral code the social acceptance of which would best promote expected well-being in the long run. This is the code we should promulgate, instill in ourselves, and teach to the next generation. The principles that make up that code are the basis for distinguishing right actions from wrong actions. As Brandt explains:

> A rule-utilitarian thinks that right actions are the kind permitted by the moral code optimal for the society of which the agent is a member. An optimal code is one designed to maximize welfare or what is good (thus, utility). This leaves open the possibility that a particular right act by itself may not maximize benefit .... On the rule-utilitarian view, then, to find what is morally right or wrong we need to find which actions would be permitted by a moral system that is "optimal" for the agent's society.[39]

The "optimal" moral code does not refer to the set of rules that would do the most good if everyone conformed to them all the time. The meaning is more complex. To determine the optimal moral code we must take into account what rules can reasonably be taught and obeyed, as well as the costs of inculcating those rules in people. As we have seen, if a principle or rule is part of a person's moral code, then it will influence the person's behavior. The person will tend to follow that principle, to feel guilty when he or she does not observe it, and to disapprove of others who fail to conform to it. Rule utilitarians must consider not only the benefits of having people motivated to act in certain ways but also the social, psychological and other costs of instilling those motivations in them. As Brandt writes:

> The more intense and widespread an aversion to a certain sort of behavior, the less frequent the behavior is apt to be. But the more intense and widespread, the greater the cost of teaching the rule and keeping it alive, the greater the burden on the individual, and so on. (42)

[39] Brandt, "Real and alleged problems of utilitarianism," 38.

Thus, the "optimality" of a moral code encompasses both the benefits of reducing objectionable behavior and the long-term costs of doing so. Perfect compliance is an unrealistic goal. "Like the law," Brandt continues, "the optimal moral code normally will not produce 100 percent compliance with all its rules; that would be too costly."

Brandt strenuously argues that the ideal moral code will not be a one rule code, commanding us always to bring about as much happiness as we can. Teaching people that their only obligation is to maximize happiness will not in fact maximize happiness. Better results, Brandt and other rule utilitarians believe, will come from instilling in people a pluralistic moral code, one with a number of different principles. The principles of the ideal code will be prima facie in the sense that any given principle can sometimes by overridden by other principles. Different principles will have different moral weights. It makes sense, for example, for people to be more averse to killing than to telling lies.

Obviously, moral codes differ in the types of actions that they require or prohibit. They can also vary in the relative intensity or strength of the motivations connected with each act-type. In addition, a moral system's rules and attendant dispositions can vary somewhat for different groups. For example, a simplified version of the ideal code will be appropriate for children, whereas physicians and other professionals will need more elaborate codes tailored to the special situations they are likely to face. Thus, for Brandt, a total moral system is optimal when, variations having been made for different groups, "the consequences of its being in force to the extent it is, taken with the costs of teaching it and having it, will maximize benefit."[40]

Between Acts and Rules

Critics of rule utilitarianism reject the idea that the rules of the optimal moral code are binding on us when other people do not accept that code or some of its tenets. The critics conjure up hypothetical situations in which it would be decidedly harmful to stick to the ideal code while others do not. Suppose the ideal code for our society bans racial discrimination or forbids people from carrying dangerous weapons in public, but in fact people are extremely bigoted and armed to the teeth. In that situation would it not be foolish and wrong to adhere to the ideal code by going about unarmed or marrying someone of a different race? To this, rule utilitarians such as

---

[40] Brandt, *Morality, Utilitarianism, and Rights*, 145.

Brandt respond that the ideal code is flexible and will offer rules about what to do in situations where others do not comply with the rules.

Brandt and other rule utilitarians make a similar response to the broader criticism that it is a kind of "rule worship" to adhere to the rules when doing so will not maximize happiness. They argue that such situations will be rare. For example, the ideal moral code will permit one to break a promise when it conflicts with a more important obligation, and it may allow, as commonsense morality does, agents to make exceptions to the normal moral rules in emergency situations. Critics of rule utilitarianism often argue that if one cares about utility, then one should violate the rules whenever one thinks that doing so will maximize well-being. But we have already seen that thoughtful utilitarians from Mill to Hare stress not only the advantages of rules and the dangers of permitting exceptions to them, but also the benefits of having agents internalize these rules.

In fact, Brandt turns this criticism around, arguing that even if act utilitarians adopt a sophisticated two-level perspective like Hare's, they will still be too ready to put aside their intuitive principles in an effort to maximize well-being. Indeed, he contends, Hare's theory requires them to do so whenever they believe that they safely can. As a result, Brandt maintains that any act-utilitarian approach is risky and potentially counterproductive. Only by letting the utility-maximizing rules determine what is right and wrong, can we eliminate entirely the temptation for utilitarians to pursue the good directly, with results that are bound to be sub-optimal.

However, Brandt's criticism of Hare is overstated because in practice his rule utilitarianism will differ little, if at all, from Hare's two-level act utilitarianism. Hare points this out, writing that his method is like Brandt's because

> it justifies the cultivation and following of dispositions (rules) by the utility of these (series of) acts of cultivation and following, and bids us *at the intuitive level* do our moral thinking (decide what we ought to do) in conformity to these rules. It thus secures the advantages claimed for rule-utilitarianism.[41]

Both Hare's theory and Brandt's rule utilitarianism emphasize the importance of instilling (in oneself and others) aversions of varying strengths toward certain kinds of conduct, along with the corresponding dispositions to feel guilty and to criticize others for engaging in the conduct. The practical distance between Brandt and Hare is further shrunk by the fact

---

[41] Hare, "Comments," 227.

that the ideal moral code will probably allow direct appeals to utility when its rules conflict or in exceptional circumstances.

This debate is still a live one, and the last word on rule utilitarianism has yet to be written. Nevertheless, I shall continue to interpret the principle of utility as laying down the fundamental standard of right and wrong. The rationale for utilitarians like Brandt to define the right in terms of adherence to rules (rather than maximization of utility) is entirely pragmatic.[42] However, once utilitarians distinguish between upholding their theory as a criterion of right and treating it as a decision procedure, then they can already achieve these pragmatic benefits without revising or abandoning their fundamental normative principle.

Furthermore, even putting aside the difficulties of identifying the ideal moral code, to view morality as an entirely rule-governed affair seems too limited a perspective. A utilitarian can appreciate the importance of moral rules – indeed, endorse some of them as virtually absolute – and yet recognize that we probably can't identify utility-maximizing rules to cover all conduct and all situations. G. E. Moore made this point clearly, as did Mill when he distinguished situations in which

> there is . . . a necessity that some rule, of a nature simple enough to be easily understood and remembered, should not only be laid down for guidance, but universally observed, in order that the various persons concerned may know what they have to expect: the inconvenience of uncertainty on their part being a greater evil than that which may possibly arise, in a minority of cases, from the imperfect adaptation of the rule to those cases

from situations

> in which there does not exist a necessity for a common rule, to be acknowledged and relied on as the basis of social life; where we are at liberty to inquire what is the most moral course under the particular circumstances of the case.[43]

Further, utilitarians have traditionally wanted to apply their standard to a wide range of objects – to the assessment of institutions, social policies, character traits, dispositions and motivations, as well as moral rules and,

---

[42] Some philosophers defend rule utilitarianism on non-utilitarian grounds. For example, Hooker argues that rule utilitarianism does a better job than rival moral theories of matching and tying together our intuitions. See his "Rule-consequentialism, incoherence, fairness," 29.
[43] Mill, *Logic*, 1154–5.

yes, individual actions. Sticking with the principle of utility as our ultimate normative gauge is more in keeping with this ambition.

Although the principle of utility remains the final standard for assessing actions, it is a self-limiting principle. First, the utilitarian principle determines whether, when, and to what degree praise or blame is appropriate. In particular, it will often be wrong on utilitarian grounds to criticize someone for failing to maximize well-being. Second, utilitarians will want to encourage in themselves and in others commitments, motivations, dispositions, and character traits that, while generally conducive to the good, occasionally or even frequently lead one to act in ways that do not maximize happiness. There are good utilitarian reasons for one to be, or try to become, the kind of person who cares about things other than maximizing general utility. Third, and related, utilitarians will seek to teach, promote, and internalize in themselves dispositions to act in accord with certain moral rules and principles, general adherence to which will be utility maximizing. The benefits that flow from people being committed to such principles and knowing that others are, too, is of the greatest importance, but people's accepting these moral principles precludes, in all but the most unusual circumstances, their putting them aside in an effort to boost utility.

6

Rights, Liberty, and Punishment

Utilitarianism ties right and wrong to the promotion of well-being, but it is not only a personal ethic or a guide to individual conduct. It is also a "public philosophy"[1] – that is, a normative basis for public policy and the structuring of our social, legal, and political institutions. Indeed, it was just this aspect of utilitarianism that primarily engaged Bentham, John Stuart Mill, his father James, and their friends and votaries. For them utilitarianism was, first and foremost, a social and political philosophy and only secondarily a private or personal moral code. In particular, they saw utilitarianism as providing the yardstick by which to measure, assess, and, where necessary, reform government social and economic policy and the judicial institutions of their day.

In the public realm, utilitarianism is especially compelling. Because of its consequentialist character, a utilitarian approach to public policy requires officials to base their actions, procedures, and programs on the most accurate and detailed understanding they can obtain of the circumstances in which they are operating and the likely results of the alternatives open to them. Realism and empiricism are the hallmarks of a utilitarian orientation, not customary practice, unverified abstractions, or wishful thinking. Promotion of the well-being of all seems to be the appropriate, indeed the only sensible, touchstone for assessing public policies and institutions, and the standard objections to utilitarianism as a personal morality carry little or no weight against it when viewed as a public philosophy.

Consider, for instance, the criticisms that utilitarianism is too impersonal and ignores one's individual attachments and personal commitments, that it is coldly calculating and concerned only with maximizing, that it

---

[1] See Goodin, *Utilitarianism as a Public Philosophy*, Ch. 1.

demands too much of moral agents, and that it permits one to violate certain basic moral restraints on the treatment of others. The previous two chapters addressed some of these criticisms; others will be dealt with in Chapter 8. The point here, though, is that far from undermining utilitarianism as a public philosophy, these criticisms highlight its strengths.[2] We want public officials to be neutral, impersonal, and detached and to proceed with their eyes firmly on the effects of the policies they pursue and the institutions that their decisions shape. Policy making requires public officials to address general issues, typical conditions, and common circumstances. Inevitably, they must do this through general rules, not on a case by case basis. As explained later in this chapter, this fact precludes public officials from violating the rights of individuals as a matter of policy.

Moreover, by organizing the efforts of countless individuals and compelling each of us to play our part in collective endeavors to enhance welfare, public officials can make it less likely that utilitarianism will demand too much of any one individual because others are doing too little. Utilitarians will seek to direct and coordinate people's actions through effective public policy and to reshape, in utility-enhancing ways, the institutions that structure the choices people face. By doing so, utilitarians can usually accomplish more good than they can through isolated individual action, however dedicated and well-intentioned. For this reason, they will strive to foster institutions that take over from individuals much of the task of promoting the general welfare of society.

General welfare is a broad goal, of course, and sensible policies and institutions will typically focus on more specific desiderata – such as promoting productivity, increasing individual freedom and opportunity, improving people's physical health, guaranteeing their personal security, and so on – that contribute significantly to people's well-being. Implementing even these goals can prove difficult. Furthermore, many of the problems facing society have no simple answers because they are tangled up with contested issues of fact and controversial questions of psychology, sociology, and economics. To the extent that utilitarians disagree among themselves over these matters, their policy recommendations will diverge. Nevertheless, by clarifying what is at stake and continually orienting discussion toward the promotion of well-being, a utilitarian approach provides the necessary framework for addressing questions of institutional design and for fashioning effective public policy.

The present chapter explicates the utilitarian approach to three matters that have long engaged social and political philosophers and that concern

---

[2] Goodin, *Utilitarianism as a Public Philosophy*, 8–10, 65–75.

society's institutional arrangements at a fundamental level: criminal justice, political and legal rights, and individual liberty. The next chapter turns to the distribution of income and wealth and related questions of economic policy.

The Criminal Justice System

A world of perfectly moral agents could do without a criminal justice system with its police, judges, and prisons, for there would be no wrongdoers to catch and punish. Laws, or at least public rules and regulations of some kind, would probably be needed to coordinate people's actions and direct them in mutually beneficial ways. However, any violations of those laws or rules would be inadvertent or unintentional, the result of accident, error, miscalculation, or minor negligence, rather than malicious intent, gross recklessness, or criminal design. Unfortunately, we live in a different world. Society needs criminal laws not only to steer the conduct of morally motivated people in socially useful directions, but also, among other things, to restrain those with weaker internal moral inhibitions from injuring others. Society also needs an apparatus to enforce those laws.

Although the details of a welfare-maximizing criminal code do not concern us here, it seems beyond debate that utilitarianism firmly underwrites the core provisions of traditional criminal law. For people's lives to go well, they must be protected from extortion, battery, and rape, their homes secured from trespass, burglary, and vandalism, and their possessions preserved from theft, embezzlement, and malicious destruction. Not only do such crimes directly harm people, but the fear and insecurity they provoke diminish people's well-being and the quality of their lives. An efficient and effective system of criminal justice is not valuable for its own sake, nor generally speaking does it directly enhance individual well-being. Rather, by making possible a civilized and secure social existence, it facilitates our obtaining various social and material goods that are central to our lives going well.

That the point of criminal law is to promote our collective welfare may seem obvious, but there are those who would deny it. On the one hand, minimalists believe that the purpose of criminal laws is more modest: not to enhance general welfare, but only to secure respect for people's rights. On the other hand, maximalists believe that the function of criminal law is broader: to root out and punish immoral conduct. This chapter later argues that utilitarianism takes rights seriously (and, in fact, provides the soundest theoretical account of them), but nevertheless the theory approaches

173

criminal justice with broader goals than just the protection of rights. Not all crimes violate people's rights. Indeed, utilitarianism can justify criminalizing conduct that is not otherwise wrongful (parking one's car on the sidewalk) or that in a particular instance risks little harm to others (the carrying of a loaded firearm by an experienced but nonviolent marksman) if the gains from doing so outweigh the costs. However, contrary to the maximalists, even when conduct is clearly wrong – for example, callously inducing an emotionally distressed person to commit suicide – utilitarian considerations may argue against criminalizing it. The criminal justice apparatus is a blunt instrument, and bringing it to bear on some types of wrongful conduct will prove too costly and intrusive. Whether a certain kind of conduct is right or wrong is one issue. Whether the state should outlaw the conduct and punish those guilty of it is an entirely separate matter.

Utilitarianism makes sense of the core content of criminal law and certain basic and familiar legal doctrines. Among these are the following principles: that laws be public; that they not be applied retroactively; that necessity or self-defense can sometimes justify conduct that would otherwise be criminal; that certain considerations are exculpatory, such as a mistake of fact or the insanity of the defendant; and that various mitigating factors may reduce the seriousness of the crime, as when one person kills another, not with premeditation, but impulsively or in the heat of passion. Putting the legal details aside, the point is that utilitarianism provides solid grounds for these and a number of other well-established principles of criminal law.

The Utilitarian Approach to Punishment

Punishment is the flip side of the criminal law: "If you can't do the time," the saying goes, "don't do the crime." Because of this, we tend to take its moral legitimacy for granted. Yet our practice of punishment is disquieting, and not just because one can question the effectiveness of existing penal institutions. Even under the best of circumstances, whenever we punish people, we are doing to them something that it is normally wrong to do to people. We restrict their liberty, take away their property, harm them physically, or even deprive them of their lives. On what basis, if any, can punishment be justified?

The utilitarian answer is straightforward. Punishment is justified if and only if (1) the pain and suffering (or, more broadly, the loss of welfare) to those who are punished is outweighed by the benefits of punishment and (2) those benefits cannot be achieved with less suffering or at a lower cost to

174

those punished. On the basis of this formula, utilitarians have something to say not only about the considerations that support the practice of punishment in general, but also about what sort of conduct should be criminalized and about the appropriateness of particular punishments for specific types of crimes. However, before we pursue these matters further, bear in mind that punishment is an after the fact response to antisocial behavior. Utilitarians, like other social theorists and reformers, will be concerned not only with society's response to criminals, but also with understanding and confronting the social and psychological circumstances that conduce to crime.

As an institutional practice, the punishment of lawbreakers benefits society as a whole by reducing the amount of criminal activity. It does this in several ways. To begin with, punishment can affect the future conduct of the criminal who has been caught, along three different avenues. First, if it involves incarceration, exile, or execution, punishment removes the delinquent from society and physically prevents him from committing any other crimes for the duration of his sentence. Second, punishing the miscreant can teach him a lesson and discourage him from violating the law in the future. Having been punished once, the ex-convict will be reluctant to risk being punished again and will therefore be more likely than he was before to abstain from illicit conduct. Third, punishment can sometimes reform or rehabilitate the criminal, making him a better person – someone who is motivated less by the threat of punishment than by the desire to be a law-abiding and productive citizen.

It is important to be clear about two things. First, the issue for utilitarians is not whether we can identify the specific benefits of punishing a given individual for a particular crime. That is usually impossible. Rather, the issue is the benefits that come from the general practice of punishing those who violate the law. Second, utilitarianism does not claim that our system of punishment, as it actually functions in the United States, succeeds in rehabilitating very many convicted criminals or in discouraging them from future wrongdoing. The evidence that it does so is slight, and many suspect that prisons, as they exist today, only harden inmates and reinforce a criminal orientation toward life.[3] To the extent that our system of punishment fails to rehabilitate the criminal or deter him from future misconduct, the less likely it is to be justified on utilitarian grounds.

Punishing a lawbreaker not only discourages him from future crimes, it can also deter other potential wrongdoers from committing the same crime. This deterrent effect is an extremely important part of the rationale

---

[3] Ten, *Crime, Guilt, and Punishment*, 8–13.

for punishment and is often singled out as if it were the one and only utilitarian reason for punishment. Deterrence reflects the sad fact that sanctions are necessary to give some people an incentive to obey the law. For example, car theft causes inconvenience, distress, and financial loss to its victims, and the specter of it spreads insecurity and worry. Although the thief profits from his larceny, there is an overall loss of welfare. Other things being equal, the less car theft there is, the better off society as a whole will be. For this reason we have laws against taking a motor vehicle without its owner's permission. Nevertheless, there are those who will be tempted to do just that, for fun or for profit. Unless we make it a practice to attempt to catch and then punish car thieves, no potential thief has an incentive to refrain from stealing cars. Thus, punishment not only dissuades the criminal who is caught from breaking the law again, but it also deters those people who would otherwise be tempted to do the crime if doing so brought no risk of punishment.

To be sure, the threat of criminal punishment is not what deters most people from criminal activity. They refrain from stealing, not because they fear punishment, but because they believe that theft is wrong and are strongly disposed not to do it. Abolishing the laws against car theft would be unlikely to cause most people to try their hand at stealing cars. Although the risk of punishment is not what prevents moral people from doing wrong, punishment may nevertheless be one factor in their moral education. It may be a component of a socialization process that has shaped their moral character so that they are strongly averse to robbing, injuring, or killing other people. Punishing a wrongdoer teaches a moral lesson to others. When society punishes someone for a crime, it sends a vivid, forceful, and public message that it rejects certain conduct, and that message can profoundly influence the norms that people absorb. The revulsion that law-abiding people feel toward serious crime and their aversion to engaging in it themselves may derive in part from the vivid association of crime with punishment.

Discussions of punishment often overlook this important utilitarian consideration, but John Stuart Mill saw it clearly. Writing about the death penalty, he refers to the "efficacy of a punishment which acts principally through the imagination . . . by the impression it makes on those who are still innocent." It does this "by the horror with which it surrounds the first promptings of guilt [and] the restraining influence it exercises over the beginning of the thought, which, if indulged, would become a temptation."[4] Mill's argument illuminates an important feature of punishment in

---

[4] Mill, "Capital punishment," 269.

general, but it is far from conclusive with respect to whether execution or life imprisonment (or some other punishment) is the most effective response to murder. Some writers believe that capital punishment teaches the enormity of murder more effectively than any other punishment.[5] Others believe that execution should go the way of torture: progress in civilization is characterized by our refusing to inflict horrible punishments even on wicked people.[6] In this view, killing criminals sends the wrong moral message. This dispute turns on controversial matters of social psychology and moral development. Although these elude simple answer, they are of crucial importance for anyone approaching capital punishment from a utilitarian perspective.

Understanding Deterrence

Most people are moral, and except in situations of unusual temptation, the prospect of punishment does not deter them from crime because their consciences already restrain them. On the other hand, some people are hot-headed or imprudent, lack the self-control of normal adults, or are prone to irrational or self-destructive behavior. The prospect of punishment may deter such people only weakly or not at all. For any given type of crime, however, there will be some people who will be deterred by the risk of punishment. Their number will vary with the likelihood and severity of the punishment in question.

Thus, as we have seen, a policy of punishing car thieves is justified because it discourages people from stealing cars who would otherwise be tempted to do so. The cost to the convicted thieves is outweighed by the greater benefit to society of a lower level of car theft. For utilitarians, however, not only must the benefits of reducing car theft be greater than the cost of enforcement and punishment, but we must be unable to achieve those benefits at a lower cost. Because utilitarians want to increase *net* welfare as much as possible, they consider both the costs and the benefits of any policy or practice. For instance, if speeding were a capital crime, far fewer drivers would violate the speed limit, and we would all be a little safer on the road. But clearly the benefit to society of increased compliance with this traffic law would be outweighed by the harm done to the executed drivers and their loved ones and by the worry and insecurity that knowledge of such draconian punishment would cause drivers in general.

[5] Goldberg, "On capital punishment."
[6] Reiman, "Justice, civilization, and the death penalty."

If the deterrent effect of two punishments is the same, then, all other things being equal, utilitarianism requires us to choose the less severe punishment. If imprisoning burglars for two years deters potential burglars as effectively as a policy of imprisoning them for three years, then one can justify the harsher sentencing policy only if it provides some non-deterrent benefit. This issue is central to the debate over capital punishment. Does execution prevent homicide more effectively than life imprisonment? In other words, can we reasonably expect the threat of capital punishment to lower the rate of murder? If it does, then executing murderers will save innocent lives, and that fact would provide a compelling utilitarian argument for capital punishment. On the other hand, if executing murderers deters potential killers no more effectively than life imprisonment does, then capital punishment would be difficult to justify on utilitarian grounds (assuming, as most people do, that it is worse to be executed than to spend one's life in prison). From a utilitarian perspective, it cannot be right to increase the harm done to wrongdoers if this brings no offsetting benefit to them or to the rest of society.

If no crime ever went unsolved and unpunished, then relatively mild penalties would suffice to deter wrongdoers. For instance, if every burglary were solved and every burglar captured, even a clement punishment would eliminate any gains to the burglar and make committing the crime pointless. Not all crimes are solved, however, and a calculating criminal might reasonably believe, let's suppose, that there is only a one out of twenty chance that he will be caught and convicted for stealing a car. If so, the punishment for car theft must be at least twenty times more costly to the thief than his gain from stealing the car. This is because the rational car thief will discount the disutility of being punished by the likelihood of capture and conviction. If few car thieves are ever caught, very severe punishments may be needed to deter car theft. Of course, real life is complicated, and thieves do not always rationally calculate the costs and benefits of the crimes they contemplate. Nevertheless, the simple but often neglected point holds that deterrence is a function of both the severity of the punishment and the likelihood of its being inflicted.

In fact, we know surprisingly little about the comparative deterrent effect of different punishments, and some commentators doubt that putting criminals in prison achieves anything that could not be accomplished by less harsh means, such as monetary fines, community service, house arrest with electronic monitoring, intermittent incarceration (on weekends, for instance), or half-way houses with close supervision.[7] Utilitarians

---

[7] Brandt, *Facts, Values, and Morality*, 258.

will consider and perhaps experiment with these and other alternatives to conventional punishment. They are not wedded to the status quo but, rather, favor whatever system of criminal justice and whatever forms and mechanisms of punishment produce the greatest expected net benefit for society as a whole. Determining this is no easy matter, and utilitarian reformers will doubtless proceed in an incremental fashion, basing their recommendations on the best available empirical data and on whatever insights psychology, social theory, and scientific criminology can provide.

Against Retributivism

Retributivists advance the non-utilitarian thesis that punishment is justified because it is the morally appropriate response to wrongdoing. It is right and fitting that wrongdoers be punished. Having done evil, they should to be paid back for what they have done; they deserve to suffer. Retributivists urge that whereas utilitarianism concerns itself with the future effects of punishment, punishment is properly backward looking. It looks to the past, to what people deserve because of what they have done. Just as someone can merit praise or reward for doing something well, so a person can deserve blame or punishment for doing wrong. No further justification, in terms of social benefit or anything else, is called for. Staunch retributivists believe that it is right to punish wrongdoers even if doing so has no positive social benefits whatsoever.

Retributivism enjoys some commonsense appeal, but it is debatable whether desert is the independent moral variable retributivists take it to be. Given an established practice, or within the context of certain rules, people can appropriately be said to deserve the rewards or penalties they incur. A prizefighter can deserve to be judged the winner of a heavyweight bout; a basketball player can deserve to be thrown out of the game for an egregious foul. Likewise, assuming that the laws are reasonable and people are aware of them, we can say that, having broken the "rules of the game" by assaulting someone, stealing a purse, or embezzling money, a person can deserve to be punished. Utilitarians have no problem with this way of talking. However, they will insist that desert is always relative to some institutional framework or to some system of rules, norms, or established expectations, which system is itself subject to consequentialist assessment. In their view, desert is not an antecedent or free-standing moral factor capable of showing what laws we should have in the first place, which transgressions we should punish, or what penalties we should mete out.

179

Likewise, utilitarians can accommodate the point (urged by a number of philosophers) that punishment is justified on grounds of fair play. Criminals take advantage of law-abiding citizens by breaking rules that those citizens have adhered to. In this way, they attempt to benefit themselves unfairly at the expense of others. Society therefore has a right to punish criminals, these philosophers argue, to restore an equitable distribution of benefits and burdens. Although utilitarians do not center their analysis of punishment on the idea of fair play, the underlying point is perfectly compatible with a utilitarian approach. Those who adhere to rules that others get away with breaking may come to feel resentful or aggrieved, especially if obeying the rules requires an effort on their part or if the rule breakers injure their interests. A failure to punish lawbreakers can jeopardize the allegiance of the law abiding. From a utilitarian perspective, this point highlights another positive social effect of punishment. Like desert, however, the idea of fair play is parasitic on existing institutional arrangements; it does not tell us what conduct should be criminalized, what type of punishment is the appropriate response, or how severe that punishment should be.

Retributivists would dispute this. They affirm, not just that criminals deserve to be punished, but also that they deserve to be punished in proportion to the evil they have done: the worse the crime, the harsher the punishment should be. This is a sensible precept, to be sure, and it is one that utilitarians can easily endorse. Unfortunately, the principle that the severity of the punishment should correspond to the gravity of the deed provides little practical guidance. Some retributivists embrace the ancient tenet of "an eye for an eye," at least in the case of murder. The thought that those who kill deserve to die has to be modified, of course, if it is to accommodate different degrees of murder (first degree, second degree, manslaughter, etc.) or to determine the appropriate punishment for attempted murder. Some people who think that they agree with "an eye for an eye" implicitly assume that execution has a greater deterrent effect than life imprisonment. If they came to believe otherwise, then they might cease to believe that the death penalty is a moral imperative. They would almost certainly cease to believe this if they thought that capital punishment actually increased the murder rate (because, say, state-sponsored executions cause some impressionable citizens to become less averse to killing people in other circumstances).

Some retributivists fear that a utilitarian approach to punishment will lead us to let criminals off too easily, not punishing them as fully as they deserve. Kant, for instance, firmly believed in capital punishment and was vexed by the thought that utilitarian reasoning might induce us to refrain

180

from executing murderers.[8] There is, however, no more substantial ground for this belief than for its opposite, that utilitarians will punish criminals too harshly. For instance, one might contend that if a certain kind of crime is very difficult to detect, then a utilitarian society might have to punish the few violators it catches more severely than they deserve. Or suppose that someone who commits a crime has himself been wronged or abused or received less than a fair share of society's resources; one might argue that the criminal is more sinned against than sinning and thus does not deserve the punishment that utilitarianism might authorize. The fact that some retributivists allege that a utilitarian approach to punishment is too harsh whereas others allege that it is too lenient highlights a weakness of retributivism. It provides no agreed upon framework from which questions of punishment can be systematically addressed. In practice, retributivists fall back on their sometimes conflicting intuitions about what criminals deserve or don't deserve under different circumstances.

The criminal justice system of any advanced society comprises several complex institutions and practices. Utilitarians seek to shape these institutions and practices so as to direct and modify people's behavior in welfare-enhancing directions. By contrast, for retributivists the prime or perhaps only point of these institutions is to see that people get what they morally deserve. But assessing people's desert is problematic.[9] Moreover, retributivists have relatively little interest in the impact that these institutions have on social well-being (for instance, their effect on the overall level of crime and anti-social behavior). This stance seems, at best, misguided.

Hanging the Innocent Man

Retributivists contend that utilitarianism ignores considerations of desert and argue that, as a result, the theory could conceivably require us to punish an innocent person if doing so maximized overall social benefit. To illustrate their point, they ask us to imagine a sheriff in a small town where

---

[8] Kant, *Practical Philosophy*, 473.
[9] If incompatibilists or hard determinists are correct that our actions are determined and that therefore we are not responsible for them, then retributivists will have a problem making sense of talk of moral desert. Their position assumes either that we have free will or that our normal ideas about responsibility are compatible with the truth of determinism. Utilitarianism, by contrast, is neutral with respect to the debate over free will, determinism, and responsibility.

a heinous, racially inflammatory crime has been committed.[10] The local community is restless and upset, demanding that the culprit be caught and punished. Unless this happens soon, there will be (the sheriff knows) violent rioting resulting in several deaths and much future bitterness. The sheriff has a suspect in custody but learns that he is innocent. Nevertheless, the sheriff could plausibly frame the suspect for the crime. If he does, then the potential riot will be averted, public faith in law enforcement renewed, and widespread fear and anxiety replaced by a sense of safety and security. The retributivist contends, then, that if the sheriff is a utilitarian, he should frame the innocent man and see him hanged because it is better that one man dies than that a riot occurs with multiple deaths. (To make his argument tighter, the critic might stipulate further imaginary details. The true criminal confesses his crime to the sheriff immediately before dying. Unfortunately, there is no other evidence of his guilt, and he is so well regarded and the circumstances so strange that nobody would be likely to believe the sheriff's report.)

To this line of argument, utilitarians respond that the imagined case is too fanciful to take seriously and that the same is true of any other story that one might concoct in an effort to show the utility of executing an innocent person. The example assumes as certainties what are only extremely risky possibilities. For one thing, the sheriff cannot know with confidence what he is supposed to know. He cannot be sure that proceeding honestly and setting the innocent man free really would have dire consequences, nor can he safely assume that no one will ever figure out what he has done. And if the truth ever leaked out, the results would be extremely bad.

Furthermore, the example rests on a naive view of human psychology and institutional life. It clearly promotes long-run utility for the rule of law to prevail and for people working in the criminal justice system to follow established professional standards. Yet we are to suppose that somehow the sheriff (and perhaps others) could decide to break the law this one time and yet on all other occasions be firmly committed to acting legally and professionally. Yet if the sheriff believes that he is right to fabricate evidence when he knows an accused person is innocent, he will surely be tempted to invent evidence against people he firmly believes to be guilty. This is something it would be madness to encourage.

There is another and deeper point here as well. Judicial punishment is part of a larger criminal justice system, and it is the rules and practices of

---

[10] This much discussed example originated in McCloskey, "An examination of restricted utilitarianism."

182

that system that utilitarianism seeks to assess and possibly reform. As a number of writers have stressed, one must distinguish between justifying a practice or institution and justifying conduct within that practice or institution.[11] With regard to the former, there are conclusive utilitarian objections to a legal (or quasi-legal) system that instructs or permits its officials to frame innocent people whenever those officials deem it necessary for the benefit of society. The potential for abuse is so great that the contention that utilitarians would favor and attempt to design such a system is preposterous.

Assume that we have a democratic society with a morally defensible criminal justice system in place. Once the legislature has decided what the punishment is for a particular crime, then it follows that although judges may have some discretion in the sentencing of individual lawbreakers (taking into account, for instance, age or prior convictions), their role is essentially to determine legal guilt or innocence and to assign a reasonable and appropriate penalty (within a predetermined range). It is not to calculate what precise social benefit, if any, will come from sentencing this particular person to jail. By analogy, in baseball the umpire's job is to call balls and strikes, rather than to determine on utilitarian grounds whether a particular batter should be allowed extra swings.

Retributivists contend that utilitarianism fails to give moral weight to the fact that criminals deserve to be punished. Utilitarianism is forward looking, they say, whereas punishment properly looks back to what the criminal has done. But we can now see that this contention is simplistic. In assessing different systems of punishment, utilitarians do, to be sure, approach the whole issue in terms of benefits and costs. If they approve of a particular system, it will be on forward-looking grounds. However, a judge within that system looks backward and attempts to determine what the accused person did and whether it fits the legally established criteria of the crime in question. Likewise, other officials will have specific institutional roles to play. For them to ignore both the rules of the system and their own institutional duties whenever they think that doing so is best would have very poor long-term results. Rather, utilitarians will want officials to stick to established institutional procedures and perform their assigned roles as well as possible.

Utilitarians believe that any acceptable criminal justice system must acknowledge various rights that individuals have, and they insist that its officials must respect those rights in practice. That is one reason why

---

[11] Rawls, "Two concepts of rules." Mill, Austin, and others anticipated this distinction.

utilitarians oppose hanging the innocent man. But what exactly are rights, and how, if at all, do they fit into a utilitarian framework?

The Nature and Function of Rights

Broadly speaking, a *right* is an entitlement to act or to have others act in a certain way. Because different rights involve different clusters of permissions and constraints on people's actions, talk of rights is sometimes ambiguous. To assert that Carlos has a right to do something can mean that he has no obligation not to do it, that others are obligated not to stop Carlos from doing it, or that others have a positive obligation to ensure that Carlos can have or do the thing he has a right to.[12] Generally speaking, though, if a person has a right to do something or to be treated in some way, then someone else has a correlative duty to act or refrain from acting in a certain way. For example, if Harriet asserts that she has a right to drive, she means that she is entitled to drive or that others should – that is, have a duty to – permit her to drive. Because her right to drive (under specified conditions and subject to certain restraints) is a function of the laws that govern her society, it is considered a *legal right*.

Legal rights depend on the rules, laws, and judicial principles of a given legal system. In addition to legal rights and other rights defined and created by specific institutions, philosophers speak of *moral rights*. Some of these moral rights derive from the special roles or relationships people are in or from undertakings they have given or expectations they have created. For example, as a student Tina has a right that her instructor grade her work fairly and professionally, and as a spouse she has a right to the material and emotional support of her husband. If Tina has borrowed Ahmad's car, promising to return it on Saturday morning, then Ahmad has a right to have Tina return his car by then. If she has agreed to water Elaine's plants while Elaine is on vacation, then Elaine has a right to expect Tina to look after the plants as she said she would.

Equally important are moral rights that are independent of special relationships, roles, or situations – for example, the rights to life, free speech, and unhampered religious affiliation. These widely accepted moral rights are not seen merely as the entitlements of some specific political or legal system, nor is their existence thought to depend on the agreements people make or the particular relationships they enter into. Such moral

---

[12] Hare, *Moral Thinking*, 149; Hausman and McPherson, *Economic Analysis*, 125.

rights are called *human rights*. They have several important character-istics.

First, human rights are universal. For instance, if the right to life is a human right, as most people believe, then everyone, everywhere, and at all times has that right. By contrast, there is nothing universal about your right that I keep my promise to help you move house or about my right to drive at 65 miles per hour on certain roads.

Second, and closely related, human rights are equal rights. If the right to free speech is a human right, then everyone has this right equally. No one has a greater right to free speech than anyone else. In comparison, your daughter has a greater right than do the daughters of other people to your emotional and financial support.

Third, human rights are not transferable, nor can they be relinquished. If we have a human right, we cannot give, lend, or sell it to someone else. We cannot waive it, and no one can take it from us. That is what is meant in the Declaration of Independence when certain rights – namely, life, liberty, and the pursuit of happiness – are described as "inalienable." By comparison, legal rights can be renounced or transferred, as when one party sells another a house or a business.

Fourth, human rights are natural rights, not in the sense that they can be derived from a study of nature, but in the sense that they do not depend on human institutions in the way that legal rights do. If people have human rights, then they have them simply because they are human beings. They do not have them because they live under a certain legal system. Human rights rest on the assumption that people have certain basic moral entitle-ments simply because they are human beings. No authoritative body assigns them human rights. The law may attempt to protect human rights, to make them explicit and safe through codification, but the law is not their source.

Utilitarianism and Rights

One of the most widespread criticisms of utilitarianism is that it cannot take rights seriously enough. Generally speaking, rights take precedence over considerations of immediate utility. They limit or restrict direct appeals to welfare maximization. For example, to have a right to free speech means that one is free to speak one's mind even if doing so will fail to maximize happiness because others will dislike hearing what one has to say. The right not to be compelled to incriminate oneself entails that it would be wrong to force a criminal defendant to testify against himself even if the results of doing so would be good. If rights are moral claims that trump straightforward appeals to utility,[13] then utilitarianism, the critics argue, cannot meaningfully respect rights because their theory subordinates them to the promotion of welfare.

However, the criticism that utilitarianism cannot do right by rights ignores the extent to which utilitarianism can, as discussed in Chapter 5, accommodate the moral rules, principles, and norms other than welfare maximization that appear to constitute the warp and woof of our moral lives. To be sure, utilitarians look at rights in a different light than do moral theorists who see them as self-evident or as having an independent deontic status grounded on non-utilitarian considerations. For utilitarians, it is not rights, but the promotion of welfare, that lies at the heart of morality. Bentham was consistently hostile to the idea of natural rights, in large measure because he believed that invoking natural rights was only a way of dressing up appeals to intuition in fancy rhetoric. In a similar vein, many utilitarians today believe that in both popular and philosophical discourse people are too quick to declare themselves possessors of all sorts of putative rights and that all too frequently these competing claims of rights only obscure the important, underlying moral issues.

Learning from Bentham. Although Bentham opposed talk of natural rights, he had no problem with legal and other institutional rights. Indeed, it is hard to see how a welfare-maximizing legal system could fail to entrench certain entitlements, such as property rights or the right to be free from bodily invasion. As a commentator on Bentham explains:

> Human well-being depends overwhelmingly on social institutions provid-
> ing favourable conditions for human enterprise in the broadest sense . . . .
> These all-important conditions are created and maintained principally by
> enforced social rules. The resulting framework of legal rights and obliga-
> tions makes normal human functioning possible and abundance achievable.
> Moreover, to maximize well-being, the framework must secure a realm of
> equal freedom and personal inviolability to all.[14]

Bentham well understood the necessity, if we are to maximize well-being, of institutionalizing certain rights that protect individuals' freedom of action from infringement by others, including the state. The task for utilitarians is to determine the exact set of rights that will produce the most desirable results. This set may change over time, and both socioeconomic

[13] Dworkin, *Taking Rights Seriously*, xi.
[14] Lyons, "Bentham, utilitarianism, and distribution," 324.

circumstances and the larger historical and cultural context will affect the precise specification and relative weight of different rights.

The establishment of a right entails that, in normal circumstances, one is free to act in a certain way (or must be treated in a certain way) without regard to considerations of overall utility. This is not a point utilitarians reluctantly acknowledge; they insist upon it. Rights provide people with certain protections or a realm of choice that is not subject to direct calculation of utility. If you have a right to control access to your home, then you may admit and exclude whomever you wish; you do not have to allow homeless people to sleep in your living room even if doing so would increase net happiness. The benefits of having rights depend upon their remaining rights, which in turn entails that one can exercise them without first determining whether doing so will maximize happiness. Part of the point of rights is that welfare is increased by sparing people the burden of gathering information about possible consequences and calculating probabilities before they act.

Utilitarians can and should structure or revise institutional rights so that, as a general matter, people's having and exercising those rights will promote well-being as much as possible. Having done this, though, it would then be counterproductive to disregard, override, or permit exceptions to these rights in an endeavor to boost well-being in particular cases. If we support a certain right on grounds of utility, then we must tolerate cases in which its exercise fails to maximize utility. Practically speaking, it is impossible to institutionalize a right (and reap the benefits that this brings) and at the same time condemn its exercise or license violations of that right in a particular situation. For example, as Russell Hardin explains, if

> enforcing the right of private ownership of property is generally better than not doing so, then it should be enforced. If there are specifiable classes of infringement of property that would be utilitarian, however, these may also be institutionalized and enforced. But it is often implausible that we can design institutions ... that could be used to make exceptions from our generally institutionalized rules.

In order to boost overall welfare, utilitarians will circumscribe the rights they endorse in various ways or build certain readily identifiable exceptions into them. The right to free speech, for example, does not permit one to holler "fire" in a crowded theater. Similarly, homeowners have rights over their property, but these rights are not unlimited, and zoning laws can restrict what they may build on their property without infringing their rights. But once we have institutionalized a right that has already been

187

specified and delimited so as to maximize well-being, there will then be no feasible way to authorize violations of it simply on the ground that doing so would increase well-being in a particular case. This is because there

> is likely to be no person or institution we would be willing to empower to decide to take A's property to benefit B simply because that would make the world better. We can, however, easily imagine laws and institutions to tax all property to benefit those in B's class. The capricious sorts of individual interventions that many moral theorists pose as counterexamples to utilitarian prescriptions can have no institutional home.[15]

Mill and moral rights. As we have seen, Bentham was attentive to the importance of legal and other institutional rights. John Stuart Mill went further and upheld, on utilitarian grounds, moral rights that are not institutionally based. In an important passage in *Utilitarianism*, Mill first explains what moral rights are and then affirms that they can be justified only in terms of utility:

> When we call anything a person's right, we mean that he has a valid claim on society to protect him in the possession of it, either by the force of law or by that of education and opinion. If he has what we consider a sufficient claim, on whatever account, to have something guaranteed to him by society, we say that he has a right to it .... To have a right, then, is, I conceive, to have something which society ought to defend me in the possession of. If the objector goes on to ask why it ought, I can give him no other reason than general utility. (52)

Today most utilitarians follow Mill in recognizing not just legal rights but also moral rights. That is, they believe that people have certain valid claims or entitlements that others act or not act in certain ways, entitlements that it promotes utility to recognize and protect, even if these rights are not legally formalized. Just as utilitarians want people in their society to have internalized certain norms and be strongly disposed to follow certain rules, so they want people to be able to recognize that others have rights and to be firmly minded to respect those rights and refrain from violating them.

In line with this, most contemporary utilitarians acknowledge the importance of upholding certain basic human rights and insisting that individuals are morally entitled to be treated in certain ways whether or not this is required by the legal system under which they live. These rights include personal liberty and freedom of movement, freedom of religion,

---

[15] Hardin, *Morality within the Limits of Reason*, 102–3.

freedom of expression and inquiry, and freedom from arbitrary imprison-ment or execution and from arbitrary deprivation of property or livelihood. Widely recognized human rights such as these correspond to certain basic human interests, which are central to our well-being. Respecting these rights promotes human flourishing; violating them almost always detracts from human welfare. By identifying as human rights certain fundamental sources of, or preconditions for, well-being, utilitarians attempt to safe-guard the most basic interests of individuals and prevent governments and other powerful groups from trampling on them.

Because human rights mark as morally impermissible certain salient and easily identifiable harms, they provide a powerful focal point for moral and political criticism. By contrast, criticism that appeals to the general good is often less effective because people disagree about what best promotes the general good in specific cases.[16] Ideally, human rights should be institu-tionalized by being incorporated into the legal or constitutional structure of all nations. In the meantime they provide an important basis for moral criticism in the court of public opinion.

It is possible, of course, for there to be exceptional circumstances when it would be better to violate someone's human rights than to respect them. But utilitarians argue that in practice we can rarely if ever reliably judge ourselves to be in such a situation. In fact, most arguments that purport to justify violating human rights on utilitarian grounds are nothing more than rationalizations, advanced by rulers intent on shoring up their regimes or protecting their privileges. And even when the arguments are in good faith, the supposed utility calculations are overwhelmingly likely to be erroneous. Thus, we do better not to countenance violations of human rights at all, treating them instead as virtually absolute. Consider torture for example. We know that those in power can sometimes convince themselves of the necessity of torturing suspects to obtain information the authorities believe to be vital; doing so, they claim, is justified on utilitarian grounds. Yet we also know that those authorities have always been wrong about this and that state-sponsored torture only diminishes social well-being, crippling its victims and sapping the humanity of its perpetrators.

For these reasons, then, instilling in people respect for the rights of others and institutionalizing in society an almost absolute commitment to the protection of certain fundamental human rights form part of a wise, long-term strategy for safeguarding people's basic welfare interests and promoting human flourishing. Far from being defensive about rights,

[16] Gibbard, "Utilitarianism and human rights," 99.

189

utilitarians argue that only their theory can give a satisfactory account of them. They reject the traditional view that the existence of moral rights is simply self-evident and that we are to settle conflicts over and between supposed rights by intuition. They maintain that utilitarianism properly justifies rights in terms of the good that comes from establishing certain entitlements or imposing certain restrictions on people's conduct – entitlements and restrictions that are not subject to direct appeals to utility. Other writers ground human rights in concepts like dignity, respect, autonomy, and self-control,[17] and these values do seem intimately linked to honoring core human rights. However, utilitarians respond either that these values just are (or reduce to) aspects of human well-being or else that they matter only insofar as they promote human well-being.

In addition to justifying rights in general, utilitarianism can delineate more precisely than most other normative theories the specific rights that people have. Because it sees rights as serving a larger function, a utilitarian approach explains why rights differ in their importance, with different rights carrying different moral weight, and it can help us to specify the contours and limits of particular rights. In this way, utilitarianism provides a methodology for adjudicating conflicting claims of rights.

Two Critics

The previous section argued not only that utilitarianism can make room for rights, but also that it provides an illuminating account of them in theory and a secure foundation for them in practice. Some contemporary philosophers resist this conclusion. They believe that utilitarianism does not deal satisfactorily with rights and that this failure betrays a deep deficiency in the theory. Two such critics are James Fishkin and David Lyons, respected moral theorists whose views on this issue are representative of those of many opponents of utilitarianism. Fishkin and Lyons, however, attack the theory on distinct grounds. Fishkin maintains that utilitarianism cannot adequately underwrite a commitment to basic human rights, whereas Lyons argues that utilitarians, including utilitarian officials, will not see themselves as bound to respect those rights that their own theory justifies and whose institutionalization it supports.

Fishkin: utilitarianism is an insecure basis for human rights. James Fishkin's main line of argument for this proposition rests on the contention that

---

[17] E.g., Meyer, "Dignity, rights, and self-control."

if the ultimate basis for institutionalizing one set of rights-defining practices rather than another is utilitarian, then those core human rights have a most uncertain basis. It is an open, quasi-empirical question whether other practices, abhorrent to rights advocates, might not produce greater aggregate utility.[18]

Fishkin rejects the utilitarian approach to rights precisely because it is consequentialist and empirical. Hence, there is no a priori guarantee that the rights that utilitarians endorse will be those favored by non-utilitarian "rights advocates" such as Fishkin. However, this line of criticism begs the question against utilitarianism. It assumes without argument that the preferences of the so-called rights advocates – preferences that are formed, as Fishkin affirms, independently of an understanding of the empirical implications of acknowledging and enforcing those putative rights – are the decisive normative test of what rights people have. Fishkin believes that utilitarianism fails to provide a secure enough basis for human rights, but he provides no alternative theory of rights, implicitly relying only on intuition and people's common moral beliefs.

Fishkin takes the existence of certain human rights as a given and then contends that it might turn out that respect for some of these rights does not promote human welfare in the long run. As a result, utilitarianism, he believes, fails to underwrite adequately certain core human rights. Fishkin's argument rests on two assumptions. First, there must be some moral right, of the existence of which we are more certain than we are of any normative theory, so that a theory's failure to acknowledge that right constitutes sufficient grounds for rejecting the theory (rather than for abandoning the right). Second, it must not be the case that recognizing and supporting this right promotes human well-being in the long term; otherwise, utilitarianism will champion it. Naturally, utilitarians reject both these assumptions. In particular, they believe that if upholding some moral prerogative that we normally take to be a right fails to promote human well-being, then our commitment to that supposed right must be rethought. We must either abandon it altogether or else revise, restrict, or reconceptualize it in some way.

To buttress his argument, Fishkin considers a stock anti-utilitarian example. We are to imagine that a hospital can save five people, each of whom desperately needs an immediate organ transplant (in one case a kidney, in another a lung, in a third a heart, and so on), by killing a healthy patient who has checked in for some routine procedure and then redis-

---

[18] Fishkin, "Utilitarianism versus human rights," 103–4; cf. Dworkin, *Law's Empire*, 290–1.

tributing his organs to the other five people. Fishkin grants that there are strong and fairly obvious utilitarian objections to killing the healthy patient to save the others; these include the fear this would create in other patients and potential patients and the bad consequences of undermining established medical norms and practices. He further allows that utilitarians can endorse the "right to protection from arbitrary loss of life and liberty" and invoke it on behalf of the patient (106).

However, Fishkin goes on to hypothesize that utilitarian calculations might favor our institutionalizing an entirely different rights-defining practice than the one we now have, for example, by setting up a system of involuntary organ donation based on a random lottery. If such a system saved lives and if people were more relieved by the prospect of receiving transplants when needed than they were worried about the risk of being forced to be donors, then, he believes, utilitarians would have to endorse such a system as a way of maximizing general welfare. Fishkin rejects such a lottery as abhorrent and repudiates utilitarianism for its alleged willingness to countenance it.

Several flaws vitiate his argument, however. First, it is implausible to suppose that a practice of involuntary organ donation would maximize well-being. If organ donors are in short supply, a variety of humane policies are possible either to encourage people to donate spare organs while they are alive or to facilitate recycling the vital organs of the recently deceased. These policies would almost certainly be as effective as trying to take people's bodily parts against their will, without having any of the drawbacks of such a system.

Second, if for the sake of argument one concedes whatever wild factual assumptions an anti-utilitarian like Fishkin needs if he is to maintain that a system of involuntary organ donation would maximize happiness, then perhaps one should reconsider one's objections to such a system *under the imagined circumstances*. Suppose, for instance, that people vote unanimously for a system of forced organ donation because they believe it will increase average longevity. Should we still insist with Fishkin that such a system odiously violates people's human rights? The answer would seem to be no. The important point, however, is that the hypothetical world supposed by the critic is not our world. Determining what might or might not maximize happiness in imaginary circumstances is irrelevant to the question of what rights we should acknowledge and respect in the world as it is now and will likely continue to be.

Lyons: utilitarians must violate rights. David Lyons grants that utilitarianism readily provides for the establishment of legal and other institutionally embedded rights, and he believes (contrary to Fishkin) that these rights will be the familiar ones protecting individuals from violations of their persons and property. Although he grants that utilitarianism will support and enforce the rights that we cherish, Lyons nevertheless argues that it "ignores" or fails to "accommodate" their moral force.[19] Utilitarianism justifies those rights at the institutional level, but it does not oblige us to obey them, and puts no moral weight on those rights when assessing individual conduct. For this reason, the whole utilitarian approach to rights is "incoherent."[20]

Lyons clarifies his position with an example. In a neighborhood where parking places are scarce, Mary rents a house with a garage and private driveway. Assuming that the relevant institutional procedures and arrangements are welfare maximizing, then from a utilitarian perspective Mary has a right to use her driveway as she wishes. Other drivers may not park there or block her access to it without her permission. If they do so, they violate her right. Of course, Mary's right to her driveway is hardly absolute. On an urgent assignment, the driver of an emergency vehicle might justifiably obstruct her driveway. In ordinary circumstances, though, the fact that Mary has a right to her driveway entails that others may not park there even if their doing so would benefit them more than it would inconvenience her.

Although Lyons stipulates that utilitarianism upholds the systems of rights of which Mary's is an instance, he nevertheless argues that from a utilitarian perspective "Mary's rights *make no difference* to what she and others may justifiably do."[21] This is because "Mary is fully justified in exercising her legal rights only when and as she can promote human welfare to the maximum degree possible, and others are fully justified in encroaching on Mary's rights in the same sort of circumstances and for the same sort of reason" (156). What supports this contention, in the eyes of Lyons, is simply the fact that it will sometimes maximize utility to deviate from a rule even though the rule itself is justified on utilitarian grounds. Accordingly, "utilitarian justification of the institution provides the utilitarian himself with no reason for conforming to its rules – not when greater utility accrues to deviation from them" (170). Lyons pushes this point further, arguing that it applies to utilitarian officials who are charged with enforcing Mary's rights. Although they acknowledge that the rules are morally justified – that better rules are impossible – they must deviate from

[19] Lyons, *Rights, Welfare, and Mill's Moral Theory*, 151, 161.
[20] Lyons, "Utility as a possible ground of rights," 25.
[21] Lyons, *Rights, Welfare, and Mill's Moral Theory*, 157.

them whenever doing so best serves overall welfare. In particular, an official who accepts utilitarianism may decide that welfare would be better served by not enforcing Mary's rights in a particular case even though the institution does not recognize this situation as a legitimate exception (and even though the rule itself could not be improved to take account of such situations).

Lyons's argument is guilty of the incoherence he accuses utilitarians of. His example supposes that utilitarians, in conformity to their theory, uphold a system that grants Mary the freedom to use her driveway as she wishes. Yet Lyons denies that they understand what they are doing when they acknowledge her right and endorse the system that underwrites it.

Let us consider this point carefully. We are to assume that utilitarians rightly believe that it maximizes welfare to have a system that (1) permits people like Mary to use their driveways as they see fit without concerning themselves, in ordinary circumstances, with the interests of others or with maximizing welfare and that (2) forbids drivers from using the private driveways of others without permission even when they calculate that doing so would maximize advantage all around. But if utilitarians support such a system, then they believe that Mary is not to be criticized for using her driveway, even when others might need it more, and that people who park there without her permission are rightly open to rebuke and punishment (for example, by being fined or having their cars towed away).

It is true, of course, that it might sometimes maximize well-being for a driver to park in Mary's driveway without her consent. But no sensible utilitarian would say that a person should violate the rights of others whenever the person believes that doing so would boost utility. Indeed, to support the institution in question, utilitarians will criticize the conduct of the rights-violator even when it can be proved to have maximized utility. To do otherwise is to undermine the very institution that utilitarians wish to reinforce. By the same token, Mary cannot be reproached for exercising her right to her driveway. If Mary is a utilitarian, then she will seek to maximize happiness through her actions, but she also knows that her having a right to her driveway – and thus being free from having to calculate the immediate welfare implications of how she uses it – is justified on utilitarian grounds. Indeed, part of the rationale of granting people such rights is to enable them to use their driveways without bothering to calculate utility.

There may, of course, be situations in which a person ought not to exercise her rights. Everyday morality recognizes that one may be within one's rights yet act in a way which, all things considered, is not morally justified. For example, a person may wrongly exercise her right to free speech when she makes true but needlessly hurtful statements about someone else. Nevertheless, it may be wrong for others to interfere with the exercise of that right. This point is a commonplace, with which utilitarians will agree. Recognizing the importance of supporting certain rights, utilitarians will rarely if ever censure people for failing to maximize utility when they exercise them. They will encourage people to act for the best, but not rebuke them for failing to do so when they act within their rights and those rights are defensible on utilitarian grounds. Still less are they likely to tolerate others interfering with those rights. Because it is beneficial for people to adhere to certain norms without calculating utilities, utilitarians will seek to encourage people to internalize a firm commitment to respecting the rights of others.

Moreover, the critics are mistaken if they suppose that a utilitarian-minded parking official will sometimes (in ordinary, non-emergency situations) choose not to enforce Mary's right to have her driveway free of obstructing vehicles. To begin with, parking control officials will rarely if ever know with certainty that making an exception to the rules will maximize well-being in the long run. Yet, they know (Lyons grants) that the system is justified, that it cannot be improved upon, and that tolerating violations weakens respect for the rights of people like Mary. And they rightly believe that it is their professional responsibility to enforce rights and regulations fairly and uniformly. Although they are presumably permitted to exercise their discretion when they encounter ambiguous, irregular, or emergency situations, it is not part of their job – indeed, it is a breach of their office – to set aside the rules in routine circumstances because of their on-the-spot estimates of welfare. Thus, even if a parking official knows that Mary is away at work and will not be inconvenienced by the shopper who has parked in front of her driveway, the official will still believe himself obliged to issue a ticket.

Lyons rejects this argument, contending that utilitarians offer no evidence that it would maximize utility for officials to internalize a commitment to upholding the rights and rules that utilitarians are seeking to institutionalize. But this assertion is tendentious and inaccurate. Because of their support for those rights and rules, utilitarians want officials to take them seriously. They appreciate the advantages of having officials feel bound to enforce the law, regardless of their personal estimates of utility. Again, the analogy with baseball is instructive. The umpire must throw the batter out after three strikes, even if he thinks permitting him one more chance would, in this particular case, make for a better game.

Lyons overlooks the fact that even if a utilitarian official acknowledges that a person's violating a right enhanced welfare in the circumstances, the official may justifiably choose to punish the person anyway. Imagine an able-bodied driver who infracts a valid moral and legal rule by parking for an hour in a place reserved for handicapped drivers and that the driver's doing so maximized good (either because no handicapped driver happened to be seeking a parking place during that time or because the benefits to the able-bodied driver outweighed whatever inconvenience the handicapped driver suffered). Although she understands these facts, a utilitarian traffic judge will nevertheless refuse to waive the fine the able-bodied driver receives in order to reinforce the general norm. Punishing the able-bodied driver will help discourage others from violating this rule whenever they calculate that it would be utility maximizing to do so, a pattern of behavior that could quickly come to destroy the practice of saving parking spaces for handicapped drivers.

Personal Liberty

Human rights designate certain important interests that people have, interests which utilitarians desire to safeguard. Those interests include having certain areas of decision-making free from the need to subordinate one's choices to the wishes and interests of others. Personal autonomy – the ability to shape for oneself the important features of one's own life – is central to well-being on any plausible conception of it. Without autonomy human beings cannot flourish; their personal and moral growth will be retarded, and some of their important talents and abilities will go unexplored and undeveloped. We promote autonomy by providing individuals with a zone of personal independence and choice, where they are free to pursue their own good by their own lights – that is, to follow their own interests and inclinations and to determine for themselves how important aspects of their lives go. Although it enhances well-being to encourage autonomy and respect personal choice, human liberty has limits. People do not have a right to do whatever they want regardless of the damage that others suffer. (When Hobbes says otherwise, he is imagining an anarchical, pre-social state of nature, which he describes as "a war of every man, against every man.") Other individuals and society as a whole have interests that legitimately constrain our choices.

How, then, are we to delineate the boundary between personal choice and individual freedom, on the one hand, and the good of others and the legitimate interests of society, on the other? When is it right for society to constrain the liberty of its members? These broad questions are difficult to answer because the underlying issues are complicated and because conflicting values seem to be at stake. As a result, many people, including a number of utilitarians, believe that we can decide only on a case by case basis where to draw the line between society's interests and individual freedom. In his famous essay *On Liberty*, however, John Stuart Mill advocated "one very simple principle" as the correct one for determining when society can justifiably restrict or interfere with the liberty of individuals to do as they wish. It is to that principle that we now turn.

Mill's Liberty Principle

Whether we have in view legal penalties or less formal social coercion, Mill urged that:

> the sole end for which mankind are warranted, individually or collectively, in interfering with the liberty of action of any of their number is self-protection. That the only purpose for which power can be rightfully exercised over any member of a civilized community, against his will, is to prevent harm to others . . . . The only part of the conduct of anyone for which he is amenable to society is that which concerns others. In the part which merely concerns himself, his independence is, of right, absolute. Over himself, over his body and mind, the individual is sovereign. (9)

Mill's principle applies only to adults of sound mind, not to children or the mentally ill, and it concerns not only legal compulsion and control but also informal sanctions and social pressure, including the coercion of public opinion.

With regard to adults, then, society may interfere only with conduct that harms or risks harming others. To say that society is entitled to restrict or regulate such conduct does not entail that society must restrict it, only that it has a right to. Society is free to decide that it is best to allow certain kinds of conduct even though they do or might harm others. For example, although the interests of others are damaged when a company drives a competitor out of business by selling a better product, society might permit such conduct because it believes that business competition improves productivity and benefits consumers. An individual's actions can injure or risk damage to the interests of others in various ways and to different degrees. But however society decides to deal with such conduct, for Mill the essential point is that society ought never to restrict conduct that is self-regarding, that is, that affects only the individual and those who freely choose to associate with her.

Mill's liberty principle implies, in particular, that society is not justified in coercing a person for his or her own benefit:

His own good, either physical or moral, is not a sufficient warrant. He cannot rightfully be compelled to do or forbear because it will be better for him to do so, because it will make him happier, because, in the opinions of others, to do so would be wise or even right. These are good reasons for remonstrating with him, or reasoning with him, or persuading him, or entreating him, but not for compelling him or visiting him with any evil in case he do otherwise. To justify that, the conduct from which it is desired to deter him must be calculated to produce evil to someone else. (9)

Because Mill's liberty principle strikes a chord that resonates with many of us, it is easy to overlook how radical it is and the extent to which we countenance violations of it every day. The evidence of this is the explosive growth in the twentieth century of paternalistic legislation.

Paternalistic laws or regulations are intended to protect people from harming themselves or behaving unwisely. Laws requiring us to keep the brakes on our cars in working order are necessary to protect others; they restrict our liberty in order to prevent us from injuring other people. By contrast, laws compelling adults to wear seat belts are paternalistic; they prevent us from hurting ourselves, not from harming others. Other examples of laws that appear to be paternalistic and thus contrary to Mill's principle are laws against swimming at certain beaches when no lifeguard is present, laws requiring motorcyclists to wear helmets, laws preventing people from choosing to take drugs like heroin or cocaine, and laws that forbid landowners from building homes on risky sites like the sides of cliffs. Although we may disagree with some of these laws, most people assume that in some cases it is sensible and perfectly legitimate for society to restrict people's conduct for their own benefit. Closely related to paternalistic laws are moralistic laws intended to prevent individuals from acting in ways that society deems immoral even though others are unaffected. Laws against selling your sexual services or that forbid adults from purchasing pornography are moralistic, as are laws outlawing homosexual acts between consenting adults (laws that the U.S. Supreme Court has upheld as constitutional).

Some laws that appear to be paternalistic or moralistic may, on closer inspection, turn out to be justified by other considerations that do not run afoul of Mill's liberty principle. For example, if drug addicts endanger others, if pornography fosters violence against women, if society must assume the burden of caring for motorcyclists who are crippled by head injuries, or if it must spend money sending out search parties to find inexperienced cross-country skiers who get lost in wilderness areas, then there are non-paternalistic grounds for interfering with the behavior in question. This is not to say that such grounds are conclusive, or that they justify outlawing the activity altogether (we might, for example, require motorcyclists to purchase disability insurance if they wish to ride without helmets). The point here is simply that these issues are often complex, and when people advocate restricting individual liberty in some way, they sometimes intermingle paternalistic and non-paternalistic considerations.

Mill's principle rules any appeal to paternalistic (or moralistic) concerns out of bounds. However, when people defend paternalistic laws, they generally do so on utilitarian (or utilitarian-sounding) grounds. Thus, the main argument for requiring people to don helmets on motorcycles is that reducing the number of serious or fatal head injuries to motorcyclists outweighs the inconvenience or loss of pleasure they suffer from having to wear helmets. But if utilitarian concerns underlie paternalism, how can Mill square his liberty principle with his commitment to utilitarianism? We will look at this question more closely later. For his part, however, Mill affirms in *On Liberty* that happiness or utility is the ultimate basis for deciding all ethical questions, "but it must be utility in the largest sense, grounded on the permanent interests of man as a progressive being." And these interests, he believes, "authorize the subjection of individual spontaneity to external control only in respect to those actions of each which concern the interest of other people" (10). When we view human well-being from a broad and long-term perspective, we see that "mankind are greater gainers by suffering each other to live as seems good to themselves than by compelling each to live as seems good to the rest" (12).

As mentioned, Mill is clear that as soon as the individual's conduct affects prejudicially the interests of others, society has jurisdiction over it. If a person's actions injure others or risk harm to them, there is a prima facie case for punishing the person through law or social disapprobation. In addition, an individual may rightfully be compelled to do certain things for the benefit of others – for example, to give evidence in court, share in the common defense, save the life of another, or protect the innocent from ill usage. "But," argues Mill,

> there is a sphere of action in which society, as distinguished from the individual, has, if any, only an indirect interest: comprehending all that portion of a person's life and conduct which affects only himself, or if it also affects others, only with their free, voluntary, and undeceived consent and participation. When I say only himself, I mean directly, and in the first instance. (11)

When "a person's conduct affects the interests of no persons besides himself, or need not affect them unless they like," society has no business

199

interfering with it. "In all such cases, there should be perfect freedom, legal and social, to do the action and stand the consequences" (73–4).

The main reason for this, Mill says, is that the individual is the person best able to judge what is good for him, as well as being the person with the strongest interest in his well-being.[22] When society interferes and overrules the individual's judgment, this is likely to be on the basis of presumptions that are either wrong or else misapplied to his own case by those who are unacquainted with his circumstances. "The strongest of all the arguments against the interference of the public with purely personal conduct is that, when it does interfere, the odds are that it interferes wrongly and in the wrong place" (81). Mill is fervent on this point. When the majority regulates the self-regarding conduct of the minority, it is at best imposing on other people its opinion of what is good or bad for them. More often, the majority simply ignores the interests of the minority in its haste to outlaw as an injury to itself conduct that it regards as foolish or distasteful.[23]

Mill is not saying that when we fault people for their self-regarding conduct, we must put our own judgment aside and continue to treat them as we did before. If we deem someone to be a blockhead, to be deficient in self-control, or to lack self-respect, we can express our opinion, and we can warn others against the person. Just as we are free to avoid people we don't like, so we can change our relations with those whose self-regarding conduct we find foolish, base, or perverse. We can, if we choose, cease to grant them favors or disassociate ourselves from them entirely. What we should not do, however, is to try to punish or retaliate against them for self-regarding behavior we disapprove of, nor should we attempt to force them to change their conduct. If your heavy drinking means (in the words of a country song) that "old friends don't come 'round much any more," you are not being punished; you are simply suffering what Mill would call a "natural penalty" of your chosen, self-regarding conduct.

---

[22] Cf. Mill, *Later Letters*, 762, and *Political Economy*, 311. Other nineteenth-century utilitarians made the same point; see Austin, *Province of Jurisprudence Determined*, 95–6.

[23] Here Mill's defense of liberty connects with his disdain for ethical intuitionism: "Nine-tenths of all moralists and speculative writers . . . teach that things are right because they are right; because we feel them to be so. They tell us to search in our own minds and hearts for laws of conduct binding on ourselves and on all others. What can the poor public do but apply these instructions and make their own personal feelings of good and evil, if they are tolerably unanimous in them, obligatory on all the world?" (*On Liberty*, 82).

200

Challenges to the Liberty Principle

Since its publication in 1859, *On Liberty* has kindled political and philosophical controversy. Some theorists reject Mill's principle on the grounds that a person's actions, even when they appear to concern only herself, almost always affect other people as well. Mill does not deny this point, and he is far from believing that each person is an island. He maintains, rather, that there is some individual conduct that has no direct or significant impact on anyone other than the individual herself. If others have an interest in what she does, that interest is only indirect and of negligible weight compared to the individual's own interest. Nor, as we have seen, is Mill denying that individuals have duties to others. Whether a bachelor gets drunk at home on his day off from work is his own business, but this is false of a police officer on duty or of a parent with children to look after. Finally, Mill insists that he is not advocating selfish individualism. Not only do we have duties to others, but we should also encourage people to choose what is best for themselves – in particular, to exercise their higher faculties and to eschew worthless or degraded activities. We can advise them, and we can warn them. "But neither one person, nor any number of persons, is warranted in saying to another human creature of ripe years that he shall not do with his life for his own benefit what he chooses to do with it" (74).

Mill anticipated the objection that society has a right to prevent an individual from setting a bad example for others. To this he rejoins that if the conduct does indeed harm the individual, then the example will be a salutary one because it shows the deleterious results of the behavior in question. Mill also reminds us that, when it comes to dissuading individuals from self-regarding conduct that is base or harmful, society already has almost absolute power over their education and upbringing. In addition, society has conventional opinion on its side as well as the "natural penalties" or inevitable ill consequences of the conduct itself. Society does not also need the power to prevent adults from engaging in freely chosen self-regarding conduct of which it disapproves.

Still, there is the question of what exactly counts as harm to others and of when our conduct can be said to directly or significantly affect their interests. A number of commentators have thought that Mill was vague on this point and that this vagueness threatens to undermine the liberty principle's viability. If your drinking upsets your friends, is this not a harm that you should consider? An apparently self-regarding action can, it seems, affect others in the sense that they dislike it, find it repugnant, or for some other reason are distressed by your doing it. Some people are bothered by knowing that others read pornography, worship Satan, or enjoy having sex with strangers, and parents sometimes lose sleep worrying about how their grown children are living their lives. This seems to make the conduct in question other regarding and hence potentially open to restriction. Mill, however, was adamant that the harm to others must be real and not imaginary or self-imposed. Mill views the supposed distress of those who disapprove of what others do in private as a "merely contingent or . . . constructive injury" (80), and he gives it no weight. The supposed harm done to the distressed person is, in a sense, self-induced because it depends solely on the person's own attitudes and desires. In Mill's view, we do not prejudice people's interests if, without causing them any discernible damage, we ignore their likes and dislikes when choosing how to live our own life.[24]

There is an extensive secondary literature probing this and other aspects of Mill's liberty principle and debating its application to specific situations. Mill devoted most of the final chapter of *On Liberty* to analyzing problematic cases, but certain theoretical puzzles remain,[25] and real life can throw up complicated factual predicaments. For example, behavior that appears self-regarding (my agreeing to work for half the minimum wage) may turn out to damage the important interests of others (whose endeavor to earn a living wage will be undercut if desperate people are permitted to work for peanuts) and thus fall outside the scope of the liberty principle after all. Difficult cases can also arise when a person's decision is not fully voluntary, rests on misinformation, or seems unreasonable or even irrational given the person's own goals and values. However, there is no reason to assume that the liberty principle must provide an immediate and facile solution to every possible question about the proper limits of liberty. For present purposes, we do not need to pursue how best to apply Mill's principle in various borderline cases. Instead, we return to the question of whether, consistent with his utilitarianism, Mill can defend his principle as firmly and unequivocally as he does.

Utilitarianism and the Liberty Principle

The philosophical problem is that Mill's commitment to personal liberty appears virtually absolute, and yet it seems that utilitarianism can at best

---

[24] Riley, " 'One very simple principle,' " 22.
[25] For example, do people have the liberty to sell themselves into slavery? Mill thought not.

supply a presumption in favor of personal freedom, not the categorical underwriting of it that Mill urges. Utilitarians recognize the importance of personal liberty for human well-being, but their support for liberty must, it seems, be empirical and contingent, allowing for possible exceptions. Mill implies as much when he writes that "the odds are" that when society interferes with individual choice, it will make things worse. This suggests that sometimes interference doesn't make things worse. Accordingly, many commentators believe that in endorsing the liberty principle almost unconditionally, Mill goes further than a utilitarian approach warrants, supplementing his argument with an implicit appeal to values other than welfare.

The commentators may be right that there are non-utilitarian aspects to Mill's stirring defense of liberty. But even if this is true (and Mill would have denied that it is), the more important question for us is whether it is possible to make a compelling case for the liberty principle on purely utilitarian grounds. Mill adduces some of the most pertinent utilitarian considerations in its favor in Chapter III of *On Liberty*, entitled "Of Individuality, as One of the Elements of Well-Being," where he upholds the value of individuality and opposes blind submission to custom and tradition.

Mill is not against custom or tradition as such; his point is that one needs to interpret and use in one's own way the ideas and experience that tradition and custom represent. As he sees it, individuality entails deliberating and choosing for oneself the direction and content of one's life. It thus requires personal liberty. When people lack liberty, they are guided not by their own character – by their own desires, needs, and choices – but by conformity to what others believe and do. When this is the case, then "there is wanting one of the principal ingredients of human happiness, and quite the chief ingredient of individual and social progress" (54). Why is this?

One might answer that liberty promotes happiness because people like making choices; they enjoy governing themselves and find it fulfilling to direct their own lives. However, it is debatable whether people always prefer to think for themselves and resist having others structure their choices or direct their lives. Certainly, psychologists have noted that people sometimes seem content to follow the crowd and that some individuals seem positively to fear personal choice and responsibility. It is probably for this reason that Mill does not claim simply that liberty makes people happy.

Instead Mill argues that liberty is valuable because without choice, individuals cannot develop any of the qualities which are the distinctive endowment of a human being. The human faculties of perception, judgment, discriminative feeling, mental activity, and even moral preference are exercised only in making a choice .... He who lets the world, or his own portion of it, choose his plan of life for him has no need of any other faculty than the ape-like one of imitation. He who chooses his plan for himself employs all his faculties.[26]

The point that liberty and choice develop our distinctively human talents might look like a perfectionist (and thus non-utilitarian) argument for liberty, but Mill's remarks suggest two possible links between personal liberty and individual well-being. First, as a rule, developing these capacities makes a person's life go better because they enhance the person's ability to negotiate her way through the world, to promote her own interests, and to satisfy her needs and desires. Second, to realize one's self by developing and exercising these higher-level abilities can itself be an important source of satisfaction. People tend to enjoy, and to derive a sense of accomplishment from, using and improving their talents, especially their mental abilities.

For these two reasons, then, the "free development of individuality is one of the leading essentials of well-being" (54). Furthermore, as people begin to develop and exercise their talents through choice, they come more and more to desire to guide their own lives. Personal liberty becomes a necessary ingredient of their happiness. Although it may be false that everyone desires the freedom to direct his or her own life, it does seem, as Mill thought, that under the right circumstances – in particular, as they experience liberty and develop the capacity to choose and think for themselves – people want increasingly to govern themselves and take satisfaction in doing so. If this is correct, then liberty not only promotes well-being, but also the exercise of choice strengthens the desire for it, thus tying well-being yet more intimately to liberty.

Mill grants that someone who lacked the necessary qualities to choose for himself might nevertheless "be guided in some good path, and kept out of harm's way" by others. But what, he asks, will be the person's "comparative worth as a human being?" What matters, Mill contends, is not merely what we do, but how and why we do it. It is in this connection that he lays such stress on what he calls "character." This is what a person has when his

---

[26] *On Liberty*, 56. In *Political Economy*, Mill writes: "To be prevented from doing what one is inclined to, from acting according to one's own judgment of what is desirable, is not only always irksome, but always tends, *pro tanto*, to starve the development of some portion of the bodily or mental faculties, either sensitive or active" (306–7).

"desires and impulses are his own – are the expression of his own nature, as it has been developed and modified by his own culture" (57). This emphasis on the value of character may sound like an argument for liberty based on the intrinsic value of autonomy or on a perfectionist ideal, rather than on welfare. But Mill is sounding some deep and properly utilitarian themes.

A central one of these is that full and profound human well-being involves activity. Happiness is not (or at least not predominantly) a passive thing – a commodity that someone can give us. Even if they protect us from harm and furnish us with the necessities of life (as parents do children), for others to choose for us and to guide our lives as adults is compatible with our achieving only rudimentary well-being. To realize greater well-being, individuals must determine their own way.

Mill believes that human nature is more like a tree than a machine; it "requires to grow and develop itself on all sides, according to the tendency of [its] inward forces" (57). Because people differ, they require different conditions to develop and be happy. Free choice makes this diversity possible. Without it, "people can neither obtain their fair share of happiness, nor grow up to the mental, moral, and aesthetic stature of which their nature is capable" (65). For this reason, a person's "own mode of laying out his existence is the best, not because it is the best in itself, but because it is his own mode" (64). This remark is more radical than the proposition that individuals are the best judge of what is good for them or that activity is essential to human satisfaction. It is more radical because it implies that something cannot be best for a person unless it is rooted in her authentic choices. Because what is good for the person must grow from her, it is impossible for something to be imposed on her and at the same time be what is best for her.

As previously noted, Mill affirms not only that liberty is central to individual happiness, but also that it is "quite the chief ingredient of individual and social progress." In this vein, he argues that the individuality that liberty makes possible is socially beneficial because it stimulates the lives of others, even those who do not desire liberty. Individuality is also a source of creativity, of novel ideas, and of fresh "experiments of living," which are needed to prevent even the best beliefs and practices from degenerating into mechanical tradition. By encouraging individuality and, thus, a "plurality of paths" and "many-sided development," respect for personal liberty is the main source of social progress (69). In line with this, Mills states in his *Autobiography* that *On Liberty* highlights "a single truth," namely, "the importance, to man and society, of a large variety in types of character, and of giving full freedom to human nature to expand itself in innumerable and conflicting directions" (150). However, if society hopes to

205

progress by fostering individuality, it cannot channel people's liberty in pre-selected directions. Society can, of course, choose to encourage personal liberty or to stifle it. But if it is to reap the benefits Mill describes, society cannot grant people freedom and yet permit them to exercise it only in certain favored ways.

This, then, is the last of the utilitarian or welfare-oriented considerations that Mill provides in favor of the liberty principle. He successfully highlights some important links between personal liberty and human well-being, but are these enough to secure the liberty principle? Do they underwrite a basic right to live our lives as we please insofar as our actions do not injure others? Ultimately, these questions must be left for the reader to answer. Mill's utilitarian case for liberty rests on his understanding of human nature and of the sources of well-being, happiness, and satisfaction and, as we saw in Chapter 2, these are matters about which there is no consensus. Philosophers disagree about the meaning of well-being, and psychologists and social scientists are a long way from comprehending all the factors that promote or retard it.

Nevertheless, I maintain that the liberty principle has a firm utilitarian basis, that there are cogent grounds for enshrining it as a basic human right, and that a failure to do so spells a significant loss in long-term human welfare for the reasons Mill discusses. The only plausible rival to a right to personal liberty is (what we might call) a "liberty presumption," that is, a prima facie or overrideable assumption in its favor. Although a liberty presumption would put the burden of proof on those wishing to restrict an individual's self-regarding conduct, it would permit them to do so if they provided credible paternalistic grounds for such interference. Yet, if personal liberty were merely a presumption and not a right, then the door would be open to abuse; in practice unnecessary and counterproductive restrictions on individuals would almost certainly be authorized.

The utilitarian philosopher Rolf Sartorius believes that we can justify exceptions to the liberty principle, without being ad hoc, when "identifiable classes of individuals can be shown to be likely to manifest choice behavior inconsistent with their [own] preferences." In these cases, "the odds may change in favor of interfering with their personal liberty, if necessary, in order to protect them against themselves. Mill's principle can and should be modified accordingly." In line with this, Sartorius defends statutes making helmets compulsory for motorcyclists as a case "in which it is empirically demonstrable that people will act against their own interests if not coerced into acting otherwise."[27] However, this defense of

[27] Sartorius, *Individual Conduct*, 157.

selective paternalism is open to criticism, criticism that highlights the strength of Mill's position.

First, it is far from obvious that the paternalist's judgment about what is good for motorcyclists is better informed than their own judgment. The paternalist believes that it is foolish not to wear a helmet, but it doesn't follow from this that it is foolish from the point of view of the motorcyclists who choose to run that risk. Second, even if riding helmetless is inadvisable given the motorcyclists' own values and desires, we mustn't forget Mill's point that there is an alternative to paternalistic coercion: we can educate people about the dangers of motorcycling without a helmet and try to convince them that the joys of doing so are not worth the gamble. Third, forcing otherwise rational people to behave a certain way because we cannot persuade them to act as we think best involves a welfare cost. In forcing them to act contrary to their own judgment of what is desirable, we do something they will find disagreeable, we restrict their individuality, and we hinder their development and growth. Moreover, when we rely on coercion, we lessen the need to treat people as adults by trying to persuade them with reason. We take the pressure off society to raise and educate people to be thoughtful and reflective choosers, which in turn makes it more likely that in the future we will have to fall back on coercion to prevent them from making poor choices. Finally, permitting paternalistic interference sets a dangerous precedent. If we applaud the regulating of self-regarding conduct we judge reckless or imprudent, we shouldn't be surprised when personal conduct we approve or think benign is restricted because others believe it misguided.

For these reasons, I believe that utilitarians should endorse the liberty principle as a basic right. They should seek to institutionalize this right and strive to inculcate in others, and internalize in themselves, a commitment to it. In some cases it may be difficult to determine precisely what the liberty principle requires, and in other cases it may be possible to square certain weak forms of paternalism with a commitment to it.[28] Nevertheless, the utilitarian case for Mill's "one very simple principle" is strong.

---

[28] For seminal discussions, see Dworkin, "Paternalism," and Feinberg, *Social Philosophy*, 45–52.

7

Justice, Welfare, and Economic Distribution

In any society, the allocation of income, land, riches, and other worldly assets can lead to contention over particular goods as well as to broader political disputes over the rules, policies, or institutions that govern the distribution of those goods. Often these disputes simply reflect conflicts of interest among individuals or groups, but sometimes they also represent disagreements over the fairness or justice of a society's way of distributing socioeconomic benefits and burdens. Given the relative scarcity of material resources, deciding who should get what – or, more fundamentally, determining the rules and procedures for deciding who should get what – is an important moral task. Put simply, the question is: on what basis should economic goods and services be allocated?

Philosophers call this the problem of distributive or economic justice, and at one level the utilitarian answer to it is simple and straightforward. Utilitarianism supports establishing and maintaining that set of economic policies and institutions, whatever it is, that will maximize social well-being in the long run. Although helpful, this general answer leaves open the exact nature of the economic arrangements that utilitarians will favor. In this chapter, we shall explore the implications of a utilitarian approach to questions of economic allocation in more detail, contrasting it with two rival contemporary theories of distributive justice, which have been enormously influential: the libertarianism of Robert Nozick and the social-contract egalitarianism of John Rawls. But first some facts.

Some Facts about Poverty and Inequality

The topic of justice and economic distribution has profound practical implications because it goes to the heart of who in society ought to get

208

what. This is evident when one considers the disparities in income, wealth, and life prospects that actually exist among the citizens of one's own country. To set the real-world context for the discussion of economic justice that follows, this section presents some facts and figures about poverty and economic inequality in the United States.

According to the U.S. Census Bureau, one in every seven Americans lives in poverty. That's over 36 million people, about 13.9 million of whom are children. An additional 12 million or more people live on incomes only slightly above the poverty line of $12,158 for a family of three and $15,569 for a family of four. Although the rate of poverty is down slightly from the early 1990s, it is still higher than it was in the 1970s.[1] Today, one out of every four Americans lives in substandard housing, and a Columbia University survey estimates that 13.5 million adult Americans have been homeless at some time.[2]

People in different walks of life and in different circumstances experience poverty. Many work but are unable to pull themselves up. The percentage of "working poor" in the United States – that is, those who work full-time, year-round while earning an income below the poverty line – is at its highest level in over twenty years. Since 1977, the poverty rate for working families with children has climbed from 7.7 percent to 11.4 percent.[3] In 1997 the minimum wage increased to $5.15, but someone working forty hours a week, every week, for that wage cannot raise his or her family above the poverty line. Today, one out of every six workers earns only a poverty-level wage.[4]

Consider now the other end of the economic scale. *Business Week*'s annual survey of the two highest-paid executives at 362 large companies shows that their average pay (salary plus bonuses) has soared to $2.2 million and their average total compensation to $7.8 million per year.[5] Among these executives, Michael Eisner of Walt Disney Co. has long been one of the highest paid. Already an extremely wealthy man, in 1997 he was offered a ten-year pay package worth an estimated $771 million – a figure that omits his annual salary and bonuses, which could bring him another $15 million per year. The pay of CEOs such as Eisner has boomed in recent years, not

[1] U.S. Bureau of Census, *Statistical Abstract of the United States 1997* (Washington, D.C., 1997), 475.

[2] "Single mothers and welfare," *Scientific American*, October 1996, 66.

[3] *Economist*, July 8, 1995; *San Francisco Chronicle*, August 22, 1988, A4; *The Nation*, February 5, 1993.

[4] *San Francisco Examiner*, July 17, 1994, A9; *San Jose Mercury News*, July 18, 1993, 7C.

[5] *Business Week*, April 20, 1998, 65.

only absolutely, but also relative to other occupational groups like engineers, schoolteachers, and factory workers. For instance, as Table 7.1 shows, since 1980 the total compensation of CEOs in the U.S. has jumped from 42 times that of a production worker to more than 300 times greater.

Table 7.1 The growing gap between CEO pay and what others make ($)[a]

	1960	1970	1980	1990	1997
CEO	90,383	548,787	624,996	1,952,806	7,800,000
Engineer	9,828	14,695	28,486	49,365	66,498
Schoolteacher	4,995	8,626	15,970	31,166	38,930
Factory worker	4,665	6,933	15,008	22,998	23,926

[a] Figures are based on *Business Week*, April 26, 1993; April 22, 1996; April 21, 1997; and April 20, 1998.

The swelling pay of CEOs and other elite groups is part of a general trend since the 1970s toward greater inequality in the distribution of income in the United States. In the 1980s the wealthiest 1 percent of the nation, those with an average household income of $548,969, increased their share of the country's total income from 8.7 percent to 13.3 percent.[6] Since 1990, income inequality has grown even more than in the preceding decade. Today the bottom 40 percent of society is worse off in inflation-adjusted terms than it was two decades earlier.[7] While the income share of the bottom 60 percent has fallen to its lowest ever (27.5 percent), the families that make up the top 20 percent income group now take home 49.1 percent of the total national income, their highest level since figures were first collected in 1947.[8] They make 12.7 times as much as families in the bottom fifth.[9]

This trend is even more striking when set against the background of an extremely unequal distribution of wealth in the U.S. Not only does the top 10 percent receive a disproportionate share of the total national income, they already have 68 percent of the nation's wealth in their hands. Even more striking, the top 1 percent owns nearly 40 percent of the nation's total net worth – more than is owned by the entire bottom 90 percent of U.S.

[6] *San Francisco Chronicle*, September 30, 1990, B5.
[7] *USA Today*, September 30, 1996, 1B.
[8] *San Jose Mercury News*, June 20, 1996, C1.
[9] *New York Times*, December 17, 1997, A14.

households. This economic elite owns 49 percent of all publicly held stock, 62 percent of all business assets, 78 percent of bonds and trusts, and 45 percent of nonresidential real estate for a net worth of $5.7 trillion.[10] It would, for instance, take a city of more than a quarter million average Americans (the size of Rochester, N.Y.) to equal the net worth of Bill Gates alone.

Although the information just presented is statistical and aggregate, it does raise the question of the justice of current social and economic arrangements and forces one to take seriously the issue of what principle or principles ought to guide us in assessing a society's distribution of economic goods. For how a society distributes possessions, services, and opportunities is not an unalterable fact of nature, but reflects institutions and policies that people could choose to alter.[11]

Thinking about Justice

Justice is an old concept with a rich philosophical history, but it is not the whole of morality. The complaint that something is "unjust" is more specific than that it is "bad" or "immoral." What, then, makes an act, policy, or institution unjust? Unfortunately, the terms *just* and *unjust* are vague, and different people use them in different ways. Still, talk of justice or injustice typically focuses on at least one of several related ideas — fairness, equality, desert, or rights.

First, justice is often used to mean *fairness*. Justice frequently concerns the fair treatment of members of groups of people or else looks backwards to the fair compensation of prior injuries. Exactly what fairness requires is difficult to say, and different standards may be pertinent in different cases. If corporate manager Smith commits bribery, he is justly punished under our laws. If other managers commit equally serious crimes but are allowed to escape punishment, then Smith suffers a comparative injustice because he was unfairly singled out. On the other hand, Smith and other white-collar criminals are treated unfairly and thus unjustly, although this time for the opposite reason, if stiffer sentences are meted out to common criminals for less grave offenses.

---

[10] *New York Times*, April 21, 1994, A1, and April 17, 1995, A1.
[11] For example, although the United States has the highest level of child poverty of any industrialized country, it chooses to spend only 0.6 percent of its gross national product on basic income support for children. *New York Times*, April 17, 1995, A1; *San Francisco Chronicle*, May 12, 1989, C5, and October 7, 1996, B2.

One way unfairness creates injustice is when like cases are not treated in the same fashion. Following Aristotle, most philosophers believe that we are required, as a formal principle of justice, to treat similar cases alike except where there is some relevant difference. This principle emphasizes the role of impartiality and consistency in justice, but it is a purely formal principle because it is silent about which differences are relevant and which are not. Furthermore, satisfying this formal requirement does not guarantee that justice is done. For example, a judge who treats similar cases alike can succeed in administering fairly and non-arbitrarily a law that is itself unjust (like a statute requiring racial segregation).

Related to Aristotle's fairness requirement is a second idea commonly bound up with the concept of justice, namely, that of *equality*. Justice is frequently held to require that our treatment of people reflect their fundamental moral equality. While Aristotle's formal principle of justice does not say whether we are to assume equality of treatment until some difference between cases is shown or to assume the opposite until some relevant similarities are demonstrated, a claim of injustice based on equality is meant to place the burden of proof on those who would endorse unequal treatment. Still, the premise that all persons are equal implies relatively little about justice in economic distribution. We all believe that some differences in the treatment of persons are consistent with equality (punishment, for example), and neither respect for equality nor a commitment to equal treatment necessarily requires an equal distribution of economic goods.

Despite equality, then, individual circumstances – in particular, what a person has done – make a difference. We think it is unjust, for example, when a guilty person goes free or an innocent person hangs, regardless of how others have been treated. This suggests that justice sometimes involves, as a third aspect, something in addition to equal or impartial treatment. Justice also requires that people get what they *deserve* or, as a number of ancient moralists put it, that each receive his or her due.

This is closely related to a fourth and final idea, namely, that one is treated unjustly when one's moral *rights* are violated. John Stuart Mill, in fact, made this the defining characteristic of injustice. In his view, what distinguishes injustice from other types of wrongful behavior is that it involves a violation of the rights of some identifiable person:

> Whether the injustice consists in depriving a person of a possession, or in breaking faith with him, or in treating him worse than he deserves, or worse than other people who have no greater claims – in each case the supposition implies two things: a wrong done, and some assignable person who is

wronged . . . . It seems to me that this feature in the case – a right in some person, correlative to the moral obligation – constitutes the specific differ- ence between justice and generosity or beneficence. Justice implies something which it is not only right to do, and wrong not to do, but which some individual person can claim from us as his moral right.[12]

Rival Principles of Distribution

Justice, then, is an important subclass of morality in general, a subclass that generally involves appeals to the overlapping notions of fairness, equality, desert, and rights. Turning to the topic of distributive justice, that is, to the proper distribution of social benefits and burdens (in particular, economic benefits and burdens), a number of rival principles have been proposed. Among the principles most frequently recommended as a basis of distribution are: to each an equal share, to each according to individual need, to each according to personal effort, to each according to social contribution, and to each according to merit. Every one of these principles has its advocates, and each seems plausible in some circumstances. But only in some. There are problems with each. For example, if equality of income were guaranteed, then the lazy would receive as much as the industrious. On the other hand, effort is hard to measure and compare, and what one is able to contribute to society may depend on one's luck in being at the right place at the right time. And so on: none of the principles seems to work in enough circumstances to be defended successfully as the sole principle of justice in distribution.

It often seems that we simply employ different principles of distributive justice in different circumstances. For example, corporations in certain industries may be granted tax breaks because of their social contribution while welfare programs operate on the basis of need, and business firms award promotions for meritorious performance. Moreover, multiple princi- ples may often be relevant to a single situation, sometimes pulling in the same direction, other times pulling in different directions. Some philoso- phers are content to leave the situation here. Adopting a pluralistic approach, they deny that there is one core principle, or one unifying theory, of distributive justice. Instead, as they see it, there are various equally valid, prima facie principles of just distribution – equality, need, effort, and so on – and one must try to find the principle that best applies in the given circumstances. If several principles seem to apply, then one must weigh them the best one can.

---

[12] Mill, *Utilitarianism*, 49.

In his book *Spheres of Justice*, Michael Walzer pursues a more sophisticated version of the pluralistic approach.[13] Skeptical of the assumption that justice simply requires us to implement (in different contexts) some basic principle or set of principles, Walzer argues

> that different goods ought to be distributed for different reasons, in accordance with different procedures, by different agents; and that all these differences derive from different understandings of the social goods themselves – the inevitable product of historical and cultural particularism. (6)

Different norms and principles govern different distributive spheres, and these norms and principles are shaped by the implicit social meanings of the goods in question. He continues:

> Every social good or set of goods constitutes, as it were, a distributive sphere within which only certain criteria and arrangements are appropriate. Money is inappropriate in the sphere of ecclesiastical office . . . . There is no single standard [against which all distributions are to be measured]. But there are standards (roughly knowable even when they are also controversial) for every social good and every distributive sphere in every particular society. (10)

As Walzer sees it, distributive criteria are determined by the particular, historically shaped social meanings of the goods in question. The philosophical task is to tease out the inner logic of each type of good, thus revealing the tacit, socially shared values that govern (or should govern) its distribution. Walzer's historically informed discussion of topics like medical care or dirty and degrading work are rich and intriguing, but his view implies that, when it comes to issues of distributive justice, the best philosophers can do is to try to unravel the implicit, socially specific norms that govern the distribution of different goods in a particular society. Utilitarians disagree. They and many non-utilitarian philosophers believe that it is both possible and desirable to step further back than Walzer does from existing norms and social arrangements and to employ some independent normative principle or set of principles to assess current social practices.

The Utilitarian View of Justice

Philosophers who see distributive justice as involving an irreducible number of distinct principles or who, like Walzer, emphasize the histor-

---

[13] See also Elster, *Local Justice*.

ically specific, socially constructed character of justice are generally hostile to utilitarianism because it approaches questions of economic allocation from a simple, unifying theoretical point of view. They see utilitarians as applying a one-size-fits-all theory of justice. It is true, of course, that for utilitarians the goal of maximizing well-being ultimately determines what is just and unjust. Yet utilitarians can take on board much of what both groups of pluralistically minded philosophers have to say.

First, utilitarians can readily agree with Walzer about the importance of grasping the established norms and implicit social understandings that currently govern the distribution of various goods. Doing so is simply part of comprehending the nature and context of existing socioeconomic institutions and practices and, thus, the likely consequences of modifying them. Second, utilitarians can agree with the idea that different principles of distribution – equality, need, social contribution, and so on – may apply in different circumstances. Utilitarians reject the idea that these principles are basic, but they can accept some or all of them as secondary principles that we should follow (either usually or always) because doing so maximizes social welfare. An advantage of this approach is that "if one should question precisely how one of these rules is to be formulated or what its relative weight will be, the utilitarian has at hand a procedure that will provide an answer."[14]

This last point is one that Mill stressed. He argued that without utilitarianism to provide a determinate standard, one will always be left with a plethora of competing principles of justice, all of which seem to have some plausibility but which are mutually incompatible. Only the utilitarian standard can provide a satisfactory and intelligent way of handling controversial questions of justice and of resolving conflicts between competing principles.

Consider, for example, whether it is just that more talented workers should receive a greater remuneration. There are, Mill wrote, two possible answers to this question:

> On the negative side of the question it is argued that whoever does the best he can deserves equally well, and ought not in justice to be put in a position of inferiority for no fault of his own; that superior abilities have already advantages more than enough . . . without adding to these a superior share of the world's goods; and that society is bound in justice rather to make compensation to the less favored for this unmerited inequality of advantages than to aggravate it.

[14] Brandt, *Morality, Utilitarianism, and Rights*, 374 (emphasis omitted).

215

This argument sounds reasonable, but then so does the alternative answer:

> On the contrary side it is contended that society receives more from the more efficient laborer; that, his services being more useful, society owes him a larger return for them; that a greater share of the joint result is actually his work, and not to allow his claim to it is a kind of robbery; that, if he is only to receive as much as others, he can only be justly required to produce as much.

Here we have conflicting principles of justice. How are we to decide between them? The problem, Mill said, is that both principles seem plausible:

> Justice has in this case two sides to it, which it is impossible to bring into harmony, and the two disputants have chosen opposite sides; the one looks to what it is just that the individual should receive, the other to what it is just that the community should give.

From his or her own point of view, each disputant is unanswerable. "Any choice between them, on grounds of justice," Mill continued, "must be perfectly arbitrary." The only sensible way to resolve such controversies, he argued, is by appealing to the utilitarian standard.[15]

What Economic Arrangements Do Utilitarians Favor?

From a utilitarian perspective, an economic system is just if and only if no alternative set of institutions would benefit society more. One might perhaps call this "an ideally just system" to distinguish it from a system that is highly conducive to human well-being even though further improvements are possible (such a system might be called "basically just"). In any case, no single system is optimal for all times and places, and the economic arrangements that work well in one society may ill suit another because of cultural variations, historical context, level of economic development, and other factors. Furthermore, designing utopias won't be a high priority for utilitarians. They are likely to be less concerned with trying to draw a detailed blueprint of the ideal system for a given society than with using the utilitarian standard to recommend more specific, welfare-enhancing improvements in the society's current way of doing things.

The particular economic arrangements utilitarians favor will depend on their understanding and assessment of the relevant social, economic, and

[15] Mill, *Utilitarianism*, 56–7; see also, *Later Letters*, 1318–19.

political facts. When addressing issues of economic justice, the utilitarian must determine the various possibilities, assess their consequences, and weigh the competing options. Obviously, this is no simple task. For instance, deciding what institutional reforms would increase well-being in a particular context requires the utilitarian to consider many things, including (1) the type of economic ownership (private, public, mixed); (2) the way of organizing production and distribution in general (pure laissez faire, markets with government planning and regulation, fully centralized planning); (3) the type of authority arrangements within the units of production (worker control versus managerial prerogative); (4) the range and character of material incentives; and (5) the nature and extent of social security and welfare provisions.

Because large issues of fact and socioeconomic theory are involved, contemporary utilitarians disagree about what economic arrangements would best increase well-being in Western, industrialized countries. However, as we shall see later in this chapter, many of them strongly favor measures that would increase economic equality. This is a point with which Mill agreed.[16] In a related vein, his *Principles of Political Economy* advocates breaking down the sharp and hostile division between the producers or workers, on the one hand, and the capitalists or owners, on the other hand. Many contemporary utilitarians would concur in thinking this a good thing. Mill himself also thought that it was something the advance of civilization was bringing about. "The relation of masters and workpeople will be gradually superseded by partnership, in one of two forms: in some cases, association of the labourers with the capitalist; in others, and perhaps finally in all, association of labourers among themselves" (129). These developments would not only enhance productivity but, even more important, promote the fuller development and well-being of the people involved. The aim, Mill thought, should be to enable people "to work with or for one another in relations not involving dependence" (128).

By the association of labor and capital, Mill had in mind different schemes of profit sharing. For example, "in the American ships trading to China, it has long been the custom for every sailor to have an interest in the profits of the voyage; and to this has been ascribed the general good conduct of those seamen" (129). This sort of association would, however, eventually give way to a more complete system of worker cooperatives:

The form of association, however, which if mankind continue to improve,

<hr>

[16] Sorting out Mill's thinking about equality is difficult. See Berger, *Happiness, Justice, and Freedom*, 157–86.

217

must be expected in the end to predominate, is not that which can exist between a capitalist as chief, and workpeople without a voice in the management, but the association of the labourers themselves on terms of equality, collectively owning the capital with which they carry on their operations, and working under managers elected and removable by themselves. (133)

In *Principles*, Mill discussed several examples of successful cooperative associations and viewed optimistically the future of the cooperative movement:

Eventually, and in perhaps a less remote future than may be supposed, we may, through the co-operative principle, see our way to a change in society, which would combine the freedom and independence of the individual, with the moral, intellectual, and economical advantages of aggregate production; and which . . . would realize, at least in the industrial department, the best aspirations of the democratic spirit. (139–40)

What that transformation implied for Mill was nothing less than "the nearest approach to social justice, and the most beneficial ordering of industrial affairs for the universal good, which it is possible at present to foresee" (140–1).

Before pursuing further utilitarianism's socioeconomic ramifications, it will prove useful to compare the theory with the two most influential, non-utilitarian approaches to distributive justice, namely, the libertarianism of Robert Nozick and the social-contract egalitarianism of John Rawls.

Nozick's Libertarianism

Nozick's influential work *Anarchy, State, and Utopia* starts from the premise that people have certain basic moral rights, which he calls "Lockean rights." By alluding to the political philosophy of John Locke (1632–1704), Nozick wishes to underscore that these rights are both negative and natural. They are negative because they require only that people forbear from acting in certain ways – in particular, that we refrain from interfering with others. Beyond this, we are not obliged to do anything positive for anyone else, nor is anyone required to do anything positive for us. We have no right, for example, to be provided with satisfying work or with any material goods that we might need. These negative rights, according to Nozick, are natural in the sense that we possess them independently of any social or political institutions.

These individual rights impose firm, virtually absolute restrictions (or, in Nozick's phrase, "side constraints") on how we may act. We cannot morally infringe someone's rights for any purpose. Not only are we forbidden to interfere with a person's liberty in order to promote the general good, we are prohibited from doing so even if violating that individual's rights would somehow prevent other individuals' rights from being violated. Each individual is autonomous and responsible, and should be left to fashion his or her own life free from the interference of others – as long as this is compatible with the right of others to do the same. Only an acknowledgment of this almost absolute right to be free from coercion, Nozick argues, fully respects the distinctiveness of individuals, each with a unique life to lead.

A belief in these rights shapes Nozick's theory of economic justice, which he calls the *entitlement theory*. Essentially, Nozick maintains that people are entitled to their holdings (that is, goods, money, and property) as long as they have acquired them fairly. Stated another way, if you have obtained your possessions without violating other people's Lockean rights, then you are entitled to them and may dispose of them as you choose. No one else has a legitimate claim on them. If you have secured a vast fortune without injuring other people, defrauding them, or otherwise violating their rights, then you are morally permitted to do with your fortune whatever you wish – bequeath it to a relative, endow a university, or squander it in riotous living. Even though other people may be going hungry, justice imposes no obligation on you to help them.

The first principle of Nozick's entitlement theory concerns the original acquisition of holdings – that is, the appropriation of unheld goods or the creation of new goods. If a person acquires a holding in accordance with this principle, then he or she is entitled to it. If, for example, you retrieve minerals from the wilderness or make something out of materials you already legitimately possess, then you have justly acquired this new holding. Nozick does not spell out this principle or specify fully what constitutes a just original acquisition, but the basic idea is clear and reflects the thinking of John Locke.

Property is a moral right, said Locke, because individuals are morally entitled to the fruits of their labor. When they mix their labor with the natural world, they are entitled to the resulting product. Thus, if a man works the land, then he is entitled to the land and its products because through his labor he has put something of himself into them. This investment of self through labor is the moral basis of ownership, Locke wrote, but there are limits to this right:

In the beginning . . . men had a right to appropriate, by their labour, each

one of himself, as much of the things of nature, as he could use . . . .
Whatsoever he tilled and reaped, laid up and made use of, before it spoiled,
that was his peculiar right; whatsoever he enclosed, and could feed, and
make use of, the cattle and product was also his. But if either the grass of his
inclosure rotted on the ground, or the fruit of his planting perished without
gathering, and laying up, this part of the earth . . . was still to be looked on
as waste, and might be the possession of any other.[17]

In this early "state of nature" prior to the formation of government,
property rights were limited not only by the requirement that one not
waste what one claimed, but also by the restriction that "enough and as
good" be left for others – that is, that one's appropriation not make others
worse off. Later, however, with the introduction of money, Locke thought
that both these restrictions were overcome. You can pile up money beyond
your needs without it spoiling; and if your property is used productively
and the proceeds offered for sale, then your appropriation leaves others no
worse off than before.

Nozick's second principle concerns transfers of already-owned goods
from one person to another: how people may legitimately transfer holdings
and how they may legitimately get holdings from others. If a person
possesses a holding because of a legitimate transfer, then he or she is
entitled to it. Again, Nozick does not work out the details, but it is clear
that acquiring something by purchase, as a gift, or through exchange
would constitute a legitimate acquisition. Gaining it through theft, force,
or fraud would violate the principle of justice in transfer.

Nozick's third and final principle states that one can justly acquire a
holding only in accord with the two principles just discussed. If you come
by a holding in some other way, you are not entitled to it. Nozick sums up
his theory this way:

> 1. A person who acquires a holding in accordance with the principle of
> justice in acquisition is entitled to that holding.
>
> 2. A person who acquires a holding in accordance with the principle of
> justice in transfer, from someone else entitled to the holding, is entitled to
> the holding.
>
> 3. No one is entitled to a holding except by (repeated) applications of 1 and
> 2. (151)

In short, the distribution of goods in a society is just if and only if all are
entitled to the holdings they possess. Nozick calls his entitlement theory
"historical" because what matters is how people come to have what they

---

[17] Locke, *Second Treatise*, 23–4.

have. If people are entitled to their possessions, then the distribution of economic holdings is just, regardless of what the actual distribution happens to look like (for instance, how far above or below the average income people are) or what its consequences are.

The Wilt Chamberlain Example

Nozick argues that respect for liberty inescapably leads one to repudiate other conceptions of economic justice in favor of his entitlement approach. One of his most memorable examples features Wilt Chamberlain, the basketball star. Suppose, Nozick says, that things are distributed according to your favorite non-entitlement theory, whatever it is. (He calls this distribution D_1.) Now imagine that Wilt Chamberlain signs a contract with a team that guarantees him $5 from the price of each ticket. Whenever people buy a ticket to a game, they drop $5 into a special box with Chamberlain's name on it. To them it is worth it to see him play. Imagine then that in the course of a season a million people attend his games and Chamberlain ends up with far more than the average income – far more, indeed, than anyone else in the society earns. This result (D_2) upsets the initial distributional pattern (D_1).

Can the proponent of D_1 complain? Nozick thinks not:

> Is [Chamberlain] entitled to this income? Is this new distribution D_2, unjust? If so, why? There is *no* question about whether each of the people was entitled to the control over the resources they held in D_1; because that was the distribution (your favorite) that (for the purposes of the argument) we assumed was acceptable. Each of these persons *chose* to give [$5] of their money to Chamberlain .... If D_1 was a just distribution, and people voluntarily moved from it to D_2, transferring parts of their shares they were given under D_1 ... isn't D_2 also just? If the people were entitled to dispose of the resources to which they were entitled (under D_1), didn't this include their being entitled to give it to, or exchange it with, Wilt Chamberlain? Can anyone else complain on grounds of justice? (161)

Having defended the legitimacy of Chamberlain's new wealth, Nozick pushes his case further, arguing that any effort to maintain some initial distributional arrangement like D_1 will interfere with people's liberty to use their resources as they wish. To preserve this original distribution, he writes, society would have to "forbid capitalist acts between consenting adults":

> The general point illustrated by the Wilt Chamberlain example ... is that no [non-entitlement] principle of justice can be continuously realized

without continuous interference with people's lives. Any favored pattern would be transformed into one unfavored by the principle, by people choosing to act in various ways; for example, by people exchanging goods and services with other people, or giving things to other people . . . . To maintain a pattern one must either continually interfere to stop people from transferring resources as they wish to, or continually (or periodically) interfere to take from some persons resources that others for some reason chose to transfer to them. (163)

The Libertarian View of Liberty

Nozick and other libertarians are committed to leaving market relations – buying, selling, and other exchanges – unregulated. Force and fraud are forbidden, of course, but there should be no interference with the uncoerced exchanges of consenting individuals. Libertarians are for economic laissez faire and against any government interference with the marketplace, even if the point of such interference is to enhance the performance of the economy. This is because their allegiance to the market is totally nonconsequentialist.

By contrast, utilitarians have sometimes defended laissez faire on the ground that an unregulated market works better than either a planned, socialist economy or the sort of regulated capitalism with some welfare benefits that we have in the United States and most other developed countries. But if a utilitarian supports laissez faire, he or she does so because of its consequences. Convince a utilitarian that some other form of economic organization better promotes human well-being, and the utilitarian will advocate that instead. With libertarians this is assuredly not the case. Most libertarians probably believe that unregulated capitalist behavior best promotes everyone's interests. But even if, hypothetically, a libertarian like Nozick were convinced that some sort of socialism or welfare capitalism outperforms laissez-faire capitalism – greater productivity, shorter working day, higher standard of living – he or she would still spurn this alternative as morally unacceptable.

Libertarians say that their commitment to an unrestricted market reflects the priority of liberty over other values. However, libertarians do not value liberty in the mundane sense of people being free to do what they want to do. Rather, libertarians understand freedom in terms of their theory of rights, thus building a commitment to private property into their concept of liberty. According to them, being able to do what you want does not automatically represent an increase in your liberty. It does so only if you remain within the boundaries set by the Lockean rights of others. Likewise, one is unfree or coerced only when one's rights are infringed.

222

Imagine, for example, that having purchased the forest in which I occasionally stroll, the new owner bars my access to it. It would seem that my freedom has been reduced because I can no longer ramble where I wish. But libertarians deny this. My liberty is restricted if and only if someone violates my Lockean rights, which no one has done. Suppose that I go for a hike in the forest anyway. If the sheriff's deputies arrest me, they prevent me from doing what I want to do. But according to libertarianism, they do not restrict my liberty, nor do they coerce me. Why not? Because my hiking in the forest violates the landowner's rights.

Here utilitarians seem driven to an unusual use of familiar terminology, but they have no choice. They cannot admit that abridging the landowner's freedom to do as he wants with his property would expand my freedom. If they did, then their theory would be in jeopardy. They would have to acknowledge that restricting the liberty or property rights of some could enhance the liberty of others. In other words, if their theory committed them simply to promoting as much as possible the goal of people doing what they want to do, then libertarians would be in the position of balancing the freedom of some against the freedom of others. But this sort of balancing and trading off of goods is just what libertarians dislike about utilitarianism.

If liberty means being free to do what you want, it's not true that libertarians value it above everything else. What they value are Lockean property rights, which then set the parameters of liberty. Libertarians frequently contend (1) that private property is necessary for freedom and (2) that any society that doesn't respect private property rights is coercive. But libertarianism makes (1) true by definition, and (2) is incorrect. Any system of property (whether Lockean, socialist, or something in between) necessarily puts restrictions on people's conduct; its rules are coercive. What one system of property permits, another forbids. Society X prevents me from hiking in your woods, whereas society Y prevents you from stopping me. Both systems of rules are coercive. Both grant some freedoms and withhold others.

Desert, Entitlement, and Property Rights

Libertarians defend market relations, then, as necessary to respect human liberty (as their theory understands liberty). However, in doing so, libertarians do not assert that, morally speaking, people deserve what they receive from others through gift or exchange, only that they are entitled to whatever they receive. Imagine that Jack makes a fortune from having been in the right place at the right time with his beanie babies, while Jill loses her investment because the market for bottled water collapses. The libertarian position is not that Jack deserves to be wealthy and Jill does not; rather, it is that Jack is entitled to his holdings if he has acquired them in accordance with the principles of justice.

The same point comes up with regard to gifts and inheritance. Inheritance strikes many people as patently unfair. How can it be just, they ask, that one child inherits a vast fortune, the best schooling, and social, political, and business connections that will ensure its future, while another child inherits indigence, inferior schooling, and connections with crime? At birth neither youngster deserves anything – a fact suggesting, perhaps, that an equal division of holdings and opportunities would be the only fair allocation. For his part, Nozick contends that deserving has no bearing on the justice of inherited wealth; people are simply entitled to it as long as it is not ill gotten. Or looking at it the other way, if one is entitled to one's holdings, then one has a right to do with them as one wishes, including using them to benefit one's children.

According to libertarians, a totally free market is necessary for people to exercise their fundamental rights. In certain circumstances, however, unregulated market transactions can lead to disastrous results. Unfortunately, this is more than just a theoretical possibility. In an important study of several of this century's worse famines, Amartya Sen has shown how in certain circumstances changing market entitlements, the dynamics of which he attempts to unravel, have led to mass starvation.[18] Although the average person thinks of famine as caused simply by a shortage of food, Sen and other experts have established that famines are frequently accompanied by no shortfall of food in absolute terms. Indeed, even more food may be available during a famine than in non-famine years – if one has the money to buy it. Famine occurs because large numbers of people lack the financial wherewithal to obtain the necessary food.

Libertarians would find it immoral and unjust to force people to aid the starving or to tax the affluent to set up programs to relieve hunger or prevent famines in the first place. Utilitarians are not alone in finding this appalling. Yet Nozick's theory treats property rights as sacrosanct. These rights are thought by him to exist prior to any social arrangements and are morally antecedent to any legislative decision that a society might make. However, Nozick's critics argue that it is a mistake to think of property as a simple, pre-social relation between a person and a physical thing.

First, property is not restricted to material objects like cars, watches, or houses. In developed societies, one may own more abstract goods, and the

[18] See Sen, *Poverty and Famines*, and Drèze and Sen, *Hunger and Public Action*.

courts have counted as property a wide range of items such as new life forms, an original idea, pension payments, the news, or a place on the welfare rolls.[19] Second, property ownership involves a bundle of different rights – for instance, to possess, use, manage, dispose of, or restrict others' access to something. The nature of this bundle differs among societies, as do the types of things that can be owned. In any society, property ownership is structured by the various implicit or explicit rules and regulations governing the legitimate acquisition and transfer of various types of goods, interests, and claims. Accordingly, most non-libertarian social and political theorists view property rights as a function of the particular institutions of a given society.

Utilitarians, of course, reject as a fiction the whole idea of a natural right to property. In their view, although various property systems can and do exist, there is no natural right that things be owned privately, collectively, or in any particular way whatsoever. The moral task is to find that property system, that way of organizing production and distribution, with the greatest utility. Yet even if one believes that under certain circumstances a person can have a natural right to some item of property, it doesn't follow, as libertarians assume, that this property right is absolute and unlimited by other moral considerations.

Rawls's Theory of Justice

John Rawls's tome *A Theory of Justice* is widely acknowledged to be the single most influential work in social and political philosophy since the Second World War, at least in the English language. Although Rawls presents his theory as an alternative to utilitarianism, he does not base his conception of justice, as Nozick does, on the postulate that individuals possess certain natural rights prior to any political or social organization. Contrary to Nozick's entitlement theory, he argues that the primary subject of justice is not, in the first instance, transactions between individuals but rather "the basic structure, the fundamental social institutions and their arrangement into one scheme." Why? As Rawls explains:

> Suppose we begin with the initially attractive idea that social circumstances and people's relationships to one another should develop over time in accordance with free agreements fairly arrived at and fully honored. Straightaway we need an account of when agreements are free and the social circumstances under which they are reached are fair. In addition, while these

[19] Becker and Kipnis, *Property*, 3–5.

conditions may be fair at an earlier time, the accumulated results of many separate and ostensibly fair agreements . . . are likely in the course of time to alter citizens' relationships and opportunities so that the conditions for free and fair agreements no longer hold. The role of the institutions that belong to the basic structure is to secure just background conditions against which the actions of individuals and associations take place. Unless this structure is appropriately regulated and adjusted, an initially just social process will eventually cease to be just, however free and fair particular transactions may look when viewed by themselves.[20]

Rawls discusses several considerations that support taking the basic structure of society as the primary subject of justice. Of particular importance is the fact that the basic structure shapes the wants, desires, hopes, and ambitions of individuals. Social conditions also affect which of our natural capacities we develop and the directions in which we develop them. Thus, an economic system is more than an institutional device for satisfying existing desires and aspirations. It also fashions those desires and aspirations.

Utilitarians will agree with the substance of these points and much else that Rawls has to say against libertarianism. They too insist on looking at the basic institutions that govern socioeconomic life and how they affect human well-being in practice, not merely at the apparent fairness or unfairness of individual transactions. However, Rawls's orientation differs from utilitarianism in some important ways. This will become clear as we examine the two main aspects of his theory: his hypothetical-contract approach and the principles of justice that he derives with it.

The Original Position

The strategy that Rawls employs to identify and justify the basic principles of justice is to imagine that people come together for the purpose of deciding on the ground rules for their society, in particular, the rules governing economic distribution. This is a thought experiment, and the question is entirely hypothetical: what principles would people choose in this sort of original position? To answer this question, one must specify the conditions that govern their choice. Rawls's idea is that people in the original position choose solely on the basis of self-interest. That is, we are to imagine that each individual wants society to be governed by the set of principles that will be best for himself or herself (and loved ones). We don't

[20] Rawls, *Political Liberalism*, 265–6.

have to imagine that people are antagonistic to one another or that they are basically selfish; we just imagine that each hopes to get the group to elect those principles that will benefit him or her more than any alternative set of principles.

The veil of ignorance. If people in the original position are supposed to choose principles on the basis of self-interest, agreement seems unlikely. Because different sets of principles would benefit different groups, conflicts of self-interest seem bound to create irreconcilable demands. As a way around this problem, Rawls asks us to imagine that people in the original position do not know what social position or status they hold in society. They do not know whether they are rich or poor, nor do they know their personal talents and characteristics – whether, for example, they are athletic or sedentary, artistic or tone-deaf, intelligent or dim-witted, physically sound or handicapped in some way. They are unaware of their race or even their sex. Behind what Rawls calls the "veil of ignorance," people in the original position know nothing about themselves personally or about what their individual situation will be once the rules are chosen and the veil is lifted. However, they do have a general knowledge of history, sociology, and psychology – although no specific information about their own society.

Because individuals in the original position are trying to advance their self-interest but are all equally ignorant of their personal predicament, they can reach agreement. The reasoning of any one person will be the same as the reasoning of each of the others. The veil-of-ignorance device thus makes agreement possible by forcing people, in effect, to be objective and impartial in their deliberations. In Rawls's view, the principles arrived at will be the principles of justice because they reflect agreement under reasonable conditions. In this respect, Rawls's method has affinities with the "ideal chooser" or "ideal observer" account of utilitarianism (mentioned at the end of Chapter 3).[21]

Choosing the principles. Although people in the original position are ignorant of their individual circumstances, they know that whatever their particular goals, interests, and talents turn out to be, they will want more, rather than less, of what Rawls calls the "primary social goods." These include not just income and wealth but also rights and liberties, powers and opportunities, and self-respect. Of course, once the veil of ignorance is lifted, people will have more specific ideas about what is good for them – they may choose a

---

[21] See also Haslett, *Equal Consideration*, 203–4.

life built around religion, one spent in commerce and industry, or one devoted to academic study. But whatever their particular goals, interests, and plans turn out to be, these will almost certainly be furthered, and definitely never limited, by the fact that people in the original position secured for themselves more rather than less in the way of primary goods.

Rawls sees no important difference between his theory and utilitarianism over the concept of a person's good, but he believes that focusing on primary goods simplifies interpersonal comparisons. Some utilitarians believe that this is a mistake, urging instead that our concern should not be with primary goods, but with the utility, welfare, well-being, or happiness that they provide. But it's not clear that they are right. Utilitarians cannot distribute happiness or welfare; they can only distribute goods and other resources that tend to promote happiness. Although, as we saw in Chapter 2, utilitarian conceptions of well-being vary, Rawls's primary goods are important means to – indeed important ingredients of – human well-being on almost any conception of it. Because of this and because Rawls's primary goods tend to be tangible and public, there's a lot to be said for utilitarians making them the principal focus of distributive issues. Still, some attention will have to be paid to well-being as well as to primary goods. This is because some people, for example, those who are blind or handicapped in some way, will require more primary goods than do others to satisfy the same needs and achieve the same level of welfare.[22]

Putting this issue aside, how are people in the original position to choose their principles? At the heart of Rawls's argument is the contention that people in the original position will be conservative and refrain from gambling with their futures. In setting up the ground rules for their society, they are determining their own fate and that of their children. With so much at stake, they will be cautious. In particular, Rawls believes that people in the original position will not seek to maximize average expected utility (or, more precisely, maximize the average bundle of primary goods), even though in most situations this would be the rational choice. Rather, they will follow what game strategists call the *maximin rule* for making decisions. This rule says that you should select the alternative

---

[22] Rawls acknowledges this point in *Political Liberalism*, 182–5. Some non-utilitarian writers believe that our concern should be neither with primary goods nor with welfare, but with something in between. For Sen, the proper focus should be "capabilities"; for Cohen, it is "midfare." (See Sen, "Capability and well-being," and Cohen, "Equality of what?") But the difference between them and a utilitarian such as Brandt is not great; see Brandt, *Facts, Values, and Morality*, 203.

under which the worst that could happen to you is better than the worst that could happen to you under any other alternative. That is, you should try to *maxi*mize the *mini*mum that you will receive.

Many philosophers and decision theorists reject this rule because it can have absurd practical implications. For example, it implies that you should stay home instead of driving your car somewhere if the worst possible outcome of driving (a fatal accident) is worse than the worst thing that could befall you at home. In most situations disregarding probabilities and ignoring outcomes other than the worst possible one is irrational. Rawls nevertheless believes the maximin rule makes sense when you cannot estimate the likelihood of possible outcomes and you are more anxious to avoid an unacceptable or disastrous result than you are to achieve more than the minimum that the maximin rule would guarantee you. In particular, he believes that people in the original position will care much more about being assured a decent life, once the veil of ignorance is lifted, than they will, say, about having a chance at great wealth in a situation where a lucky few enjoy riches and luxury but most people are impoverished slaves. On the other hand, if we reject the maximin rule as a basis for decision making and assume that each person in the original position has an equal chance of occupying any social position once the veil of ignorance is lifted, then as John Harsanyi has argued (see Chapter 3) the utilitarian standard becomes the rational principle for people in the original position to choose to govern their society.

Rawls's Two Principles

Rawls argues that, following the maximin rule, people in the original position will refuse to adopt the utilitarian standard as the governing principle of society because it might require their interests to be sacrificed for the greater good once the veil of ignorance is lifted. People in the original position, he maintains, will be unwilling to run this risk. Instead they will endorse the following two principles:

1 Each person is to have an equal right to the most extensive total system of equal basic liberties compatible with a similar system of liberty for all.[23]
2 Social and economic inequalities are to satisfy two conditions: first, they are to be attached to positions and offices open to all under conditions

[23] Rawls, *Theory of Justice*, 302; cf. *Political Liberalism*, 291.

of fair equality of opportunity; and second, they are to be to the greatest expected benefit of the least advantaged members of society.[24]

According to Rawls, the first principle takes priority over the second, at least for societies that have attained a moderate level of affluence. The liberties Rawls has in mind are the traditional ones of freedom of thought, conscience, and religious worship, as well as freedom of the person and political liberty. He explicitly omits the right to own certain kinds of property (in particular, the means of production) and freedom of contract as understood by the doctrine of laissez faire. The first principle guarantees not only equal liberty to individuals, but also as much liberty as possible, compatible with others having the same degree of liberty. There is no reason why people in the original position would settle for less. Utilitarians, too, will happily endorse a liberty principle like Rawls's for reasons discussed in the previous chapter. In particular, liberty promotes autonomy and control over one's life, which are essential to human well-being.

Rawls's second principle states that if any inequalities are permitted, then the jobs or positions that bring greater rewards must be open to all. In other words, there must be meaningful equality of opportunity in the competition among individuals for those positions with superior economic and social benefits. This is a familiar ideal, but Rawls seeks to do more than remove formal barriers to competition. By fair equality of opportunity he also has in mind eliminating the effect of social class on one's life prospects. Utilitarians will support something like Rawls's ideal of equality of opportunity because, in the real world, equality of opportunity promotes total social well-being. Policies, institutions, or social structures that restrict some individuals from meaningful competition for economic and social goods cause unhappiness and frustration and undermine the bonds of solidarity that hold society together – all for little or no social benefit.

The other part of the second principle is less familiar and more controversial. Called the *difference principle*, it is one of the most distinctive features of Rawls's theory. It states that inequalities are justified only if they maximally benefit the least advantaged group in society. By "least advantaged," Rawls simply means those who are least well off in terms of primary goods. But what does it mean to require that inequalities work to the benefit of this group?

---

[24] *Political Liberalism*, 6; cf. *Theory of Justice*, 60, 83, 302.

· To answer this, imagine that we are in the original position. Following the maximin decision rule, we wish to make sure that, under the principles we choose, the worst that can happen to us once the veil of ignorance is lifted is still better than the worst that might have happened under some other arrangement. We might, therefore, choose strict social and economic equality. With an equal division of goods, there's no risk of doing worse than anyone else. And in the case of liberty, people in the original position would insist on full equality. But when it comes to economic equality and inequality, the matter is different.

Suppose, for instance, that as a result of dividing things up equally, people lack an incentive to undertake some of the more difficult work that society needs done. It might then be the case that allowing certain inequalities – for example, paying people more for being particularly productive or for undertaking the necessary training to perform some socially useful task – would work to everyone's benefit, even those who are now earning less. If permitting those inequalities resulted in a larger economic pie for society to divide, then those who were least well off would still be doing better than they would have been if things had simply been divided equally. Rawls is not trying to prove that the existence of inequalities always or even usually benefits those on the bottom. His point is that people in the original position would not insist on social and economic equality at all costs. If permitting some people to be better off than others resulted in the least well-off segment of society being better off than it would otherwise have been (and better off than it would be under a strictly equal division), then this is what people in the original position would want.

Utilitarianism and the Difference Principle

A Theory of Justice maintains that inequalities are justified only to the degree necessary to improve the lot of the least advantaged; any inequalities beyond that are unjust. The difference principle thus

> represents, in effect, an agreement to regard the distribution of natural talents as a common asset and to share in the benefits of this distribution whatever it turns out to be. Those who have been favored by nature, whoever they are, may gain from their good fortune only on terms that improve the situation of those who have lost out. The naturally advantaged are not to gain merely because they are more gifted, but only to cover the costs of training and education and for using their endowments in ways that help the

231

less fortunate as well. No one deserves his greater natural capacity nor merits a more favorable starting place in society. (101–2)

Because people have done nothing to deserve the particular talents, personal characteristics, or social advantages they were born with, they cannot claim that society's basic institutions should be shaped to benefit them. They cannot insist on receiving the economic rewards that those talents, characteristics, and advantages might have brought them in a free, Nozickian marketplace. Rather, individuals are entitled to what their natural endowments bring them only within the context of a structure that works to everyone's advantage.

Utilitarians agree with this. For them, as for Rawls, desert, rights, and entitlements are at best derivative moral concepts, a function of the particular rules and institutions that constitute a justly organized society. However, utilitarians only partly agree with Rawls's belief that the basic structure should minimize the social consequences of purely arbitrary, natural differences. Minimizing the social consequences of such differences may be the best way to promote total social well-being, but in the eyes of utilitarians it is not a good in and of itself.

For utilitarians, socioeconomic inequalities are, in themselves, neither a good thing nor a bad thing. What matters are the comparative welfare consequences of different systems of equality or inequality. Considered abstractly, inequalities of a particular kind and degree are fully justified if and only if they are a necessary part of a system of socioeconomic arrangements that benefits society as a whole more than any alternative system involving either greater or lesser inequality. In any particular socioeconomic context, utilitarians will favor increasing or decreasing inequalities to the extent that doing so boosts welfare in the long run.

However, given the poverty and extremely unequal distribution of wealth and income that exist in most countries, in practice there is likely to be little difference between adhering to Rawls's difference principle and following a utilitarian approach to distributive justice. This is because improving the lot of the least well off is, in the world we live in, almost certainly the best way to increase total social well-being. The next section will provide further reasons for this, but a deficiency of primary goods undermines people's well-being at the most basic level. Because such shortfalls spoil people's lives, preventing them will have a far higher priority for utilitarians than will supplying further primary goods to those whose basic needs have already been met. Indeed, as a general matter, it is usually easier and more fruitful for utilitarians to proceed negatively, rather than positively – that is, to focus, not so much on trying to increase happiness, but rather on alleviating pain, distress, and misery and on tackling oppression and other institutional obstacles to well-being.[25] From a utilitarian perspective, a society should, before pursuing other welfare goals, first strive to eradicate obvious sources of ill-being (such as malnutrition) and to ensure that people's elementary needs are met and that they are provided with the basic powers and opportunities necessary for them to endeavor to procure their own happiness. Seeking to better the condition of the least well off is in line with this strategy.[26]

Critics of utilitarianism such as Rawls worry that furthering the long-run well-being of society might somehow or other necessitate crushing the life prospects of some group. If no alternative set of institutions would prove as beneficial to society as a whole, then utilitarianism would have to license as just the sacrifice of this group's basic interests. As we saw in Chapter 4, however, this is one of the bogeyman stories that opponents of utilitarianism like to make up. There is no credible or realistic scenario in which a socioeconomic system built on the systematic frustration of the basic interests of some group would maximize net social well-being in the long run. This is, of course, an assertion of fact, not of logic, but it is nevertheless an important truth about the human condition.

Imagine, however, an affluent and fairly egalitarian society in which the least well off enjoy a comfortable life and are not much worse off than others in society. In these circumstances, it is perhaps not so far-fetched to imagine that permitting certain relatively minor economic inequalities might enhance total social well-being, even though the lot of the worse-off group is not improved or, indeed, is made slightly worse. However, it is far from obvious that one should follow the difference principle in rejecting these minor inequalities as unjust.

Suppose, for instance, that in this reasonably equal society a lottery is proposed. Tickets sell for $1, and anyone who chooses to can buy one. Lottery winners receive an all-expenses-paid cruise around the world, with the number of winners being a function of the number of tickets sold. Because, as in all other lotteries, overhead and other expenses must be subtracted from the funds used to pay for the prizes, the expected dollar

---

[25] So-called negative utilitarianism elevates this strategic dictum to a first principle so that the sole moral goal is to eliminate suffering, rather than to promote happiness. But the distinction between the positive goal of increasing happiness and the negative goal of decreasing unhappiness is too shaky to make this proposal plausible. See Quinton, *Utilitarian Ethics*, x–xi; Scarre, *Utilitarianism*, 17–18; Griffin, *Well-Being*, 84.

[26] For one utilitarian's recommendations for tackling poverty, see Haslett, *Capitalism with Morality*, 199–226.

233

value of a ticket (the value of the cruises divided by the number of tickets sold) will be less than $1. In terms of primary goods, therefore, buying a lottery ticket is (as it is in real life) a losing proposition. However, given that the cruise is a once in a lifetime experience and that the losers are only ever so slightly worse off, the lottery might increase net social utility. Nevertheless, it will fail to improve the lot of the worst off.[27] Accordingly, Rawls would reject the lottery whereas utilitarians would favor it. Simple imaginary examples are rarely decisive in moral philosophy, and it can't be claimed that this one proves much. But it does raise the following possibility: if there turn out to be real-world situations in which utilitarianism supports inequalities that the difference principle forbids (which is not obvious), then this fact (if that is what it is) may tell in favor of utilitarianism, not against it.

Most discussions of these issues focus only on the possibility that utilitarianism might permit inequalities that the difference principle disallows, but one must not overlook the possibility that utilitarianism might reject inequalities that the difference principle permits. Because the difference principle concerns primary goods, rather than well-being, it is possible that making the worst-off group better off in terms of primary goods could make it (and society as a whole) worse off in welfare terms. How might this happen? The difference principle licenses inequalities that increase the worst off's absolute share of primary goods while simultaneously reducing its relative share. But, in some circumstances, permitting inequalities to increase might weaken feelings of fraternity and social solidarity (by fostering elitist attitudes, say, or increasing envy, resentment, and disaffection), and thus reduce overall well-being. If so, then utilitarians, but not Rawlsians, would stand against these inequalities. The possibility that utilitarianism might sometimes be more, rather than less, egalitarian than Rawls's theory is an intriguing one, even though commentators rarely entertain it.[28]

---

[27] One might deny this on the ground that some of the winners will be from the worst-off group so that the group as a whole is better off than it was before the lottery. But as Rawls understands it, the identity of the least well-off group is not set through time. Inequalities are justified, not because they improve the lot of those particular individuals who were the least well off, but because they make those who are least well off after the inequality is introduced better off than those who were previously least well off. Whatever they were before, lottery winners will not, after the drawing, be among the least well-off group. On the other hand, the least well-off group will be worse off than if there had been no lottery (because of the money they have lost).

[28] Haslett, *Equal Consideration*, 213; cf. Pogge, *Realizing Rawls*, 46–7, 114–15. Rawls discusses the problem of envy in *Theory of Justice*, 530–41.

234

Utilitarianism and Distributive Equality

As we have seen, egalitarians such as Rawls discard utilitarianism on the ground that it might tolerate too much economic inequality. In the real world, however, utilitarianism's distributive implications are strongly egalitarian. Consider, for instance, the following distributive principle which Richard B. Brandt has put forward as one utilitarians should support:

> The real income ... after any taxes should be equal, except (a) for supplements to meet special needs, (b) supplements recompensing services to the extent needed to provide desirable incentive and allocate resources efficiently, and (c) variations to achieve other socially desirable ends such as population control.[29]

Many utilitarians would accept a principle like Brandt's, although more needs to be said about the nature of the supplements and other variations, and about the institutional structures best suited to implement the principle. Here our concern is not with these issues,[30] but rather with the general proposition that utilitarianism has robustly egalitarian implications for economic distribution.

Brandt's principle concerns the allocation of money both as a matter of simplicity and because, a few exceptions aside, it is more efficient and better promotes welfare to allow individuals to make their own purchasing decisions. Although motivated by the goal of welfare maximization, the principle tends strongly toward equality of welfare. Not only does equality of real income promote equality of welfare, but so also do (a) and (b), which authorize exceptions to income equality. These exceptions move society away from an equal distribution of income, but they move it toward greater equality of welfare by removing inequalities due to special needs and by compensating those "who are willing to work rather than enjoy leisure time" (310).

Various consequentialist considerations can be marshaled on behalf of equality of income or, at least, against significant economic inequality: (1) economic inequality promotes snobbishness, indolence, and pursuit of (relatively less satisfying) luxury and status goods at one end of the social spectrum, social stigmatization, discontent, resentment, and envy at the

---

[29] Brandt, *Theory of the Good and the Right*, 310.
[30] For Brandt's own thinking on these matters, see *Theory of the Good and the Right*, 306–26; *Morality, Utilitarianism, and Rights*, 370–87; and *Facts, Values, and Morality*, 199–221.

other end; (2) economic inequality warps the marketplace because, where supply is limited, those who have more money will simply outbid those who have less regardless of the value the latter place on the goods in question or the benefit they would receive from them; and (3) economic inequality translates swiftly into political inequality and other forms of domination, with untoward welfare consequences. However, the most important utilitarian argument for an equal distribution of income, and the one on which Brandt himself relies, rests on the declining marginal utility of money.

The Declining Marginal Utility of Money

Economists have long pointed out that additional units of a commodity are worth less and less to a consumer. As Paul Samuelson explains: "As you consume more and more, your total utility will grow at a slower and slower rate. This slower growth in total utility arises because your marginal utility (the extra utility added by the last unit consumed of a good) diminishes as more of the good is consumed."[31] Although economists call this the law of diminishing marginal utility, it is really only an empirical generalization, to which there may be exceptions. Still, introspection, everyday observation, and commonsense psychology support the proposition that, for most people and for most goods, one's appreciation or taste for a good drops off as one consumes more of it. If I have only one pair of shoes, the benefit I receive from another pair is much greater than if I already possess twenty-five pairs. I may enjoy or benefit from having twenty-six pairs of shoes more than from having two pairs (or even twenty-five), but the incremental or marginal gain in my well-being from my twenty-sixth pair is much less than it was from my second pair.

Money is no exception to this principle. An additional $100 brings more satisfaction to a person when she has only $5000 than it does when she has $50,000. More generally, "expenditure of successive increments to one's income produces less happiness or welfare than that of the preceding increments, on the average and in the long run."[32] The reason for this is simply that people want some things more strongly than others and arrange their purchases accordingly. As Brandt explains:

> So a person, when deciding how to spend his resources, picks a basket of groceries which is at least as appealing as any other he can purchase with the money he has. The things he does not buy are omitted because other things

---

[31] Samuelson and Nordhaus, *Economics*, 412.
[32] Brandt, *Theory of the Good and the Right*, 312.

are wanted more. If we double a person's income, he will spend the extra money on items he wants less (some special cases aside), and which will give him less enjoyment than will the original income. The more one's income, the fewer preferred items one buys and the more preferred items one already has. On the whole, then, when the necessities of life have been purchased and the individual is spending on luxury items, he is buying items which will give less enjoyment.[33]

At this point, the distributive implications of the declining marginal utility of money should be obvious. The economist A. C. Pigou puts the point clearly and succinctly:

> Any transference of income from a relatively rich man to a relatively poor man of similar temperament, since it enables more intense wants to be satisfied at the expense of less intense wants, must increase the aggregate sum of satisfaction. The old "law of diminishing utility" thus leads securely to the proposition: Any cause which increases the absolute share of real income in the hands of the poor, provided that it does not lead to a contraction in the size of the national dividend . . . will, in general, increase economic welfare.[34]

Are Our Income-Utility Levels Alike?

Even if the declining marginal utility of monetary income is a general truth, this does not, by itself, entail that income should be distributed equally. One reason it does not (a second is discussed in the next section) is that people may derive different amounts of happiness or welfare from the same amount of money. According to standard economic theory, if people's income-utility curves differ (that is, if they derive different amounts of welfare from various levels of income), and if we know what those curves are, then the way to maximize welfare is to distribute income, not equally, but so as to equalize marginal utilities. This is why Pigou, aware of this, refers in the passage just quoted to the "transference of income from a relatively rich man to a relatively poor man *of similar temperament*." Given the declining marginal utility of money, increasing the poorer person's share of real income increases net welfare only if we assume that people's

---

[33] Brandt, *Theory of the Good and the Right*, 312. Brandt's argument is based on Lerner, *Economics of Control*, 26.

[34] Pigou, *Economics of Welfare*, 89. Economists credit Daniel Bernoulli in the eighteenth century with having been the first to discuss explicitly the declining marginal utility of money. Bentham viewed with favor the argument for equality based on it in his "Principles of the Civil Code," Chapter VI ("Propositions of Pathology upon which the Advantage of Equality Is Founded").

temperaments are similar or, in other words, that they have similar income-utility levels.

This is an assumption that Pigou, for one, is happy to make. He rejects the idea that rich and poor have different mental constitutions – either inherently or as a result of upbringing and training – so that the rich are able to derive more satisfaction from a given income than are the poor. And he deals effectively with the class-biased contention that any sudden rise in the income of the poor is likely to lead to "a great deal of foolish expenditure which involves little or no addition to economic welfare" (89). That the rich operate at a higher utility level than the poor is a proposition most people today would find both false and distasteful, but few philosophers or economists would assert that we know to be true Pigou's postulate that people have similar income-utility levels.

Although Pigou's postulate is unproved, the proposition that people benefit equally from any given level of income can be claimed to be a plausible working hypothesis. "In the ordinary affairs of life," Pigou writes, "we always assume that groups of *prima facie* similar men will be mentally affected by similar situations in much the same way . . . . We *expect* similar situations to produce similar mental effects." Or as another economist writes with regard to taxation:

> The assumption that wants are equal ... though obviously not true, approximates more nearly to the truth than any other working assumption that could possibly be invented. Since the state must collect a revenue, it must have some definite assumption upon which it can proceed. The question is not, therefore, whether men's wants are equal, but whether there is any rule of inequality of wants upon which the apportionment of taxes could be made with a nearer approximation to the truth.[35]

The argument here involves two steps: first, that Pigou's postulate is more credible that any alternative supposition and, second, that because we must make some assumption about individuals' utility curves, we should act on the one that is most plausible.

In addition to its inherent plausibility, because Pigou's assumption is simpler than its rivals, it provides an easier and more straightforward basis on which to design institutions and to implement policies. By analogy, the law frequently ignores individual differences and acts on the assumption that people are the same, for example, when it sets one standard of negligence for all. In addition, the assumption of human equality fits better

[35] Both quotations are from Blum and Kalven, *The Uneasy Case for Progressive Taxation*, 61.

238

with the principles and values that utilitarians would want to inculcate in their society than does the rival proposition that human beings differ significantly in their ability to enjoy similar goods. Given our democratic tradition and culture, publicly defending that rival premise as a morally legitimate basis for policy would be difficult, if not impossible.

Brandt, however, does not avail himself of Pigou's assumption, granting instead that "the correlation between income and happiness-level . . . varies from one person to another, depending on personality."[36] Nevertheless, we lack reliable information about individuals' (differing) income-utility levels. This lack of reliable information, Brandt explains, is the reason why utilitarians cannot maximize welfare simply by distributing money to those whose well-being will be most enhanced by it.[37] There are not publicly identifiable classes into which individuals with high, medium, or low levels of income-utility fall. And there is no straightforward way in which individuals could hope to show that they would benefit more from extra income than would other people whose income is now the same as theirs. Furthermore, even if people could show this, permitting them to try would be socially divisive and would channel their energies in counter-productive directions.

Thus, even if we grant that people differ in their levels of income-utility, we are in no position to adopt the strategy of maximizing utility by distributing the national income so that the extra enjoyment produced by the last dollar each person receives is exactly the same. Accordingly, the welfare-maximizing strategy is (all other factors being equal) to divide things equally, for whenever we move away from an egalitarian division, the probable size of the welfare loss is greater than the probable size of the welfare gain.[38]

Incentives

The declining marginal utility of money has powerful egalitarian implications, but it has them only if one grants an important further assumption. According to most economists,[39] one must also assume that transfers from

---

[36] Brandt, *Theory of the Good and the Right*, 312.

[37] Except in the case of the ill or handicapped; see *Theory of the Good and the Right*, 312, 316–19.

[38] For a proof of this, see Lerner, *Economics of Control*, 32; Brandt, *Theory of the Good and the Right*, 313–15; and Barry, *Theories of Justice*, 176–7. But cf. Pogge, "Does utilitarianism favor economic equality?"

[39] For example, Pigou, *Economics of Welfare*, 89, and Friedman, "Lerner on the economics of control," 410.

rich to poor leave the total amount of income to be distributed undiminished. Strictly speaking, though, the argument for income equality requires only the weaker assumption that the welfare gains from income transfers outweigh any loss of welfare stemming from a contraction of total national income. Because money is not happiness, a relatively equal distribution of a total national income of x might well produce more total welfare than an unequal distribution of a larger national income of $x + n$.

Nevertheless, moving from the status quo toward equality of income is a process, the dynamic effects of which could have unfavorable welfare consequences. Depending on the socioeconomic institutional framework of the society in question and the motivations of its citizens, some ways of pursuing income equality or pursuing it too rapidly or too relentlessly may be, or after a certain point come to be, counterproductive. This could happen for a variety of reasons. Among the more interesting and important is the possibility that people will lack sufficient economic incentive to invest in certain ways, to pursue certain careers, or to work at certain jobs. They might lack sufficient incentive if, say, the tax system deprives them of all income above a certain level and gives it to those who earned less than that amount. The result could be a reduction in national income sufficient to lower net social welfare despite the welfare gains from income transfers.

As we have seen, Brandt's principle addresses this problem by allowing equality of income to be modified by "supplements recompensing services to the extent needed to provide desirable incentive and allocate resources efficiently." For instance, the principle might permit financial rewards to individuals beyond their (hypothetical) equal share of national income if this is necessary for people (1) to enter unpleasant, stressful, or dangerous occupations, (2) to work well in certain boring and monotonous jobs, (3) to put in long hours, or (4) to sacrifice current enjoyments in order to undergo training or acquire the skills necessary for pursuing certain socially beneficial careers. In such ways, a system permitting income differentials might entice people more successfully, than would a system of equal income, to behave in ways that expand society's wealth and, thus, its total welfare.

Although such supplements undermine equality of income, they promote equality of welfare. By recompensing people for extra efforts, they tend "to make the total prospects for different persons equal."[40] In this respect, such payments are analogous to the extra income allocated to the ill and the handicapped because they serve to equalize people's welfare. However, the phrase "supplements recompensing services" obscures a

[40] Brandt, *Theory of the Good and the Right*, 320.

240

contrast between payments necessary simply to offset the welfare losses one would otherwise incur by undertaking a certain job or pursuing a certain career, and payments that reward people above and beyond that level. For example, people in a given society might be so motivated that extra payments are needed to entice those with special talents to apply themselves to tasks that only they can do or that they can do better than others. If the benefits to society from the talented applying themselves are great enough, utilitarians might approve their receiving a financial reward that goes beyond what is necessary to recompense their welfare sacrifices. Incentive payments of this sort – call them "pure incentives" – smack of extortion, and paying them will run counter to both equality of income and equality of welfare.

On further refection, however, there are reasons for doubting that utilitarians would authorize pure incentive payments – by contrast with "welfare equalizing" supplements that eliminate disincentives – or, at least, that utilitarians would authorize them routinely. First, in our society the comparatively lush rewards of many talented professionals are due, at least in part, to restrictions on entry into those professional fields. Control over the number of medical school places, for example, has enabled the American Medical Association to boost physicians' earnings enormously over the decades, both absolutely and in comparison to other professions. In various areas, licensure and other occupational restrictions buoy the incomes of relatively privileged professionals by preventing paraprofessionals and others from performing equivalent services for less. Removal of unnecessary restrictions would go a long way towards freeing society from having to pay pure incentive payments.

Second, many of the most talented members of society, those with socially useful skills in limited supply, possess the talents they do, not because of innate ability alone, but also because of the comparative advantages they enjoyed in education, upbringing, and social environment. A society committed, as a utilitarian society would be, to substantive (as opposed to merely formal) equality of opportunity would find itself with a larger pool of talented or potentially talented citizens, thus reducing the ability of any group to successfully demand pure incentive payments.

A third point supports the previous two: jobs that only the talented can perform tend to be more intrinsically engaging and rewarding than other jobs, in large measure because they permit greater autonomy and involve the exercise of skill and expertise. Imagine, for example, that medical training and subsequent hospital apprenticeship were recompensed equally with other jobs and that young interns were no longer initiated into their profession by overwork. Suppose further that a practicing physician's work

241

week was only as long as that of a hospital orderly. Under those circumstances, it is hard to believe that people with the temperament and talent for being physicians would prefer to be orderlies instead and that pure incentive payments would be necessary to entice them to undertake the more challenging and satisfying work of being a doctor. Many are the jobs whose salary and other advantages are significantly higher than necessary to induce people to do them – jobs, in other words, whose occupants enjoy what economists call "employment rent."

Fourth, society has strong utilitarian grounds for resisting demands for pure incentive payments, even if acceding to them seems expedient at the time, because it will not want to encourage such claims nor to affirm the social legitimacy of such motivation. Considerations of long-run social welfare thus undergird social efforts to promote the norm of equality and to reinforce job-related motivational considerations other than the desire for an extra and disproportionately high monetary reward.

Allocation of Material Resources

The previous section focused on job income, but the need for incentives poses an additional obstacle to equal distribution when one considers entrepreneurship, investment, and the efficient utilization of capital assets and material resources. That is, one might reject equality of income on the grounds (1) that the prospect of fairly spectacular reward is necessary to entice independent inventor-entrepreneurs to spend the time and take the risks necessary to develop new products and services, or (2) that the prospect of a less spectacular, but nonetheless equality-busting reward is necessary to entice those with capital to invest it productively. Although these two issues deserve more complete discussion, two brief comments must suffice here.

First, one needs to examine whether contention (1) really represents a problem and, to the extent that it does, whether the problem might be addressed in ways other than by licensing significant income inequality. One cannot simply assume that the creative impulse responds only to financial incentives or that these incentives must be inegalitarian in character. For example, grants, subsidies, risk-pooling, insurance and other forms of assistance might be designed to encourage independent inventor-entrepreneurs to tackle problems that others are ignoring.

Second, contention (2) points to the question of exactly what sort of economic system and what sort of property arrangements would be welfare maximizing. That's a big issue, but if, for the sake of discussion, we consider only market-oriented societies in which people have private

242

control of most productive assets, an important point can be made. People are in a position to demand pure incentive payments that distort income equality just to the extent that they control productive resources – either human or material – that others lack. Equalizing people's productive resources would minimize this problem. Milton Friedman makes this point when discussing the possibility that redistributive taxation of income for egalitarian purposes can reduce people's incentives to act in wealth-producing ways:

> This difficulty could have been largely avoided by considering instead the distribution of resources . . . . Measures to reduce inequality by altering the distribution of resources (such as social investment in the training of individuals, inheritance taxation, etc.) may interfere less with the optimum utilization of resources than measures that seek to redistribute income directly.[41]

Because a people's capitalism made up of citizens with roughly equal productive assets would enjoy a fairly high degree of income equality prior to any redistributive taxation, equality of income could be maintained and promoted with less market distortion and less day-to-day reallocation of resources.

In terms of parental wealth, social position, and educational background, one's starting position in life greatly affects one's later ability to command a high salary. Reducing inequalities here will enhance equality of opportunity and thus equality of income. In addition, of course, the declining marginal utility of money provides a direct and independent case for reducing inequality of wealth. A tax on non-income assets is one possibility.[42] Even more important, ending or at least limiting the inheritance of wealth would have enormous welfare-enhancing effects and go a very long way toward creating a more equal society. Moreover, it has been argued that doing so would fit well with the basic values underlying capitalism by promoting freedom, equality of opportunity, and distribution according to productivity.[43]

Although utilitarianism has strongly egalitarian implications, identifying the exact policies and the specific institutional reforms that would do the most in a particular social and historical context to enhance people's well-being is a difficult task, involving as it does debatable empirical

---

[41] Friedman, "Lerner on the economics of control," 410.
[42] See Michalos, "A progressive annual net wealth tax."
[43] Haslett, *Capitalism with Morality*, 238–44. See also, Ascher, "Curtailing inherited wealth."

claims and controversial issues in economics and other social sciences. For this reason, when it comes to schemes for reallocating society's material resources, would-be utilitarian reformers should proceed cautiously and with a sense of their own fallibility. Putative social reforms often have severely negative side effects that policy makers neither intended nor foresaw. Although the anti-reform conclusion that reactionary thinkers draw from this fact is too broad and too pessimistic, experience nevertheless counsels us to aim at modest and incremental reforms rather than a wholesale upsetting of the status quo.

Utilitarians since Bentham have understood the importance that human beings attach to stability and security, and they have appreciated the welfare costs of disturbing expectations formed under existing socio-economic arrangements. Ramming through unpopular or misunderstood reforms can easily prove counterproductive. For these reasons, too, gradual-ism may be the surest course. Because utilitarians are concerned to maximize society's well-being over the long run, they can and should take a far-sighted, long-term approach. Part of doing so involves persuading people that utilitarianism provides the appropriate framework from which to address issues of economic justice. Whether people should be so persuaded is, of course, precisely the question with which this chapter has been occupied.

8

Virtue, Personal Life, and the Demands of Morality

Chapter 5 argued that utilitarianism does not instruct people to attempt to maximize welfare with each and every action they perform. Rather, the theory usually recommends promoting the general good in less direct ways. Although the utilitarian standard remains the ultimate criterion of right and wrong, it functions only occasionally as the immediate guide to one's conduct. In line with this, Chapter 6 focused on the institutional side of utilitarianism – that is, on the public structure of rules, rights, and liberties that utilitarians will favor as devices for enhancing collective well-being – while Chapter 7 probed the theory's approach to questions of economic justice and the distribution of income, wealth, and other social resources. These issues especially engaged Bentham, the two Mills, and their utilitarian compatriots, who tended to be less interested in utilitarianism as a personal ethic than as a public philosophy.

Today, there are philosophers – some sympathetic to utilitarianism, others hostile – who believe that the theory has whatever plausibility it has only (or primarily) in the public domain. They believe that utilitarianism falters as a personal ethic, having nothing serviceable to say about how individuals should live their lives or about what kind of people they should strive to be. This is not the position endorsed here. We have already seen that utilitarianism is concerned with the moral rules people embrace, with their motivations and dispositions, and with the characters it would be good for them to have. Against this, however, it has been urged that one cannot live a coherent and satisfying life as a utilitarian. Utilitarianism, it is alleged, is a profoundly deficient vantage point from which to view one's life, in particular, one's moral life.

Two different lines of thought have led some philosophers to this conclusion. The first is general: our moral lives are too rich and too embedded in particular relationships and communities for any abstract

245

normative theory, utilitarian or not, to do them justice. The second is specific: utilitarianism, in particular, cannot provide a satisfactory personal ethic because adhering to it thwarts close personal relationships, undermines our integrity and autonomy, and sabotages the projects that give our lives meaning. This chapter rebuts these two lines of criticism and tries to show that utilitarianism constitutes a plausible and coherent basis for understanding and directing one's life.

Good-Bye to Normative Theory?

Believing that the major task of ethics is to delineate the correct or best justified principle or set of principles for distinguishing right from wrong, moral philosophers have advanced an impressively diverse array of normative theories. Kantians, social contract theorists such as Rawls, utilitarians, commonsense pluralists, and others less easily categorized have put forward a plethora of rival principles, intended to guide our moral decision-making and to explain why certain acts are right and others wrong. Much of academic moral philosophy consists in dialogue and argument among and between representatives of these different camps. Some contemporary philosophers, however, have grown disenchanted with these debates and, indeed, with the whole idea of normative theory. These "anti-theorists" are not only critical of utilitarianism and other existing normative theories, they "reject normative theory [itself] as unnecessary, undesirable, or impossible."[1]

The Anti-Theorists

The anti-theorists point out that no normative theory has won general philosophical acceptance. From this fact they infer that the whole enterprise is mistaken. But this is a hasty conclusion. Neither in ethics nor in any other intellectual field does a lack of consensus imply that no progress has been made or that the whole endeavor is on the wrong track. In exculpation of normative theory, one can also argue, as Derek Parfit has, that non-religious ethics is still a very young discipline; it has, he writes, "been systematically studied, by many people, only since about 1960."[2]

The anti-theorists are particularly hostile to what they see as the rationalism of contemporary normative ethics, in particular, the assumption "that morality is rational only insofar as it can be formulated in, or

---

[1] Clarke and Simpson, *Anti-Theory in Ethics*, 3.
[2] Parfit, *Reasons and Persons*, 453.

grounded on, a system of universal principles."[3] According to the anti-theorists, moral decisions are irreducibly particular and contextually circumscribed, and moral conflicts and dilemmas are ubiquitous and inescapable. Because of this, no normative theory can successfully identify universal principles of conduct that hold for all moral agents. The anti-theorists thus reject the neo-Kantianism of writers like Alan Donagan, who states that morality is "a system of laws or precepts, binding upon rational creatures as such, the content of which is ascertainable by human reason."[4] They are also skeptical of the reflective equilibrium method (see Chapter 3), dismissing theories like Rawls's as fanciful constructions that bear little relevance to our real moral lives.

Whatever force these criticisms may have against neo-Kantians and Rawlsians, they do not tell against utilitarians. For one thing, utilitarians since Bentham have been staunch critics of those who rest their moral theories on intuitions about right and wrong. Even more important is the fact that utilitarianism, especially the indirect, pragmatic, and open-ended utilitarianism defended here, is a long way from Kantian rationalism. Although utilitarians believe that an impartial commitment to well-being is reasonable, few, if any of them, would claim that the utilitarian standard is a dictate of pure reason, logically binding on all rational creatures. In thinking about the rules, rights, and institutions that would be best for their society, utilitarians are engaged in a practical and empirical project, one which implicitly views morality as a human creation, not a deductive enterprise. Utilitarians do not seek universal and exceptionless ethical rules that are valid for all times and places.

The anti-theorists doubt the need for normative theory at all. We need knowledge about how the world works, they say, but not fancy theories about what we ought to do. But it is far from evident that their doubts reasonably bar one from adopting a utilitarian orientation to ethics. In fact, the anti-theorists frequently turn out to be less radical than they sound. When pressed by their critics, many of them deny abandoning the idea of universal human rights and appear willing to accept certain basic moral prescriptions. But if so, they open the door to normative theory. Often, what the anti-theorist repudiates is merely the notion that normative theorists can produce an ethical algorithm, some mechanical procedure for resolving all moral questions. Some commentators believe Bentham guilty

---

[3] Clarke and Simpson, *Anti-Theory in Ethics*, 3. "Today's moral theorists," Annette Baier complains, "are all Kantians in their prejudice in favor of formulated general rules" ("Doing without moral theory?" 36).

[4] Donagan, *The Theory of Morality*, 7; Baier, "Doing without moral theory?" 36.

of such vaulting ambition, but even if they are right, this is not a charge that will stick against contemporary utilitarianism.

The anti-theorists stress that we can have moral knowledge without having moral theory. What exactly they mean by moral knowledge is unclear, but utilitarians can certainly agree that people can have firm convictions about what is right or wrong, convictions that it is good for them to have, without having studied moral philosophy. The anti-theorists argue that thinking of morality in terms of theory is misguided. Living a moral life is more like mastering a craft than it is like studying mathematics or learning a scientific theory. By analogy, although it is possible to have theories of friendship, it is not knowledge of a theory that makes one a good friend or that makes a friendship work; rather it is sensitivity, instinct, and affection. Similarly, it is not because they follow different rules that one painter's landscape is great and another's is mediocre or that one actor's performance of Hamlet is riveting while another's is pedestrian.

Furthermore, the anti-theorists argue, even if we had a fully satisfactory set of moral rules, the difficult part would still remain: how to apply those rules in particular situations. What one really needs is not rules, but moral discernment and practical wisdom. Martha Nussbaum makes this point, writing that "moral knowledge . . . is not simply intellectual grasp of propositions; it is not even simply intellectual grasp of particular facts." Rather, "it is perception. It is seeing a complex, concrete reality in a highly lucid and richly responsive way; it is taking in what is there, with imagination and feeling." And again: "Situations are all highly concrete, and they do not present themselves with duty labels on them. Without the abilities of perception, duty is blind and therefore powerless."[5]

However, not all moral choices require great discernment or subtle judgment. Many are clear cut and straightforward, even if carrying them out sometimes requires strength of character. Although overstated, Nussbaum's point is nevertheless important. There is more to moral conduct than apprehending a set of moral rules. Utilitarians, however, can readily agree with this. They are interested in moral education in its broadest sense – not simply teaching certain rules, but promoting certain dispositions, desires, and sensitivities in people. Because we need both moral rules and moral discernment, it is a false dilemma to disparage the former in favor of the latter, as the anti-theorists do. They may be right to contend that most discussions of moral decision-making pay too much attention to rules and too little attention to the role of perception and judgment in applying

[5] Nussbaum, "'Finely aware and richly responsive,'" 116, 121.

those rules, but this is a point that utilitarianism is particularly well positioned to take account of.

Feminism and the Ethics of Care

Among philosophers sympathetic to feminism, there is no consensus about what it means to be a feminist in ethics. Some feminists believe that traditional normative theories such as utilitarianism can accommodate feminist concerns, whereas others think that it is necessary to elaborate a distinctively feminist ethic from the ground up. Although this latter camp is diverse, many of its members side with the anti-theorists in holding that a whole new way of thinking about ethics is needed. In so thinking, they have been influenced by Carol Gilligan.

Gilligan is a critic and former colleague of the psychologist and educator Lawrence Kohlberg, who developed an influential model of the stages of moral development. The highest stage, Kohlberg thought, involves the ability to apply universal principles to situational facts and thus determine in a logical way what one should do. Kohlberg developed his model by analyzing the answers that children and adults give to various moral dilemmas. In one of his best-known experiments, Kohlberg and his colleagues would tell children that a man named Heinz needs a certain drug to save his wife's life. However, he cannot afford to buy it, and the druggist refuses to lower his price to help Heinz. The researchers then ask the children, Should Heinz steal the drug?

In discussing the Heinz dilemma in her book *In a Different Voice*, Gilligan draws our attention to the contrasting responses of two 11-year-olds, called Jake and Amy. Jake argues that Heinz should steal the drug, but Amy doesn't think so:

> JAKE'S RESPONSE: For one thing, a human life is worth more than money, and if the druggist only makes $1000, he is still going to live, but if Heinz doesn't steal the drug, his wife is going to die. (*Why is life worth more than money?*) Because the druggist can get a thousand dollars later from rich people with cancer, but Heinz can't get his wife again. (*Why not?*) Because people are all different and so you couldn't get Heinz's wife again. (26)

> AMY'S RESPONSE: Well, I don't think so. I think there might be other ways besides stealing it, like if he could borrow the money or make a loan or something, but he really shouldn't steal the drug – but his wife shouldn't die either . . . . If he stole the drug, he might save his wife then, but if he did, he might have to go to jail, and then his wife might get sicker again, and he couldn't get more of the drug, and it might not be good. So, they should really just talk it out and find some other way to make the money. (28)

249

Gilligan points out that from Kohlberg's perspective Jake displays the higher level of moral development. He appears able to think abstractly, stepping back from conventional norms (such as "Do not steal!") and analyzing the situation in terms of more general moral principles. He describes the Heinz dilemma as "sort of like a math problem with humans." By contrast, Amy, who believes that Heinz and the druggist "should really just talk it out," seems not to come to grips with the dilemma at all. Apparently unable to think about the situation in an abstract, principle-oriented way, she wants it somehow to be the case both that Heinz not steal and that his wife live.

Gilligan argues that the difference between Jake and Amy reflects a more general contrast between the moral thinking of boys and girls, and the men and women they grow up to be. Men, she believes, tend to think in terms of abstract rights and systems of rules. They see morality as a matter of law and logic. By contrast, women are the traditional care-givers and tend to be more intuitive and less interested in following abstract principles. Concerned with sustaining personal relationships and meeting the needs of particular people, women seek to mediate and to arrive at concrete solutions based on their detailed knowledge of the situation. In Gilligan's view, men are oriented toward justice, women toward care. If this is correct, then on a model like Kohlberg's, "the very traits that traditionally have defined the 'goodness' of women, their care for and sensitivity to the needs of others, are those that mark them as deficient in moral development" (18). Gilligan repudiates this conclusion, however, and defends the value of the female moral perspective as at least as legitimate as the one favored by Kohlberg's model.

Most moral philosophers agree that Gilligan is right to criticize Kohlberg, whose understanding of moral theory they find unsophisticated and even rather confused. They are skeptical of stage theory and believe that his model of ideal moral reasoning is rigid and implausible.[6] However, the evidence for Gilligan's positive thesis that women speak "in a different voice" from men is shaky. There may be, in our culture, some subtle gender-linked differences in people's thinking about moral matters, but empirical investigators have yet to succeed in identifying and corroborating any pronounced and stable variations in moral reasoning between men and women. Just as one can find plenty of 11-year-old boys who think like Amy and countless 11-year-old girls who think like Jake, so it appears that there are elements of justice and care in the thinking of both men and

---

[6] For useful critiques, see Barry, *Justice as Impartiality*, 234–46, and Flanagan, *Varieties of Moral Personality*, 182–95.

women about a range of moral topics. Still, Gilligan's work has resonated with a number of feminists who have been attracted to the idea of developing an ethic based, not on a supposedly masculine concern for rights and rules, but on the moral traits traditionally associated with women.

Nel Noddings and several other feminist philosophers have begun elaborating just such an ethic of care, according to which our moral responsibilities are a function of the particular, context-specific needs of the people with whom our lives are entangled. Although it springs from an appreciation of the moral characteristics traditionally associated with women, an ethic of care is not for women only. In the eyes of Noddings and like-minded thinkers, what matters morally is that we develop the disposition to care for others. As Rita Manning explains, this disposition involves "a willingness to receive others, a willingness to give the lucid attention required to appropriately fill the needs of others."[7] An ethic of care, she continues,

> is not an appeal to abstract principles but to the use of our moral imaginations, where our attention to the particulars of a situation is infused by our involved concern about the other(s) .... While the practice involves moral imagination, this moral imagination is directed by a concern to advance the good of the other(s) in the context of a network of care. (89)

Although the obligation to care is rooted in our relations with others, a concern with formal rules or explicitly formulated duties tends only to get in the way of one's ability to care for others and determine the most appropriate way of expressing that care. In other words, Amy's way of thinking about things is better than Jake's.

Because it is personal, context specific, and based on the particular relationships involved, an ethic of care refrains from offering rules or precise guidelines. Although Noddings, Manning, and other writers illustrate their position with anecdotes and examples, critics find it vague and elusive and argue that caring has to fit into a larger structure of rights and duties. They also believe that benevolence can be harmful when unenlightened, shortsighted, or not guided by general principles.[8] Its defenders respond that an ethic of care accurately reflects the way many people, women in particular, experience their moral obligations and that it captures the

---

[7] Manning, *Speaking from the Heart*, 61.
[8] In the "Subjection of women" Mill held that women tended to be guilty of this because their upbringing and moral education traditionally (but wrongly) emphasized sentiment at the expense of understanding (Mill and Mill, *Essays on Sex Equality*, 226–7). See also Nussbaum, "The feminist critique of liberalism," 29–32.

251

intuitive concerns that guide their moral thinking. Yet, our moral culture, in which both men and women participate, gives ample space to more abstract claims of utility and right, and it often requires us to be prepared to defend our conduct by appeal to general principles and objective moral considerations rather than to an intuitive discernment of what the situation calls for, given the needs of those around us. This, too, is part of the moral experience of most of us. There are times when we should think like Jake, just as there are times when we should think like Amy.

Because of this, it seems doubtful that the whole of morality, in all its complexity, can be based on a single virtue, that of caring for those with whom we are in relationship. The world would, no doubt, be a better place if people were more thoughtful and caring toward those around them, and utilitarians will certainly encourage benevolence and sensitivity to the needs of others. But utilitarianism goes beyond advocating a situation-specific concern for those in our network of care. It is, in a sense, a second-order theory of care because a concern for the well-being of all is the basis upon which our duties, rights, and obligations ultimately rest.

Virtue Ethics

Virtue ethicists join anti-theorists and proponents of an ethics of care in rejecting conventional moral philosophy as too oriented toward moral rules and its practitioners as obsessed with designing fancy normative theories. They believe that moral philosophy should concern itself less with the assessment of actions, and more with the character of the agent who performs them – in particular, with the virtues that make a good person good. By contrast with an ethics of care, virtue theorists are interested in understanding the nature and interrelationship of a wide range of virtues, not just the virtue of caring for others.

Virtue ethicists see themselves as standing in the tradition of Aristotle (384–322 BC). Aristotle did not formulate a general account of right and wrong, nor was he concerned to lay down specific moral rules like "Keep your promises." Instead of searching, as modern philosophers tend to do, for general ethical principles, he focused on moral education and the formation of virtue. For Aristotle, the good life for human beings is one that consists in the exercise of *aretê* (excellence or virtue), and the *Nicomachean Ethics* provides his account of the principal virtues, both those of the intellect and, more relevant here, those of character.

Achieving excellence or virtue involves acquiring certain habits of action and emotion. A virtue is a kind of disposition or character trait, and one acquires a virtue, not by memorizing certain rules, but by acting in certain

252

ways until those ways of acting become firm dispositions. One develops a particular virtue such as bravery or generosity by acting as the brave or generous person does. This is not a matter of following a moral rule, but of coming to have the dispositions, habits, and character traits that mark a person as brave, say, or just, or generous. It may sound circular to say that to act justly or bravely or generously is simply to act as the just, brave, or generous person would act, but Aristotle was not trying to formulate a general account of right and wrong. He was trying to help his listeners understand and improve their moral lives.

More specifically, Aristotle contended that a virtue is the mean between two extremes, each of them a vice. Courage, for example, represents the mean between cowardice and foolhardiness, whereas generosity embodies the mean between prodigality and stinginess. As Aristotle explains in the *Nicomachean Ethics*:

> Both fear and confidence and appetite and anger and pity and in general pleasure and pain may be felt both too much and too little, and in both cases not well; but to feel them at the right times, with reference to the right objects, towards the right people, with the right aim, and in the right way, is what is both intermediate and best, and this is characteristic of excellence. (1106b16-23)

Finding that mean is not easy:

> Anybody can get angry – that is easy – or give or spend money; but to do this to the right person, to the right extent, at the right time, with the right aim, and in the right way, *that* is not for everybody, nor is it easy; that is why goodness is both rare and laudable and noble. (1109a26-29)

For Aristotle, becoming virtuous is like acquiring a skill, and the exercise of virtue requires experience and judgment or what he calls "practical wisdom."

Although inspired by Aristotle, contemporary virtue ethicists do not necessarily endorse his theory of virtue as a mean. They believe, though, that in deviating from Aristotle, moral philosophy of the last several hundred years has taken a wrong turn. Instead of emphasizing abstract concepts of duty and obligation, and instead of searching for general moral principles, moral philosophy, the virtue ethicists believe, should recognize that morality is essentially a matter of habits of feeling and acting – a matter of character – and that moral rules are, at best, of only secondary importance. Full-fledged virtue ethicists hold further that one can derive

253

the moral status of actions entirely from the moral evaluation of persons, character traits, and motivations. In their view, an action is right if and only if it is what a virtuous person would do in the circumstances.[9]

Virtue ethicists are right to emphasize the importance of character, virtue, and judgment and to remind us of the limits to rule-oriented approaches to morality. However, a concern to distinguish good agents from bad agents cannot entirely supplant our interest in distinguishing right acts from wrong acts, or take absolute priority over the establishing of general principles, rules, rights, and normative guidelines. Often, it is acts rather than agents that need to be our focus. For one thing, even good people can act wrongly, and we need standards for assessing their actions independently of their character. In addition, people sometimes face moral problems and dilemmas, and the morality of rival social policies and institutions may be open to debate. In these cases, where people need the guidance that principles afford, virtue ethics tends to be unhelpfully vague.

In trying to ground morality on virtue, virtue ethics faces the further problem that there is no consensus on the meaning, value, or implications of different virtues. For instance, is humility a virtue? Is innocence? What is it to be benevolent in a world where millions live in poverty? What are the limits to loyalty? As a result, opinions differ as to what precisely is involved in being truly virtuous. This problem is compounded by the fact that even the lives of those few souls that most of us would rightly consider to be saints, exemplars, or moral heroes conspicuously lacked some important virtues.[10] In this respect, Aristotle had it easier. He wrote against the backdrop of a small homogeneous society, whose members shared an implicit, largely uncritical understanding of what ways of living were admirable and noble, and what ways were base and deplorable. Not all of Aristotle's virtues are virtues for us and, of those that are, we see some as personal virtues rather than moral virtues (for example, wittiness). Not only does the modern world lack a shared understanding of the virtues, but it is unimaginable that we could return to a world like Aristotle's, in which it is taken for granted by everybody that certain traits of character and certain particular ways of living are superior to all others.

For these reasons, then, we require a more satisfactory theoretical framework than that provided by Aristotle, from which to analyze and assess different virtues and vices and, more generally, determine the traits

---

[9] Oakley, "Varieties of virtue ethics," 129; Hursthouse, "Virtue theory and abortion," 225.
[10] Flanagan, *Varieties of Moral Personality*, 9.

and motivations it is desirable for people to have. Utilitarianism provides just such a framework.

Utilitarianism and the Virtues

Some writers define the virtues as dispositions to adhere to the basic rules of morality and not violate them without justification.[11] Thus, honesty and truthfulness are virtues because they are dispositions that correspond to certain elementary moral duties. This is a common way of thinking about virtue, but a virtue ethicist would probably reject it because it focuses on rules, thus making the concept of virtue parasitic on a prior account of right and wrong. A broader and more neutral account of virtue defines it as a "trait of character, manifested in habitual action, that it is good for a person to have."[12] Thus understood, our culture identifies a wide range of traits as virtues – for example, courage, conscientiousness, cooperativeness, compassion, circumspection, consistency, civility (just to name some that begin with the letter "c"). Some virtues (like trustworthiness) are quite general; others are virtues only in certain contexts or only for those in certain occupations (aggressiveness on the football field). Most virtues are a matter of one's attitude and conduct toward others, but some (such as self-respect or prudence) primarily concern oneself.

From a utilitarian perspective, the precise definition of virtue may not matter much. Nor does utilitarianism, as a normative theory, have a stake in how one chooses to delineate different traits of character. In some contexts, it can accept the commonsense criteria of various traits such as honesty or courage; in others, it can draw on the efforts of psychologists to identify different traits and to understand how they are formed and their relation to one another. The important point is that utilitarians step back and ask about any trait, disposition, or motivational pattern whether one's possessing it is a good thing, and if so, why. Because people can possess traits to a greater or lesser degree, we might say, more precisely, that utilitarians want to know not just whether, but also to what extent, it would be good for a person or for persons in general to possess a certain trait. For instance, we want people to be honest, but not so obsessed with honesty that they walk twenty miles to return a nickel to its rightful possessor.

[11] E.g., Gert, *Morality*, 184.
[12] Rachels, *Elements of Moral Philosophy*, 163.

Utilitarians, then, assess habits, traits, and habitual motivations just as they do actions, policies, and institutions; that is, by reference to the utilitarian standard. They favor traits and dispositions, the having of which tends to promote the well-being of the agent and others, and they typically describe those favored traits and dispositions as virtues. Utilitarianism's instrumental approach to virtue is thus analogous to its treatment of moral rights. Whereas virtue theorists take the virtues as their moral starting point, and natural rights theorists take rights as theirs, for utilitarians establishing a right or identifying a trait as a virtue represents the conclusion of an ethical argument, not the premise of one.

One might suppose that there is only one character trait that utilitarians would approve: namely, the disposition to maximize well-being, whenever and wherever possible. However, we have already seen that there are solid utilitarian reasons against encouraging people to use the utilitarian standard as their direct guide to quotidian decision-making. Although utilitarians want people to be benevolent and generally sensitive to the needs and well-being of others, they also desire, as we have seen, that people internalize certain relatively specific action-guiding rules and principles, rules and principles that are necessary for social coordination and that promote the well-being of all in the long run. Small children, for instance, need to learn not to hit their younger siblings, to share their toys, to help around the house, and not to grab the largest piece of cake. Schoolchildren need to be taught not to lie, not to cheat on tests, not to be cruel to animals, not to get into fights with classmates, and so on.[13] Adults, of course, should have dispositions and motivations corresponding to other, rather more complex constraints on their conduct, some of them reflecting the special responsibilities they have, for instance, to their children, spouses, and colleagues or employees.

Determining whether particular dispositions are useful (and thus virtues) is an empirical issue, and a virtue in one time or place may not be a virtue in another. This is because whether a particular disposition has good results can vary among societies and between historical periods. Further, people differ in their talents, personalities, and temperaments. For this reason, utilitarians will probably follow G. E. Moore in rejecting the assumption that it is good for everyone to cultivate the same virtues.[14] In any case, the key point is that utilitarians appeal to an external standard to determine whether particular dispositions, motivations, and character traits are virtues. By contrast, virtue theorists start from the premise that

[13] Brandt, *Facts, Values, and Morality*, 146.
[14] See Moore, *Principia Ethica*, 166.

certain specific traits are virtues and are then faced with the project of defining them (What is generosity?), deciding whether certain other traits are or are not among them (Is chastity a virtue?), reconciling different virtues (Can one display courage in a cause one knows to be unjust?), and using them to provide people with some kind of ethical guidance.

A few paragraphs above, virtue was defined as a "trait ... that it is good for a person to have," but this phrase is open to different interpretations. Utilitarians would interpret it to mean that a virtue is a trait that it promotes well-being generally for people to have. In other words, a trait such as truthfulness or honesty is a virtue, and thus to be valued, because those who possess it are disposed to respond to certain sorts of situations in ways that, in general, not only have good results for all but also have better results than do the actions of those who lack that trait. In addition, part of what makes a trait a virtue may be the indirect benefits it brings to its possessor. A particular virtue, for example, might reinforce other useful dispositions, enhance one's mental health, or have other positive psychological side effects.

Virtue theorists, however, look at the matter differently. First, they believe that virtue is good, not instrumentally (or not only instrumentally), but in itself. In other words, a trait like honesty is to be valued for its own sake, rather than merely because it has good results. This is in line with the belief that traits have priority over actions so that an act is right if and only if it reflects a good character or is the kind of thing that a virtuous person would do. Second, most virtue theorists believe that virtue is "good for a person to have" in the sense that virtue benefits its possessor. To be virtuous is in a person's interest. Aristotle believed both these things. He held that the exercise of virtue or the achieving of excellence benefits a person, and he also speaks of virtues as being fine, excellent, or noble, which suggests he was praising them for their own sake.

Are the Virtues Good in Themselves?

Because we often sing their praises without qualification, it may appear that we do indeed value certain virtues for their own sake. But appearances can be misleading. We value impartiality in judges, but is this for its own sake or because impartiality leads to better (that is, more reasonable and accurate) decisions? If it somehow turned out that partial judges typically delivered sounder verdicts than impartial judges did, we would probably value judicial impartiality less. When people hold up a certain trait as admirable, they usually have no reason to clarify whether they do so because possession of the trait is valuable in itself or because it has good results.

Indeed, distinguishing between these two things can be tricky. Would we value kindness if acts of kindness typically had bad results? The question barely makes sense. We can imagine kindness that is misplaced (as when, for example, a charming serial killer talks a naive and tender-hearted soul into assisting him to escape the police), but it is bizarre to hypothesize a systematic wedge between kindness and the happy results of kind acts. It may be that when a trait is so tightly linked to good results, we come, by a process of transference, to think of it as valuable in and of itself. Thus, the approbation we feel, say, for kindness and honesty may lead us to attribute intrinsic value to them.

In fact, it may be good on utilitarian grounds to praise certain virtues such as honesty as if they were good in themselves, and not just instrumentally valuable. This is because we want to encourage people to be honest, and a good way to achieve this goal is for people to value honesty and to be motivated to be honest, not merely as a means, but also for its own sake.[15] This point also clarifies why we praise self-regarding virtues less than other-regarding virtues. The reason is simply that people need less encouragement to develop habits that benefit them than they do habits that benefit others.

Some writers criticize the utilitarian account of virtue on the ground that people admire certain traits independently of the happiness or unhappiness they produce.[16] Now, one can certainly imagine admiring someone for her integrity or perseverance even in a situation where this trait leads her to a course of action that has poorer results both for herself and for others than if the trait had been a weaker component of her personality. But this is no different than esteeming a person for sticking to a moral rule that it was difficult for her to adhere to, when doing so did not have particularly good results. Utilitarians assess neither character traits nor adherence to rules on a case by case basis. Good rules and good traits are to be encouraged and reinforced even though they can occasionally produce suboptimal results.

Although a utilitarian approach to the virtues appears to square with our ordinary attitudes, the virtue ethicist might still insist that the possession of certain traits is valuable in and of itself. This assertion rests on an intuition, and people's intuitions differ. Christians value humility whereas Nietzsche repudiates it. Aristotle values the great-souled man, who builds

---

[15] Thus, Mill writes that "the utilitarian standard ... enjoins and requires the cultivation of the love of virtue up to the greatest strength possible" (*Utilitarianism*, 37; cf. *Logic*, 952).
[16] Slote, *From Morality to Virtue*, 236.

monuments and entertains lavishly, whereas we would probably consider him vulgar. Intuitions can be neither proved nor disproved; that is why we call them intuitions. Still, we can reflect on whether we would truly value traits that did not ultimately promote human well-being and whether, if we did, that valuation would really be a moral one, as opposed, perhaps, to an aesthetic judgment.

A character trait is a standing disposition to perform acts of a certain type or, better perhaps, a standing disposition to notice (or not notice) certain features of a situation and to have certain sorts of considerations motivate (or fail to motivate) one to act in a certain way. It's easy to understand why we commend an honest action (like returning a mislaid wallet to its owner) and laud the person who always acts honestly. However, it's difficult to see how the mere disposition to act honestly could have value in and of itself. Even if we put aside latent or unexercised dispositions and focus on dispositions that occasionally manifest themselves in conduct, many virtues seem too mechanical or unwitting to have intrinsic value.[17] One might, for instance, habitually abstain from stealing in situations where some persons would be strongly tempted to do so and yet this very valuable trait be as unthinking as one's disposition to put on one's right shoe before the left.

Are the Virtues Good for Us?

Aristotle and most contemporary virtue ethicists believe that it is good for a person to possess virtue, meaning that doing so is in the person's own best interest. Are the traits that utilitarianism identifies as virtues also good for their possessors? Those traits are virtues because they promote human flourishing in general, but does their possession necessarily promote one's own flourishing? The short answer is no. Just as doing the right thing can, according to any normative theory other than egoism, diverge from doing what is in one's own interest, so for utilitarians there is no logically necessary connection between one's possessing a virtue and one's doing well. Courageousness, for example, can lead to one's premature demise.

There is more to be said, however. First, it can be argued that as a general proposition a person's life goes better if it displays certain key virtues. Virtue may not be cost free, but it has its rewards. People tend to like and respect those who are fair and upright, and honest and trustworthy people tend to get on better with others and to develop closer and more rewarding ties with them. Second, possessing a virtue typically involves a distinctive

---

[17] Moore, *Principia Ethica*, 175–7.

pattern of commitments and motivations, so that it can be argued that the interests of the generous or kind or courageous person differ from those of the selfish, mean, or cowardly person. The generous person values generosity, desires to do generous things, and finds the exercise of generosity satisfying. For this reason, although being generous may involve personal cost, it may not be contrary to the interests of the generous person.

In the *Nicomachean Ethics* Aristotle maintains that a virtuous person takes pleasure in the exercise of his virtue. At one point, though, he puzzles over whether the brave man really takes pleasure in the painful blows that he receives when acting bravely in combat (III.9). Aristotle concludes, in effect, that what the brave man really takes pleasure in, what he really desires, is not the blows; rather, it is not acting cowardly. Given this desire, and the self-image, aspirations, and motivational dispositions built up around it, it is not absurd to say that there is a sense in which it is in the interest of the brave man to accept the painful blows, rather than run away. Aristotle can also be interpreted as saying that it can be in one's interest to have a certain sort of character, that is, to be a certain kind of person, even if, in acting from that character, one sometimes acts against one's immediate interests.

As we saw in Chapter 2, Aristotle held an objective, perfectionist account of well-being, according to which certain traits are part of what constitutes human well-being. It's not that virtue promotes one's well-being; rather, it's that well-being consists in the possession of virtue. Just as having disease-free lungs is an objective component of physical well-being, so a person is inherently better off possessing certain moral traits. This is a debatable proposition, tied up as it is with a controversial conception of human nature and well-being. Alternatively, and more plausibly, one can argue that people who possess certain virtues typically have happier and more satisfying lives. This is a not an assertion about the meaning of well-being, but an empirical claim about the connection between personal well-being and the possession of certain traits. As a general matter, this proposition is almost certainly correct, but the devil is in the details: which virtues are the ones that do the most to make our lives go well?

Unfortunately, there is no ready answer to this question; nor, as we have seen, do utilitarians have a handy list specifying the exact traits that we should endeavor to instill in ourselves and others because of their overall benefit. In large measure this is because we know too little about moral psychology. As one writer explains:

We do not yet understand what sort of thing a virtue is from a psychological

260

point of view . . . . Nor do we understand very well how traits, assuming they are individual dispositions, interact with one another in an overall psychological economy. In part our ignorance is due to the fact that within psychology itself we do not fully understand the nature of traits and dispositions, how they interact, and what topological varieties they contain.[18]

Two things further complicate matters. First, people differ. Even if they had the same basic traits, their moral personalities would still differ (e.g., not all generous people are generous in the same way). Thus, as previously noted, it will be neither desirable nor possible for people to attempt to cultivate exactly the same traits. Second, utilitarians wish to take into account the costs of trying to instill a trait in people (to some specified degree), not just the benefits of their having that trait. Nevertheless, despite the shortfalls in our knowledge, utilitarians endeavor to assess possible dispositions and character traits in a way that is as open minded and as empirically informed as possible.

Moral Fanaticism and the Things We Value

Utilitarians approach issues of character and conduct from several distinct angles. First, about any action they can ask whether it was right in the sense of maximizing expected well-being. Second, they can ask whether it was an action the agent should have performed, knowing what she knew (or should have known) and feeling the obligation she should have felt to adhere to the rules that utilitarians would want people to stick to in her society. Third, if the action fell short in this respect, utilitarians can ask whether the agent should be criticized and, if so, how much. This will involve taking into account, among other things, how far the agent fell short, whether there were extenuating factors, what the alternatives were, what could reasonably have been expected of someone in the agent's shoes, and, most important, the likely effects of criticizing the agent (and others like her) for the conduct in question. Finally, utilitarians can then ask whether the agent's motivations are ones that should be reinforced and strengthened, or weakened and discouraged, and they can ask this same question about the broader character traits of which these motivations are an aspect. Looking at the matter from these various angles produces a nuanced, multi-

---

[18] Flanagan, *Varieties of Moral Personality*, 11.

dimensional assessment, one which reflects the complicated reality of our moral lives.

As they go through life, thoughtful people inevitably survey their own characters, assess their traits and dispositions, and reflect on the kind of person they want to be and on the kind of people they wish others to be. They will ponder how best to raise and educate their children, and they will sometimes take steps to modify and improve their own habits, traits, and dispositions. Utilitarians naturally approach these issues with a desire to identify the motivations and habitual patterns of conduct that conduce to the well-being of both the agent and others, and they want to understand the costs and psychological feasibility of trying to cultivate those dispositions.

Utilitarianism is a theory, but we are individuals long before we are old enough self-consciously to embrace any normative theory. If we come to accept utilitarianism, we do so as human beings with settled personalities, character traits, and dispositions, with established likes, dislikes, hopes, projects, goals, and ambitions, and with pre-existing, frequently long-term emotional attachments to other human beings. This fact does not rule out change, nor does it imply that we cannot refashion and improve our future selves; it implies only that we do so in a certain context and that we cannot alter our psychological make-up with a snap of the fingers. We are not blank disks waiting to be formatted.

Some critics of utilitarianism seem to believe that the theory requires people to shed their personal interests and normal human attachments in order to devote themselves to maximizing general well-being. With so much good waiting to be done in the world, they argue, utilitarians should be working around the clock, and not wasting time dallying with their friends, going to the movies, reading Plato, or listening to old jazz records. But an impossible personality type cannot be the utilitarian ideal for the simple reason that it is impossible. Perhaps, though, utilitarians should strive to come as close to this ideal as they can, even if no human being can fully achieve it. But this conclusion is wrong for two reasons.

The first is pragmatic: such an effort, so against the grain of human nature, is bound to collapse. With great exertion, perhaps, one might sustain the sort of utilitarian fanaticism envisioned by the critics for a year or two, but a collapse of these efforts seems inevitable, most likely followed by a repudiation of the whole endeavor.

The second reason is deeper. The ideal that the critics attribute to utilitarianism overlooks a basic fact about human beings: namely, that one's personal attachments, interests, and goals are central to one's welfare. To strip oneself of them, even if it were possible, would be to denude oneself of the very things that give meaning, zest, and interest to life – they are cardinal components of human well-being. Moreover, one has, as a rule, far and away greater power to affect positively one's own well-being than that of any other person. This was one of the guiding thoughts in Chapter 6's endorsement of Mill's liberty principle. To turn around now and adopt the idea that the utilitarian injunction to promote the general good requires one to systematically deprive oneself of the major sources of well-being seems absurd.

Wolf on Moral Saints

One contemporary philosopher who advances the argument I have been criticizing is Susan Wolf. In an influential essay, Wolf rejects moral saintliness as a personal ideal, writing that she is glad that neither she nor those she cares about are moral saints. She defines a moral saint as "a person whose every action is as morally good as possible . . . who is as morally worthy as can be."[19] Wolf believes such a person would be an unappealing figure because the person would lack the time to develop any significant non-moral interests and skills. If a saint is spending all her waking moments, say, feeding the hungry, then she can't be playing the trumpet, reading poetry, or backpacking. Lacking any non-moral virtues or without the interests that ordinary people have, saints will tend to be bland and colorless. They will be nice, but boring.

There probably aren't any saints in Wolf's sense. Certainly, those real people whom we think of as moral exemplars have real, sometimes quirky, personalities; they also have non-saintly interests. This misses the point, however. Wolf's beef is with moral saintliness as an ideal and, defined as she defines it, saintliness does seem drab and unappealing. Instead of moral fanatics, we would all prefer to be persons who are, to be sure, virtuous but who also have other interests, passions, and abilities – persons who are morally upright but who also, perhaps, are crazy about opera and skiing, like to poke fun at pretentious people, or know how to make great chili.

To her credit, Wolf recognizes that utilitarians approve our having these sorts of interests, talents, and attractive personality traits. After all, such traits enhance the well-being both of the person himself and those with whom he associates. Further, Wolf acknowledges that a world in which most people strove to achieve sainthood would probably be less happy than a world in which people pursued a diversity of ideals and projects. Looking

[19] Wolf, "Moral saints," 419.

at the matter pragmatically, utilitarians will accomplish more, she concedes, by encouraging individuals to pursue the goals that attract them, rather than strive for a saintliness that is probably beyond the reach of the average person.

Nevertheless, Wolf argues that utilitarians themselves should privately aspire to moral saintliness. Although utilitarians will not advocate saintliness as a universal ideal, she believes it should be their personal ideal. This is because the

> gain in happiness that would accrue to oneself and one's neighbors by a more well-rounded, richer life than that of the moral saint would be pathetically small in comparison to the amount by which one could increase the general happiness if one devoted oneself explicitly to the care of the sick, the downtrodden, the starving, and the homeless. (428)

Of course, there are limits to how much good a saint can do before burning out, and wise utilitarians will therefore allot some of their time to pursuing their non-moral interests and developing some of their non-moral talents. In this way, they may accomplish more good in the long run than if they permitted themselves no indulgences at all. Wolf grants this, but she still believes that utilitarians will have to restrict severely – too severely, in her view – these extracurricular pursuits if they are to promote the general good as much as possible.

Later in this chapter we return to the vexed question of the limits, if any, to the burden that utilitarianism imposes upon us to aid people in distress – "the sick, the downtrodden, the starving, and the homeless." What I want to examine here is Wolf's contention that those who embrace utilitarianism are required to value their various passions, projects, and non-moral interests only "under the description 'a contribution to the general happiness.'" In her view, utilitarians can value their non-saintly interests "only because of and insofar as they *are* a part of the general happiness." In contrast to the alleged single-mindedness of utilitarians, Wolf writes that someone who is not a utilitarian:

> might love literature because of the insights into human nature literature affords. Another might love the cultivation of roses because roses are things of great beauty and delicacy. It may be true that these features of the respective activities also explain why these activities are happiness-producing. But, to the nonutilitarian, this may not be to the point .... From that point of view, it is not because they produce happiness that these activities are valuable; it is because these activities are valuable in more direct and specific ways that they produce happiness. (429)

264

Is it really true that utilitarians cannot love roses for their beauty? Wolf's argument that they cannot rests on an error, one that is recurrent in contemporary critiques of utilitarianism.

For utilitarians, to be sure, the ultimate value of either literature or roses lies in human well-being. Reading good books, cultivating flowers, listening to opera, and climbing mountains are among the many activities that can and do enrich people's lives. But from this fact it does not follow that a utilitarian who loves opera loves it because she thinks that listening to opera promotes her well-being and thus, in a small way, the general good. She may well believe that opera is important to her happiness and listening to it promotes her well-being, but this belief is not the reason why she loves opera. It does not, for instance, explain why she adores opera but not backpacking, gardening, or baking bread even though she knows that these activities can also enhance one's well-being. A utilitarian who cares for opera will do so because she finds it thrilling, or an emotional release, or for any of a number of other reasons that people love opera. If she cultivates roses, it will likely be because she appreciates their beauty and values the feelings that come from nurturing it. She also knows that cultivating roses contributes to her happiness and thus, by definition, to general happiness, but that is another matter.

Wolf and other critics of utilitarianism err in assuming that a person's reason for liking, enjoying, or participating in an activity must be identical to the person's reason for thinking it valuable that she likes, enjoys, or participates in that activity. Felicia likes carrots because of their crunch, their texture, and their flavor. She also thinks that carrots are good for her and that her eating them is beneficial. That thought may influence her eating habits (she doesn't feel guilty when she indulges in carrots as she does when she eats chocolate pie). But it doesn't explain why she eats carrots. After all, she believes broccoli is good for her, but she doesn't eat it because she doesn't like its taste.

The Mental Crisis of the Young Mill

Properly understood, utilitarianism does not imply that we should become persons fanatically devoted to doing good, nor does it say that as utilitarians we should love the things we do only because and insofar as our doing so promotes the general good. John Stuart Mill's own life illustrates these points.

Mill's father James educated John Stuart at home in an effort to mold his development along utilitarian lines. By all accounts, the Mill household was not a particularly warm and loving one, and James Mill deprived the younger Mill of contact with boys his own age so as not to impede the rigorous, accelerated, and demanding educational program he had designed for him. So successful was this program, in one respect, that as an adolescent Mill was the intellectual peer of writers and thinkers much older than he was. Although Mill had already absorbed implicitly utilitarian values from his father, reading Bentham at age 15 gave his life intellectual coherence and moral purpose. Thereafter, he was an active writer, debater, and organizer in the cause of utilitarian social reform.

At 20, however, Mill fell into what he called "a crisis in my mental history," the onset of which he described in his *Autobiography*:

> It was in the autumn of 1826. I was in a dull state of nerves, such as everybody is occasionally liable to ... one of those moods when what is pleasure at other times, becomes insipid or indifferent .... In this frame of mind it occurred to me to put the question directly to myself, "Suppose that all your objects in life were realized; that all the changes in institutions and opinions which you are looking forward to, could be completely effected at this very instant: would this be a great joy and happiness to you?" And an irrepressible self-consciousness distinctly answered, "No!" At this my heart sank within me: the whole foundation on which my life was constructed fell down. All my happiness was to have been found in the continual pursuit of this end. The end had ceased to charm, and how could there ever again be any interest in the means? I seemed to have nothing left to live for. (80–1)

Following this disturbing realization, Mill slumped into a dark period of depression that lasted for several years. Gradually, Mill emerged from his misery and began to enjoy life again. Although he remained a utilitarian, and indeed went on to write his classics *Utilitarianism* and *On Liberty*, he advocated, as we have seen, a subtle and moderate form of utilitarianism. He was no longer the single-minded utilitarian fanatic he had been.

As an adolescent, Mill's life approximated what critics like Wolf take to be the utilitarian ideal: he had been, Mill said later, "a mere [Benthamite] reasoning machine." However, his mental breakdown illustrates both the pragmatic and deeper reasons for rejecting this supposed ideal as a caricature of utilitarianism. Mill himself drew two explicit conclusions from his experiences, both of which are relevant here.

First, although he remained firmly convinced "that happiness is the test of all rules of conduct, and the end of life," he came to believe that

> this end was only to be attained by not making it the direct end. Those only are happy ... who have their minds fixed on some object other than their

266

own happiness; on the happiness of others, on the improvement of mankind, even on some art or pursuit, followed not as a means, but as itself an ideal end. Aiming thus at something else, they find happiness by the way. (85–6)

This passage suggests two different but related ideas. One is that happiness is a by-product of things or activities that we pursue for other reasons. If you aim directly at happiness, it is likely to elude you. This is sometimes called the *paradox of hedonism*. To take an everyday analogy, recreational tennis players know that tennis is only a game, which one plays for fun. Whether one wins or loses is unimportant; indeed, in the larger scheme of one's life it is totally meaningless. However, those Saturday-morning players who pretend that winning is important and take their matches seriously, trying hard to win, usually end up having more fun than do those players who, because they just want to have fun, simply lob the ball back and forth without trying earnestly to score.

The passage also suggests another way in which happiness is best achieved indirectly. This is the idea that people who are exclusively concerned with their own interests tend to have less happy and less satisfying lives than those whose desires extend beyond themselves. Individuals who care only about their own happiness will generally be less happy than those who care about the well-being of others.[20] If so, then happiness is indirect in two ways. It is a by-product of activities that we pursue for reasons other than happiness, and it comes more readily to those who, rather than being preoccupied with their own concerns, are sincerely interested in the lives and well-being of others and for whom they feel genuine concern. Both these propositions are psychological generalizations, to which exceptions are possible, but they nevertheless contain important truths.

The second general conclusion that Mill drew from his own experience was the importance, "among the prime necessities of human well-being," of what he called "the internal culture of the individual":

> I ceased to attach almost exclusive importance to the ordering of outward circumstances, and the training of the human being for speculation and for action. I had now learnt by experience that the passive susceptibilities needed to be cultivated as well as the active capacities, and required to be

---

[20] "When people who are tolerably fortunate in their outward lot do not find in life sufficient enjoyment to make it valuable to them, the cause generally is caring for nobody but themselves" (*Utilitarianism*, 13).

nourished and enriched . . . . The cultivation of the feelings became one of the cardinal points in my ethical and philosophical creed. (86)

As a result, Mill began to attach new importance to music, poetry, and the imaginative arts. Personally, Mill found solace in the beauty of nature, long country walks being among his greatest joys. Philosophically, he realized that there is more to human welfare than physical comfort. The development of our emotions and the refinement of our feelings contribute significantly to our well-being.[21] By cultivating roses we cultivate an appreciation of their beauty and delicacy, and in this way develop aspects of ourselves, of our "internal culture," that enhance our lives and promote our well-being. Once again, though, a utilitarian who loves raising roses may believe that cultivating them enhances her life, but – contrary to Wolf – this is not why she loves growing them.

Those Who Are Near and Dear

Most of us cherish our close personal relationships and take them to be of central importance to our lives. We have strong and deep-seated ties to family, friends, spouses, and lovers; we care about them and want them to fare well, and they care about us. These bonds are not only a source of mutual pleasure and satisfaction but also of self-knowledge, a sense of self-worth, and personal and moral growth.[22] We are partial to those who are near and dear to us, and we treat their interests with a solicitude and regard that we do not extend to mere acquaintances, still less to strangers. This display of concern and the special bonds and affection that underlie it are part of what it means to be intimate with another person. However, some critics object to utilitarianism because they believe that it requires moral agents to be totally impartial and objective, thus forbidding them from exhibiting any special regard for family, friends, and loved ones.

Unfortunately, some utilitarians have erroneously believed that their theory does indeed entail this conclusion. In a famous passage in his *Enquiry Concerning Political Justice*, first published in 1793, the early utilitarian William Godwin argued that one should save the life of the illustrious archbishop Fénelon rather than that of his valet, if one cannot rescue both from a burning building, because saving Fénelon would have better consequences. He continues: "Suppose the valet had been my brother, my

---

[21] "Next to selfishness, the principal cause which makes life unsatisfactory is want of mental cultivation" (*Utilitarianism*, 13).
[22] See LaFollette, *Personal Relationships*, 85–92.

father or my benefactor. This would not alter the truth of the proposition" (71).

This looks like impartialism with a vengeance. Our special ties to others, Godwin is saying, should not lead us to deviate from the utilitarian goal of doing what produces the most good. However, he does try to mute the harsh implications of his view. He accepts that, as a matter of human nature, we have a special concern for those we know, and he acknowledges that the disposition to act in their favor is a generally beneficial one. Still, in his eyes, this fact does not make it objectively right to rescue one's brother or father, even if it absolves one of blame. He grants, further, that the rule that we should provide for our families before we provide for strangers makes sense in ordinary cases.

In his later writings, Godwin softened his position further. In a memoir of his wife, he wrote warmly of the importance of our emotional attachments to others. After underscoring that "it is impossible we should not feel the strongest interest for those persons, whom we know most intimately, and whose welfare and sympathies are united to our own," he continues:

> True wisdom will recommend to us individual attachments; for . . . it is better that man should be a living being, than a stock or a stone. True virtue will sanction this recommendation, since it is the object of virtue to produce happiness, and since the man who lives in the midst of domestic relations, will have many opportunities of conferring pleasure, minute in the detail, yet not trivial in the amount, without interfering with the purposes of general benevolence. Nay, by kindling his sensibility, and harmonizing his soul, they may be expected . . . to render him more prompt in the service of strangers and of the public.[23]

Here Godwin is rightly stressing the importance, from a utilitarian perspective, of close personal relationships. First, these ties do not merely bring us happiness; their contribution to our well-being goes far deeper than that. They make one a living being rather than "a stock or a stone." Second, people's affection for family, friends, and loved ones leads them to daily acts of assistance, consideration, and kindness, which add up to a significant contribution to the well-being of others – perhaps the most significant contribution one can normally make. Third, close relationships stimulate feelings of benevolence, caring, and concern that can extend outside one's own circle. Without the attachments that are nurtured at home, people could never come to have feelings of sympathy or the moral

[23] Godwin, *Memoirs*, 274.

imagination to act beneficently toward casual acquaintances and strangers.[24]

Where does that leave us with regard to Godwin's original dilemma? Should one save the archbishop or one's father? The answer is simple. Utilitarians would want themselves and others to be people who, in an emergency, would act without hesitation or question to save their loved one. Does this imply that they will sometimes do the wrong thing? Yes, perhaps, but the motivation is still one that utilitarians will approve.[25] We must also bear in mind that uncertainty about the future may prevent one from confidently judging that more good really will come from saving the archbishop than from saving one's father or some other ordinary person. It is one thing to stipulate this for purposes of argument, and quite another for one reasonably to believe it at the time. (This is not to say that one may do anything whatsoever to save a loved one. Even Godwin's critics believe that one ought to rescue a bus full of schoolchildren instead of one's father and that it would be wrong to plant a bomb that will kill several innocent people in order to comply with the demands of a terrorist and thus secure the release of one's child who is being held hostage.)

For a number of reasons, then, utilitarians will uphold the idea that the particular relations we have to family, friends, and loved ones give rise to special claims and duties. In arguing for this point, Sidgwick endorsed several of the considerations Godwin mentions. Utilitarianism, he wrote, approves the "cultivation of affection and the performance of affectionate services." But these affections are inevitably limited in scope:

> Most persons are only capable of strong affections towards a few human beings in certain close relations, especially the domestic: and that if these were suppressed, what they would feel towards their fellow-creatures generally would be, as Aristotle says, "but a watery kindness" and a very feeble counterpoise to self-love: so that such specialised affections as the present organisation of society normally produces afford the best means of developing in most persons a more extended benevolence, to the degree to which they are capable of feeling it. (434)

Several other considerations supplement Sidgwick's and Godwin's defense of our special affections. First, we are particularly well positioned to help those who are near and dear to us. We know their needs and

---

[24] For more on this point, see LaFollette, *Personal Relationships*, 208.

[25] Godwin himself later wrote that in (wrongly) saving my loved one, I nevertheless show that "I have *my heart in the right place*." See *Enquiry Concerning Political Justice*, 325.

personalities. We can coordinate our actions with theirs, and the relations of trust, respect, and understanding that we share with them facilitate our acting effectively to promote their good. Second, the affection we feel for them makes it more likely that we will in fact attempt to benefit them and that we will stick to long-term endeavors aimed at promoting their good. Because my well-being is often closely tied to theirs, acting to advance the interests of friends and loved ones – unlike acting to promote the interests of strangers – may involve little or no sacrifice on my part. Indeed, some philosophers describe my benefiting those I care about as extended egoism or self-referential altruism.[26] Finally, in our society, at least, people expect their loved ones to act with special consideration for their interests, and will be hurt and disappointed if they do not.

Can Utilitarians Be True Friends?

Central to one's well-being is having close personal relations with others, and we have reviewed a number of reasons for believing that utilitarians will encourage people to cultivate deep ties to others and to act with special regard for those they are close to. Some critics of utilitarianism concede these points, yet doubt that utilitarians can be true friends, where true friendship is understood to involve loving one's friend for the friend's own sake, for the distinctive individual he or she is.

In discussing this question, Peter Railton asks us to imagine a person he calls John. John feels great affection for his wife Anne, is acutely sensitive to her needs, and goes out of the way to meet them. When asked about the indulgence he shows Anne, John explains:

> I've always thought that people should help each other when they're in a specially good position to do so. I know Anne better than anyone else does, so I know better what she wants and needs. Besides, I have such affection for her that it's no great burden – instead, I get a lot of satisfaction out of it. Just think how awful marriage would be, or life itself, if people didn't take special care of the ones they love.[27]

Railton suggests that Anne might justifiably feel hurt by John's way of looking at things. She might have hoped that it was at least in part for her sake and the sake of their love that he paid special attention to her:

> It is as if John viewed her, their relationship, and even his own affection for her from a distant, objective point of view . . . . His wife might think a more

[26] Mackie, *Ethics*, 132.
[27] Railton, "The demands of morality," 135.

personal point of view would also be appropriate, a point of view from which "It's my wife" or "It's Anne" would have direct and special relevance, and play an unmediated role in his answer to the question, "*Why* do you attend to her so?" (136)

John is a good person, but Railton believes that he is alienated in the sense that an abstract and universalizing point of view mediates his responses both to Anne and to his own feelings.

A number of philosophers believe that this describes the plight of utilitarians, who are thus, they allege, incapable of true friendship. The critics suppose that, according to utilitarianism, what should move us to help a friend is only the desire to maximize the general good. We should not benefit a friend merely because we care for the person, nor should we be motivated by the thought that the person is our friend. Rather, we should assist our friends only if (and to the extent that) doing so maximizes net benefit to all. The critics then contend that this sort of attitude is incompatible with true friendship. Endeavoring always to maximize good is, they believe, inconsistent with the motivations characteristic of true love and friendship.

One might doubt this last proposition and wonder whether John's supposed alienation is really all that troubling. In the real world, friendships and other personal relations sometimes go sour because we come to believe that people we took to be our friends acted selfishly or used us for their own purposes. John, however, is not acting selfishly, and the only sense in which he "uses" his friends is that he acts the way he does toward them because of a general commitment to doing good. Is Anne right to be distressed by what John says? Should we be disturbed to learn that someone we took to be a true friend was a utilitarian? The answers are at least open to debate.

In any case, Railton argues that the distinction we have previously encountered between utilitarianism understood as a criterion of right and utilitarianism understood as a decision-making procedure solves the alienation problem. Utilitarians can reasonably believe that it maximizes well-being in the long run for them to have strong personal attachments, attachments that lead them to act directly for the sake of their friends and loved ones without immediate calculation of utility. Because love and friendship are such important human goods, one's having those attachments and commitments can maximize well-being even if they sometimes cause one to act for the sake of one's friends in ways that run contrary to the general good. In Railton's view, a sophisticated utilitarian is motivated directly by feelings of love and friendship (and not by the goal of maximizing good); yet the person would live a different life if she didn't believe that her life was morally defensible.

In Defense of Railton

Although Railton's reasoning tallies with the indirect utilitarianism this book has championed, several philosophers have attacked it. Neera Badhwar Kapur, for one, concedes that Railton has shown that there is no psychological incompatibility between being a utilitarian and being committed to one's friends, but she argues that there is still "a logical incompatibility between them."[28] This is because utilitarianism demands that "from the moral point of view I give no special weight to my own friendship." It requires that "as between my own friendship and those of others, I be as strictly impartial as a disinterested benevolent spectator." The utilitarian justifies friendship instrumentally, and this, Kapur says, "is logically inconsistent with the attitudes and motivations of [true] friendship" (488). Although she grants that utilitarians can value friendship as both an intrinsic and an instrumental good, the theory still "sees the moral worth of friendship as entirely dependent on its total consequences, with no independent moral weight assigned to its worth for the individuals involved" (498).

Kapur's criticism of Railton misconstrues the utilitarian approach to friendship. She is right, of course, that utilitarians believe that their friendships and, indeed, their personal well-being are, in and of themselves, no more important than anyone else's. Indeed, how could anyone believe otherwise? My relationship to my wife may be the most important thing in my life, but I cannot reasonably believe that my relationship to her is of greater significance than the relationship of any other husband to his wife, just because it is my relationship. However, for reasons we have already canvassed, it does not follow from this, as Kapur apparently believes, that I should be impartial between the needs of my wife and the needs of other men's wives (or other women generally). Likewise, the fact that utilitarians value friendship because of its centrality to human well-being does not imply that one is wrong to love and appreciate one's friends for the particular people they are.

Dean Cocking and Justin Oakley have criticized Railton along related lines. They grant that the sophisticated utilitarian does not ordinarily act as he does out of a desire to promote total well-being; he can, as Railton

---

[28] Kapur, "Why it is wrong to be always guided by the best," 487.

explains, act on the basis of more particular dispositions and motivations, for example, out of love and affection for his friends. However, the utilitarian "would nevertheless alter his dispositions and the course of his life if he thought they did not most promote the good."[29] In their view, this fact implies that the utilitarian should be prepared to terminate a friendship if he finds that it is failing to maximize well-being. Cocking and Oakley believe that being so disposed is incompatible with being a true friend. To measure one's relationships, even occasionally, against the utilitarian standard is too instrumental a way of looking at friendship for their taste.

Like Kapur, Cocking and Oakley have a romantic and rather rarefied view of friendship, and their complaints dissipate when we reflect more closely on how utilitarians would view their friends. Consider a person who has emotional bonds and commitments to friends, spouse, and family members. She cares about these particular people, and her concern and affection for them guide much of her day-to-day conduct. (All parties to the debate agree that on utilitarian grounds it is good for her to have such relationships.) Now, if this person is a utilitarian, then she believes that it would be right for her to alter the terms of those relationships, or even end them altogether, if doing so would be best for everyone affected. This is something she only rarely reflects on. When she does, she hopes that circumstances never arise that would oblige her to alter, or end, her existing relationships. In some cases, her attachments are so strong that she may doubt her ability to end the relationship, even if doing so would be for the best. Still, as a utilitarian, she agrees that if altering the relationship would advance the interests of all, then that is what one should do.

It is difficult to believe that this person's utilitarian perspective alienates her in any objectionable sense or that it is incompatible with being a true friend. Cocking and Oakley wrongly make it sound as if this utilitarian is continually monitoring her relationships with an eye to terminating them as quickly as possible as soon as they appear somehow suboptimal. They also write as if the good that the utilitarian seeks to promote is something entirely divorced from the interests of the people around her. One must bear in mind, further, that no human relationships are unconditional. Relationships change; friendships cease; people divorce. Believing that there are circumstances under which one ought to alter or end a relationship and that you would try to act accordingly, does not necessarily undermine love or true friendship. It depends, to use Cocking and Oakley's phrase, on what those "terminating conditions" are. Cocking and Oakley

[29] Cocking and Oakley, "Indirect consequentialism," 89.

believe that if the terminating condition for you is "it would be best for everyone," then you can't be a friend. This seems daft.

The Personal Point of View

Kapur complains that utilitarianism requires one to take an "agent-neutral or impersonal point of view," from which "my own or my friends' ends and perspectives count for no more than anyone else's" (488). Her contention that utilitarianism cannot do justice to friendship thus connects to a more general criticism of the theory, namely, that it fails to respect one's personal point of view. Utilitarianism, it is alleged, forces the agent to view things from an impartial perspective that regards his own values, projects, and commitments as of no more worth than those of anyone else. Critics of utilitarianism find this unsatisfactory. Our personal projects and commitments, they urge, are what gives value and meaning to our lives. These freely chosen ends have an importance to us that the ends of others do not and, indeed, cannot possibly have (unless, of course, they come to be our ends as well).

The critics charge that utilitarianism obliges us to treat our projects and ends as having no special importance, requiring us to be prepared and willing to drop them at a moment's notice if this is what the overall calculus of utility dictates. As a result, they argue, the theory fails to recognize the importance of a central component of human existence. This line of argument is associated with the writings of the anti-utilitarian philosopher Bernard Williams, whose advocacy of it has been enormously influential. In an important passage, Williams writes that a person

> is identified with his actions as flowing from projects and attitudes which in some cases he takes seriously at the deepest level, as what his life is about . . . . It is absurd to demand of such a man, when the sums come in from the utility network which the projects of others have in part determined, that he should just step aside from his own project and decision and acknowledge the decision which utilitarian calculation requires. It is to alienate him in a real sense from his actions and the source of his action in his own convictions. It is to make him into a channel between the input of everyone's projects, including his own, and an output of optimific decision; but this is to neglect the extent to which *his* actions and *his* decisions have to be seen as the actions and decisions which flow from the projects and attitudes with which he is most closely identified. It is thus, in the most literal sense, an attack on his integrity.[30]

[30] Williams, "Critique of utilitarianism," 116–17.

Williams's integrity objection can be understood in two ways. The first is that utilitarianism threatens one's integrity because it could conceivably require one to do something dreadful (such as kill an innocent person) if this is absolutely necessary for the greater good (for example, to save the lives of several innocent people). However, previous chapters have established that utilitarians will want people to develop moral characters that would make it extremely difficult, even psychologically impossible, for them to slay an innocent person under any circumstance. This is because we are far better off in such a society than in one where people's inhibitions against killing are so weak that they are prepared to kill whenever they believe the likely gain to be worth the cost. Thus understood, Williams's criticism is easily met.

However, the integrity objection can be understood in another way. Now the complaint is not that utilitarianism might require one to do evil, but that it requires one continually to do good. Williams and other critics see utilitarianism as enslaving us to the general happiness. They urge that in deciding how to act a person may properly tilt the scales in her favor, putting more weight on her projects and less on the good of others. This is the argument that concerns us now.

Projects and Well-Being

One's fundamental projects, deep goals, and basic commitments are central to one's identity and self-understanding, to one's integrity in the sense of one's wholeness as a person. On any plausible conception of human good, people's well-being will be intimately connected to the success or failure of their projects, and in Chapter 6 we saw the importance that Mill and other utilitarians place on people's being free to develop and pursue their own plan of life. To be obliged to subordinate one's projects to others or, worse, relinquish them altogether can spell a significant sacrifice, threatening one's identity and cutting at the core of one's well-being. But this is a point about projects and well-being in general, not just about you or me. Utilitarians have reason to value everyone's fulfilling those projects that matter to them; there is nothing special about my particular projects. Because they are mine, I naturally have a concern for them that I do not have for the projects of others, but I can also see that the projects of others are as central to their well-being as mine are to me.

We must not exaggerate, however. We pursue our projects and goals in a world that we do not make, against a changing backdrop of actions and decisions by others. The world is not always conducive to our desires. In navigating our way through life, we must often adjust, modify, and

276

sometimes abandon our plans and projects. Circumstances may eventually oblige Sarah to give up her dream of Hollywood stardom, Kim to exchange a hoped-for career in philosophy for one in computer science, and Eloise to acknowledge that she will never win the Boston Marathon.

Not all of one's goals and projects are fundamental; some are transient or of relatively little importance. Even when we are considering projects that are fundamental, not all projects are of equal value. They can be misconceived or based on false preconceptions; they can be shallow or unsatisfying, and they can be harmful to others or even to one's self. The fact that human beings typically have goals and commitments that are deeply linked to their well-being does not imply that we cannot and should not discriminate among those projects. There are projects that people should abandon, either for their own sake or for the sake of others.

No matter how central our projects are to us, circumstances can compel us to subordinate them to the greater good. In the film *Casablanca* the expatriate adventurer Rick (played by Humphrey Bogart) gives up the love of his life because of her importance to another man. Although she loves this other man less, she sustains him in his crucial work as a leader of the anti-fascist resistance. In explaining his decision, Rick says that in the world they face, it's easy to see that their private concerns do not amount "to a hill of beans" and that their love must yield to larger and weightier concerns. Rick abandons his project at great cost to his well-being, but his sacrifice furthers the projects and well-being of others. Williams's writings sometimes seem to imply that Rick made the wrong choice by putting aside what was of central importance to him in order to advance the greater well-being of others. But this position, which smacks of egoism, is too extreme to be credible.

Influenced by Williams, many contemporary moral theorists insist that morality should respect the deep importance that our projects have for our lives by permitting us to pursue at least our most central or basic projects free from the imperative to promote the general good. Samuel Scheffler calls this freedom an "agent-centred prerogative" and argues that any plausible moral theory must "allow each agent to assign a certain proportionately greater weight to his own interests than to the interests of other people."[31] This prerogative is not boundless. Scheffler does not believe that self-interest takes priority over all moral demands. However, he and likeminded philosophers insist that, when deciding how to act, we are permitted to treat our own projects, desires, and interests as having more significance than those of others. We do not have to give equal considera-

[31] Scheffler, *The Rejection of Consequentialism*, 20.

tion to their interests. In weighing what we should do, we are permitted to put our thumb on the scale.

The Utilitarian Case for Agent-Centered Prerogatives

Although Scheffler, as we shall see, grants that utilitarians can make a case for agent-centered prerogatives, he assumes (as do Williams and others) that in its pure form utilitarianism instructs us to maximize utility in each and every action. These philosophers interpret the theory as holding that people should be motivated only by the goal of maximizing well-being and that this goal should guide every step they take. We have seen, however, that this interpretation is incorrect.

Utilitarians will monitor their conduct by the light of a variety of secondary principles, rules, and norms, general adherence to which tends to promote well-being. Although these rules are not absolute, they do forbid people from doing certain things, for example, lying, stealing, or intentionally injuring others even when they believe that doing so will have favorable results. We have also seen that utilitarianism favors people's developing close personal relationships and acting directly on the basis of their concerns for friends and loved ones, instead of always endeavoring impartially to maximize the good. And, as argued in Chapter 6, there are good utilitarian grounds for giving people reasonably wide scope to live their lives as they see fit, leaving them free from criticism or punishment as long as they fulfill their duties and do not harm others.

G. E. Moore, however, argued that moral agents should seek always to maximize the good to the extent that they can do so without shirking their duties or violating any moral rules. Although he was adamant, as we saw in Chapter 5, that one should never violate moral rules validated on grounds of utility, Moore also held that there is only a limited number of such rules and that they do not cover all situations. In situations not governed by rules, one should always strive to produce as much good as possible. However, Moore mitigates the demanding practical implications of his position by defending two propositions: first, that it is better for one to aim at lesser goods that capture one's interest or for which one has a strong preference (say, coaching a children's baseball team) than at greater goods that move one less (for example, succoring adults with terminal diseases) and, second, that one should aim at goods affecting oneself and those to whom one is strongly attached rather than "attempt a more extended beneficence."[32] In both cases, the rationale is practical: it is better to pursue

---

[32] Moore, *Principia Ethica*, 166–7; Shaw, *Moore on Right and Wrong*, 167–74.

a lesser goal toward which one is inclined and which one is, thus, more likely to accomplish than to aim at an objectively greater good that one will probably fail to achieve for want of perseverance.

Following our discussion of Williams, we can now see a deeper reason for resisting the idea that utilitarianism places us under a general obligation to maximize well-being (except insofar as the moral rules forbid this). This rests on the contribution to well-being that comes from granting an agent-centered prerogative that gives people some scope to develop and pursue their own projects without having to worry whether each step they take contributes maximally to the general good. Just as we obtain better results by encouraging agents to stick to certain reasonably specific rules, so it will maximize well-being in the long run to permit people to pursue (within limits) their interests and freely chosen goals. Freedom to pursue one's projects and goals is basic to human fulfillment, but this fundamental human good cannot be harvested without an agent-centered prerogative. Indeed, as a practical matter, human beings cannot function effectively unless they are able to devote relatively greater attention to their own well-being. In addition, of course, people can generally promote their own well-being and advance their own projects better than they can those of others. For this reason, Mill asserted that "mankind ... obtain a greater sum of happiness when each pursues his own, under the rules and conditions required by the good of the rest, than when each makes the good of the rest his only object, and allows himself no personal pleasures not indispensable to the preservation of his faculties."[33]

For his part, Scheffler grants that the utilitarian case for recognizing agent-centered prerogatives suffices for all practical purposes, but he judges it deficient in theory. He believes that "the independence of the personal point of view is an important fact for morality" because it is an important fact about how people view the world and "not just because of its role in determining the nature of human fulfillment" (62). In other words, respecting the personal point of view by granting people scope to pursue their own interests is important in its own right, not merely because doing so tends to maximize well-being. Instead of trying to vindicate an agent-centered prerogative on utilitarian grounds, we should embrace it as a necessary and appropriate "response to ... the way in which concerns and commitments are *naturally* generated from a person's point of view quite independently of the weight of those concerns in an impersonal ranking of overall states of affairs" (9).

However, it is unclear why the naturalness of the personal point of view

---

[33] Mill, "August Comte," 337. See also *Later Letters*, 762.

gives it intrinsic moral importance. It is easy to see that respecting it is important for promoting human well-being, but difficult to see why it should be respected for its own sake. Further, there is the problem of where, when, and why one is to limit the claims of the personal. Scheffler refers to a "discrepancy" between the personal and impersonal points of view, and indeed every moral theory (aside from egoism) recognizes that self-interest and the demands of morality can diverge and, thus, that we must sometimes subordinate our own projects to the interests of others. But where precisely is the line to be drawn? Delimiting the claims of the personal requires a comprehensive moral perspective. This is what utilitarianism offers.

Scheffler concedes, as I have said, that in practice utilitarianism provides ample scope for the personal point of view, but some critics deny this. They contend either that the utilitarian concern to maximize well-being will restrict an agent-centered prerogative too much, or that the utilitarian approach requires a kind of bifocal vision that continues to undercut or in some way alienate one from one's projects. The first of these contentions is an empirical one. It imagines that it will turn out that more good will come from giving less scope to the personal than has been implicitly assumed heretofore. This, of course, is a hypothesis which requires evidence to back it up. Suppose, however, that the assertion is true. If so, it discredits utilitarianism only if one assumes that our present intuitions about how much scope should be granted to the personal have foundational moral status. Yet if anything reflects one's cultural background and historical circumstances, it will be one's intuitive sense of where the proper balance lies between one's interests and those of others. We return to this issue in the next section.

The second contention is a variation of one of the criticisms of the utilitarian perspective on friendship. The critic reminds us that even if utilitarianism acknowledges the importance of the personal point of view by making space for an agent-centered prerogative, it still requires agents, at least occasionally, to step back and assess their projects, commitments, and relationships from the larger utilitarian perspective. This, it is argued, is either impossible or else alienating and subversive of one's projects and undertakings. But this complaint is misguided. Far from being impossible, an ethical and reflective life requires one periodically to take stock and to reassess and possibly alter one's projects in light of larger moral considerations. Doing so need not alienate a person from his or her commitments, nor does it in any way undermine or deny the importance of the personal.

The Needs of Strangers

Critics of utilitarianism inveterately complain that the theory is unacceptably demanding because it requires us, in the name of the general good, to sacrifice our most basic interests – our projects, close personal relations, and defining commitments. As we have seen, utilitarians respond by arguing that collective, long-term well-being is best served (1) by encouraging individuals to develop close personal relations and to act on the basis of those affections and (2) by permitting them to pursue their own goals and plans without endeavoring in every action they take to advance the general good as much as possible. This chapter has marshaled various considerations in support of this proposition and has argued that utilitarianism, properly understood and applied, does not routinely command moral agents to relinquish their most basic interests.

This conclusion may be premature, however, because we live in a world in which many human beings, perfect strangers to us, are in great distress. Famine, malnutrition, disease, and extreme poverty undermine the well-being and destroy the lives of millions of our fellow creatures. Many of us in the affluent countries would like to believe that there is little or nothing we can do to alleviate or prevent such suffering, but this notion is demonstrably false. None of us can single-handedly eradicate poverty or stop famine, but we could, each of us, act in ways that would help to save numerous lives and alleviate the misery and distress of many.

To focus on just one issue, aid organizations could prevent the deaths of millions of Third World children – if they had more money. Every year three million unfortunate children die from dehydrating diarrhea alone; yet a packet of the oral rehydration salts that would save a diarrhetic child's life costs only 15 cents. Even making generous allowance for overhead, transportation, and other costs, a check for $100 could permit thirty children to have reasonably long lives instead of dying painfully at a young age. Measles kills an additional million children a year; yet for $17 UNICEF can vaccinate a child against measles as well as tuberculosis, whooping cough, diphtheria, tetanus, and polio, giving them lifetime protection.[34] So there is plenty one could do to help. If we sent to Oxfam, CARE, or UNICEF the money we would otherwise spend on new clothes, entertainment, or eating out, each of us could save hundreds of children. The more money we send, the more good we do. Because we are talking about rescuing children from death or crippling disease, on almost any conception of well-being a person

[34] See Unger, *Living High*, 3–7.

could easily donate most of what she owns and most of what she earns before the cost to her begins to match the good that she is doing.

Many people believe that although it would be good for us to help Oxfam or CARE, there is nothing wrong about not doing so. They believe that giving money to save children from debilitating disease is like supporting the soccer program at the local elementary school. It is a worthy cause, and donating to it is generous and charitable, but we are not morally obliged to give. This common belief is almost certainly mistaken. Consistency with the values and principles implicit in everyday commonsense morality requires those of us who live in the affluent countries to do significantly more than most of us now do (which is almost nothing).[35] This concurs with most normative theories. For example, a Kantian approach to ethics supports the proposition that both as nations and as individuals we have a strict duty to give at least our fair share to relieve the suffering of those in distress.[36] And from a utilitarian perspective there is a very strong case for establishing a general norm that we should aid strangers when the benefit to them is great and the cost to ourselves is comparatively minor. Practically speaking, a norm requiring people in the affluent countries to contribute 5 or 10 percent of their incomes toward alleviating disease, malnutrition, and grinding poverty would, if generally acted upon, probably suffice to eliminate in a few decades much of the misery that now exists in the world.[37]

Many philosophers believe that utilitarianism commands us to do much, much more than this. They believe the theory requires those of us who are relatively well off to devote most of our time, money, and energy to eradicating extreme poverty. Although the sacrifice involved would be significant, the resultant good would easily counterbalance it. Weighed against the lives I would be saving, it is of little moment that I relinquish my creature comforts, shelve the novel I have been trying to write, and stop spending time playing with my young niece and nephew. A few utilitarian-minded philosophers embrace this conclusion. "Given the parameters of the actual world," one writes, "there is no question that promoting the good would require a life of hardship, self-denial, and austerity."[38] Some other writers arrive at a similar conclusion on grounds independent of utilitarianism.[39] Nevertheless, it's fair to say that most contemporary

---

[35] Singer, *Practical Ethics*, Ch. 8; Unger, *Living High*; Cullity, "International aid."
[36] Van Wyk, "World hunger," 80–3.
[37] Cf. Brandt, *Facts, Values, and Morality*, 229–32.
[38] Kagan, *The Limits of Morality*, 360.
[39] Unger, *Living High*, Ch. 6; Cullity, "International aid."

philosophers believe this conclusion to be untenable. It cannot be the case, they think, that morality ordains this sort of sacrifice. If utilitarianism entails that it does, then the theory is to be rejected.

There are compelling reasons, however, for believing that utilitarians will not advocate a moral norm requiring people to give away most of what they have to help those in distress. Instead, utilitarians will uphold the less demanding norm mentioned earlier (namely, that we should aid strangers when the benefit to them is great and the cost to ourselves comparatively minor). First, trying to instill the more demanding norm would be difficult, and the psychological and other costs of doing so (that is, of getting people to feel guilty about not giving away most of what they have) would be high. Second, and related, it is doubtful whether we could ever succeed in motivating most people to comply with such a norm – at least not over the long run. Third, even if most people did adhere to the norm, the price to them would be high, requiring them, as we have seen, to relinquish, or at least be prepared to relinquish, their basic projects and attachments.[40]

One might argue that, however difficult and costly it might be to instill such a norm, still it would be beneficial for utilitarians to push in this direction. But the truth of this assertion is far from obvious. For one thing, if a moral rule places demands on people that they repudiate as unreasonable or that it is unrealistic to expect them to live up to, their commitment to other norms may weaken. Just as impractical or unworkable laws can enfeeble respect for the law in general, so attempts to foist ill-considered moral demands on people can prove counterproductive. There is, in any case, a kind of unreality to the idea that the best results would come from people accepting and acting on the principle that they must give away almost all they have to combat the distress of strangers. Suppose that society began moving gradually to embrace this norm, with more and more people beginning to make larger and larger sacrifices. Long before the norm was generally accepted – that is, long before most people were prepared to live as monks in order to help the Third World – people would de facto be living up to the weaker norm by making comparatively modest but still significant efforts to help. But if most people were complying with this weaker norm, then the problem of Third World children dying needlessly would be solved, and there would be little need for people to sacrifice more.

In this context, it is important to recall one of the themes of Chapter 6,

---

[40] See Hooker, "Brink, Kagan, utilitarianism," and Haslett, *Capitalism with Morality*, 13–17.

namely, the importance from a utilitarian perspective of designing institutions that structure people's conduct in welfare-promoting ways. As Russell Hardin writes:

> The chief result of successful utilitarian actions over the long run, therefore, must be the creation of institutions that will take over the task of enhancing the general welfare. This means that the chief aim of utilitarianism in many contexts must be to reduce the need for individual beneficence and even to eliminate it in many contexts.[41]

Similarly, Peter Railton argues for the necessity of "altering social and political arrangements" so that "we can lessen the disruptiveness of moral demands on our lives, and in the long run achieve better results than freelance good-doing."[42] For example, with an adequately funded system of disaster relief in place, it would probably be a poor idea for people to interrupt their normal lives to help. Their ill-informed and uncoordinated efforts would interfere with skilled relief work and be economically disruptive as well.

In trying to alleviate hunger and distress, the first and highest priority of utilitarians will be to establish (or strengthen) institutions dedicated to this task. Because of the state's superior ability to mobilize resources, state-funded or state-sponsored humanitarian organizations will inevitably play a leading role. Moreover, through taxation and other revenue-generating devices the state can spread the costs so that no individual is required to shoulder an inordinate burden. One must also bear in mind that tackling famine, poverty, and disease is more than a matter of donating money; taking on these problems will require long-term, structural changes in the social and economic arrangements of the afflicted countries. Outsiders can encourage the relevant changes, but assuming responsibility for the management of another nation's affairs would almost certainly be counterproductive.

Let us assume, then, that rather than advocating a stringent norm that requires people in the affluent countries to give up most of what they have to assist strangers in distress, utilitarians will, instead, devote their energies to setting up the institutions necessary to effectively address problems like famine relief. In this context, Railton makes two further points. The first is that

---

[41] Hardin, *Morality within the Limits of Reason*, 13.
[42] Railton, "The demands of morality," 161.

such social and political changes cannot be made unless the lives of individuals are psychologically supportable in the meanwhile, and this provides substantial reason for rejecting the notion that we should abandon all that matters to us as individuals and devote ourselves solely to net social welfare.

The second is that

what matters most is *perceived* rather than actual demandingness or disruptiveness, and this will be a relative matter, depending upon normal expectations. If certain social or political arrangements encourage higher contribution as a matter of course, individuals may not sense these moral demands as excessively intrusive. (161–2)

Nevertheless, it is a fact that most people are not now living up to the weaker norm of making a modest effort to help, and that the institutions and government policies that would be desirable on utilitarian grounds are not in place. As a result, there is clearly room for the individual to do more. Knowing this, the argument goes, I should respond by increasing my own efforts, spending more and more of my time, money, and energy to alleviate misery in the Third World – if not directly, then indirectly, by fighting for appropriate government action.[43] And I should keep on increasing my efforts up to the point of diminishing marginal utility, that is, up to the point where the cost to me of doing more would outweigh whatever good I could achieve. This point runs in harness with Wolf's earlier contention that utilitarians should strive to be moral saints themselves even if they shouldn't advocate saintliness to others.

There are several responses to this argument. First, one should not feel guilty, nor criticize others, for not doing more than is required by the weaker norm.[44] This is what it means for there to be a moral norm or rule in the first place. By analogy, utilitarians should not feel guilty about, or criticize others, for refusing to violate rules that are justified on utilitarian grounds (like those against stealing or harming innocent people) in an

---

[43] The United States now spends only $43 per capita on non-military aid to developing countries (and not all of this is directed toward those who are most in need). Germany spends twice as much per capita, France three times as much, and Norway six times as much. *San Francisco Chronicle*, April 27, 1997, "Sunday," 3.

[44] Mill writes: "It is not good that persons should be bound, by other people's opinion, to do everything that they would deserve praise for doing. There is a standard of altruism to which all should be required to come up, and a degree beyond it which is not obligatory, but meritorious" ("August Comte," 337).

effort to maximize the good in particular cases. Nor should utilitarians regret having the dispositions and attachments that their theory thinks it is good for people to have, even though this means that they do not always act as impartial utility-maximizing machines. Second, one can praise and hold up as moral exemplars those who do more than is required of them without rebuking others for doing less. Positive reinforcement can influence how people act without incurring the costs involved in trying to establish a moral rule that few, if any, of them can live up to.

Third, one may choose as an individual to do more than the general norm requires. The utilitarian R. M. Hare suggests that one can accept for oneself personal but fairly general principles "which I do not expect to be the same for everybody, but which are suited to my own capacities and condition."[45] Hare goes on to stress that these principles must be based on honest self-assessment; they should be realistic and not demand what is impossible. Even if an individual doesn't set for herself higher ideals or more exacting principles than she advocates for others, the person will, if she has the benevolent instincts that utilitarians would want themselves and others to have, be moved by the distress of strangers and desire to alleviate it. Not only will she willingly embrace and advocate the weaker norm, but she may also adjust and modify her life and projects in ways beyond what the norm requires. For instance, without seeking to be a saint, she may involve herself in political efforts to alleviate poverty in the Third World, or join a charitable organization devoted to famine relief or to inoculating poor children against measles. She may even become an expert on the problems facing particular regions or the needs of specific villages. This sort of involvement means, however, that relieving famine or reducing infant morbidity becomes one of her personal projects, perhaps even a life-defining project. Instead of being experienced as a sacrifice, her efforts may be part of what brings meaning and satisfaction to her life.[46]

The argument over utilitarianism and our duties to strangers has a curious dialectic. Utilitarianism is accused of requiring excessive sacrifice on our part, undermining our personal projects, and effacing our attachments to those who are near and dear to us. Critics contend that because utilitarianism is so demanding, it can and must be repudiated. At this point, many people breathe a sigh of relief, comforted that they can continue their lives as before, free from moral censure. For the message that we have nothing to feel guilty about is clearly the subtext of what the critics are saying, even when they give lip service to the idea that we should

---

[45] Hare, *Moral Thinking*, 200.
[46] Jackson, "Decision-theoretic consequentialism," 477–8.

all be doing more than we now do to save the lives of Third World children.

Most of us are all too eager to be reassured that we are living upright lives, beyond moral reproach. Yet almost all of us could be doing substantially more to assist needy Third World children without diminishing in the least our own well-being or that of those who are near and dear to us. Indeed, without any significant loss to ourselves, most of us could be doing much more than we do now for those who need help in our own communities – homeless families, children growing up in poverty, elderly people who are lonely or ill. In fact, concerning ourselves with the travails and tribulations of those who are less fortunate would probably enrich our lives and bring us significant long-term satisfaction. This point may seem banal, and indeed it is one that ethicists of various stripes affirm. Nevertheless, much of our capitalist, materialist culture promotes patterns of value and behavior, in particular, a self-indulgent consumerism, that can blind us to the needs of those in distress, both in our own communities and in far away places.

In this context, living up to the norm of assisting those in distress (at least where doing so involves no serious sacrifice to us), encouraging others to do the same, and helping to build the institutions and public policies necessary to make that commitment effective, especially in the case of Third World poverty, is of the utmost importance. Professional philosophers, however, have been more interested in using the issue of famine relief as a club with which to beat utilitarianism over the head for its allegedly extreme demandingness than they have been in upholding the moral necessity of doing far more than most of us do now to aid those in distress – or in exploring why our culture is resistant to that message.

Bibliography

Adams, Robert Merrihew. "Motive utilitarianism." *Journal of Philosophy*, vol. 73, no. 14 (August 12, 1976): 467–81.

Alexander, Larry. "Comment: personal projects and impersonal rights." *Harvard Journal of Law and Public Policy*, vol. 12, no. 3 (Summer 1989): 813–26.

Alexander, Larry. "Pursuing the good – indirectly." *Ethics*, vol. 95, no. 2 (January 1985): 315–32.

Allison, Lincoln, ed. *The Utilitarian Response: The Contemporary Viability of Utilitarian Political Philosophy*. London: Sage Publications, 1990.

Anderson, John. *Studies in Empirical Philosophy*. Sydney: Angus and Robertson, 1962.

Annas, Julia. "The good life and the good lives of others." *Social Philosophy and Policy*, vol. 9, no. 2 (Summer 1992): 133–48.

Aristotle, *The Nichomachean Ethics*, trans. D. Ross and J. O. Urmson. Oxford: Oxford University Press, 1980.

Arthur, John and William H. Shaw, eds. *Justice and Economic Distribution*, 2nd edn. Englewood Cliffs, N.J.: Prentice-Hall, 1991.

Ascher, Mark L. "Curtailing inherited wealth." *Michigan Law Review*, vol. 89, no. 1 (October 1990): 69–151.

Austin, John. *The Province of Jurisprudence Determined*, ed. W. E. Rumble. Cambridge: Cambridge University Press, 1995.

Baier, Annette, "Doing without moral theory?" In Stanley G. Clarke and Evan Simpson, eds., *Anti-Theory in Ethics and Moral Conservatism*. Albany, N.Y.: State University Press of New York, 1989.

Bailey, James Wood. *Utilitarianism, Institutions, and Justice*. New York: Oxford University Press, 1997.

Barrow, Robin. *Utilitarianism: A Contemporary Statement*. Aldershot, Hants: Edward Elgar, 1991.

Barry, Brian. *Justice as Impartiality*. Oxford: Oxford University Press, 1995.

Barry, Brian. *Theories of Justice*. Berkeley: University of California Press, 1989.

Barry, Norman. *Welfare*. Minneapolis: University of Minnesota Press, 1990.

Becker, Lawrence C. "Good lives: prolegomena." *Social Philosophy and Policy*, vol. 9, no. 2 (Summer 1992): 15–37.

Becker, Lawrence C. and Kenneth Kipnis, eds. *Property: Cases, Concepts, Critiques*. Englewood Cliffs, N.J.: Prentice-Hall, 1984.

Bennett, Jonathan. *The Act Itself*. Oxford: Oxford University Press, 1995.

Bentham, Jeremy. "A fragment on government." In *The Works of Jeremy Bentham*, vol. 1, ed. J. Bowring. New York: Russell & Russell, 1962.

Bentham, Jeremy. "Principles of the civil code." In *The Works of Jeremy Bentham*, vol. 1, ed. J. Bowring. New York: Russell & Russell, 1962.

Bentham, Jeremy. *The Principles of Morals and Legislation*. Buffalo: Prometheus, 1988.

Bentham, Jeremy. "The rationale of judicial evidence, specially applied to English practice." In *The Works of Jeremy Bentham*, vol. 6, ed. J. Bowring. New York: Russell & Russell, 1962.

Bentham, Jeremy. "The rationale of reward." In *The Works of Jeremy Bentham*, vol. 2, ed. J. Bowring. New York: Russell & Russell, 1962.

Berger, Fred R. *Happiness, Justice, and Freedom: The Moral and Political Philosophy of John Stuart Mill*. Berkeley: University of California Press, 1984.

Berkeley, George. "Passive obedience." In *The Works of George Berkeley, Bishop of Cloyne*, vol. 6, ed. A. A. Luce and T. E. Jessop. London: Thomas Nelson, 1953.

Blum, Lawrence. "Moral perception and particularity." *Ethics*, vol. 101, no. 4 (July 1991): 701–25.

Blum, Walter J. and Harry Kalven, Jr. *The Uneasy Case for Progressive Taxation*. Chicago: University of Chicago Press, 1953.

Bok, Sissela. *Lying: Moral Choice in Public and Private Life*. New York: Random House, 1978.

Braithwaite, John and Philip Pettit. *Not Just Deserts: A Republican Theory of Criminal Justice*. Oxford: Oxford University Press, 1990.

Brandt, Richard B. *Ethical Theory*. Englewood Cliffs, N.J.: Prentice-Hall, 1959.

Brandt, Richard B. *Facts, Values, and Morality*. Cambridge: Cambridge University Press, 1996.

Brandt, Richard B. "Fairness to indirect optimific theories in ethics." *Ethics*, vol. 98, no. 2 (January 1988): 341–60.

Brandt, Richard B. "Happiness." In Paul Edwards, ed., *The Encyclopedia of Philosophy*, vol. 3. New York: Macmillan, 1967.

Brandt, Richard B. *Morality, Utilitarianism, and Rights*. Cambridge: Cambridge University Press, 1992.

Brandt, Richard B. "The real and alleged problems of utilitarianism." *The Hastings Center Report*, vol. 13, no. 2 (April 1993): 37–43.

Brandt, Richard B. *A Theory of the Good and the Right*. Oxford: Oxford University Press, 1979.

Brandt, Richard B. "Toward a credible form of utilitarianism." In Hector-Neri Castañeda and George Nakhnikian, eds., *Morality and the Language of Conduct*. Detroit: Wayne State University Press, 1963.

Brink, David O. "Mill's deliberative utilitarianism." *Philosophy and Public Affairs*, vol. 21, no. 1 (Winter 1992): 67–103.

Brink, David O. *Moral Realism and the Foundations of Ethics*. Cambridge: Cambridge University Press, 1989.

Brink, David O. "The separateness of persons, distributive norms, and moral theory." In R. G. Frey and Christopher W. Morris, eds., *Value, Welfare, and Morality*. Cambridge: Cambridge University Press, 1993.

Broome, John. "A Reply to Sen." *Economics and Philosophy*, vol. 7, no. 2 (October 1991): 285–7.

Broome, John. "Utility." *Economics and Philosophy*, vol. 7, no. 1 (April 1991): 1–12.

Broome, John. *Weighing Goods*. Oxford: Blackwell, 1991.

Clarke, Stanley G. and Evan Simpson, eds. *Anti-Theory in Ethics and Moral Conservatism*. Albany, N.Y.: State University Press of New York, 1989.

Cocking, Dean and Justin Oakley. "Indirect consequentialism, friendship, and the problem of alienation." *Ethics*, vol. 106, no. 1 (October 1995): 86–111.

Cohen, G. A. "Equality of what? On welfare, goods, and capabilities." In Martha C. Nussbaum and Amartya Sen, eds., *The Quality of Life*. Oxford: Oxford University Press, 1993.

Cohen, G. A. *Self-Ownership, Freedom, and Equality*. Cambridge: Cambridge University Press, 1995.

Crisp, Roger, ed. *How Should One Live? Essays on the Virtues*. Oxford: Oxford University Press, 1996.

Crisp, Roger, ed. *Mill on Utilitarianism*. London: Routledge, 1997.

Crisp, Roger, "Utilitarianism and the life of virtue." *Philosophical Quarterly*, vol. 42, no. 167 (April 1992): 139–60.

Crisp, Roger and Michael Slote, eds. *Virtue Ethics*. Oxford: Oxford University Press, 1997.

Cullity, Garrett. "International aid and the scope of kindness." *Ethics*, vol. 105, no. 1 (October 1994): 99–127.

Darwall, Stephen. "Moore to Stevenson." In Robert J. Cavalier, James Gouinlock, and James P. Sterba, eds., *Ethics in the History of Western Philosophy*. Basingstoke: Macmillan, 1989.

Darwall, Stephen, Allan Gibbard, and Peter Railton. "Toward *fin de siècle* ethics: some trends." *Philosophical Review*, vol. 101, no. 1 (January 1992): 115–89.

Davis, Michael. "Recent work in punishment theory." *Public Affairs Quarterly*, vol. 4, no. 3 (July 1990): 217–32.

Den Uyl, Douglas and Tibor R. Machan. "Recent work on the concept of happiness." *American Philosophical Quarterly*, vol. 20, no. 2 (April 1983): 115–34.

Dinwiddy, John. *Bentham*. Oxford: Oxford University Press, 1989.

Dolinko, David. "Some thoughts about retributivism." *Ethics*, vol. 101, no. 3 (April 1991): 537–59.

Donagan, Alan. "Consistency in rationalist moral systems." *Journal of Philosophy*, vol. 81, no. 6 (June 1984): 291–309.

Donagan, Alan. "Moral dilemmas, genuine and spurious: a comparative anatomy." *Ethics*, vol. 104, no. 1 (October 1993): 7–21.

Donagan, Alan. *The Theory of Morality*. Chicago: University of Chicago Press, 1977.

Dore, Clement. *Moral Scepticism*. Basingstoke: Macmillan, 1991.

Drèze, Jean, and Amartya Sen. *Hunger and Public Action*. Oxford: Oxford University Press, 1989.

Duff, R. A. and David Garland, eds. *A Reader on Punishment*. Oxford: Oxford University Press, 1994.

Dworkin, Gerald, ed. *Mill's* On Liberty: *Critical Essays*. Lanham, Md.: Rowman & Littlefield, 1997.

Dworkin, Gerald. "Paternalism." In Richard A. Wasserstrom, ed., *Morality and the Law*. Belmont, Calif.: Wadsworth, 1971.

Dworkin, Ronald. *Law's Empire*. Cambridge, Mass.: Harvard University Press, 1986.

Dworkin, Ronald. *Taking Rights Seriously*. Cambridge, Mass.: Harvard University Press, 1977.

Ellis, Brian. "Retrospective and prospective utilitarianism." *Noûs*, vol. 15, no. 3 (September 1981): 325–39.

Elster, Jon. *Local Justice: How Institutions Allocate Scarce Goods and Necessary Burdens*. New York: Russell Sage, 1992.

Elster, Jon and John E. Roemer, eds. *Interpersonal Comparisons of Well-Being*. Cambridge: Cambridge University Press, 1991.

Eriksson, Björn. "Utilitarianism for sinners." *American Philosophical Quarterly*, vol. 34, no. 2 (April 1997): 213–28.

Ewing, A. C. *Ethics*. London: English Universities Press, 1953.

Farina, Francesco, Frank Hahn, and Stefano Vannucci, eds. *Ethics, Rationality, and Economic Behaviour*. Oxford: Oxford University Press, 1996.

Feinberg, Joel. *Social Philosophy*. Englewood Cliffs, N.J.: Prentice-Hall, 1973.

Feldman, Fred. *Confrontations with the Reaper: A Philosophical Study of the Nature and Value of Death*. New York: Oxford University Press, 1992.

Feldman, Fred. *Introductory Ethics*. Englewood Cliffs, N.J.: Prentice-Hall, 1978.

Finnis, John. *Natural Law and Natural Rights*. Oxford: Oxford University Press, 1980.

Fishkin, James. "Utilitarianism versus human rights." *Social Philosophy and Policy*, vol. 1, no. 2 (Spring 1984): 103–7.

Flanagan, Owen. *Varieties of Moral Personality: Ethics and Psychological Realism*. Cambridge, Mass.: Harvard University Press, 1991.

Foot, Philippa. "Utilitarianism and the virtues." *Mind*, vol. 94, no. 374 (April 1985): 196–209.

Frankfurt, Harry. "Equality and respect." *Social Research*, vol 64, no. 1 (Spring 1997): 3–15.

Freeman, Samuel. "Utilitarianism, deontology, and the priority of the right." *Philosophy and Public Affairs*, vol. 23, no. 4 (Fall 1994): 313–49.

Frey, R. G. "Act-utilitarianism, consequentialism, and moral rights." In R. G. Frey, ed., *Utility and Rights*. Minneapolis: University of Minnesota Press, 1984.

Frey, R. G. *Rights, Killing, and Suffering: Moral Vegetarianism and Applied Ethics*. Oxford: Blackwell, 1983.

Frey, R. G., ed. *Utility and Rights*. Minneapolis: University of Minnesota Press, 1984.

Frey, R. G., and Christopher W. Morris, eds. *Value, Welfare, and Morality*. Cambridge: Cambridge University Press, 1993.

Fried, Charles. *Right and Wrong*. Cambridge, Mass.: Harvard University Press, 1978.

Friedman, Jeffrey. "What's wrong with libertarianism." *Critical Review*, vol. 11, no. 3 (Summer 1997): 407–67.

Friedman, Milton. "Lerner on the economics of control." *Journal of Political Economy*, vol 55, no. 5 (October 1947): 405–16.

Gauthier, David. *Practical Reasoning: The Structure and Foundations of Prudential and Moral Arguments and their Exemplification in Discourse*. Oxford: Oxford University Press, 1962.

Gert, Bernard. *Morality: A New Justification of the Moral Rules*. New York: Oxford University Press, 1988.

Gibbard, Allan. "Inchoately utilitarian common sense: the bearing of a thesis of Sidgwick's on moral theory." In Harlan B. Miller and William H. Williams, eds., *The Limits of Utilitarianism*. Minneapolis: University of Minnesota Press, 1982.

Gibbard, Alan. "Utilitarianism and human rights." *Social Philosophy and Policy*, vol. 1, no. 2 (Spring 1984): 92–102.

Gilligan, Carol. *In a Different Voice: Psychological Theory and Women's Development*. Cambridge, Mass.: Harvard University Press, 1982.

Glover, Jonathan. *Causing Death and Saving Lives*. Harmondsworth: Penguin, 1977.

Glover, Jonathan, ed. *Utilitarianism and Its Critics*. New York: Macmillan, 1990.

Godwin, William. *Enquiry Concerning Political Justice. With Selections from Godwin's Other Writings*, ed. K. C. Carter. Oxford: Oxford University Press, 1971.

Godwin, William. *Memoirs of the Author of* The Rights of Woman. In Mary Wollstonecraft and William Godwin, *A Short Residence in Sweden* and *Memoirs of the Author of* The Rights of Woman, ed. R. Holmes. Harmondsworth: Penguin, 1987.

Goldberg, Steve. "On capital punishment." *Ethics*, vol. 85, no. 1 (October 1974): 67–79.

Goldstick, D. "Distributive justice and utility." *Journal of Value Inquiry*, vol. 25, no. 1 (January 1991): 65–71.

Goldsworthy, Jeffrey. "Well-being and value." *Utilitas*, vol. 4, no. 1 (May 1992): 1–26.

Goodin, Robert E. "Actual preferences, actual people." *Utilitas*, vol. 3, no. 1 (May 1991): 113–19.

Goodin, Robert E. *Utilitarianism as a Public Philosophy*. Cambridge: Cambridge University Press, 1995.

Goodin, Robert E. "Utility and the good." In Peter Singer, ed., *A Companion to Ethics*. Oxford: Blackwell, 1991.

Gorovitz, Samuel, ed. *Mill's* Utilitarianism: *Text and Critical Essays*. Indianapolis: Bobbs-Merrill, 1971.

Gray, John. *Liberalisms: Essays in Political Philosophy*. London: Routledge, 1989.

Griffin, James. "The human good and the ambitions of consequentialism." *Social Philosophy and Policy*, vol. 9, no. 2 (Summer 1992): 118–32.

Griffin, James. *Value Judgement: Improving Our Ethical Beliefs*. Oxford: Oxford University Press, 1996.

Griffin, James. *Well-Being: Its Meaning, Measurement, and Moral Importance*. Oxford: Oxford University Press, 1986.

Grote, John. *An Examination of the Utilitarian Philosophy*. Cambridge: Deighton, Bell, and Co., 1870.

Hall, Everett W. "The 'proof' of utility in Bentham and Mill." *Ethics*, vol. 60, no. 1 (October 1949): 1–18.

Hamlin, Alan. "Rights, indirect utilitarianism, and contractarianism." *Economics and Philosophy*, vol. 5, no. 2 (October 1989): 167–87.

Hamlin, Alan. "Welfare." In Robert E. Goodin and Phillip Pettit, eds., *A Companion to Contemporary Political Philosophy*. Oxford: Blackwell, 1993.

Hardin, Russell. *Morality within the Limits of Reason*. Chicago: University of Chicago Press, 1988.

Hare, R. M. "Comments." In Douglas Seanor and N. Fotion, eds., *Hare and Critics: Essays on* Moral Thinking. Oxford: Oxford University Press, 1988.

Hare, R. M. "Could Kant have been a utilitarian?" *Utilitas*, vol. 5, no. 1 (May 1993): 1–16.

Hare, R. M. *Freedom and Reason*. New York: Oxford University Press, 1963.

Hare, R. M. *The Language of Morals*. Oxford: Oxford University Press, 1952.

Hare, R. M. *Moral Thinking: Its Levels, Method, and Point*. Oxford: Oxford University Press, 1981.

Hare, R. M. "Principles." *Proceedings of the Aristotelian Society*, vol. 73 (1972/73): 1–18.

Hare, R. M. "What is wrong with slavery." *Philosophy and Public Affairs*, vol. 8, no. 2 (Winter 1979): 103–21.

Harman, Gilbert. *The Nature of Morality*. New York: Oxford University Press, 1977.

Harrison, Jonathan. "Rule utilitarianism and cumulative-effect utilitarianism." *Canadian Journal of Philosophy*, suppl. vol. 5 (1979): 21–45.

Harrison, Ross. *Bentham*. London: Routledge and Kegan Paul, 1983.

Harsanyi, John C. "Expectation effects, individual utilities, and rational desires." In Brad Hooker, ed., *Rationality, Rules, and Utility: New Essays on the Moral Philosophy of Richard B. Brandt*. Boulder, Colo.: Westview, 1993.

Harsanyi, John C. "Morality and the theory of rational behaviour." In Amartya Sen and Bernard Williams, eds., *Utilitarianism and Beyond*. Cambridge: Cambridge University Press, 1982.

Hart, H. L. A. *The Concept of Law*. Oxford: Oxford University Press, 1961.

Harwood, Sterling. "Eleven objections to utilitarianism." In Louis Pojman, ed., *Moral Philosophy: A Reader*. Indianapolis: Hackett, 1993.

Haslett, D. W. *Capitalism with Morality*. Oxford: Oxford University Press, 1994.

Haslett, D. W. *Equal Consideration: A Theory of Moral Justification*. Newark, N.J.: University of Delaware Press, 1987.

Haslett, D. W. "On life, death, and abortion." *Utilitas*, vol 8, no. 2 (July 1996): 159–89.

Haslett, D. W. "What is utility?" *Economics and Philosophy*, vol. 6, no. 1 (April 1990): 65–94.

Hausman, Daniel M. and Michael S. McPherson. *Economic Analysis and Moral Philosophy*. Cambridge: Cambridge University Press, 1996.

Häyry, Matti, *Liberal Utilitarianism and Applied Ethics*. London: Routledge, 1994.

Held, Virginia, ed. *Justice and Care*. Boulder, Colo.: Westview, 1995.

Henson, Richard G. "Utilitarianism and the wrongness of killing." *Philosophical Review*, vol. 80, no. 3 (July 1971): 320–37.

Holbrook, Daniel. "Consequentialism: the philosophical dog that does not bark?" *Utilitas*, vol. 3, no. 1 (May 1991): 107–12.

Holbrook, Daniel. *Qualitative Utilitarianism*. Lanham, Md.: University Press of America, 1988.

Hooker, Brad. "Brink, Kagan, utilitarianism, and self-sacrifice." *Utilitas*, vol. 3, no. 2 (November 1991): 263–73.

Hooker, Brad. "Compromising with convention." *American Philosophical Quarterly*, vol. 31, no. 4 (October 1994): 311–17.

Hooker, Brad, ed. *Rationality, Rules, and Utility: New Essays on the Moral Philosophy of Richard B. Brandt*. Boulder, Colo.: Westview, 1993.

Hooker, Brad. "Rule-consequentialism." *Mind*, vol. 99, no. 393 (January 1990): 67–77.

Hooker, Brad. "Rule-consequentialism, incoherence, fairness." *Proceedings of the Aristotelian Society*, vol. 95 (1994/95): 19–35.

Howard-Snyder, Frances. "The rejection of objective consequentialism." *Utilitas*, vol. 9, no. 2 (July 1997): 241–8.

Hurka, Thomas. *Perfectionism*. Oxford: Oxford University Press, 1993.

Hurka, Thomas. "Virtue as loving the good." *Social Philosophy and Policy*, vol. 9, no. 2 (Summer 1992): 149–68.

Hursthouse, Rosalind. "Virtue theory and abortion." *Philosophy and Public Affairs*, vol. 20, no. 3 (Summer 1991): 223–46.

Hutcheson, Francis. *An Inquiry into the Original of Our Ideas of Beauty and Virtue*. New York: Garland, 1971.

Jackson, Frank. "Decision-theoretic consequentialism and the nearest and dearest objection." *Ethics*, vol. 101, no. 3 (April 1991): 461–82.

Johnson, Conrad D. *Moral Legislation: A Legal-Political Model for Indirect Consequentialist Reasoning.* Cambridge: Cambridge University Press, 1991.

Kagan, Shelly. *The Limits of Morality.* Oxford: Oxford University Press, 1989.

Kagan, Shelly. "The limits of well-being." *Social Philosophy and Policy,* vol. 9, no. 2 (Summer 1992): 169–89.

Kagan, Shelly. *Normative Ethics.* Boulder, Colo.: Westview, 1997.

Kamm, F. M. "Non-consequentialism, the person as an end-in-itself, and the significance of status." *Philosophy and Public Affairs,* vol. 21, no. 4 (Fall 1992): 354–89.

Kant, Immanuel. *Practical Philosophy,* ed. M. J. Gregor (Cambridge Edition of the Works of Immanuel Kant). Cambridge: Cambridge University Press, 1996.

Kapur, Neera Badhwar. "Why it is wrong to be always guided by the best: consequentialism and friendship." *Ethics,* vol. 101, no. 3 (April 1991): 483–504.

Kelly, P. J. "Utilitarian strategies in Bentham and John Stuart Mill." *Utilitas,* vol. 2, no. 2 (November 1990): 245–66.

Keyes, John. *The Examined Life.* Cranbury, N.J.: Associated University Presses, 1988.

Kilcullen, John. "Utilitarianism and virtue." *Ethics,* vol. 93, no. 3 (April 1983): 451–66.

Korn, Fred and Shulamit R. Decktor Korn. "Where people don't promise." *Ethics,* vol. 93, no. 3 (April 1983): 445–50.

Korsgaard, Christine M. "Two distinctions in goodness." *Philosophical Review,* vol. 92, no. 2 (April 1983): 169–95.

Kraut, Richard. "Two conceptions of happiness." *Philosophical Review,* vol. 88, no. 2 (April 1979): 167–97.

Kymlicka, Will. *Contemporary Political Philosophy.* New York: Oxford University Press, 1990.

LaFollette, Hugh. *Personal Relationships: Love, Identity, and Morality.* Oxford: Blackwell, 1996.

Lemos, Noah H. *Intrinsic Value: Concept and Warrant.* Cambridge: Cambridge University Press, 1994.

Lerner, Abba P. *The Economics of Control.* New York: Macmillan, 1944.

Levy, Sanford S. "The coherence of two-level utilitarianism: Hare vs. Williams." *Utilitas,* vol. 6, no. 2 (November 1994): 301–9.

Levy, Sanford S. "Utilitarian alternatives to act utilitarianism." *Pacific Philosophical Quarterly,* vol. 78, no. 1 (March 1997): 93–112.

Lewis, C. I. *Values and Imperatives: Studies in Ethics,* ed. John Lange. Stanford: Stanford University Press, 1969.

Locke, John. *Second Treatise of Government,* ed. C. B. Macpherson. Indianapolis: Hackett, 1980.

Lyons, David. "Bentham, utilitarianism, and distribution." *Utilitas,* vol. 4, no. 2 (November 1992): 323–8.

Lyons, David. *Forms and Limits of Utilitarianism.* Oxford: Oxford University Press, 1965.

Lyons, David, ed. *Mill's* Utilitarianism: *Critical Essays*. Lanham, Md.: Rowman & Littlefield, 1997.

Lyons, David. *Rights, Welfare, and Mill's Moral Theory*. New York: Oxford University Press, 1994.

Lyons, David. "Utility as a possible ground of rights." *Noûs*, vol. 14, no. 1 (March 1980): 17–28.

McCloskey, H. J. "An examination of restricted utilitarianism." *Philosophical Review*, vol. 66, no. 4 (October 1957): 466–85.

Mack, Eric. "Moral individualism: agent-relativity and deontic restraints." *Social Philosophy and Policy*, vol. 7, no. 1 (Autumn 1989): 81–111.

Mackie, J. L. *Ethics: Inventing Right and Wrong*. Harmondsworth: Penguin, 1977.

Mackie, J. L. "Sidgwick's pessimism." *Philosophical Quarterly*, vol. 26, no. 104 (July 1976): 317–27.

Manning, Rita C. *Speaking from the Heart: A Feminist Perspective on Ethics*. Lanham, Md.: Rowman & Littlefield, 1993.

Mason, Elinor. "Can an indirect consequentialist be a real friend?" *Ethics*, vol. 108, no. 2 (January 1998): 386–93.

Meyer, Michael J. "Dignity, rights, and self-control." *Ethics*, vol. 99, no. 3 (April 1989): 520–34.

Michalos, Alex C. "A case for a progressive annual net wealth tax." *Public Affairs Quarterly*, vol. 2, no. 2 (April 1988): 105–40.

Mill, John Stuart. "August Comte and positivism." In *Essays on Ethics, Religion and Society* (*Collected Works of John Stuart Mill*, vol. X), ed. J. M. Robson. Toronto: University of Toronto Press, 1969.

Mill, John Stuart. *Autobiography*, ed. J. Stillinger. Boston: Houghton Mifflin, 1969.

Mill, John Stuart. "Bentham." In *Essays on Ethics, Religion and Society* (*Collected Works of John Stuart Mill*, vol. X), ed. J. M. Robson. Toronto: University of Toronto Press, 1969.

Mill, John Stuart. "Capital punishment." In *Public and Parliamentary Speeches* (*Collected Works of John Stuart Mill*, vol. XXVIII), ed. J. M. Robson and B. L. Kinzer. Toronto: University of Toronto Press, 1988.

Mill, John Stuart. *The Later Letters of John Stuart Mill, 1849–1873* (*Collected Works of John Stuart Mill*, vols. XV, XVI), ed. F. E. Mineka and D. N. Lindley. Toronto: University of Toronto Press, 1972.

Mill, John Stuart. *On Liberty*, ed. E. Rapaport. Indianapolis: Hackett, 1978.

Mill, John Stuart. *Principles of Political Economy*, ed. D. Winch. Harmondsworth: Penguin, 1970.

Mill, John Stuart. "Remarks on Bentham's philosophy." In *Essays on Ethics, Religion and Society* (*Collected Works of John Stuart Mill*, vol. X), ed. J. M. Robson. Toronto: University of Toronto Press, 1969.

Mill, John Stuart. "Sedgwick's discourse." In *Essays on Ethics, Religion and Society* (*Collected Works of John Stuart Mill*, vol. X), ed. J. M. Robson. Toronto: University of Toronto Press, 1969.

Mill, John Stuart. "The subjection of women." In John Stuart Mill and Harriet Taylor Mill, *Essays on Sex Equality*, ed. A. S. Rossi. Chicago: University of Chicago Press, 1970.

Mill, John Stuart. *A System of Logic (Collected Works of John Stuart Mill*, vol. VIII), ed. J. M. Robson. Toronto: University of Toronto Press, 1974.

Mill, John Stuart. *Utilitarianism*, ed. G. Sher. Indianapolis: Hackett, 1979.

Mill, John Stuart. "Whewell on moral philosophy." In *Essays on Ethics, Religion and Society (Collected Works of John Stuart Mill*, vol. X), ed. J. M. Robson. Toronto: University of Toronto Press, 1969.

Mill, John Stuart, and Harriet Taylor Mill, *Essays on Sex Equality*, ed. A. S. Rossi. Chicago: University of Chicago Press, 1970.

Miller, Harlan B., and William H. Williams, eds. *The Limits of Utilitarianism*. Minneapolis: University of Minnesota Press, 1982.

Moore, G. E. *Ethics*. New York: Oxford University Press, 1965.

Moore, G. E. "The nature of moral philosophy." In *Philosophical Studies*. Paterson, N.J.: Littlefield, Adams, and Company, 1959.

Moore, G. E. *Principia Ethica*. Cambridge: Cambridge University Press, 1968.

Moore, G. E. "A reply to my critics." In Paul Arthur Schilpp, ed., *The Philosophy of G. E. Moore*, 2nd edn. New York: Tudor, 1952.

Nagel, Thomas. *The Possibility of Altruism*. London: Oxford University Press, 1970.

Nagel, Thomas. *The View from Nowhere*. New York: Oxford University Press, 1986.

Narveson, Jan. *Morality and Utility*. Baltimore: Johns Hopkins Press, 1967.

Narveson, Jan. "Rawls and utilitarianism." In Harlan B. Miller and William H. Williams, eds., *The Limits of Utilitarianism*. Minneapolis: University of Minnesota Press, 1982.

Nietzsche, Friedrich. *Basic Writings of Nietzsche*, ed. W. Kaufman. New York: Modern Library, 1968.

Nietzsche, Friedrich. *Untimely Meditations*. Cambridge: Cambridge University Press, 1983.

Noble, Cheryl N. "Normative ethical theories." In Stanley G. Clarke and Evan Simpson, eds., *Anti-Theory in Ethics and Moral Conservatism*. Albany, N.Y.: State University Press of New York, 1989.

Noddings, Nel. *Caring: A Feminine Approach to Ethics and Moral Education*. Berkeley: University of California Press, 1984.

Norcross, Alastair. "Comparing harms: headaches and human lives." *Philosophy and Public Affairs*, vol. 26, no. 2 (Spring 1997): 135–67.

Nozick, Robert. *Anarchy, State, and Utopia*. New York: Basic Books, 1974.

Nussbaum, Martha C. "The feminist critique of liberalism" (The Lindlay Lecture). Lawrence, Kansas: Department of Philosophy, University of Kansas, 1997.

Nussbaum, Martha C. " 'Finely aware and richly responsive': literature and the moral imagination." In Stanley G. Clarke and Evan Simpson, eds., *Anti-Theory in Ethics and Moral Conservatism*. Albany, N.Y.: State University Press of New York, 1989.

Nussbaum, Martha C. and Amartya Sen, eds. *The Quality of Life*. Oxford: Oxford University Press, 1993.

Oakley, Justin. "Varieties of virtue ethics." *Ratio*, vol. 9, no. 2 (September 1996): 128–52.

Oddie, Graham and Peter Menzies. "An objectivist's guide to subjective value." *Ethics*, vol. 102, no. 3 (April 1992): 512–33.

Paley, William. *The Principles of Moral and Political Philosophy*. New York: Garland, 1978.

Parekh, Bhikhu. "Bentham's justification of the principle of utility." In Bhikhu Parekh, ed., *Jeremy Bentham: Ten Critical Essays*. London: Frank Cass, 1974.

Parfit, Derek. *Reasons and Persons*. Oxford: Oxford University Press, 1984.

Pettit, Philip. "Consequentialism." In Peter Singer, ed., *A Companion to Ethics*. Oxford: Blackwell, 1991.

Pigou, A. C. *The Economics of Welfare*, 4th edn. London: Macmillan, 1952.

Pogge, Thomas W. "Does utilitarianism favor economic equality?" In Edgar Morscher, Otto Neumaier, and Peter Simons, eds., *Applied Ethics in a Troubled World*. Dordrecht: Kluwer Academic Publishers, 1998.

Pogge, Thomas W. *Realizing Rawls*. Ithaca, N.Y.: Cornell University Press, 1989.

Prior, Arthur. "The consequences of actions." In *Papers on Time and Tense*. London: Oxford University Press, 1968.

Prior, Arthur. *Logic and the Basis of Ethics*. Oxford: Oxford University Press, 1949.

Quinton, Anthony. *Utilitarian Ethics*, 2nd edn. La Salle, Ill.: Open Court, 1989.

Rachels, James. "Active and passive euthanasia." *New England Journal of Medicine*, vol. 292, no. 2 (January 8, 1975): 78–80.

Rachels, James. *The Elements of Moral Philosophy*, 2nd edn. New York: McGraw-Hill, 1993.

Railton, Peter. "Alienation, consequentialism, and the demands of morality." *Philosophy and Public Affairs*, vol. 13, no. 2 (Spring 1984): 134–71.

Railton, Peter. "How thinking about character and utilitarianism might lead to rethinking the character of utilitarianism." *Midwest Studies in Philosophy*, vol. 8 (1988): 398–416.

Railton, Peter. "Naturalism and prescriptivity." *Social Philosophy and Policy*, vol. 7, no. 1 (Autumn 1989): 151–74.

Raphael, D. D. "J. S. Mill's proof of the principle of utility." *Utilitas*, vol. 6, no. 1 (May 1994): 55–80.

Rawls, John. *Political Liberalism*. New York: Columbia University Press, 1993.

Rawls, John. *A Theory of Justice*. Cambridge, Mass.: Harvard University Press, 1971.

Rawls, John. "Two concepts of rules." *Philosophical Review*, vol. 64, no. 1 (January 1955): 3–32.

Rees, John C. *John Stuart Mill's On Liberty*. Oxford: Oxford University Press, 1985.

Regan, Donald H. *Utilitarianism and Co-operation*. Oxford: Oxford University Press, 1980.

Reiman, Jeffrey H. "Justice, civilization, and the death penalty: answering van den Haag," *Philosophy and Public Affairs*, vol. 14, no 2 (Spring 1985): 115–48.

Rescher, Nicholas. *Distributive Justice: A Constructive Critique of the Utilitarian Theory of Justice*. Indianapolis: Bobbs-Merrill, 1966.

Riley, Jonathan. *Liberal Utilitarianism: Social Choice Theory and J. S. Mill's Philosophy*. Cambridge: Cambridge University Press, 1988.

Riley, Jonathan. "'One very simple principle.'" *Utilitas*, vol. 3, no. 1 (May 1991): 1–35.

Rosen, F. "Utilitarianism and the punishment of the innocent: the origins of a false doctrine." *Utilitas*, vol. 9, no. 1 (March 1997): 23–37.

Ross, W. D. *Foundations of Ethics*. Oxford: Oxford University Press, 1939.

Ross, W. D. *The Right and the Good*. Oxford: Oxford University Press, 1930.

Russell, Bertrand. "The elements of ethics." In Wilfrid Sellars and John Hospers, eds., *Readings in Ethical Theory*. New York: Appleton-Century-Crofts, 1952.

Russell, Bertrand. "The meaning of good." *Independent Review*, vol. 2 (March 1904): 328–33.

Ryan, Alan. "Conservatives, nice and nasty." *New York Review of Books*, June 26, 1997: 27–32.

Ryan, Alan. *John Stuart Mill*. New York: Pantheon, 1970.

Samuelson, Paul A. and William D. Nordhaus. *Economics*, 12th edn. New York: McGraw Hill, 1985.

Santayana, George. "Hypostatic ethics." In Wilfrid Sellars and John Hospers, eds., *Readings in Ethical Theory*. New York: Appleton-Century-Crofts, 1952.

Sartorius, Rolf E. *Individual Conduct and Social Norms: A Utilitarian Account of Social Union and the Rule of Law*. Encino, Calif.: Dickenson, 1975.

Scanlon, Thomas. "Contractualism and utilitarianism." In Amartya Sen and Bernard Williams, eds., *Utilitarianism and Beyond*. Cambridge: Cambridge University Press, 1982.

Scanlon, Thomas. "Value, desire, and quality of life." In Martha C. Nussbaum and Amartya Sen, eds., *The Quality of Life*. Oxford: Oxford University Press, 1993.

Scarre, Geoffrey. *Utilitarianism*. London: Routledge, 1996.

Scheffler, Samuel. "Agent-centred restrictions, rationality, and the virtues." *Mind*, vol. 94, no. 375 (July 1985): 409–19.

Scheffler, Samuel, ed. *Consequentialism and Its Critics*. Oxford: Oxford University Press, 1988.

Scheffler, Samuel. *Human Morality*. New York: Oxford University Press, 1992.

Scheffler, Samuel. *The Rejection of Consequentialism: A Philosophical Investigation of the Considerations Underlying Rival Moral Conceptions*, rev. edn. Oxford: Oxford University Press, 1994.

Schneewind, J. B. *Sidgwick's Ethics and Victorian Moral Philosophy*. Oxford: Oxford University Press, 1977.

Schultz, Bart, ed. *Essays on Henry Sidgwick*. Cambridge: Cambridge University Press, 1992.

Scoccia, Danny. "Utilitarianism, sociobiology, and the limits of benevolence." *Journal of Philosophy*, vol. 87, no. 7 (July 1990): 329–45.

Seanor, Douglas and N. Fotion, eds. *Hare and Critics: Essays on Moral Thinking.* Oxford: Oxford University Press, 1988.

Sen, Amartya. "Capability and well-being." In Martha C. Nussbaum and Amartya Sen, eds., *The Quality of Life.* Oxford: Oxford University Press, 1993.

Sen, Amartya. *Poverty and Famines.* New York: Oxford University Press, 1981.

Sen, Amartya. *The Standard of Living.* Cambridge: Cambridge University Press, 1987.

Sen, Amartya. "Utility: ideas and terminology." *Economics and Philosophy*, vol. 7, no. 2 (October 1991): 277–83.

Sen, Amartya and Bernard Williams, eds. *Utilitarianism and Beyond.* Cambridge: Cambridge University Press, 1982.

Shaw, William H. *Moore on Right and Wrong: The Normative Ethics of G. E. Moore.* Dordrecht: Kluwer Academic Publishers, 1995.

Shaw, William H. "On the paradox of deontology." In John Heil, ed., *Rationality, Morality, and Self-Interest: Essays Honoring Mark Carl Overvold.* Lanham, Md.: Rowman & Littlefield, 1993.

Shaw, William H. "Welfare, equality, and distribution: Brandt from the left." In Brad Hooker, ed., *Rationality, Rules, and Utility: New Essays on the Moral Philosophy of Richard B. Brandt.* Boulder, Colo.: Westview, 1993.

Sher, George. *Beyond Neutrality: Perfectionism and Politics.* Cambridge: Cambridge University Press, 1997.

Sidgwick, Henry. *The Methods of Ethics.* New York: Dover, 1966.

Simmons, A. John. "Utilitarianism and unconscious utilitarianism." In Harlan B. Miller and William H. Williams, eds., *The Limits of Utilitarianism.* Minneapolis: University of Minnesota Press, 1982.

Simmons, A. John, Marshall Cohen, Joshua Cohen, and Charles R. Beitz, eds. *Punishment.* Princeton, N.J.: Princeton University Press, 1995.

Singer, Marcus G. "Actual consequence utilitarianism." *Mind*, vol. 86, no. 341 (January 1977): 67–77.

Singer, Marcus G. "Further on actual consequence utilitarianism." *Mind*, vol. 92, no. 366 (April 1983): 270–4.

Singer, Marcus G. *Generalization in Ethics.* New York: Knopf, 1961.

Singer, Peter. *Animal Liberation*, 2nd edn. New York: Random House, 1990.

Singer, Peter, ed. *A Companion to Ethics.* Oxford: Blackwell, 1991.

Singer, Peter. *Practical Ethics*, 2nd edn. Cambridge: Cambridge University Press, 1993.

Singer, Peter, Leslie Cannold, and Helga Kuhse. "William Godwin and the defence of impartialist ethics." *Utilitas*, vol. 7, no. 1 (May 1995): 67–86.

Sinnott-Armstrong, Walter and Mark Timmons, eds. *Moral Knowledge? New Readings in Moral Epistemology.* New York: Oxford University Press, 1996.

Skorupski, John, ed. *The Cambridge Companion to Mill.* Cambridge: Cambridge University Press, 1998.

Skorupski, John. *John Stuart Mill.* London: Routledge, 1989.

Slote, Michael. *Common-Sense Morality and Consequentialism.* London: Routledge, 1985.

Slote, Michael. *From Morality to Virtue.* New York: Oxford University Press, 1992.

Slote, Michael. "Utilitarian virtue." *Midwest Studies in Philosophy*, vol. 8 (1988): 384–97.

Smart, J. J. C. "An outline of a system of utilitarian ethics." In J. J. C. Smart and Bernard Williams, *Utilitarianism: For and Against.* Cambridge: Cambridge University Press, 1973.

Smart, J. J. C. "Utilitarianism and its applications." In Joseph P. DeMarco and Richard M. Fox, eds., *New Directions in Ethics: The Challenge of Applied Ethics.* New York: Routledge and Kegan Paul, 1986.

Sobel, David. "On the subjectivity of welfare." *Ethics*, vol. 107, no. 3 (April 1997): 501–8.

Sosa, David. "Consequences of consequentialism." *Mind*, vol. 102, no. 405 (January 1993): 101–22.

Sprigge, T. L. S. "The greatest happiness principle." *Utilitas*, vol. 3, no. 1 (May 1991): 37–51.

Sprigge, T. L. S. *The Rational Foundations of Ethics.* London: Routledge and Kegan Paul, 1988.

Sprigge, T. L. S. "Utilitarianism and respect for human life." *Utilitas*, vol. 1, no. 1 (May 1989): 1–21.

Starr, William C. and Richard C. Taylor. *Moral Philosophy: Historical and Contemporary Essays.* Milwaukee: Marquette University Press, 1989.

Sumner, L. W. "The evolution of utility: a philosophical journey." In Brad Hooker, ed., *Rationality, Rules, and Utility: New Essays on the Moral Philosophy of Richard B. Brandt.* Boulder, Colo.: Westview, 1993.

Sumner, L. W. "Is virtue its own reward?" *Social Philosophy and Policy*, vol. 15, no. 1 (Winter 1998): 18–36.

Sumner, L. W. *The Moral Foundation of Rights.* Oxford: Oxford University Press, 1987.

Sumner, L. W. "Rights denaturalized." In R. G. Frey, ed., *Utility and Rights.* Minneapolis: University of Minnesota Press, 1984.

Sumner, L. W. "Two theories of the good." *Social Philosophy and Policy*, vol. 9, no. 2 (Summer 1992): 1–14.

Sumner, L. W. *Welfare, Happiness, and Ethics.* Oxford: Oxford University Press, 1996.

Sumner, L. W. "Welfare, happiness, and pleasure." *Utilitas*, vol. 4, no. 2 (November 1992): 199–223.

Sumner, L. W. "Welfare, preference, and rationality." In R. G. Frey and Christopher W. Morris, eds., *Value, Welfare, and Morality.* Cambridge: Cambridge University Press, 1993.

Taylor, Paul. *Principles of Ethics: An Introduction.* Encino, Calif.: Dickenson, 1975.

Temkin, Jack. "Actual consequence utilitarianism: a reply to Professor Singer." *Mind*, vol. 87, no. 347 (July 1978): 412–14.

Temkin, Jack. "Singer, Moore, and the metaphysics of morals." *Philosophy Research Archives*, vol. 10 (March 1985): 567–71.

Temkin, Larry. "Weighing goods: some questions and comments." *Philosophy and Public Affairs*, vol. 23, no. 4 (Fall 1994): 350–80.

Ten, C. L. *Crime, Guilt, and Punishment*. Oxford: Oxford University Press, 1987.

Ten, C. L. *Mill on Liberty*. Oxford: Oxford University Press, 1980.

Thomson, Judith Jarvis. "On some ways in which a thing can be good." *Social Philosophy and Policy*, vol. 9, no. 2 (Summer 1992): 96–117.

Tong, Rosemarie. *Feminine and Feminist Ethics*. Belmont, Calif.: Wadsworth, 1993.

Trianosky, Gregory. "What is virtue ethics all about?" *American Philosophical Quarterly*, vol. 27, no. 4 (October 1990): 335–44.

Unger, Peter. *Living High and Letting Die*. New York: Oxford University Press, 1996.

Vallentyne, Peter. "Utilitarianism and the outcomes of actions." *Pacific Philosophical Quarterly*, vol. 68, no. 1 (March 1987): 57–70.

Van Wyk, Robert N. "Perspectives on world hunger and the extent of our positive duties." *Public Affairs Quarterly*, vol. 2, no. 2 (April 1988): 75–90.

Walzer, Michael. *Spheres of Justice*. New York: Basic Books, 1983.

Williams, Bernard. "A critique of utilitarianism." In J. J. C. Smart and Bernard Williams, *Utilitarianism: For and Against*. Cambridge: Cambridge University Press, 1973.

Williams, Bernard. *Ethics and the Limits of Philosophy*. Cambridge, Mass.: Harvard University Press, 1985.

Williams, Bernard. "The structure of Hare's theory." In Douglas Seanor and N. Fotion, eds., *Hare and Critics: Essays on Moral Thinking*. Oxford: Oxford University Press, 1988.

Wolf, Susan. "Moral saints." *Journal of Philosophy*, vol. 79, no. 8 (August 1982): 419–39.

Index

abortion, 5–6
actions
  content of, 98
  results of, 12–14
act utilitarianism, 10, 164
actual-outcome utilitarianism, 30–1
agent-centered prerogatives, 277–80
aid
  to developing countries, 285n
  to strangers in need, 281–7
Alexander, Larry, 162n
altruism, 130, 132, 285n
Americans, moral views of, 5
animals, 14–15, 41–2
anti-theory, in ethics, 246–9
archangel, 159–60
Aristotle, 36, 37, 270
  fairness requirement of, 212
  perfectionism of, 58–9
  on virtue, 252–4, 257, 258, 259
asceticism, principle of, 70–1
Ascher, Mark L., 243n
Austin, John, 142, 145n, 156n, 165,
  183n, 200n
autonomy, 32, 196, 219, 230
average-happiness utilitarianism, 32

bad examples, 156, 201
Baier, Annette, 247n
Barrow, Robin, 65n
Barry, Brian, 147, 150n, 239n, 250n

basic structure, of society, 225–6
beauty, value of, 61
Becker, Lawrence C., 225n
beetles, 62
benevolence, 79, 99, 269–70, 286
Bennett, Jonathan, 28n, 29n, 93n, 134n
  on demandingness of utilitarianism,
  131, 132
Bentham, Jeremy, 86, 140, 145n, 171,
  244, 245
  argument for utilitarianism, 69–72
  on benevolence, 99
  definition of utilitarianism, 8–9, 69
  on distributive equality, 118n, 237n
  on falsehood, 108
  historical importance of, 7–8
  on rights, 71–2, 186–8
  rejection of moral intuition, 71–2, 84,
  247
  on pleasure and happiness, 11–12,
  38–40, 52, 69
Berger, Fred R., 217n
Berkeley, George, 165
Bernoulli, Daniel, 237n
biodiversity, value of, 62–3
blame, 134–6, 158, 170, 179
Blum, Walter J., 238n
Bok, Sissela, 109n
Brandt, Richard B., 65n, 77n, 150n,
  178n, 215n, 228n, 256n

Rawls's theory of, 76–7, 225–35
see also economic distribution
economic system, favored by utilitarians, 216–18, 222
egalitarians, economic, 119, 120
egoism, 17, 89–91, 259, 280
Eisner, Michael, 209
Elster, Jon, 214n
employment rent, 242
Enquiry Concerning Political Justice (Godwin), 268
entitlement theory, 219–21
entrepreneurship, 242
envy, 234n
equality
    of income, 213, 217, 231, 235–6, 240, 243
    of opportunity, 230, 241, 243
    as part of justice, 212
    as a postulate, 238–9
    utilitarianism and, 118–21, 234–44
    see also inequality
ethical intuitionism, *see* commonsense morality; moral intuition
ethical relativism, 5–7
ethics of care, 249–52
Ewing, A. C., 103
exchange promises, 111
expected-outcome utilitarianism, 30–1
expected utility, 29
experience machine, 50–1, 63
exploitation, 108–9
eye for an eye, 180

fairness, as part of justice, 211–12
fair play, 180
famine, 224
    obligation to relieve, 129, 130, 131, 281–7
Feinberg, Joel, 207n
feminism, 249–52
Finnis, John, 56n, 57, 58
first principles, in ethics, 70, 73, 77–8, 95
Fishkin, James, 190–2
Flanagan, Owen, 250n, 254n, 260n

Foot, Philippa, 156n
Fotion, N., 84n
Frankfurt, Harry, 121n
free will, 181n.
    see also determinism
freedom, *see* liberty
Frey, R. G., 42n
Fried, Charles, 108n
Friedman, Milton, 240n, 243
friendship, 271–5, 280
future generations, obligations to, 33

Gates, Bill, 211
Gauthier, David, 126
Gert, Bernard, 255n
Gilligan, Carol, 249–52
Godwin, William, 268–70
Goldberg, Steve, 177n
Goldstick, D., 118n
Goldsworthy, Jeffrey, 51n, 58n
good
    as additive, 38, 46n, 68
    encompasses good of individual, 78–9
    instrumental vs. intrinsic, 36–7
    objectivity of, 80–1
Good Samaritan laws, 4, 19
good will, in Kant's theory, 19
Goodin, Robert E., 171n, 172n
"greatest happiness of the greatest number," 8, 13
greatest happiness principle, 9, 37
    See also utilitarianism
Griffin, James, 56n, 233n
guilt, feelings of, 134, 150, 283, 285
Gulf war, 139

hanging the innocent man, 181–4
happiness
    affective and cognitive components of, 65–6
    average vs. total, 31–5
    Bentham's view of, 37, 38–40, 48
    expected, 29
    knowledge of, 15–16, 66–7
    Mill's view of, 37, 45–8, 205